Structured Programming in

COBOL

Second Edition

B.J.Holmes B.Sc,M.Sc,MBCS,Cert.Ed.

Principal Lecturer in the
School of Computing and Mathematical Sciences,
Oxford Polytechnic, Headington, Oxford, OX3 0BP

DP PUBLICATIONS LTD
Aldine Place, 142/144 Uxbridge Road,
Shepherds Bush Green, London W12 8AW

1991

ii

Disclaimer

The programs presented in this book have been included for their instructional value. They have been computer-tested with considerable care and are not guaranteed for any particular purpose. The author does not offer any warranties or representations, nor does he accept any liabilities with respect to the programs.

A CIP catalogue record for this book is available from the British Library

First Edition 1984
Second Edition 1991
Reprinted 1992

ISBN 1 870941 82 9

©1991 B.J.Holmes

Typeset and illustrated by B.J.Holmes

Printed by The Guernsey Press Company Ltd, Braye Road, Vale, Guernsey, Channel Islands.

Contents

Preface

This text can be used as either *a first course in programming* or as *a conversion course* from another high-level computer language, for readers who want to learn structured program design and COBOL programming in a thorough and methodical manner.

The first edition of the text proved to be very popular amongst students studying for degrees in Computer Studies, BTEC Higher National and National awards in Computer Studies and City & Guilds examinations in programming

From this success it is natural that the second edition should be recommended to all students studying commercial programming in both Higher and Further Education.

Structured Programming in COBOL adopts a different approach to many texts on COBOL. The author has written the book around two complementary themes. The design of structured computer programs based on techniques, first expounded by Michael Jackson, known as Jackson Structured Programming (JSP), and the methods available for implementing these designs using the COBOL language. Throughout the text the two themes are shown to complement each other, with programming solutions to problems being designed using JSP and the designs being translated into COBOL programs.

The JSP method for program design has been chosen by the author for the following reasons. JSP has become adopted, by many in the computing industry, as a standard for designing structured programs. The techniques are well defined and provide a prescriptive means for teaching about program design. JSP is particularly applicable to problem solving in the commercial programming environment. The method produces a complete documentation for all programs. Program testing and program maintenance is made easier. The amount of COBOL coding can be reduced to a minimum if the program design stage is implemented using JSP/COBOL code generator software production tools.

The author has used Standard COBOL in the translation of the JSP program designs into COBOL code. The programs in the text have been compiled using an ANS 1985 COBOL compiler. Because of the subset of language statements used it is also possible to compile the programs using older compilers that conform to the ANS 1974 Standard. However, when using an older compiler it may be necessary to make very minor amendments to the programs in the text. The nature of such amendments, where applicable, are fully described.

The material found in this book is computer-tested and classroom tested to guarantee its reliability and use as a teaching text.

No previous knowledge of computer programming or computer concepts is assumed.

The development of the language statements and programs are taken in manageable steps to enable a reader to build a firm foundation of knowledge. The type of programming examples used in both the text and self-test questions are simple enough to give a reader confidence at each stage of learning the language. The text is full of documented worked examples and exercises with answers.

The book is equally suitable as a course text or a self-instruction text. Questions are provided at the end of the majority of chapters for readers to test their knowledge of the topics found in the chapters. The answers to selected self-test questions are given in the first appendix.

Those questions where the answers require original thought and development, and can be used for coursework or homework, have the answers in a separate Answer Supplement, supplied on a PC-compatible disc. In addition to the Answer Supplement, all the illustrative programs found in the text, are also stored on the disc. The immediate availability of these programs saves the time needed to accurately key the programs into the computer, and allows them to be used for demonstration and development purposes by lecturers and students. The disc is available, free of charge, only to lecturers and teachers using this book as a course text.

The majority of chapters contain a summary section, including a list of keywords. This provides a precis on the contents of each chapter and acts as a check-list of topics that should be understood before a reader progresses to the next chapter.

Within a single book there is enough information to provide a foundation for any reader who wishes to develop and implement a wide variety of software systems in JSP and COBOL.

Notes on the Second Edition.

In producing a second edition, Structured Programming in COBOL has been completely re-written. Substantial modifications have been made to the book, together with the introduction of a considerable amount of new material.

The contents of the old edition has been reordered, with several of the shorter chapters being consolidated into larger chapters.

There are new chapters on the Computer Environment, Structured Design, Program Development, Software Development Tools and Structured Programming with COBOL-85.

The JSP material has been brought forward and expanded to enable program designs to be produced before the introduction of COBOL coding.

For the major part of the book the method of coding the JSP program designs uses hierarchical code. However, flat or in-line code is introduced and used from chapter thirteen.

BJH, Oxford, May 1991.

Acknowledgements

The author wishes to express his thanks to Learmonth & Burchett Management Systems Plc for their cooperation in the evaluation of the software tools JSP-COBOL and PDF.

COBOL is an industry language and is not the property of any company or group of companies, or any organisation or group of organisations.

No warranty expressed or implied, is made by any contributor or by the CODASYL COBOL Committee as to the accuracy and functioning of the programming system and language. Moreover, no responsibility is assumed by any contributor, or by the committee, in connection therewith.

The authors and copyright holders of the copyrighted material used herein:

FLOW-MATIC (trademark of the Sperry-Rand Corporation), Programming for Univac(R)I and II, Data Automation Systems copyrighted 1958, 1959 by Sperry-Rand Corporation; IBM Commercial Translator, Form No. F28-8013, copyrighted 1959 by IBM; FACT DSI 27A5260-2760, copyrighted 1960 by Minneapolis-Honeywell

have specifically authorised the use of this material in whole or in part, in the COBOL specifications. Such authorisation extends to the reproduction and use of COBOL specifications in programming manuals or similar publications.

1

Computer
Environment

The purpose of this chapter is to describe a typical computer environment for the development of COBOL programs. The reader will be introduced to equipment and programs that make up a computer system, and the stages in the production of a program.

1.1 Programs, Data and Results.

A computer program is a series of coded instructions for the computer to obey and represents a method of processing the data.

Data is the name given to facts. For example, in a business the number of hours worked by employees or the level of items of stock represent data. Data is input to a computer, processed under the direction of a program into results that are output in the form of say, a payslip, or a report on out of stock items.

1.2 A Digital Computer.

A digital computer is an electronic machine capable of storing and obeying instructions at a very high speed. For example, an instruction can be obeyed in one hundred millionth of one second. The term digital implies that all information is represented by numbers within the computer. The numbers are stored as binary numbers, base 2, since it is convenient to physically represent the binary digits 1 and 0 as two respective voltage levels.

A digital computer is divided into two areas, the main memory and the central processing unit (CPU).

The main memory is used to temporarily store program instructions and data. A computer can only obey program instructions that are stored in the main memory.

The CPU consists of two sub-units, the arithmetic and logic unit (ALU) and the control unit. The ALU performs the processes of arithmetic, logical operations and comparisons on data. Whereas the control unit fetches the instructions from main memory, interprets and obeys them, and coordinates the flow of information about the computer system.

1.3 A Computer Model.

Figure 1.1 illustrates a computer model containing the CPU, main memory and in addition three other units, input, secondary storage and output units, known as peripheral units.

An input unit allows data and computer programs to be input into the computer model.

Since the main memory is only used to temporarily store programs and data, it is necessary to have secondary storage units to provide a permanent storage facility. Programs and data are transferred to and from the secondary storage units to the main memory only when they are required. The information is said to be on-line to the computer. The rate of transfer of information is fast and the speed is dependent upon the type of secondary storage unit being used.

In order to transfer results from the main memory and secondary storage units to the outside world it is necessary to provide an output unit.

1.4 Input and Output Units.

The most popular input unit used in computer systems is a keyboard. The keyboard consists of keys similar to those of a typewriter; both data and programs can be input into the computer by depressing the appropriate keys. A television screen or monitor can be used to simultaneously display the information that is being typed into a computer. Such a display is meant to provide a means of visually checking that the correct information is being entered.

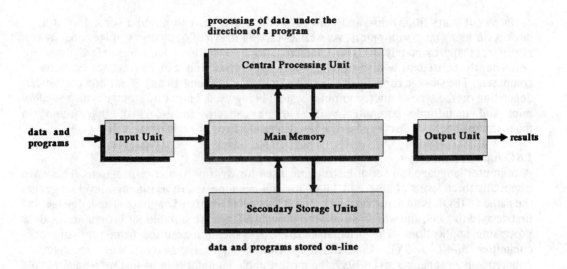

processing of data under the
direction of a program

Central Processing Unit

data and
programs → Input Unit → Main Memory → Output Unit → results

Secondary Storage Units

data and programs stored on-line

Figure 1.1 A Computer Model

A monitor has a dual function, as well as displaying the information that is typed at a keyboard it is also used as an output unit in its own right. Information that has been processed by a computer can also be displayed on a screen. A single input/output device called a visual display unit (VDU) combines both a keyboard and screen.

The major disadvantage of using a monitor as an output unit stems from the inability of the unit to provide a hard copy of the output. Because information on a printed page is so convenient it is necessary to include a printer as another output unit.

There are other types of input units, for example, card and paper tape readers were both common forms of input devices to computers in the 1960's and 70's. Programs and data were encoded by punching holes in paper tape or cards. Bar code readers are used to detect stock codes on supermarket merchandise. Magnetic ink character readers detect bank account numbers and branch codes on bank cheques. Optical character and mark readers are used to detect information written on documents.

Similarly, output units are not only limited to monitors and printers but can include graph and map plotters, synthesised speech units and digital to analogue output for controlling machinery.

1.5 Secondary Storage Units.
These units allow large quantities of information to be stored permanently on some form of magnetic medium such as magnetic tapes or discs. A standard reel of magnetic tape can store up to 40 million characters. A multiple platter magnetic disc pack can store up to 300 million characters. Both magnetic tape and disc units transfer information to, and receive information from, the CPU at speeds of many hundred thousand characters per second.

In recent years floppy disc and hard disc units have become popular secondary storage devices on many microcomputers. As well as varying in size, floppy disc storage capacity can range from approximately 100,000 characters to one million characters. Hard discs are permanently housed in a disc unit, unlike floppy discs that can be transferred between computers. The storage capacity of a hard disc will vary between 10 and 80 million characters, depending on the type of microcomputer system being used. Hard disc storage is also used on mini and mainframe computers with storage capacity in excess of that found on microcomputers. Such discs can be contained in either fixed or exchangeable disc-packs.

1.6 Computer Languages.

A computer language is a set of instructions used for writing computer programs. There are essentially three levels of language, high, low and machine. COBOL is a high-level language, the name COBOL is an acronym for **Common Business Oriented Language**. The language was first devised in 1959, and was an attempt to provide a language suitable for programming data processing applications. The original COBOL specification resulted from the work of a committee of CODASYL (Conference on Data Systems Languages). The language has undergone many changes since 1959, the most notable landmarks in its history being in 1968, 1974 and 1985. The following segment of code illustrates several statements in a COBOL program.

```
DISPLAY "input hours worked " WITH NO ADVANCING.
ACCEPT hours.
IF hours > 40
    COMPUTE Overtime-Pay = (hours - 40) * Overtime-Rate
ELSE
    MOVE ZERO TO Overtime-Pay.
DISPLAY "overtime £ ", Overtime-Pay.
```

As this example illustrates, high-level languages contain statements that are written in English words and symbols. Such languages are not designed specifically for any one brand of computer. A program written in COBOL to run on a Prime computer that also runs on an IBM PC is said to be portable between the two computers. There is an agreed standard defined by both ANS (American National Standards) and ISO (International Standards Organisation) for the COBOL language. All COBOL compilers comply with this standard, however, compiler writers tend to enhance the language by introducing extra features that are not part of the agreed standard. If programs are written using only those statements that conform to the standard then the programs can remain portable between computers.

Low level languages contain statements that are written using mnemonic codes (codes suggesting their meaning and, therefore, easier to remember) to represent operations and addresses that relate to the main memory and storage registers of a computer. Each low level language has instructions which correspond closely to the inbuilt operations of a specific computer. Since different brands of computer use different low level languages a program written for one brand of computer will not run on another brand. Despite the many low level languages in existence they all adhere to the same broad principles of language structure. An example of statements from a typical low level language is:

```
LDA 5000
ADD 6000
STA 5000
```

This program segment adds two numbers and stores the result in a memory location! This type of programming is obviously not as clear as writing *ADD number-1 TO number-2* which is the equivalent operation in COBOL.

Machine level statements are even worse to mentally interpret. They are normally written using one of the number bases 2, 8 or 16. For example the program segment coded in base 2 binary as:

```
11011101 1011011
01001100 1011100
11011100 1011011
```

would require the aid of a reference manual in order to decipher the meaning of each code.

1.7 Language Translation.
A computer stores and uses information in a binary format, therefore, the computer cannot understand programs written in either high or low level languages. Program code written in either a high or low level language must be translated into a binary machine code that the computer recognises. Translation is possible by using a supplied program to translate high or low level language statements into machine code.

Translation to machine code from a high level language is by compiler, and from a low level language by assembler. The translator, compiler or assembler, is resident in the main memory of the computer and uses the high or low level program code as input data. The output from the translator is a program in machine readable code. In addition to translation, a compiler or assembler will report on any grammatical errors made by the programmer in the language statements of the program.

1.8 Operating Environment.
There are two methods of configuring a computer to run programs. However, the choice of method is dictated by the nature of the application the program has been written for.

Interactive processing allows a two-way communication between the user and the computer. If a program is being developed under such a system, changes can be made to the program and the effects immediately noted. This system of processing is common to all microcomputers and time-sharing systems.

Batch processing allows programs to be put into a queue and processed one after another. The programmer cannot intervene during the processing to perform amendments to the program as was possible during interactive processing. In batch processing a program must wait its turn before processing data. This necessarily means that there will be a delay in obtaining results. Consequently batch processing cannot be used when results are needed immediately. A suitable application for batch processing would be running a payroll program, where for example, details of hours worked by employees could be collected one week and processed as a batch to provide payslips the next week.

The reader should be aware that there exists a higher layer of software that controls the computer system above a user's program. Regardless of the mode of processing all computer systems are supplied with an operating system. The role of an operating system covers many areas, however, one important aspect is that of supervising the execution of user written programs. Such supervision includes the premature termination of user programs in the event of attempting to execute illegal operations such as dividing a number by zero or reading from a data file that had not been opened.

1.9 Program Development Environment.

Having given the reader an introduction into the fundamental components of a typical computing environment it is now possible to outline the specific requirements of an environment for the development of COBOL programs.

Hardware

Input: keyboard.

Output: monitor and printer.

Computer: a university or polytechnic environment will probably use a VAX, ICL, IBM or Prime mini/mainframe configuration that supports a large number of users simultaneously. Alternatively, a desk-top microcomputer such as an IBM PC or Apple Macintosh can be used for a single user. In recent years a third configuration has become possible, where several microcomputers are networked together to share common secondary storage devices.

Secondary Storage: fixed or exchangeable hard discs if using a mini/mainframe system or floppy disc/ hard disc if using a microcomputer system.

Software

Editor: In order to type a COBOL program at the keyboard and save the program on a disc it will be necessary to run a program called an editor. In addition to program entry an editor allows a program to be retrieved from disc and amended as necessary. A COBOL program is stored in a text mode so that the programmer can read the program as it was written. No translation of the COBOL program to a machine recognisable form has been necessary at this stage.

Compiler: This will translate a COBOL program stored in text mode on disc to the program stored in a machine-oriented language on disc. There are several dialects of COBOL available, for example Prime COBOL-85 written specifically for Prime computers, Microsoft COBOL written for personal computers, etc. Each dialect will have its own compiler for a specific brand of computer. A program written in COBOL for a Prime computer would require translation using a COBOL-85 compiler. However, the same program, in text form, could be transferred to an IBM PC and translated into machine-oriented language using the Microsoft COBOL compiler. Note the portability of the language only refers to the language in text mode not machine code, and is only possible if both compilers conform to the same subset of statements taken from the Standard of the language.

Within the context of this book, all the programs have been developed using a COBOL-85 compiler on a Prime computer. However, the statements from the language have been chosen so that the programs can also be compiled using COBOL compilers that also conform to the 1974 Standard of the language. The language statements that have been chosen are portable between Prime COBOL-85 and Prime CBL (1974) compilers. However, when using an ANS 1974 Standard compiler for a different computer it may be necessary for the reader to make very minor amendments to the programs in the text. The nature of such amendments, where applicable, are fully described.

Link/Loader: Before a compiled COBOL program can be run or executed by the computer it must be converted into an executable form. One function of the link/loader is to take the machine-oriented program and combine it with any necessary software (already in machine-oriented form) to enable the program to be run. For example, input and output routines that are supplied by the system will need linking into the program to allow data to be input at a keyboard and results displayed on a monitor. The complete machine code program is then loaded into memory ready for execution.

Throughout the phases of editing, compilation, link/loading and running it is assumed that the reader will be using an interactive processing environment. The four phases illustrated in figure 1.2 summarise the stages necessary in the development of a COBOL program.

1.10 Summary.

A digital computer consists of input, output and secondary storage units that are peripheral to the central processing unit and main memory.

Data is input to the computer and processed under the direction of a program to produce results at an output unit.

There are three levels of computer language, high (COBOL language, etc), low (assembly level language) and machine code (binary patterns).

Programs written in a high-level language such as COBOL, must be compiled and link-loaded into memory before they can be executed on the computer.

The supervision of the running of a program on the computer is one of the tasks of the operating system.

Keywords

Software:

programs, data, results;
high, low and machine level languages;
compiler, assembler, editor, link/loader;
interactive and batch processing, operating systems;
portability.

Hardware:

digital computer, main memory, CPU, ALU;
peripheral units, keyboard, monitor, printer, magnetic tape
and disc units.

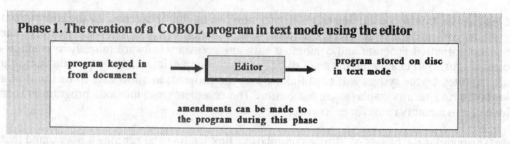

Phase 1. The creation of a COBOL program in text mode using the editor

program keyed in from document → Editor → program stored on disc in text mode

amendments can be made to the program during this phase

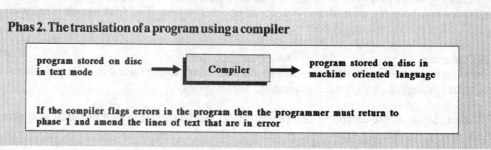

Phas 2. The translation of a program using a compiler

program stored on disc in text mode → Compiler → program stored on disc in machine oriented language

If the compiler flags errors in the program then the programmer must return to phase 1 and amend the lines of text that are in error

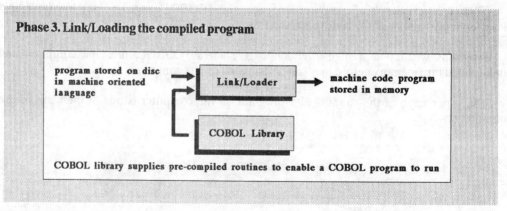

Phase 3. Link/Loading the compiled program

program stored on disc in machine oriented language → Link/Loader → machine code program stored in memory

COBOL Library

COBOL library supplies pre-compiled routines to enable a COBOL program to run

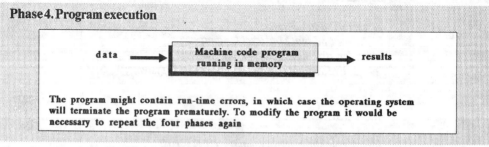

Phase 4. Program execution

data → Machine code program running in memory → results

The program might contain run-time errors, in which case the operating system will terminate the program prematurely. To modify the program it would be necessary to repeat the four phases again

Figure 1.2 The four phases of program development

1.11 Questions.
1. What are the five major hardware units of a digital computer system?

[2]. List three input units and three output units. What are the most common input and output units in a COBOL development environment?

3. Why is it necessary to translate a COBOL program into a machine-oriented language?

4. List the four stages that are necessary before a COBOL program can be executed by a computer.

[5]. What is meant by program portability? Why are low level languages not considered to be portable ?

Note. A question number printed within [ ] indicates that the answer is available in a separate Answer Supplement, only available from DP Publications Ltd, to lecturers and teachers using this book as a course text.

2

Structured Design

The purpose of this chapter is to introduce the reader to the technique of designing solutions to problems using Jackson Structured Programming - JSP. Despite no COBOL language statements being introduced at this stage it is possible to produce diagrammatic solutions that can be programmed in later chapters.

2.1 Why design programs?

Would you attempt to build a house without the use of plans, or construct a complex electronic circuit without having first drawn a circuit diagram? Clearly the answer is no! Obviously any form of construction usually requires planning and design phases prior to the actual construction work being carried out. The construction of computer software is no exception to this. The production of quality software should also include planning and design phases.

The novice programmer may well question why it is necessary to design programs at all. Indeed some programmers produce rough and ready solutions at the keyboard of a computer and continue to amend a program until eventually the program appears to do what was expected. This is not a recommended approach to programming for the following reasons.

The final program is probably not easy to read since it was no more than cobbled together. No pun intended on the word COBOL !

The documentation of what each part of the program is meant to do is probably non-existent.

The program may not have been broken down into logical tasks, with each specific task programmed as a distinct group of statements that can be used when required.

There was probably no plan for testing the program and indeed the program might easily fail. Remember that such programs are produced by continuous amendments until the program appears to work. This changing or tinkering with program statements often leads to unforeseen side effects that may not manifest themselves for quite some time.

Lastly, what of the programmer who is asked to maintain (modify) the code at a later date? Without sufficient documentation such a task is normally preceded by tracing through the program in order to gain an insight into how the program functions. Since program maintenance accounts for a substantial proportion of programming budgets, clearly any improvement in programmer productivity must be a saving.

The answer to the question *why design programs?* is so as to avoid the pitfalls that I have just listed, but how and what do you use to design a computer program. There have been many techniques used, since the dawn of programming, to design programs. Such methods include flowcharts, step-wise refinement, pseudo-code, Jackson Structured Programming (JSP), to name but a few. JSP was first described by Michael Jackson in his book on *Principles of Program Design - Academic Press, 1975.* The method became popular in commercial programming circles and was adopted by the Civil Service under the name of *Structured Design Method (SDM)* as a Central Government mandatory standard for use by civil servants.

JSP has evolved over many years and is fully supported by a set of software tools to aid in the production of programs. Designing a computer program using the JSP approach will provide the documentation for the program to be constructed. From this documentation it is possible to thoroughly test the design before even a single program statement has been coded. Thus any errors that are detected can be rectified at the design phase rather than the programming phase. With the aid of a code generator it is possible for the computer to accurately code a program from a JSP design. This is obviously an aid towards programmer productivity. Program maintenance involves changing the design of a program and not directly changing statements within a program. Having changed the design the code generator will produce the updated program code. Since the changes were made at the design phase the documentation for this phase will have been updated to reflect the changed program. The use of JSP tools together with COBOL code generators will be described in chapter 15.

2.2 JSP Notation.

Structured computer programs will contain up to three identifiable program structures, known as sequence, selection and repetition. From figure 2.1 it can be seen that JSP has a diagrammatic notation for these structures.

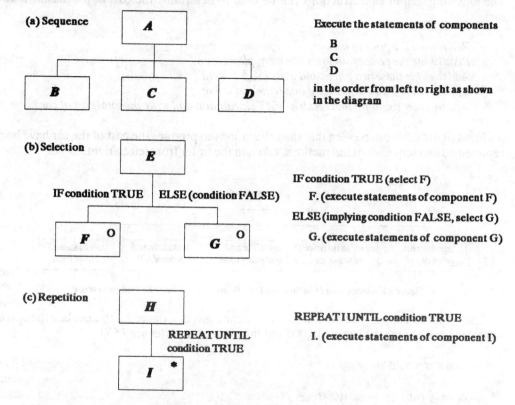

(a) Sequence

Execute the statements of components

B
C
D

in the order from left to right as shown in the diagram

(b) Selection

IF condition TRUE (select F)

F. (execute statements of component F)

ELSE (implying condition FALSE, select G)

G. (execute statements of component G)

(c) Repetition

REPEAT I UNTIL condition TRUE

I. (execute statements of component I)

IMPORTANT NOTE. In diagram (c) the component I can be repeated ZERO or MORE times. The use of the words REPEAT UNTIL in this and subsequent diagrams should NOT be confused with the statement repeat .. until found in many programming languages. The word REPEAT has been used to signify repetition and has no further connotations. For simplicity of coding REPEAT UNTIL maps into the COBOL code PERFORM UNTIL without having to negate the condition.

Figure 2.1 JSP Notation for sequence, selection and repetition

In figure 2.1(a) box A represents a sequence of instructions to be obeyed (executed) in the order box B, box C and box D (taken from left to right in the diagram). Where the boxes B,C and D represent executable statements for the computer to obey in the order given. In figure 2.1(b) box E represents a selection dependent upon a condition being either true or false. If the condition for selection is true the statements of box F are executed, however, if the condition for the selection is false then the statements of box G are executed. Note the use of the symbol o in each option box F and G.

Finally in figure 2.1(c) box H represents repetition. The statements in box I will be repeated zero or more times dependent upon the condition associated with the repetition. Note also the use of the symbol * in box I whose component is to be repeated.

This explanation of the three structures may seem a little daunting on the first reading. In order to clarify their use each structure will be fully explained using worked examples.

2.3 Sequence.
The following simplified instructions can be used to determine the cost of purchasing a new car.

> *Read/write the price of the car*
> *Read/write the price of sundries (delivery, plates, etc)*
> *Add together these two prices and write the sub-total*
> *Calculate VAT on the sub-total and write this value*
> *Add together sub-total and result of VAT calculation and write the total cost of car*

From figure 2.2 it can be seen that the calculations to produce the cost of the car have been represented as a sequence of instructions, taken in the order from left to right.

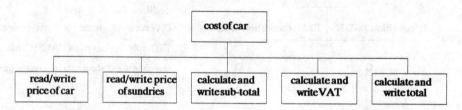

Figure 2.2 A sequence of instructions for calculating the cost of buying a new car

The reader is recommended to follow the structure given in figure 2.2 to calculate the cost of a car if the price of the vehicle is £10,000 and the price of sundries are £500.

The answer would be:

Price of car	*£10,000*
Price of sundries	*£500*
Sub-total	*£10,500*
VAT @ 15%	*£1,575*
Total cost of car	*£12,075*

2.4 Selection.
If a building society pays interest at 7% per annum on investments up to £10,000 and a higher rate of interest at 8% per annum on total investments above £10,000 then the method of selecting the appropriate rate of interest can be represented by the JSP notation shown in figure 2.3.

The notation for a selection is not limited to only a two-way selection. Each item of choice must be represented by a separate box and appropriate condition. If a building society has three rates of interest based upon different amounts being invested, such that investments up

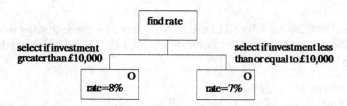

Figure 2.3 illustrates a two-way selection based upon the size of the investment

to £10,000 attract 7% per annum, investments exceeding £10,000 and up to £20,000 attract 8% per annum and investments exceeding £20,000 attract the top rate of 9%, then the method for selecting the appropriate rate of interest can be represented by the JSP notation shown in figure 2.4.

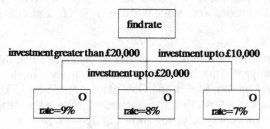

Figure 2.4 An illustration of a three-way selection

If the annual simple interest on an investment account was to be calculated then it would be necessary to use a sequence of instructions to:

Read/write the amount invested
Find the appropriate rate of interest
Write the rate of interest
Calculate and write the annual interest

These instructions can be incorporated into the JSP diagram shown in figure 2.5, where the instruction to find the appropriate rate of interest has been represented as a three-way selection.

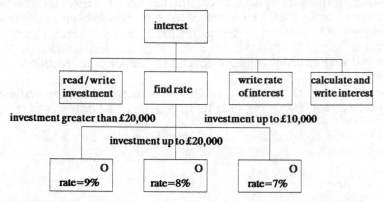

Figure 2.5 An illustration of a method of calculating interest based upon varying rates

Once again the reader is advised to use the diagram with the following information in order to calculate the appropriate annual interest on, say, £15,000 being invested; followed by, say, £25,000 being invested.

amount invested	*£15,000*
rate of interest	*8%*
annual interest of	*£1200*
amount invested	*£25,000*
rate of interest	*9%*
annual interest	*£2250*

In this example it should be clear to the reader for the necessity to incorporate a structure for repetition since the calculations were made twice on different amounts invested.

2.5 Repetition.

A salesperson visits up to three different cities in a week. Over a five-day working week several visits to the same city might be made. Only one return journey is made in a day. If the distances from the sales office to London, Exeter and Oxford are 65, 155 and 35 miles respectively, then as a continuation from the last section the method of finding the distance to the destination can be represented as a three-way selection shown in figure 2.6.

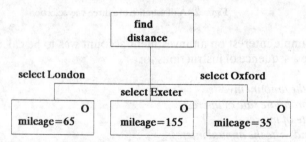

Figure 2.6 JSP notation showing sequence, selection and repetition

However, it will be necessary to repeat this selection, as shown in figure 2.7, for each of the destinations over the five working days. To control the number of times the item *find distance* is repeated a counter can be used. This will need to be set at zero before a destination is read/written, and increased by 1 after every destination has been read/written. Figure 2.7 illustrates the modifications needed to control the number of times a destination is read/written, and clearly shows that a JSP structure contains sequences, selections and repetition.

The reader should work through the following structure using the destinations *Exeter, London, Oxford, London and Oxford* in order to determine the distances of the destinations.

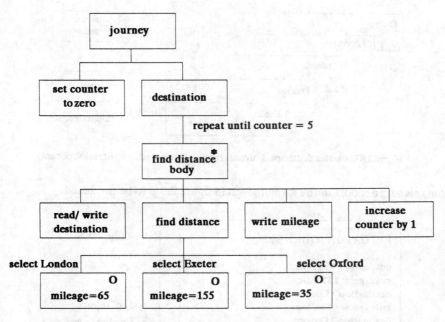

Figure 2.7 JSP notation showing sequence, selection and repetition

The results should appear as:

counter=0	*destination ? Exeter*
	mileage = 155 miles
counter=1	*destination ? London*
	mileage = 65 miles
counter=2	*destination ? Oxford*
	mileage = 35 miles
counter=3	*destination ? London*
	mileage = 65 miles
counter=4	*destination ? Oxford*
	mileage = 35 miles
counter=5	

2.6 Basic Program Structure.

Since the last example contained the three structures to be found in most programs, it will serve as a good starting point in explaining how a program structure is developed. The destinations could be stored on cards, one destination per card. Figure 2.8 illustrates that the pack of cards can be represented in a JSP notation as a repetition of card, and is the input structure in the problem.

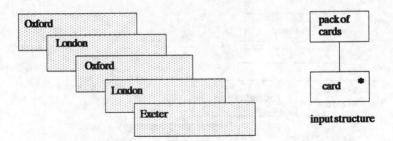

Figure 2.8 Illustrates that the pack of cards can be represented as an iteration of card

From this data a report in the format given in figure 2.9 is to be produced.

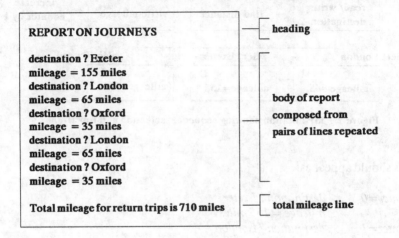

Figure 2.9 Format of report

The report can be treated as a sequence of sections *heading, body* and *total mileage* that make up the report.

and the body of the report is an iteration of journey.

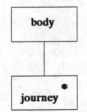

In the report a journey consists of two lines, a destination followed by the mileage.

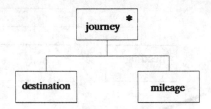

The output structure for the report is represented in JSP notation as:

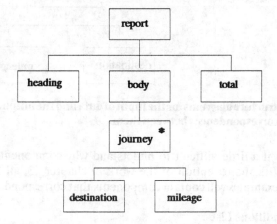

A basic program structure is produced by fusing together the input structure diagram and the output structure diagram. It is an amalgam of both structures under the following conditions.

Each component in the input structure MUST correspond with a component in the output structure under the following conditions:

(i)   Each component must occur the same number of times.
(ii)   Each component must occur in the same order.
(iii)   Each component must exist under the same circumstances.

Figure 2.10 shows arrowed lines that indicate correspondence between the pile of cards and the report, since it is necessary to read the pile in order, to produce the report. A correspondence also exists between the card and journey, since each card read will correspond with the details of a journey printed. The number of cards read and journeys printed is the same and in the same order.

In this example the basic program structure is identical to the output structure of the report.

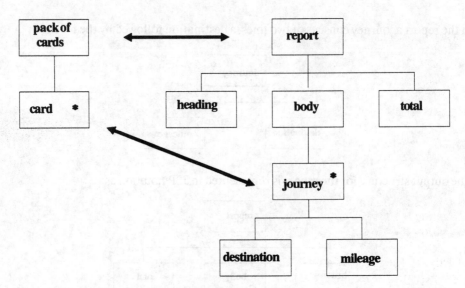

Figure 2.10 structure diagrams for the input of data and the output of a report showing the correspondences between them.

If the reader finds it a little difficult to understand why components should correspond, then do not worry. With the exception of the work in chapter 13, all the input and output structures used in the examples will contain components that correspond.

2.7 Functions and Conditions Lists.

The next stage in developing a program structure is to identify all the operations that must be obeyed in order to solve the problem. In sections 2.3, 2.4 and 2.5 methods were described to solve problems. Each method contained statements of what to do. These statements are known as functions. Within the methods discussed in sections 2.4 and 2.5 it was also necessary to introduce conditions under which a selection should be made or repetition should finish.

In developing a set of functions and conditions the order in which they are thought of does not matter. Therefore, it is possible to have a brainstorming session on what functions and conditions are necessary in the solution of a problem with little regard to the order in which the functions should be obeyed or conditions tested.

In the example given in the last section the functions and conditions necessary to read the pile of cards and produce the report are as follows. Notice that each function and each condition is given a number.

Functions List.

1. read/write destination
2. write heading to report
3. write total mileage
4. multiply total mileage by 2
5. distance becomes 65
6. distance becomes 155

7. distance becomes 35
8. increase total mileage by distance
9. initialise total mileage to zero
10. initialise counter to zero
11. write distance on report
12. add 1 to counter
13. finish

Conditions List.

1. counter = 5
2. destination = London
3. destination = Exeter
4. destination = Oxford

Strictly speaking this last condition is not necessary. If the destinations printed on the cards can be guaranteed as being either London, Exeter or Oxford then if a destination is not London or Exeter then it must, by default, be Oxford. Therefore, there is no need to explicitly test for Oxford.

2.8 Detailed Program Structure.

The final stage in the production of a program structure is to distribute the functions and conditions over the basic program structure, showing the order in which functions are to be obeyed and conditions tested.

Functions must always be attributed to boxes that have no further sub-structure. Such boxes are known as elementary components of the structure diagram. In order to distribute all the functions it may be necessary to introduce extra elementary components. The extra components are to cater for functions that cannot be assigned to existing elementary components. In order for the correctness of the structure to remain the addition of extra components is only possible if:

(i) the extra components have an obvious and constant position in the program structure, and

(ii) when they are included the structure must remain logically sound.

In other words extra boxes can be added to a structure if the sequence, selection or repetition that they are included in, remains unchanged in structure.

For example extra boxes need to be added to the basic program structure in order to represent the functions numbered 1, 4, 8, 9, 10, 11, 12. These boxes have been deliberately shaded in the detailed program structure given in figure 2.11. The letters written against each box in this figure indicates the order in which the detailed program structure is processed. Notice that box P has been used to represent two functions. Despite the comment inside the box being *write final total*, which is associated with function 3, a further function 13 has been included after function 3. Function 13 is an instruction to finish processing. An extra box to the right of box P could have been drawn, however, in the interests of economy of space this was not done. Whenever several functions are listed together under the same box the functions must be processed in the order left to right.

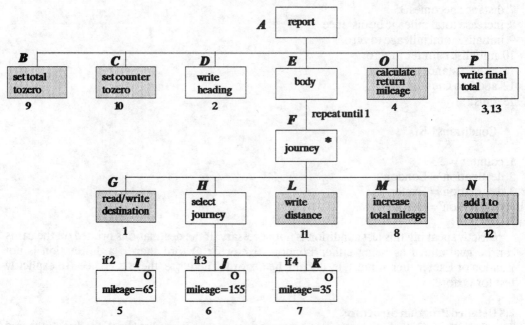

Figure 2.11 detailed program structure used to define the solution to the problem

2.9 Testing a Program Structure.

Whenever a program structure has been created it is good practice to check the logical correctness of the structure by tracing through the structure with suitable test data.

A table of values that change with the test data should be derived, showing the output from the design.

Box	Function	Condition	result (output in italics)
A			
B	9	total=0	
C	10	counter=0	
D	2		*REPORT ON JOURNEYS*
E		1 false	
F			
G	1		*destination ? Exeter*
H		3 true	
J	6	distance=155	
L	11		*distance = 155*
M	8	total=155	
N	12	counter=1	
E		1 false	
F			
G	1		*destination ? London*
H		2 true	

Box	Function		Condition	result(output in italics)
I	5	distance=65		
L	11			*distance = 65*
M	8	total=220		
N	12	counter=2		
E			1 false	
F				
G	1			*destination ? Oxford*
H			4 true	
K	7	distance=35		
L	11			*distance = 35*
M	8	total=255		
N	12	counter=3		
E			1 false	
F				
G	1			*destination ? London*
H			2 true	
I	5	distance=65		
L	11			*distance = 65*
M	8	total=320		
N	12	counter=4		
E			1 false	
F				
G	1			*destination ? Oxford*
H			4 true	
K	7	distance=35		
L	11			*distance = 35*
M	8	total=355		
N	12	counter=5		
E			1 true	
O	4	total=710		
P	3, 13			*total mileage for return trips 710 miles*

2.10 Summary

Designing a computer program provides documentation of what the program is meant to do.

The design can be checked for correctness before the program has been written.

With the use of code generators it is possible for the program design to be automatically transformed into a coded program.

The majority of programs contain groups of statements that represent sequence, selection and repetition.

The JSP method uses a specific notation for each of the constructs sequence, selection and repetition.

A detailed program structure is produced in JSP by the following steps.

The input and output structures for the data to be read and results to written are drawn.

The input and output structures are examined for correspondences between components in each structure and only if correspondence exists can the two structures be fused into one basic program structure.

The functions and conditions lists are documented.

Finally the basic program structure is enlarged to allow for all the functions to be inserted into the elementary components of the detailed program structure. The conditions associated with selection and repetition must also be inserted on to the diagram.

A detailed program structure should always be tested before any attempt is made to construct a computer program from it.

Keywords

Jackson Structured Programming (JSP);
sequence, selection, repetition;
input and output structures;
basic program structure, correspondence;
functions and conditions lists;
detailed program structure;
elementary item, testing.

2.11 Questions

Derive complete detailed program structure diagrams as answers to the following questions. A complete answer should contain the following parts.

(i)   Structure diagrams for the input and output components.
(ii)   An indication of the correspondences between components on the input structure with components on the output structure.
(iii) A basic program structure.
(iv)   Functions and conditions lists.
(v)   A detailed program structure.
(vi)   A documented test of the program structure using the data given in the output reports.

1. Using the price of a car example in section 2.3 as the basis of a program structure, read the cost of a car and the cost of the sundries and produce a report in the format shown.

COST OF CAR

Price of vehicle?   10000
Price of sundries? 500
Sub-total = 10500
VAT @ 15% = 1575
Total = 12075

2. Using the building society example in section 2.4 as the basis of a program structure, read the amounts invested by, say, five investors and output a report in the format shown.

> **XYZ Building Society**
>
> amount of investment ? 20000
> rate of interest = 8%
> annual interest = 1600
>
> amount of investment ? 10000
> rate of interest = 7%
> annual interest = 700
>
> amount of investment ? 05000
> rate of interest = 7%
> annual interest = 350
>
> amount of investment ? 25000
> rate of interest = 9%
> annual interest = 2250
>
> amount of investment ? 15000
> rate of interest = 8%
> annual interest = 1200

3. The figure below shows a pile of price tags as the input data and a bill of sale as the output report. Design a program structure to read each price tag in the pile and produce the bill of sale. You may assume two separate read/write statements, one for the description of an article, and the other for the price of an article.

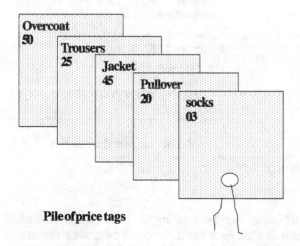

Overcoat
50

Trousers
25

Jacket
45

Pullover
20

socks
03

Pile of price tags

> **BILL OF SALE**
> article ? socks
> price ? 03
> article ? pullover
> price ? 20
> article ? jacket
> price ? 45
> article ? trousers
> price ? 25
> article ? overcoat
> price ? 50
>
> TOTAL = 143

Report on the sale from the pile of price tags

4. The figure below shows a pile of time cards for named employees. Each time card shows the number of hours an employee has worked in the previous week. If overtime is paid for hours in excess of 40, at a rate of £10 per hour then design a program structure to read the pile of time cards and produce a report showing the total amount of overtime to be paid, with an itemised billing of which employees are to receive the overtime payment. Again assume separate read/ write statements for the name and for the hours worked.

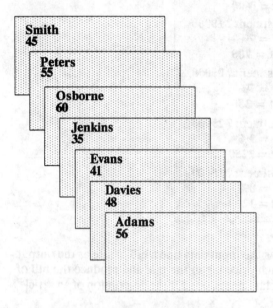

Pile of time cards for named employees

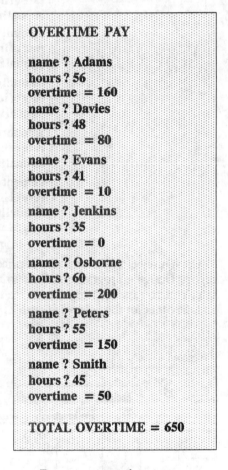

Report on overtime to pay

[5]. The figure over the page shows a pile of record cards indicating the names of pupils and the examination scores in computer programming for each pupil. Design a program structure to read the pile of cards and print the report shown. Assume separate read/ write statements for the name and for the examination mark. The pass mark for the examination is 40%.

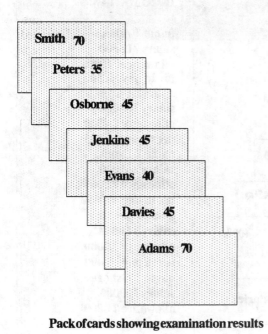

Pack of cards showing examination results

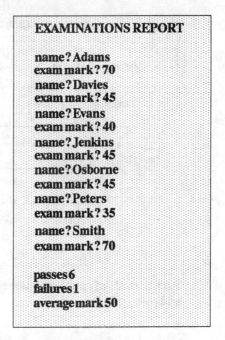

EXAMINATIONS REPORT

name? Adams
exam mark? 70
name? Davies
exam mark? 45
name? Evans
exam mark? 40
name? Jenkins
exam mark? 45
name? Osborne
exam mark? 45
name? Peters
exam mark? 35

name? Smith
exam mark? 70

passes 6
failures 1
average mark 50

Report on examination results

[6]. A simplified income tax system might use the following rules. Every wage earner will be eligible to claim a personal allowance to set against their gross salary before paying tax on the remainder of their salary. The personal allowance is based on their ability to pay income tax. Taxable income is calculated by subtracting the personal allowance from the gross salary. Income tax is calculated on taxable income according to the following tax bands.

The first £1000 is free of tax; the next £2000 is taxed at 20%; the next £2000 is taxed at 25% and all taxable income above £5000 is taxed at 30%.

From the figure over the page design a program to read the details from the cards and print a report on income tax. Assume separate read/ write statements for the name, salary and allowance.

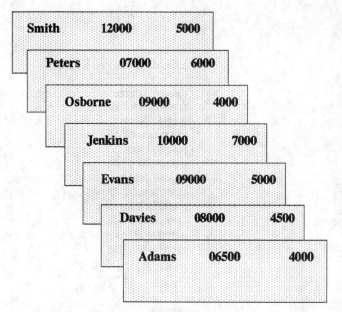

Pack of cards of employees names, gross salaries and personal allowances.

INCOME TAX

name ? Adams
salary ? 06500
allowance ? 4000
tax to pay = 300
name ? Davies
salary ? 08000
allowance ? 4500
tax to pay = 525
name ? Evans
salary ? 09000
allowance ? 5000
tax to pay = 650
name ? Jenkins
salary ? 10000
allowance ? 7000
tax to pay = 400
name ? Osborne
salary ? 09000
allowance ? 4000
tax to pay = 900
name ? Peters
 salary ? 07000
allowance ? 6000
tax to pay = 0
name ? Smith
salary ? 12000
allowance ? 5000
tax to pay = 1500

TOTAL TAX DUE = 4275

Report on tax to pay

3
Elements of COBOL

The purpose of this chapter is to give the reader an initial overview of the structure of a COBOL program and an introduction to the Procedure Division. Sufficient Procedure Division verbs will be introduced to enable the reader to program a complete Division in the next chapter.

3.1 Structure of a COBOL Program.

A COBOL program normally consists of up to four Divisions, in the order presented below, and with the following names.

IDENTIFICATION DIVISION.
ENVIRONMENT DIVISION.
DATA DIVISION.
PROCEDURE DIVISION.

The last three divisions can be subdivided into sections. Figure 3.1 illustrates a typical structure of a COBOL program. The reader should note that it is possible to write a somewhat restricted COBOL program using the minimum of two divisions - IDENTIFICATION DIVISION and PROCEDURE DIVISION. The four divisions and their respective sections have the following functions.

Identification Division - This allows the programmer to give a name to the program and provide useful comments such as the name of the author of the program, the date the program was written and compiled and remarks relating to the security of the program.

Environment Division - The CONFIGURATION SECTION is used to describe the make and model of the computer used to compile and run the program. The INPUT-OUTPUT SECTION has the primary function of describing the relationship between hardware devices (magnetic tape unit, magnetic disc unit, printer, etc) and the attributes of the files that use those devices.

Data Division - All Data Division statements relate to the format in which data is either input, stored or output. The FILE SECTION describes the format of records and data held on computer files. The WORKING-STORAGE SECTION is used to describe data that is local to the computer program. The LINKAGE SECTION describes data that is to be passed between COBOL programs when several programs are used for one particular application.

Procedure Division - The DECLARATIVES SECTION provide a method for including procedures which are invoked when a condition occurs which cannot be tested by the programmer. These sections are optional and a PROCEDURE DIVISION normally consists of procedural sections. These contain instructions that form the coded algorithm of the solution to a problem.

The last four paragraphs serve only as an introduction to the Divisions. Each division will be written about in detail, in context, later in the book. The first division to receive a more rigorous treatment is the Procedure Division, since it is through this division that the logical solution to a problem is expressed.

3.2 The Procedure Division.

The Procedure Division has a hierarchical structure. Procedure Division code can be optionally subdivided into sections; sections are subdivided into paragraphs; paragraphs are subdivided into sentences; sentences are subdivided into one or more COBOL statements.

Sections and paragraphs must be given a name according to the following convention. Some compilers will allow paragraphs to be empty, that is, the paragraph is given a name but does not contain any sentences. The use of such a technique would be for documentation purposes.

A paragraph can contain zero, one or more sentences and is referenced by a paragraph name. A paragraph name can contain up to thirty characters taken from the characters A through to Z, a through to z, 0 through to 9, or a combination of the alphabetic letters and digits, and the name may contain embedded hyphens.

Paragraph names must not be taken from the list of COBOL reserved words (Appendix III). An example of legal paragraph names would be:

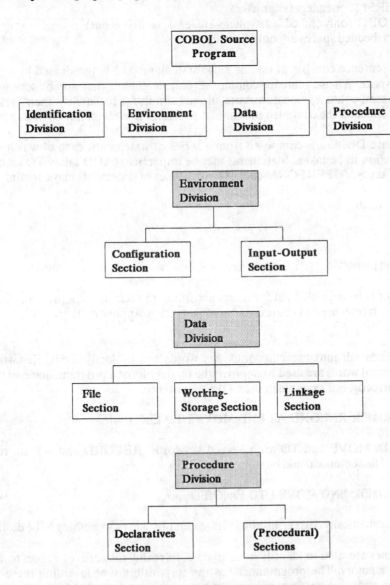

Figure 3.1 Composition of a COBOL program

TAX-SEQ
CALC-ITER
CODE-SEL
A
B3
Begin-Report

Illegal paragraph names would be:

START (reserved word)
ANSWERS? (? not a legal character)
-END-POINT (only embedded hyphens are legal the first is not)
E O F (embedded spaces are not allowed)

A COBOL sentence consists of one or more statements and is terminated by a full-stop (period) and a space. When a sentence contains several statements they may be separated by a comma (,) or a semi-colon (;). Separators are allowed simply for readability, their presence or absence has no effect on the compiled program. A separator must be followed by a space.

The Procedure Division is composed from a series of statements, each of which calls for some kind of action to be taken. Statements may be imperative (ADD salary TO account) or conditional (IF tax > 500 PERFORM code-X). Both types of statements may contain:

reserved words
variables
literals
symbols
paragraph names.

Reserved words have predefined meanings according to their use in a program. Reserved words must be correctly used in context and spelt correctly. Appendix III gives a list of Cobol reserved words.

Reserved words fall into two categories, key words and optional words. Key words are obligatory. Optional words are used to improve the readability of a program, however, if used, must be used correctly. For example in the COBOL sentence:

READ DataFile RECORD AT **END MOVE** 1 **TO** EndOfFile.

READ, END, MOVE and TO are reserved keywords, RECORD and AT are reserved optional words. The sentence could be shortened to:

READ DataFile **END MOVE** 1 **TO** EndOfFile.

and it would be syntactically correct, although its readability leaves something to be desired!

Variable names are used to identify items of data. In reality they are references to areas of the computer's memory. The programmer has the responsibility of inventing these names. Variable names should therefore convey the meaning and nature of the data and be documented in the form of a glossary. Remember the author of a program is not always the person who has to maintain the program, and there is nothing more frustrating when attempting to maintain a program than to have to guess the meaning and nature of variable names that are not your own creation.

The rules of composition of variable names are similar to those for paragraph names. However, the first character must be alphabetic (A through to Z) or (a through to z) and the variable name is not terminated by a full-stop (period) unless the variable name is the last word of a sentence. An example of legal variable names would be:

    TAX-IN-HAND
    P35
    point-of-sale
    Gross-Salary

and illegal variable names would be:

    COUNT (reserved word)
    8XKT (begins with a non-alphabetic character)
    BANK-NO- (hyphens must be embedded)
    ! COST (! and embedded space illegal)
    PRICE£ (£ is illegal)

Literals give an actual value that is used in a program. They fall into two categories - numeric literals (numeric constants) and non-numeric literals (character strings). Numeric literals contain up to eighteen characters taken from the digits (0 through to 9), and the characters plus (+), minus (-) and the decimal point (.). Note the hyphen and minus sign are the same character, so to is the decimal point and full-stop. The + and - sign is optional, if it is used it should precede the digits. Examples of numeric literals are:

    3   +17.8 -132   0.00394   -526.2 +0.1509

Non-numeric literals are character strings containing up to 160 characters taken from either the ASCII or EBCDIC character sets. The character set used will be dependent upon the make of computer being used. For example Prime use ASCII, IBM use EBCDIC.

The character string must be delimited by either identical apostrophes or quotation marks, according to the COBOL compiler being used.

Examples of non-numeric literals are:

    'EMPLOYEE DETAILS' '123456'   "TAX POINT" 'DIVISION'
    "DO'S & DON'TS"   'stock item'

A special case can be made for a third type of literal. This is the figurative constant which strictly speaking falls into the category of reserved words. The figurative constants that are commonly used within this book are:

    ZERO represents numeric 0

SPACE or SPACES represent one or more space characters
HIGH-VALUE or HIGH-VALUES represents one or more of the character that has
the highest ordinal position in either the ASCII or EBCDIC codes.

There are other figurative constants but they will not be considered here.

3.3 COBOL Character Set.

This must not be confused with either the ASCII or EBCDIC character sets. The COBOL
character set describes those characters that are used to write COBOL computer programs
and is a subset of the ASCII or EBCDIC character sets.

The COBOL character set consists of:

```
0,1, ..., 9 digit
A,B, ..., Z uppercase letter
a,b, ..., z lowercase letter
+ plus sign
- minus sign (hyphen)
* asterisk (multiplication sign)
/ slash (division sign)
= equal sign
$ currency sign
, comma
; semicolon
. full-stop (decimal point)
" quotation mark
( left parenthesis open
) right parenthesis closed
> greater than
< less than
: colon
    space
```

3.4 COBOL Program Sheet.

The programmer, regardless of experience, should refrain from composing programs at the
computer terminal. The purpose of the COBOL program sheet is for writing or coding a
COBOL program having first carefully designed and tested the algorithm. Figure 3.2 shows the
layout of a COBOL program sheet.

Columns 1 through 6, and 73 through to 80 are part of a hangover from the use of punched
cards as an input medium. Their purpose is of no importance here.

The three important areas of the COBOL program sheet are as follows.

Column 7 - this is known as the indicator area. If a hyphen (-) is present in this column it
indicates that the current line, containing the hyphen, is to be used as a continuation from the
previous line. In the context of this book the hyphen in column 7 will only be used to continue a
non-numeric literal from one line to another. This will be explained later in the text.

If an asterisk (*) is used in column 7 then the remainder of the line can be used for writing comments into the program.

Columns 8 through to 11 represent zone A or area A. In the context of this chapter Division and section headings and paragraph names must begin in zone A, and be terminated by a full-stop (period).

There are other entries in a COBOL program that must begin in zone A but these will be dealt with in later chapters.

Columns 12 through to 72 represent zone B or area B. Again in the context of this chapter all sentences in the Procedure Division must be confined to this zone.

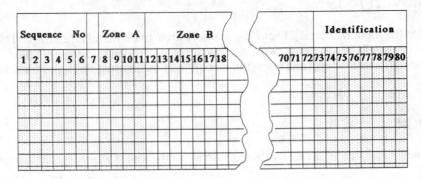

Figure 3.2 COBOL Program Sheet

3.5 Language Notation.
In defining COBOL statements the following notation will be used.

All reserved words are printed in upper-case letters. Key reserved words are printed in bold type, with the exception of Appendix II where they are underlined, optional reserved words are printed in normal type.

The use of square brackets [ ] indicates that items within the square brackets can be omitted. The use of braces { } indicates that a choice must be made between the various contents of the braces. If the braces contain a single entry then no choice is implied.

The use of ellipsis ..... represents the position at which the user elects repetition of a portion of the format. The portion of the format that may be repeated is determined as follows.

Given ..... in a format, scanning right to left, determine the closing] or } delimiter immediately to the left of ..... ; continue scanning right to left and determine the logically matching opening [or { delimiter; the ..... applies to the portion of the format between the determined pair of delimiters.

The author has introduced only the minimum syntax for the COBOL statements that follow. This is a deliberate policy so as to avoid cluttering-up the reader's mind with unnecessary syntax at such early stage in the book. The reader can always refer to Appendix II for the full syntax of each statement.

3.6 Data Movement.
The MOVE statement transfers data from one area of main memory to another.

Format   **MOVE** $\left\{ \begin{array}{l} \text{identifier-1} \\ \text{literal-1} \end{array} \right\}$ **TO**   {identifier-2} ....

Note: the term identifier has the same meaning as data name or variable.

Examples.
        MOVE 21 TO age

will move the numeric literal 21 into the memory area given the identifier age. The original contents of age will be lost or overwritten. This can be illustrated by using a simple before (the execution of the instruction) and after (the execution of the instruction) representation.

	age
before	56
after	5̶6̶21

The next example shows that it is possible to move the same value to more than one area of memory.

        MOVE 16 TO a,b,c

	a	b	c
before	12	9	-14
after	1̶2̶16	9̶16	-̶1̶4̶16

Note: a comma (,) although not part of the format of a MOVE statement can be used to separate identifiers.

        MOVE "GB" TO codes

	codes
before	SA
after	S̶A̶ GB

The MOVE statement is not confined to moving literals, the contents of identifiers can also be moved.

        MOVE a TO b, c

	a	b	c
before	21	13	-9
after	21	1̶3̶ 21	-̶9̶21

Note: the original contents of a remains unchanged, only the contents of b and c are overwritten.

Figurative constants can also be used in a MOVE statement.

>MOVE ZERO TO total   or
>MOVE ZERO TO total-a, total-b, total-c

Both statements move numeric zero to the respective destination identifiers.

3.7 Arithmetic.
The ADD statement adds together two or more numeric values and stores the resulting sum.

Format 1.   **ADD** $\begin{Bmatrix} \text{identifier-1} \\ \text{literal-1} \end{Bmatrix}$ ..... **TO**   identifier-2

Format 2.   **ADD** $\begin{Bmatrix} \text{identifier-1} \\ \text{literal-1} \end{Bmatrix}$ ..... TO $\begin{Bmatrix} \text{identifier-2} \\ \text{literal-2} \end{Bmatrix}$ **GIVING** identifier-3

Note: in format 2 the reserved word TO is optional, when TO is omitted this format will conform to the 1974 standard.

Examples.
>ADD a TO b

the contents of a is added to the contents of b and the sum is stored in b.

	a	b
before	17	19
after	17	19 36

>ADD a, b GIVING c

the contents of a is added to the contents of b and the sum is stored in c.

	a	b	c
before	5	9	12
after	5	9	12 14

>ADD 36.1 TO alpha

	alpha
before	20.7
after	20.7 56.8

>ADD j, k, l, m GIVING n

	j	k	l	m	n
before	2	3	4	5	6
after	2	3	4	5	6 14

Note: the commas between the operands are optional separators.

The SUBTRACT statement subtracts one or more numeric data items from a specified item and stores the difference.

Format   **SUBTRACT**   {identifier-1 / literal-1}   ..... **FROM**   {identifier-2 [**GIVING** identifier-3] / literal-2}

Examples.
SUBTRACT a FROM b

the contents of a is taken from b and the result is stored in b, overwriting the original contents of b.

	a	b
before	16	24
after	16	2̶4̶8

SUBTRACT a FROM b GIVING c

this is similar to the last example only the result is stored in c thus preventing the original contents of b from being overwritten.

	a	b	c
before	17	32	19
after	17	32	1̶9̶15

SUBTRACT a, b, c FROM d

the contents of a, b and c are added together and the result is subtracted from d.

	a	b	c	d
before	1	2	3	4
after	1	2	3	4̶-2

SUBTRACT k, l, m FROM n GIVING x

this is similar to the last example only the result is stored in x.

	k	l	m	n	x
before	5	6	7	8	9
after	5	6	7	8	9̶-10

The MULTIPLY statement computes the product of two numeric data items.

Format   **MULTIPLY**   {identifier-1 / literal-1}   **BY**   {identifier-2 / literal-2}   [**GIVING** identifier-3]

Examples
MULTIPLY 12 BY years

the contents of years is multiplied by 12 and the result stored in years.

	years
before	5
after	~~5~~60

>   MULTIPLY units BY price GIVING cost

the contents of units is multiplied by the contents of price and the result is stored in cost.

	units	price	cost
before	10	20	30
after	10	20	~~30~~200

The DIVIDE statement divides one numeric data item into another and stores the result.

Format **DIVIDE** $\left\{ \begin{array}{l} \text{identifier-1} \\ \text{literal-1} \end{array} \right\}$ **INTO** $\left\{ \begin{array}{l} \text{identifier-2} \\ \text{literal-2} \end{array} \right\}$ [**GIVING** identifier-3]

Examples
>   DIVIDE 5 INTO sum

the contents of sum is divided by 5 and the result is stored in sum.

	sum
before	36.20
after	~~36.20~~7.24

>   DIVIDE counter INTO total GIVING mean

the contents of total is divided by counter and the result is stored in mean.

	counter	total	mean
before	10	140	23
after	10	140	~~23~~14

The COMPUTE statement evaluates an arithmetic expression, a numeric literal or an identifier and stores the result.

Format. **COMPUTE** identifier-1 = $\left\{ \begin{array}{l} \text{identifier-2} \\ \text{literal-1} \\ \text{arithmetic expression} \end{array} \right\}$

Examples
>   COMPUTE allowance = 2300

the contents of allowance is changed to 2300.

	allowance
before	1200
after	~~1200~~2300

COMPUTE allowance = child-benefit

the contents of allowance is changed to the contents of child-benefit.

	allowance	child-benefit
before	1200	240
after	~~1200~~240	240

COMPUTE gross-wage = hourly-rate * 1.5 * (hours-worked - 20)

the arithmetic expression is evaluated using the contents of hourly-rate and hours-worked, the result is stored in gross-wage.

Notes: parenthesis ( ) may be used in arithmetic expressions to specify the order in which operands are used for arithmetic. A hierarchy of evaluation for operators exists for non-parenthesised expressions:

highest priority	+ or - unary (single) sign		
	** exponentiation		
	* multiplication	/	division (same priority)
lowest priority	+ addition	-	subtraction (same priority)

If an expression contains operators of the same priority and is not parenthesised then evaluation is from left to right in the expression.

An operator must always be preceded and followed by a space.

A left parenthesis is preceded by one or more spaces, a right parenthesis is followed by one or more spaces.

Comment. The reader may wonder from looking at Appendix II what the options ROUNDED and ON SIZE ERROR do. The options are of little importance in this chapter, however, they will be explained in full in the context of a later chapter.

3.8 Input and Output.
The ACCEPT statement causes low volume data to be made available to the specified identifier.

Format.   **ACCEPT** identifier-1

Example.   ACCEPT alpha

When this statement is executed the computer will wait for a value for alpha to be input. If a keyboard is used to input data into the computer system then a value corresponding to alpha, terminated by an enter or return key being pressed, must be typed at the keyboard. The computer will then continue with the execution of the rest of the program. In the execution of the ACCEPT statement the computer does not output a prompt on to, say, the screen of a visual display unit, and so there is no way of knowing when to input the data!

The DISPLAY statement causes low volume data to be transferred to an appropriate hardware device (screen of a visual display unit).

Format. **DISPLAY** $\begin{Bmatrix} \text{identifier-1} \\ \text{literal-1} \end{Bmatrix}$ ..... [WITH **NO ADVANCING**]

Examples.
DISPLAY beta

the value of beta would be displayed upon the screen of a visual display unit, and the cursor would move to the left-hand end of the next line down.

DISPLAY "interest gained over one year .. "

the string literal *interest gained over one year ..* would be displayed on the screen and the cursor would move down to the next line.

DISPLAY "interest gained over one year .. ", interest

the string literal *interest gained over one year ..* would be displayed followed by the value of interest. The cursor would then advance to the next line. Note the comma has been used as an optional separator in the statement.

DISPLAY "input price .. " WITH NO ADVANCING
the string *input price ..* would be displayed and the cursor would remain on the same line. Therefore, the combined statements:

DISPLAY "input price .. " WITH NO ADVANCING, ACCEPT price

would be used to display the prompt *input price ..* on the screen, leaving the cursor in the position on the same line and immediately after the prompt. The computer would then be ready to accept a value for price from the keyboard.

Note: The WITH NO ADVANCING option is not defined in the ANS 1974 Standard for COBOL. However, you may find that the option has been included as an extension to the Standard and is peculiar to the dialect of the language for the compiler being used. If your compiler does not support this option then you must modify all the DISPLAY statements that use it in the programs in this book, otherwise they will not compile correctly. The modification of deleting the words WITH NO ADVANCING will have the effect of positioning the cursor at the left-hand end of the next line.

3.9 Selection.
The IF statement causes a condition to be evaluated. The subsequent action of the computer depends upon whether the value of the condition is true or false.

Format.   **IF** *condition* {statement-1} .....
           [**ELSE** {statement-2} .....]

Where the *condition* can be defined as:

operand-1   *relational operator*   operand-2

where each operand can be a variable name, an arithmetic expression, a literal, or a figuartive constant, although both operands cannot be literals or constants. The *relational operators* are defined as:

EQUAL TO	*or* **=**		
LESS THAN	*or* **<**	**LESS THAN OR EQUAL TO**	*or* **<=**
GREATER THAN	*or* **>**	**GREATER THAN OR EQUAL TO**	*or* **>=**

Every operator may be preceded by IS [**NOT**] with the exception of **>=** and **<=** or the equivalent operator using reserved words.

Two or more conditions can be combined by the logical operators AND and OR. The format of a combined condition would be:

$$\text{IF condition-1} \begin{Bmatrix} \text{AND} \\ \text{OR} \end{Bmatrix} \text{condition-2} \begin{Bmatrix} \text{AND} \\ \text{OR} \end{Bmatrix} \text{condition-3} \ldots$$

Examples.
IF a > 23 MOVE ZERO TO a.
next sentence

If the condition *a > 23* is true then the statement *MOVE ZERO TO a* will be executed and the computer will execute the statement in the next sentence. If the condition *a > 23* is false the computer will execute the statement in the next sentence. The period at the end of the statement MOVE ZERO TO a is extremely important since it marks the end of the sentence that will be executed if the condition was true.

IF a IS NOT ZERO ADD c TO d, MOVE x TO y, SUBTRACT 6 FROM d.
next sentence

If the condition *a IS NOT ZERO* is true then the three statements *ADD c TO d, MOVE x TO y, SUBTRACT 6 FROM d* that make up a sentence will be executed, and the computer will then obey the statement(s) of the next sentence that follows the IF statement. If the condition is false the computer will only execute the statement(s) in the next sentence.

IF age > 18 AND height > 68
        ADD 1 TO count-person
ELSE
        ADD 1 TO reject-person.
next sentence

If both the conditions age > 18 and height > 68 are true then the statement ADD 1 TO count-person will be executed by the computer, however, if either or both conditions are false then the computer will execute the statement ADD 1 TO reject-person. Regardless of which statement was executed by the computer the machine will go on to execute the statement(s) of the next sentence.

```
IF a > b
     IF c > d
          ACCEPT alpha
     ELSE
          ACCEPT beta
ELSE
     ACCEPT gamma.
```
next sentence

If the condition $a > b$ is true then computer will test the condition $c > d$, if this is also true then the statement ACCEPT alpha will be executed; if the condition c > d is false then the statement ACCEPT beta will be executed. After the execution of either statement the computer will execute the statement(s) of the next sentence. If the condition a > b is false then the computer will execute the statement ACCEPT gamma, followed by the statement(s) of the next sentence.

Note: no period appears after the statement *ACCEPT beta* since this would violate the syntax of the outer IF .. ELSE .. statement.

3.10 Repetition.

The out-of-line PERFORM statement enables statements to be repeated until a condition becomes true.

PERFORM paragraph-name-1 $\left\{\begin{matrix} \text{THROUGH} \\ \text{THRU} \end{matrix}\right\}$ paragraph-name-2 [UNTIL condition-1]

Examples of using out-of-line perform.
If the UNTIL option is omitted control passes to paragraph-name-1 and all the statements contained within the two paragraphs are executed once. Control then returns to the next executable statement after the perform.

```
          PERFORM para-1 THRU para-2

para-1.
          ADD a TO b.
          MULTIPLY 2.3 BY c.
          SUBTRACT b FROM c.
para-2.
          DISPLAY a,b,c.
```

When the UNTIL option is specified the PERFORM mechanism just described is repeated until the exit condition is true. The test for the exit condition will be prior to the execution of the PERFORM. If the condition is false the COBOL statements contained in para-1 and para-2 will be executed repeatedly until the exit condition is true.

```
        MOVE 5 TO counter.
        PERFORM para-1 THRU para-2 UNTIL counter = 0
        next statement

para-1.
        ACCEPT price.
        ADD price TO total.
para-2.
        SUBTRACT 1 FROM counter.
```

If the exit condition is true prior to the execution of the PERFORM statement then PERFORM will not be obeyed, but control will revert to the next statement.

3.11 Program Termination.
The execution of a program is terminated by the statement STOP RUN.

3.12 Summary.
A COBOL program contains up to four Divisions. The Identification and Procedure Divisions are mandatory. However, the inclusion of a Data Division is normally essential.

The elements of a Procedure Division contain section and paragraph names; paragraphs containing sentences; sentences containing statements; statements containing reserved words, variable names and symbols.

COBOL programs must only use characters taken from the COBOL character set, which is a subset of the ANSI and EBCDIC sets.

COBOL programs cannot be written using a free-format. Division, section and paragraph names must start between columns 8 through 11 (zone A); other COBOL statements must be written between columns 12 through to 72 (zone B). When column 7 contains an asterisk a single-line comment may be written, otherwise if it contains a hyphen it can be used for the continuation from the previous line of a string literal. Columns 1 through 6 and columns 73 through 80 are no longer relevant.

The lines in a COBOL program may be spaced apart by the inclusion of blank lines.

In the Procedure Division data is transferred between areas of computer memory (between variable names) by the MOVE statement.

Arithmetic is performed on data by using the statements ADD, SUBTRACT, MULTIPLY, DIVIDE and COMPUTE.

The ACCEPT statement will allow low-volume keyboard input, and the DISPLAY statement will allow low-volume screen output.

Selection is possible by the the use of IF statements.

Repetition is possible by the use of the out-of-line PERFORM.

The execution of a program is terminated by using STOP RUN.

Keywords

*Identification, Environment, Data and Procedure Divisions;
paragraph, sentence, reserved words, literals, variables;
COBOL character set, COBOL program sheet;
MOVE, ADD, SUBTRACT, MULTIPLY, DIVIDE, COMPUTE;
IF .. ELSE .. , out-of-line PERFORM;
ACCEPT, DISPLAY, STOP RUN.*

3.13 Questions.

[1]. Deduce answers to the following statements that relate to the COBOL language.

(a) A COBOL program must have all four divisions present.
(b) The order in which divisions are written is not important.
(c) A sentence may contain one statement.
(d) Variable names and paragraph names can be the same.
(e) The characters , and ; can be used in a sentence.
(f) Each paragraph may contain one sentence.
(g) Paragraph names are not necessary in a Procedure Division.

2. Which characters belong to the COBOL character set?

     + ! ? * / < [^ a A

3. Which variable names are illegal, state why?

(a) Gross-Salary   (b) wage/3   (c) 23   (d) DATA   (e) DATA-VALUE
(f) *para 1   (g) count   (h) 247.34   (i) a3   (j) tax allowance

4. Which paragraph names are illegal, state why?

(a) para 1   (b) DATA DIVISION   (c) c-iter   (d) c end
(e) 1   (f) * begin   (g) start   (h) max val out
(i) "a-seq"   (j) a-end

5. Identify the various types of literals listed.

(a) 123.96   (b) "ABCD" (c) "ADDRESS" (d) 0.01478   (e) ZERO
(f) -36   (g) +6.4   (h) SPACE   (i) HIGH-VALUE

6. Comment upon the errors in the following literals.

(a) 3,649   (b) HIGH VALUES   (c) "BANK" ACCOUNT   (d) -.215
(e) 467. 63   (f) NOUGHT   (g) "name   (h) +0. 147
(i) DATA

7. Which literals or variables can be used in arithmetic?

(a) thirty-two   (b) "thirty-two"   (c) 1234   (d) "1234"   (e) SPACE
(f) ZERO

[8]. Deduce answers to the following statements.

(a) A paragraph name may start in column 9.
(b) Procedure Division statements can be split over several lines on a program sheet provided a hyphen is present in column 7.
(c) A sentence may be coded between columns 30 to 70 on one line.
(d) A comment line requires an asterisk in column 1.
(e) Columns 1 through 6 and 73 through 80 must never be used when coding a COBOL program.

9. Identify the syntax errors in the following arithmetic statements.

(a) ADD a TO 3.5
(b) SUBTRACT X FROM Y Z
(c) ADD A TO B GIVING C
(d) MULTIPLY X TIMES Y
(e) DIVIDE X INTO 5
(f) COMPUTE = 3.4 * a * b
(g) COMPUTER a = b + c

10. What are the values of the following identifiers after the execution of the respective instructions?

(a) MOVE a TO b, c, d   a   b   c   d
                        36 98 45 29
(b) ADD a, b, c TO d   a   b   c   d
                        10 14 29 36
(c) ADD a, b GIVING c   a   b   c
                        24 98 23
(d) SUBTRACT x FROM y   x   y
                        17 32
(e) SUBTRACT u, v, w FROM x   u   v   w   x
                            29 32 84 78
(f) SUBTRACT 3 FROM a GIVING b   a   b
                                16 22
(g) MULTIPLY x BY y GIVING z   x   y   z
                            18 3   27
(h) DIVIDE a INTO b   a   b
                        6   42
(i) COMPUTE a = a + b   a   b
                        3   9
(j) COMPUTE u = v + w * x   u   v   w   x
                            17 13 6   4

[11]. Evaluate the following expressions given that a=6, b=4, c=2 and d=16.

(a) a + b / c   (b) a / (b + c)   (c) a * b / (c * d)
(d) (d - b) / 2 / a   (e) (a - b) * (c - d)

[12]. What are the errors in the following COBOL expressions?

(a) a.b (b) x*-y   (c) (64 + b)/-6   (d) ((a + b) / (c + d) (e) (a - b) (a + b)

[13]. Re-write the following COBOL expressions as mathematical expressions.

(a) x + y * 3 (b) x + 2 / Y + 4   (c) a * b / (c + 2)   (d) a / b + c * d / (f * g * h)
(e) 1 / (x + y) * 2   (f) a / b + c / d + e / f

14. Identify the syntax errors in the following statements.

(a) ACCEPT alpha, beta, gamma
(b) PRINT "tax allowance" tax-allowance
(c) IF a > 3 THEN ADD b TO c
(d) PERFORM ADD a TO b UNTIL b > 1000
(e) DIVIDE x BY y

15. If the initial values of a,b and c are always 2, 3 and 4 respectively, what are their values after the execution of the following statements?

(a)   IF a > b ADD a, b GIVING c.

(b)   IF c > a MOVE ZERO TO a.

(c)   IF a > b
            ADD a, b GIVING c
        ELSE
            SUBTRACT c FROM b.

(d)   IF b > a
            IF c < b
                ADD a,b GIVING c
            ELSE
                MOVE ZERO TO a
        ELSE
            ADD a TO b.

16. If the initial values of x, y and z are always 7, 3 and 5 respectively what are the values of x, y and z after the following statements have been executed?

(a)   PERFORM para-1.
        STOP RUN.
para-1.
        ADD x,y GIVING z.

(b)   PERFORM para-1 THRU para-2.
        STOP RUN.
para-1.
        ADD 1 TO x.
        ADD 2 TO y.
para-2.
        SUBTRACT 3 FROM z.

(c)   PERFORM para-1 UNTIL z=0.
        STOP RUN.
para-1.
        MULTIPLY 2 BY y.
        SUBTRACT 1 FROM z.

(d)   PERFORM para-1 THRU para-2 UNTIL x > 10.
        STOP RUN.
para-1.
        ADD 5 TO y.
        SUBTRACT 3 FROM z.
para-2.
        ADD 1 TO x.

17. The following code is a complete Procedure Division for a COBOL program. When the program is executed by the computer what will be output to the screen of a VDU if the values of a and b are input at the keyboard as 4 and 5 respectively?

```
PROCEDURE DIVISION.
para-1.
        DISPLAY "input a " WITH NO ADVANCING, ACCEPT a.
        DISPLAY "input b " WITH NO ADVANCING, ACCEPT b.
        PERFORM para-2 UNTIL a=0.
        STOP RUN.
para-2.
        IF a > b
            DISPLAY " World! ", SUBTRACT 2 FROM a
        ELSE
            DISPLAY " Hello " WITH NO ADVANCING, SUBTRACT 2 FROM b.
```

4

A Complete Program

This chapter illustrates how to code the Procedure Division of a COBOL program. The final program design developed in Chapter 2 and the COBOL statements discussed in the last chapter are combined to produce a Procedure Division. The Identification and Data Divisions are explained in more detail and coded and combined with the Procedure Division to produce a complete program.

4.1 Procedure Division Coding.

In chapter 2 it was stated that structured computer programs would contain up to three identifiable program structures known as sequence, selection and repetition, and the JSP method had a diagrammatic notation for each structure.

From the last chapter it should be clear to the reader that the COBOL language can also cater for these three structures. A sequence would be coded as a series of COBOL statements or sentences that can be invoked using an out-of-line PERFORM .. THROUGH .. statement; a selection would be coded using the IF .. ELSE .. statement; and a repetition would be coded using an out-of-line PERFORM .. UNTIL statement.

The final program structure diagram given in chapter 2 has been re-drawn on the next page as figure 4.1. Each box in the diagram has been given a letter of the alphabet from A to P inclusive, and each row of boxes has been given a level number from level 1 to level 5 inclusive. The boxes have been alphabetically labelled in the order that the structure diagram must be traversed if it is to represent the solution to the problem. From the structure diagram, components can be identified as either a sequence (seq), selection (sel) or repetition (rep) by considering the nature of the components at the next level down in the diagram.

Starting at level 1, box A is a sequence (A-seq) since the boxes B,C,D,E,O and P appear diagrammatically as items in a sequence (note the absence of * or o in each of these boxes). Progressing down the structure to level 2, boxes B,C,D,O and P are elementary items and box E is a repetition (E-rep) with box F, at level 3, being the component that is repeated (presence of * in box F). Upon inspecting level 4 below box F, it is clear that box F is a sequence (F-seq) since the boxes G,H,L,M and N appear diagrammatically as items in a sequence. Boxes G,L,M and N are elementary items and box H is a selection (H-sel). Finally at level 5 in the program structure boxes I, J and K are elementary items.

The notation given to each box in the structure diagram will be used as a paragraph name in the Procedure Division. This will provide a one-to-one correspondence between the diagram and the code of the Procedure Division.

With reference to the detailed program structure on the opposite page, starting at level 1, since box A is a sequence it will be coded using a PERFORM .. THROUGH .. as:

```
A-seq.
    PERFORM B THROUGH P.
```

Moving down the structure diagram to level 2, all the elementary items can be coded into COBOL sentences. For example, the function for box B is number 9, *Initialise total mileage to zero*, which is coded as:

```
B.    MOVE ZERO TO total.
```

The function for box C is number 10, *Initialise counter to zero* which is coded as:

```
C.    MOVE ZERO TO counter.
```

The function for box D is number 2, *Write heading to report*, which is coded as:

```
D.    DISPLAY "REPORT ON JOURNEYS". DISPLAY SPACE.
```

The DISPLAY SPACE produces a blank line after the heading.

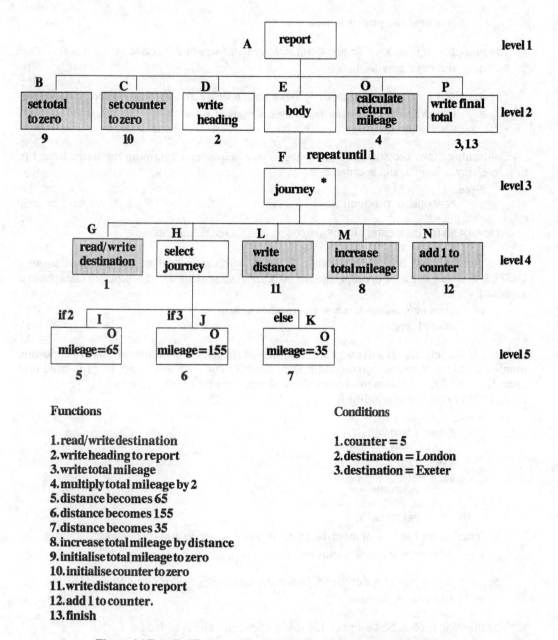

Functions

1. read/write destination
2. write heading to report
3. write total mileage
4. multiply total mileage by 2
5. distance becomes 65
6. distance becomes 155
7. distance becomes 35
8. increase total mileage by distance
9. initialise total mileage to zero
10. initialise counter to zero
11. write distance to report
12. add 1 to counter.
13. finish

Conditions

1. counter = 5
2. destination = London
3. destination = Exeter

Figure 4.1 Detailed Program Structure taken from section 2.8 in chapter 2

Since E is a repetition it will be coded using a PERFORM .. UNTIL statement, where condition number 1, *counter = 5* is incorporated into the PERFORM and coded as:

```
E-rep.
        PERFORM F-seq UNTIL counter = 5.
```

The function for box O is number 4, *Multiply total mileage by 2* is coded as:

```
O.      MULTIPLY 2 BY total.
```

The functions for box P are number 3, *Write total mileage* and 13, *Stop* which are coded as:

```
P.      DISPLAY "total mileage for return trips is " total, " miles".
        STOP RUN.
```

Continuing down the structure to level 3, F is a sequence containing the items from the next level down, level 4, and is coded as:

```
F-seq.
        PERFORM G THROUGH N.
```

At level 4 all the elementary items are coded into COBOL sentences.

The function for box G is number 1, *Read/write destination* which is coded using a DISPLAY statement as a prompt and an ACCEPT statement for the input of data from a keyboard.

```
G.      DISPLAY "destination ? " WITH NO ADVANCING.
        ACCEPT city.
```

Since H is a selection it will be coded using nested IF .. ELSE .. statements, where condition number 2, *city = "London"* ; and condition number 3, *city = "Exeter"* ; are incorporated into each IF .. ELSE .. statement respectively. Each branch of the selection is coded as a PERFORM to the corresponding item at level 5.

```
H-sel.
        IF city = "London"
            PERFORM I
        ELSE
            IF city = "Exeter"
                PERFORM J
            ELSE
                PERFORM K.
```

The function for box L is number 11, *Write distance to report* and is coded as:

```
L.      DISPLAY "distance = ", distance.
```

The function for box M is number 8, *Increase total mileage by distance* and is coded as:

```
M.      ADD distance TO total.
```

The function for box N is number 12, *Add 1 to counter* and is coded as:

```
N.      ADD 1 TO counter.
```

Finally at level 5, the function for box I is number 5, *Distance becomes 65* and is coded as:

```
I.      MOVE 65 TO distance.
```

Similarly the functions for box J and box K are respectively numbers 6, *Distance becomes 155* and 7, *Distance becomes 35,* and can be coded as:

J.   **MOVE 155 TO distance.**

K.   **MOVE 35 TO distance.**

These COBOL statements should be coded on to a COBOL coding sheet as depicted in figure 4.2. Notice that both the Division heading and paragraph names are coded from column 8. The procedural statements, that are instructions to the computer, are coded from column 12.

Sequence No							Zone A												Zone B														
1	2	3	4	5	6	7	8	9	10	11	12	13	14	15	16	17	18	19	20	21	22	23	24	25	26	27	28	29	30	31	32	33	34
							P	R	O	C	E	D	U	R	E		D	I	V	I	S	I	O	N	.								
							A	-	s	e	q	.																					
										P	E	R	F	O	R	M		B		T	H	R	O	U	G	H		P	.				
							B	.		M	O	V	E		Z	E	R	O		T	O		t	o	t	a	l	.					
							C	.		M	O	V	E		Z	E	R	O		T	O		c	o	u	n	t	e	r	.			
							D	.		D	I	S	P	L	A	Y		"	R	E	P	O	R	T		O	N		J	O	U	R	N
										D	I	S	P	L	A	Y		S	P	A	C	E	.										
							E	-	r	e	p	.																						

Figure 4.2   Layout of code on a COBOL coding sheet

A complete Procedure Division that represents the structure diagram given in figure 4.1 follows. Although the column numbers are not marked in this computer listing it is assumed that the Division heading and paragraph names start in column 8, and the procedural statements start from column 12. The use of columns should be evident to the reader from the indentation used. Comments have been inserted into this code to show how each level relates back to the detailed program structure given in figure 4.1. A comment can be made on a line by coding an asterisk * in column 7.

```
        PROCEDURE DIVISION.

*  --------------------- level 1 ---------------------------------


        A-seq.
            PERFORM B THROUGH P.


*  --------------------- level 2 ---------------------------------


        B.  MOVE ZERO TO total.
        C.  MOVE ZERO TO counter.
        D.  DISPLAY "REPORT ON JOURNEYS".
            DISPLAY SPACE.
        E-rep.
            PERFORM F-seq UNTIL counter = 5.
```

```
O.   MULTIPLY 2 BY TOTAL.
P.   DISPLAY "total mileage for return trips is ", total, " miles".
     STOP RUN.


* ----------------------- level 3 -----------------------------


F-seq.
     PERFORM G THROUGH N.


* ----------------------- level 4 -----------------------------


G.   DISPLAY "destination ? " WITH NO ADVANCING.
     ACCEPT city.
H-sel.
     IF city = "London"
        PERFORM I
     ELSE
        IF city = "Exeter"
           PERFORM J
        ELSE
           PERFORM K.
L.   DISPLAY "distance = ", distance, " miles".
M.   ADD distance TO total.
N.   ADD 1 TO counter.


* ----------------------- level 5 -----------------------------


I.   MOVE 65 TO distance.
J.   MOVE 155 TO distance.
K.   MOVE 35 TO distance.
```

4.2 Picture Clauses.

The variable names used in the Procedure Division are *total, distance, counter* and *city*. The type of data that the variable name relates to, and the size of each datum can be summarised in the table shown in figure 4.3. The term type of data implies either numeric, alphabetic or alphanumeric.

Numeric data consists of digits 0 through to 9 with or without an operational sign. A decimal point is not included as a legal character for a datum that is defined as being numeric.

Alphabetic data consists of the letters of the alphabet (uppercase) A through Z and (lowercase) a through z, and a space character.

Alphanumeric data consists of any of the characters of the ASCII or EBCDIC character sets.

Each variable name must be coded by data type and the maximum number of characters that make up the largest data value. This information is coded into a PICTURE clause.

Variable Name	data type	maximum size	range
total	numeric	4 digits	350 - 1550
distance	numeric	3 digits	35 - 155
counter	numeric	1 digit	0 - 5
city	alphabetic	6 characters	-

Figure 4.3 Type and range of data used in the example on journeys

The following characters have specific meanings within a PICTURE clause and represent the position of each character.

> 9 - a numeric digit
> A - an alphabetic character
> X - an alphanumeric character
> V - the position only of the decimal point
> S - the datum has an operational sign (+ or -).

The format of a PICTURE clause is $\begin{Bmatrix} \textbf{PICTURE} \\ \textbf{PIC} \end{Bmatrix}$ IS character-string

where the character-string is composed from the character subset 9, A, X, V and S. This is purposely described as a subset, since the reader will soon discover that there are many more characters that can be found in a picture character-string.

The following PICTURES, abbreviated to PIC, can be used to define the format of the data represented by the four variable names.

> total PIC 9999 - consists of 4 digits
> distance PIC 999 - consists of 3 digits
> counter PIC 9 - consists of only 1 digit
> city PIC AAAAAA - consists of 6 letters of the alphabet

Where a PICTURE descriptor is repeated a shorter notation may be used. For example PIC 9999 is the same as PIC 9(4) indicating that the item is numeric and contains 4 digits. Similarly PIC AAAAAA is the same as PIC A(6) indicating that the item is alphabetic and contains 6 letters of the alphabet.

Every PICTURE clause has a level number associated with it. The variable names *total, distance, counter* and *city* are not sub-components of other items of data and are designated the level number 77. The correct format for describing the four variable names is:

> 77 total PIC 9(4).
> 77 distance PIC 999.
> 77 counter PIC 9.
> 77 city PIC A(6).

4.3 Data Division.

In the last chapter it was stated that the Data Division consisted of up to three sections. The four variable names in this problem relate to data that is local to this program, that is the data is stored in the main memory of the computer and not from secondary storage, and will, therefore, be assigned to the WORKING-STORAGE SECTION of the DATA DIVISION. At this stage the FILE SECTION and LINKAGE SECTION can be omitted and the DATA DIVISION coded as:

```
DATA  DIVISION.
WORKING-STORAGE   SECTION.
77 total PIC 9(4).
77 distance PIC 999.
77 counter PIC 9.
77 city PIC A(6).
```

4.4 Identification Division.

The format of the Identification Division is given as:

```
IDENTIFICATION DIVISION.
PROGRAM-ID. program-name.
[AUTHOR. comment-entry.]
[INSTALLATION. comment-entry.]
[DATE-WRITTEN. comment-entry.]
[DATE-COMPILED. comment-entry.]
[INSTALLATION. comment-entry.]
[SECURITY. comment-entry.]
```

However, it is only necessary to include the first two statements of this Division in a COBOL program. The remaining entries are for documentary purposes.

```
IDENTIFICATION  DIVISION.
PROGRAM-ID.   Journey.
```

is sufficient for our requirements, where the name of the program *Journey* was invented by the programmer.

4.5 A Complete Program.

The three divisions are listed in the order specified in the last chapter. The ENVIRONMENT DIVISION has been omitted in this solution since the author wants the reader to be able to write complete COBOL programs as quickly as possible and with the minimum of coding. Since the first part of the ENVIRONMENT DIVISION is documentary and the second part relates primarily to external data files, that are not used in this program, the author feels justified in omitting this division at this stage.

Over the page is a computer-generated listing of the program.

```
IDENTIFICATION DIVISION.
PROGRAM-ID. Journey.

DATA DIVISION.
WORKING-STORAGE SECTION.
77 total PIC 9(4).
77 distance PIC 999.
77 counter PIC 9.
77 city PIC A(6).

PROCEDURE DIVISION.
A-seq.
    PERFORM B THROUGH P.

B.  MOVE ZERO TO total.
C.  MOVE ZERO TO counter.
D.  DISPLAY "REPORT ON JOURNEYS".
    DISPLAY SPACE.
E-rep.
    PERFORM F-seq UNTIL counter = 5.
O.  MULTIPLY 2 BY TOTAL.
P.  DISPLAY "total mileage for return trips is ", total, " miles".
    STOP RUN.

F-seq.
    PERFORM G THROUGH N.

G.  DISPLAY "destination ? " WITH NO ADVANCING.
    ACCEPT city.
H-sel.
    IF city = "London"
        PERFORM I
    ELSE
        IF city = "Exeter"
            PERFORM J
        ELSE
            PERFORM K.
L.  DISPLAY "distance = ", distance, " miles".
M.  ADD distance TO total.
N.  ADD 1 TO counter.

I.  MOVE 65 TO distance.
J.  MOVE 155 TO distance.
K.  MOVE 35 TO distance.
```

4.6 Summary.

Having completed a detailed program structure as the solution (algorithm) to a problem it is possible to directly code the functions, conditions and structure of the solution into a COBOL Procedure Division.

The hiearchical nature of the structure diagram is preserved in the COBOL statements, since each level in the diagram can be identified as separate groups of code in the Procedure Division.

The alphabetical labels given to each box in the structure diagram are used to denote sequence (seq), selection (sel), repetition (rep) and elementary items (box letter only). Each label is used as a paragraph name in the Procedure Division.

A sequence is coded as a series of COBOL statements or sentences that are referenced using the PERFORM .. THROUGH .. statement.

Selection is coded using the IF .. ELSE .. statement(s) and associated condition(s).

Repetition is coded using the out-of-line PERFORM .. UNTIL and associated condition(s).

Every variable name used in the Procedure Division must appear as an entry in the Data Division. Variable names that represent data local to the program will have their associated PICTURE clauses declared in the Working-Storage Section.

The range of each item of data must be known in advance so that a suitable PICTURE clause can be coded representing the maximum number of digits or characters for each respective data item.

A complete program will contain an Identification Division, Data Division and Procedure Division in that order.

> **Keywords**
>
> *Hierarchical coding of Procedure Division;*
> *PICTURE clause;*
> *data type, numeric, alphabetic, alphanumeric;*
> *9, A, X, V, S;*
> *level number 77;*
> *Data Division, Working-Storage section;*
> *Identification Division.*

4.7 Questions.

In the six questions that follow you are required to code complete COBOL programs from the detailed program structures that you derived in your answers to the questions at the end of chapter 2.

For each question the variable names that should be used in the Procedure Division and Data Division have been included. You must of course determine the maximum values for the data associated with these variable names and code a PICTURE clause for each variable name in the Working-Storage Section of the Data Division.

As an aid the answers to the first four questions from section 2.11 have been included for questions 1 to 4 inclusive. The answers from section 2.11 for questions 5 and 6 are given in the Answer Supplement.

1. Names and meanings of variables are as follows:

Price-of-car *initial price of the car input to the computer*
Price-of-sundries *price of extras input to the computer*
sub-total *sum of Price-of-car and Price-of-sundries*
vat-amount *15% of sub-total*
grand-total *sum of sub-total and vat-amount*

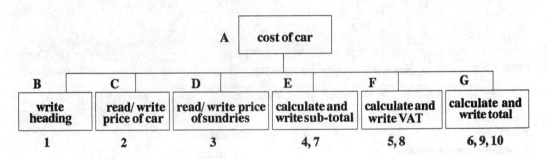

Functions

1. write heading
2. read/write basic price of car
3. read/write price of sundries
4. add price and sundries to give sub-total
5. calculate VAT @ 15% on sub-total
6. add sub-total and VAT to give total
7. write sub-total
8. write VAT
9. write total
10. finish

2. Names and meanings of variables are as follows:

investment *amount of money to be invested*
interest *amount of interest paid on annual investment*
rate *rate of interest*
counter *control loop counter for PERFORM loop*

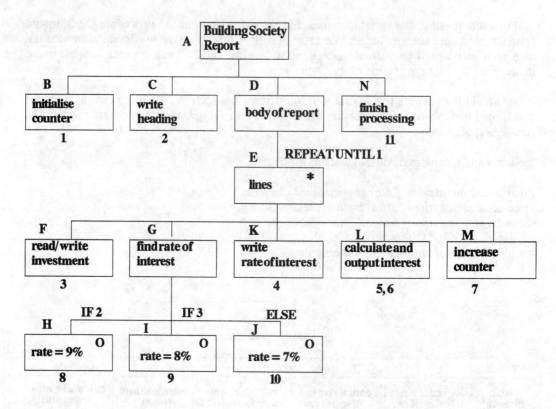

Functions

1. initialise counter to zero
2. write heading
3. read/write amount of investment
4. write rate of interest
5. calculate interest on investment
6. write interest
7. increase counter by 1
8. rate becomes 9%
9. rate becomes 8%
10. rate becomes 7%
11. finish

Conditions

1. counter = 5
2. investment > 20000
3. investment > 10000

3. The names and meanings of the variable are as follows:

total *sum of all the items*
price *cost of each item*
article *name of each item*
counter *control loop counter used in the PERFORM loop*

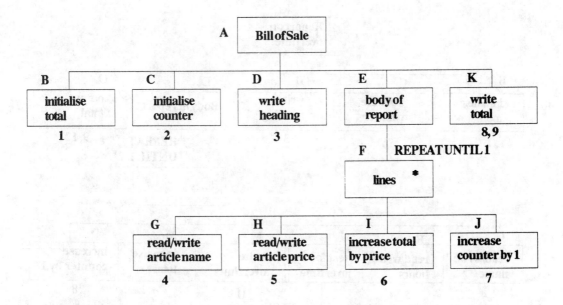

A — Bill of Sale

B — initialise total — 1
C — initialise counter — 2
D — write heading — 3
E — body of report
K — write total — 8, 9

F — REPEAT UNTIL 1 — lines *

G — read/write article name — 4
H — read/write article price — 5
I — increase total by price — 6
J — increase counter by 1 — 7

Functions

1. initialise total to zero
2. initialise counter to zero
3. write title
4. read/write description of article
5. read/write price of article
6. increase total by price
7. increase counter by 1
8. write total cost of article
9. finish

Conditions

1. counter = 5

4. The names of the variables are as follows:

total *sum of all the overtime paid*
hours *number of hours worked per week by each employee*
overtime *amount of overtime paid to each employee*
counter *control loop counter used in the PERFORM loop*
employee *name of employee*

The structure diagram for the solution to this problem is over the page.

[5]. The names of the variables are as follows:

name *name of pupil*
mark *examination mark for pupil*
counter *control loop counter used in PERFORM loop*
pass *number of pupils passing the exam*
fail *number of pupils failing the exam*
total *number of pupils taking the exam*
average *mean examination mark*

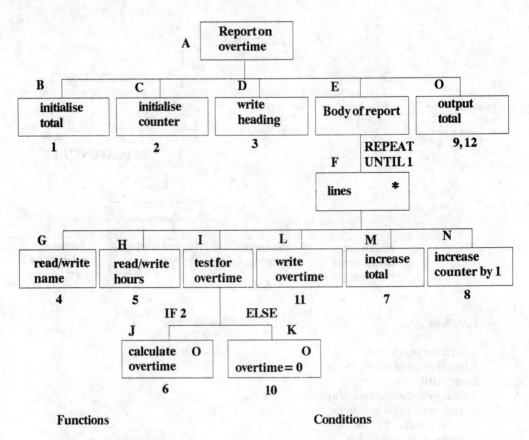

Functions

1. initialise total to zero
2. initialise counter to zero
3. write heading
4. read/write name of employee
5. read/write weekly hours worked
6. calculate overtime pay
7. add overtime pay to total
8. increase counter by 1
9. write total
10. overtime becomes zero
11. write overtime
12. finish

Conditions

1. counter = 7
2. hours > 40

[6]. The names of the variables are as follows:

name *name of person*
salary *gross salary of person*
allowance *pre-tax allowance for person*
counter *control loop counter used in PERFORM loop*
total *sum of all the tax payments for every person*
tax *amount of tax to pay by each person*
taxable-income *difference between the gross salary and allowance*

5

Program Development

This chapter can be regarded as a milestone within the text. It brings together the work of the first four chapters by considering the development of a small information system. From a problem specification the reader is guided through the stages of design, testing, coding, compilation and the implementation on a computer of the information system.

The chapter also contains information on how to deal with errors that appear at compilation and during program execution, and introduces the topic of data validation.

5.1 Problem Specification.

The XYZ Building Society requires an interactive computer system so that its' customers can obtain information about three savings accounts. The system will be switched on in the morning and will close down at 5.00 pm each day and will invite customers to view the details of up to three of the following savings accounts.

Flexisaver Account.

Pays interest at the basic rate of 9.5%.
Minimum investment is £10.
No minimum term of investment, immediate access to savings.

Supersaver Account.

Pays interest at 1.75% above the basic rate of interest.
Minimum investment is £1000.
Minimum term of investment with no loss of interest upon withdrawal is 3 years.

Moneymiser Account.

Pays interest at 2.5% above the basic rate of interest.
Minimum investment is £5000.
Minimum term of investment with no loss of interest upon withdrawal is 5 years.

After a customer has chosen a particular account the system will invite the customer to input an amount of money to be saved over a period of years. The growth of the account, using compound interest, is calculated on the size of the investment over the period stated. The arithmetic expression for the amount of money saved (A) including compound interest at R%, over a period of N years from an original investment of £P is:

$$A = P \left(1 + \frac{R}{100}\right)^N$$

The growth of the investment on the amount the customer wants to save over the period stated, based upon current interest rates, is then displayed on a screen for the customer to see. The information screens that are to be used in the system follow.

Screen 0 - initial screen inviting the customer to choose an account, by typing F, S or M. If the customer types the wrong information the screen will clear and the user must re-input the choice again. The screen will continue to behave in this manner until a correct choice has been made.

Welcome to the XYZ Building Society

SAVINGS ACCOUNTS
Do you want information on:

[F]lexisaver,
[S]upersaver, or
[M]oneymiser

Type F, S or M M

Screen 1 - details of the Flexisaver account and an invitation to input an amount of money to be invested over a period of time. If the customer types illegal data the screen will clear and they must re-input the data again. The screen will continue to behave in this manner until the correct data has been input to the system.

```
FLEXISAVER ACCOUNT

* Rate of interest    9.5 %
* Minimum investment £10
* Immediate access to your money

How much money do you want to save (6 digits) ?
  001000
and for how many years (2 digits) ?
  02
```

Screen 2 - details of the Supersaver account and an invitation to input an amount of money to be invested over a period of time. The error correction mechanism is the same as for screen 1

```
SUPERSAVER ACCOUNT

* Rate of interest    11.25 %
* Minimum investment £1000
* Minimum investment term 3 years

How much money do you want to save (6 digits) ?
  001000
and for how many years (2 digits) ?
  03
```

Screen 3 - details of the Moneymiser account and an invitation to input an amount of money to be invested over a period of time. The error correction mechanism is the same as for screen 1.

```
MONEYMISER ACCOUNT

* Rate of interest    12 %
* Minimum investment £5000
* Minimum investment term 5 years

How much money do you want to save (6 digits) ?
  005000
and for how many years (2 digits) ?
  05
```

Screen 4 - details of the name of the account, amount invested over a period of time and the growth of the account at the end of the period. Having read the information, the customer is then requested to press the return key, in order that the system returns to screen 0, the opening screen.

```
┌─────────────────────────────────────────────────┐
│  XYZ  BUILDING  SOCIETY                          │
│                                                  │
│  name of account   MONEYMISER                    │
│  amount saved         5000                       │
│  period (years)        5                         │
│                                                  │
│  amount saved at end of period      8811         │
│  based upon the current rate of interest         │
│                                                  │
│  press return key to continue                    │
└─────────────────────────────────────────────────┘
```

In order to keep the solution to this problem simple, the author has assumed that the basic rate of interest is fixed at 9.5%. There will be no need to input to the system, on a daily basis, the basic rate of interest.

5.2 Program Design.

Input Structure. Each customer of the XYZ Building Society will key in at least three items of data. Menu code F, S or M from screen 0, investment amount or principal, and the period of investment or term. For example the data M 005000 05 represents the Moneymiser account for an investment of £5000 over a period of 5 years. If the data is in error or the customer requires details of other accounts then more than three items of data will be input. There will be many customers using the system during the opening hours of the building society. The input data can be regarded as a stream of data which is in effect a repetition of single items of data. Hence the most appropriate initial structure for the input of data to the system will be:

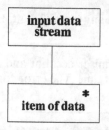

Output Structure. If a screen of information can be regarded as a basic building block in the output, in the same way as, say, a heading to a report would be viewed, then the series of screens can be represented as shown over the page.

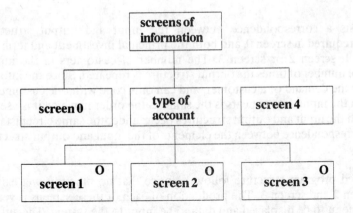

The termination of the system depends upon the time of day, and the number of customers using the system is regulated by the availability of the system.

When the building society is closed no customers can use the system, whether they want to or not! Therefore, the number of times the output structure is repeated is solely determined by the number of customers using the system when the building is open. The number of times the screens appear is a function of the customer demand for the system, which must stop after 5.00 pm (17.00) when the building society closes.

The output structure can, therefore, be modified to include the repetitive demand upon the system.

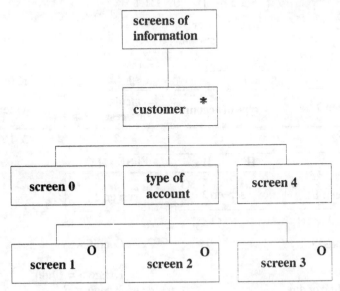

There exists a correspondence between the input and output structures since the menu-code is required in screen 0, and both the principal investment and term are required in either screen 1, screen 2 or screen 3. The number of customers in the input structure is identical to the number of times the output structure is repeated. Since the information system is activated by the demand of a customer, and can only cope with one customer at a time, the order in which the input data appears is the same as the order in which it is used by the output structure. Both the input and output structures occur under the same circumstances. The three criteria for correspondence between the elements of the input and output structures have been satisfied.

The detailed program structure follows. Notice that no functions yet exist for screen 0, screen 1, screen 2 and screen 3. The production of each of these screens is very similar. They all require a menu to be displayed and data to be input to the system. The authenticity of the data is examined, and if it is in error then the screen of the visual display is cleared and the appropriate menu is re-displayed.

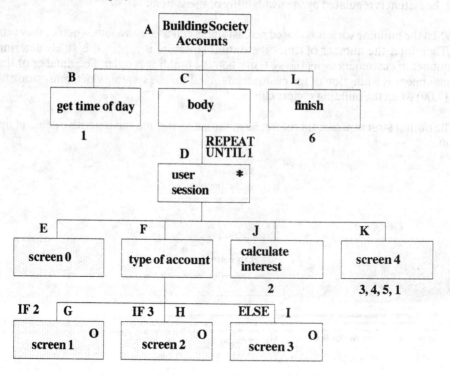

Functions

1. get time of day
2. calculate investment growth
3. clear screen
4. write investment details
5. read/write prompt to continue
6. finish

Conditions

1. time >= 17.00
2. code = F
3. code = S

To prevent too much information appearing in one detailed program structure chart it will be necessary to refine the structure diagram into several sub-structure charts. The boxes E, G, H and I, can each be expanded into a sub-structure chart as follows. Notice that the lettering of each box denotes the box from which it came in the main structure chart. Clearly letters EA, EB and EC all relate to box E in the main structure chart. Notice also that the lettering for box I does not include a box labelled as ID. Since each box label will be used as a paragraph name in the subsequent COBOL program, and ID is a COBOL reserved word, ID has been replaced by IE. The message is clear, beware of confusing COBOL reserved words with structure diagram box-labels.

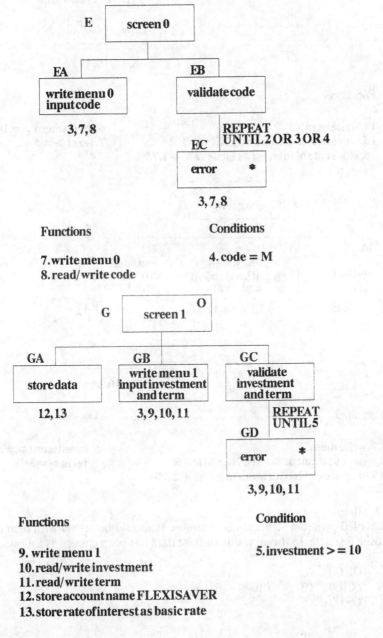

Functions

7. write menu 0
8. read/write code

Conditions

4. code = M

Functions

9. write menu 1
10. read/write investment
11. read/write term
12. store account name FLEXISAVER
13. store rate of interest as basic rate

Condition

5. investment > = 10

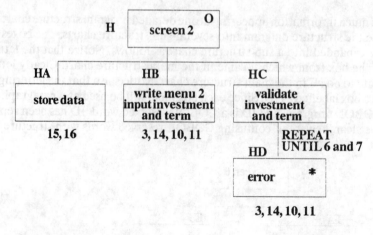

Functions

14. write menu 2
15. store account name SUPERSAVER
16. store rate of interest as basic rate + 1.75%

Conditions

6. investment > = 1000
7. term > = 3

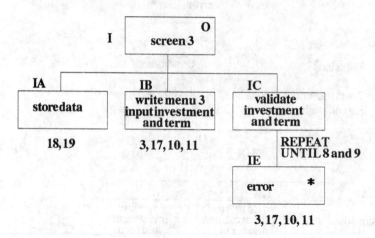

Functions

17. write menu 3
18. store account name MONEYMISER
19. store rate as basic rate of interest + 2.5%

Conditions

8. investment > = 5000
9. term > = 5

5.3 Design Testing.

Once the detailed program structure is complete it should be tested with a small amount of suitably chosen test data. In this example the test data has been chosen as follows.

```
F     001000   02
s  S  000100   03     001000   03
M     005000   05
```

with two items of data, s and 000100 being deliberately chosen to test the system for trapping error data.

Since the details of the screens have already been given they will not be printed in this test of the design. It is enough to state that a menu of a screen is output by writing the name of the menu in italics (e.g. *menu 0*). The time of day has deliberately been chosen to start at 16.57, and increment in one minute intervals per customer. Since the data has been chosen for three customers the design can be tested for system close down at 17.00.

Box	Function	Condition	Result from function being executed
A			
B	1		TimeOfDay = 16.57
C		1 false	
D			
E			
EA	3,7		*menu 0*
	8		MenuCode = F
EB		2 or 3 or 4 true	
G		2 true	
GA	12		AccountName = FLEXISAVER
	13		rate = 9.5%
GB	3,9		*menu 1*
	10		investment = 001000
	11		term = 02
GC		5 true	
J	2		growth = 1199.03
K	3,4,5		*screen 4*
	1		TimeOfDay = 16.58
C		1 false	
D			
E			
EA	3,7		*menu 0*
	8	MenuCode = s	
EB		2 or 3 or 4 false	
EC	3,7		*menu 0*
	8	MenuCode = S	
EB		2 or 3 or 4 true	
F		3 true	
H			
HA	15		AccountName = SUPERSAVER
	16		rate = 11.25%
HB	3,14		*menu 2*
	10		investment = 000100
	11		term = 03
HC		6 and 7 false	
HD	3,14		*menu 2*
	10		investment = 001000
	11		term = 03

Box	Function	Condition	Result (output in italics)
HC		6 and 7 true	
J	2		*growth = 1376.90*
K	3,4,5		*screen 4*
	1		*TimeOfDay = 16.59*
C		1 false	
D			
E			
EA	3,7		*menu 0*
	8	MenuCode = M	
EB		2 or 3 or 4 true	
F		4 true	
I			
IA	18		*Accountname = MONEYMISER*
	19		*rate = 12%*
IB	3,17		*menu 3*
	10		*investment = 005000*
	11		*term = 05*
IC		8 and 9 true	
J	2		*growth = 8811.71*
K	3,4,5		*screen 4*
	1		*TimeOfDay = 17.00*
C		1 true	
L	6		

5.4 Coding from the design.

If the reader looks back at the sub-structure diagrams for boxes E, G, H and I, it should be clear that in each respective structure the functions are repeated twice. For example the functions at EA are the same as the functions at EC; the functions at GB are the same as functions at GD; similarly HB and HD have the same functions and so too does IB and IE. Since the function to write a menu requires several lines of COBOL code it would seem foolish to duplicate the same code again in the program. The answer is to treat each group of COBOL statements as a *subroutine*. In COBOL this implies writing the code away from its normal position in the sequential flow of statements, so that the code can be performed from different parts of the program. The COBOL code is only written once and performed as many times as necessary.

There is a great temptation amongst programmers to reduce the amount of repeated code in any program. However, be warned, such pruning of repeated code can lead to a program that was once structured becoming unstructured. The outcome of such an action would result in a program that is more difficult to maintain and more prone to errors.

The technique of making a program smaller by reducing the amount of code is one of the techniques under the heading of optimisation. The other technique of optimisation is the tuning of a program to make it run faster. The reader who contemplates optimising program code should consider Michael Jackson's rules for optimisation in his book on the *Principles of Program Design*. They are:

Rule 1: Don't do it.

Rule 2: Don't do it yet.

The first rule implies that a positive quantified justification for optimisation is necessary before commencing the technique. For example, to spend time trying to make a program run faster is no justification if the computer is idle for a large percentage of its time and the output is not required within a time-critical period.

The second rule implies that the original program design should be created without any form of optimisation even though optimisation is planned at a later stage. In this worked example optimisation of code was only contemplated at the coding stage and not at the design stage.

From the structure diagrams, functions 3,7, 8; functions 3, 9, 10, 11; functions 3, 14, 10, 11 and functions 3, 17, 10, 11 will be coded towards the end of the program, out of their normal sequential position, under the paragraph names:

FUNCTIONS-3-7-8, FUNCTIONS-3-9-10-11, FUNCTIONS-3-14-10-11, and FUNCTIONS -3-17-10-11 respectively. Therefore, the translation of the functions at box EA would be:

EA. PERFORM FUNCTIONS-3-7-8.

and at box EC as:

EC. PERFORM FUNCTIONS-3-7-8.

Similar perform statements are used to call the remaining subroutines.

The Procedure Division is coded from the structure diagrams using the same hierarchical technique that was described in the last chapter.

The order in which the paragraph names appear and the associated control structures, form the following skeletal outline of the Procedure Division code. The reader is advised to trace through this code in conjunction with the structure diagrams in order to appreciate the order in which the structures have been coded into the Procedure Division. This order is important. If you get the order wrong the program will not behave in the manner intended!

```
PROCEDURE DIVISION.
A-seq.
        PERFORM B THROUGH L.

B.
C-rep.
        PERFORM D-seq UNTIL (condition 1)
L.

D-seq.
        PERFORM E-seq THROUGH K.

E-seq.
```

```
        PERFORM EA THROUGH EB-rep.
F-sel.
        IF (condition 2)
            PERFORM G-seq
        ELSE
            IF (condition 3)
                PERFORM H-seq
            ELSE
                PERFORM I-seq.
J.
K.


EA.
EB-rep.
        PERFORM EC UNTIL (conditions 2, 3 or 4)
EC.

G-seq.
        PERFORM GA THROUGH GC-rep.
GA.
GB.
GC-rep.
        PERFORM GD UNTIL (condition 5)
GD.


H-seq.
        PERFORM HA THROUGH HC-rep.
HA.
HB.
HC-rep.
        PERFORM HD UNTIL (conditions 6 and 7)
HD.

I-seq.
        PERFORM IA THROUGH IC-rep.
IA.
IB.
IC-rep.
        PERFORM IE UNTIL (conditions 8 and 9)
IE.


-------------------- subroutines -----------------


FUNCTIONS-3-7-8.
FUNCTIONS-3-9-10-11.
FUNCTIONS-3-14-10-11.
FUNCTIONS-3-17-10-11.
```

The variable names and corresponding data types and ranges follow on the next page.

Identifier	Data Type	size	range
BasicRate	numeric	4 dec. pl	0.950 - .1200
growth	numeric	8 digits	1 - 99,999,999
MenuCode	alphabetic	1 character	F, S or M
investment	numeric	6 digits	1 - 999,999
term	numeric	2 digits	1 - 99
rate	numeric	4 dec. pl.	.0950 - .1200
AccountName	alphabetic	10 characters	-
TimeOfDay	numeric	4 digits with 2 dec. pl. ?	00.00 - 23.59
prompt	alphanumeric	1 character	-

From this information it is possible to have a first attempt at coding the Data Division.

77 BasicRate PIC V9999.
77 growth PIC 9(8).
77 MenuCode PIC A.
77 investment PIC 9(6).
77 term PIC 99.
77 rate PIC V9999.
77 AccountName PIC A(10).
77 TimeOfDay PIC 99V99. *The next section will show that this declaration is incorrect.*
77 prompt PIC X.

5.5 The Value Clause.

The VALUE clause defines the initial values of WORKING-STORAGE SECTION items of data. The format of the clause is:

VALUE IS literal

where the literal will depend upon the data type of the item. The literal could be numeric, alphabetic, alphanumeric or a literal constant.

The clause is appended to the PICTURE clause of the item of data that is to be initialised. For example the basic rate of interest has been quoted as 9.5%, this could be incorporated into the PICTURE clause for the constant BasicRate as follows.

77 BasicRate PIC V9999 VALUE IS 0.0950.

By assigning a value to a variable in the WORKING-STORAGE SECTION, saves the value from being input at the keyboard using an ACCEPT statement. However, if the basic rate of interest was to change then the program would need to be modified! Clearly program modification to cater for changes in the values of data is not a good idea.

The VALUE clause can also be used in conjunction with a condition name. When the value or range of values of a variable name are known in advance of program execution, they can be specified in the DATA DIVISION using a level 88 entry.

The format of a level 88 entry is:

$$88\text{condition-name} \begin{Bmatrix} \textbf{VALUE IS} \\ \textbf{VALUES ARE} \end{Bmatrix} \text{literal-1} \begin{Bmatrix} \textbf{THROUGH} \\ \textbf{THRU} \end{Bmatrix} \text{literal-2}$$

where the level 88 entry must follow directly after the description of the variable name that has these values.

For example, in the information system a legal response to menu 0 of screen 0 is F, S or M, therefore, the WORKING-STORAGE entry for the menu code can be written as:

```
77 MenuCode PIC A.
   88 LegalCode VALUES 'F', 'S', 'M'.
```

where LegalCode is a *condition* name that can be used in place of a condition in either an IF or PERFORM .. UNTIL statement. In the context of the information system LegalCode is used in the validation of the input data for screen 0 as:

```
EB-rep.
       PERFORM EC UNTIL LegalCode.
```

An alternative method of coding this statement would have been

```
EB-rep.
       PERFORM EC UNTIL MenuCode = 'F' OR 'S' OR 'M'.
```

Notice the method of abbreviating the condition by only using the variable MenuCode once and not three times. The longer form would have been:

```
EB-rep.
       PERFORM EC UNTIL    MenuCode = 'F' OR
                           MenuCode = 'S' OR
                           MenuCode = 'M'.
```

Many implementations of COBOL use the reserved word TIME to store an eight-digit representation of the current time of day. TIME is composed from the data elements hours, minutes, seconds and hundredths of a second, and is based upon elapsed time after midnight on a 24-hour clock basis. Thus 5.00 pm would be expressed as 17000000. The close down time for the system can be represented by a constant CloseDown that is coded as:

```
77 CloseDown PIC 9(8) VALUE IS 17000000.
```

The current time of day is input to the computer system using the ACCEPT statement as follows.

```
ACCEPT TimeOfDay FROM TIME
```

where TimeOfDay is described in the WORKING-STORAGE SECTION as:

77 TimeOfDay PIC 9(8).

5.6 Program Implementation.

There are two methods of preparing a written program for entry to a computer. The first method involves using software, known as an editor, and typing a line-by-line copy of the program at the keyboard of an on-line terminal and storing the program on magnetic disc.

The second method, that is out-of-date, involved typing a line-by-line copy of the program at the keyboard of an off-line key-punch device and storing the program on either punched paper-tape or punched cards. The prepared program was then read by an on-line input device, such as a paper-tape reader or card reader, and transferred to the main memory of the computer.

It is quite probable at this stage, regardless of the method of program entry used, that transcription errors (keying errors) have been introduced into the program. Often double entry preparation techniques are used in order to reduce such errors to the very minimum.

The first method of program entry is the most common today. The program is stored on a disc, as a series of characters forming a file, and is given a name (filename). The program can be retrieved by stating the name of the file so that the information in the file may be used (copied, amended, deleted, printed, etc). The commands used to manipulate the contents of a file are system specific. Such commands will not be considered here and the reader is advised to consult the appropriate operating system and editor guides for the computer system being used.

Having stored the COBOL program, the next stage is to compile it. The commands required to invoke a COBOL compiler and compile the source program are machine and software specific. The reader is advised to consult the COBOL manual for the compiler and computer being used.

At the compilation stage a listing of all the syntax errors can be obtained together with a computer generated compiled listing of the source program. To demonstrate this feature the current program has deliberately had syntax errors introduced into it. These errors could have come from either of two sources; the programmer and/or the keyboard operator.

The COBOL program has been coded from the detailed program structure diagrams. The results of the compilation are as follows. Beginners to programming in COBOL can find that the error diagnostics can be very confusing and they often become daunted by the number of errors that a COBOL compiler will flag from what appears to be very trivial mistakes. When the compilation of a program reveals that the program contains errors the next stage is to trace through every line of code that has caused an error and annotate the correction on the page of the source listing.

```
COBOL85 ERROR1
[COBOL85 Rev. 1.0-22.0 Copyright (c) 1988, Prime Computer, Inc.]
[Serial £S033-1RQH8L-NW62 (Oxford Polytechnic)]


ERROR 29  SEVERITY 3  LINE 9  COLUMN 35  [FATAL, SEMANTICS]
Beginning quotation mark must be preceded by a space or "(".

ERROR 29  SEVERITY 3  LINE 9  COLUMN 39  [FATAL, SEMANTICS]
Beginning quotation mark must be preceded by a space or "(".

ERROR 300  SEVERITY 3  LINE 6  COLUMN 21  [FATAL, SYNTAX]
"IDENTIFIER" found when expecting one of {"PERIOD, END OF DIVISION, STATEMENT
SEPARATOR, INTEGER LITERAL, FILE, WORKING-STORAG"}.
  [syntax checking suspended at THE IDENTIFIER "V9999"]
  [syntax checking resumed at THE RESERVED WORD "VALUE"] ( LINE 6  COLUMN 27

ERROR 55  SEVERITY 3  LINE 6  COLUMN 11  [FATAL, SEMANTICS]
A picture clause is required for all data ("BASICRATE") not defined as COMP,
COMP-1,
COMP-2, or INDEX.

ERROR 177  SEVERITY 2  LINE 6  COLUMN 27  [WARNING, SEMANTICS]
The data type of the VALUE literal does not match that of the item
"BASICRATE".  The initial value may be unpredictable.


ERROR 300  SEVERITY 3  LINE 8  COLUMN 11  [FATAL, SYNTAX]
"CODE" found when expecting one of {"PERIOD, END OF DIVISION, STATEMENT
SEPARATOR, INTEGER LITERAL, FILE, WORKING-STORAGE"}.
  [syntax checking suspended at THE RESERVED WORD "CODE"]
  [syntax checking resumed at THE RESERVED WORD "PICTURE"] ( LINE 8  COLUMN 16


ERROR 300  SEVERITY 3  LINE 26  COLUMN 8  [FATAL, SYNTAX]
"PARAGRAPH" found when expecting one of {"INTEGER LITERAL, ARITHMETIC LITERAL,
FLOATING PT LITERAL, ALPHANUMERIC LITERAL"}.
  [syntax checking suspended at THE PARAGRAPH]
  [syntax checking resumed at  "."] ( LINE 26  COLUMN 13 )

ERROR 329  SEVERITY 3  LINE 33  COLUMN 15  [FATAL, SEMANTICS]
"MENUCODE" is an undefined data reference.

ERROR 329  SEVERITY 3  LINE 33  COLUMN 26  [FATAL, SEMANTICS]
"F" is an undefined data reference.

ERROR 329  SEVERITY 3  LINE 36  COLUMN 18  [FATAL, SEMANTICS]
"MENUCODE" is an undefined data reference.
```

```
ERROR 329  SEVERITY 3  LINE 36  COLUMN 29  [FATAL, SEMANTICS]
"S" is an undefined data reference.

ERROR 300  SEVERITY 3  LINE 41  COLUMN 12  [FATAL, SYNTAX]
"IDENTIFIER" found when expecting one of {"END OF DIVISION, SECTION, PARAGRAPH,
COBOL_VERB, END"}.
  [syntax checking suspended at THE IDENTIFIER "GROWTH"]
  [syntax checking resumed at  "."] (  LINE 41  COLUMN 52 )

ERROR 329  SEVERITY 3  LINE 54  COLUMN 19  [FATAL, SEMANTICS]
"PROMPT" is an undefined data reference.

ERROR 300  SEVERITY 3  LINE 107  COLUMN 19  [FATAL, SYNTAX]
"CODE" found when expecting one of {"IDENTIFIER"}.
  [syntax checking suspended at THE RESERVED WORD "CODE"]
  [syntax checking resumed at  "."] (  LINE 107  COLUMN 23 )

ERROR 407  SEVERITY 2  LINE 6  COLUMN 11  [WARNING, SEMANTICS]
The initial value for "BASICRATE" exceeds the range of values allowed by
 the PICTURE or by the default implementation size.  The initial value
 may be truncated or unpredictable.

[13 FATALS 2 WARNINGS IN PROGRAM: <SYSF02>U10>PS0054610>DPCOBOL2>ERROR1.COBOL85]
```

```
001     IDENTIFICATION DIVISION.
002     PROGRAM-ID. BuildingSoc.
003
004     DATA DIVISION.
005     WORKING-STORAGE SECTION.
006     77 BasicRate V9999 VALUE IS 0.0950.
007     77 growth PIC 9(8).
008     77 code PIC A.
009        88 LegalCode VALUES 'F','S','M'
010     77 investment PIC 9(6).
011     77 term PIC 99.
012     77 rate PIC V9999.
013     77 AccountName PIC A(10).
014     77 TimeOfDay PIC 9(8).
015     77 CloseDown PIC 9(8) VALUE IS 17000000.
016     77 ClearScreen PIC X(4) VALUE ''.
017
018     PROCEDURE DIVISION.
019     A-seq.
020        PERFORM B THROUGH L.
021     B.  ACCEPT TimeOfDay FROM TIME.
022     C-rep.
```

RESERVED WORD PICTURE MISSING

RESERVED WORD USED AS A VARIABLE

EACH OPENING APOSTROPHE MUST BE PRECEDED BY A SPACE

```
023         PERFORM D-seq UNTIL TimeOfDay > CloseDown.
024     L.  STOP
025
026     D-seq.
027         PERFORM E-seq THROUGH K.
028
029     E-seq
030         PERFORM EA THROUGH EB-rep.
031
032     F-sel.
033         IF MenuCode = F
034             PERFORM G-seq
035         ELSE
036             IF MenuCode = S
037                 PERFORM H-seq
038             ELSE
039                 PERFORM I-seq
040
041     J.  growth = investment * (1 + rate) ** term.
042
043     K.  DISPLAY ClearScreen.
044         DISPLAY 'X Y Z    B U I L D I N G    S O C I E T Y'.
045         DISPLAY SPACE.
046         DISPLAY 'name of account ', AccountName.
047         DISPLAY 'amount saved ', investment.
048         DISPLAY 'period (years) ', term.
049         DISPLAY SPACE.
050         DISPLAY 'amount saved at end of period ', growth.
051         DISPLAY 'based upon the current rate of interest'.
052         DISPLAY SPACE
053         DISPLAY 'press the return key to continue ' WITH NO ADVANCING.
054         ACCEPT prompt.
055         ACCEPT TimeOfDay FROM TIME.
056
057     EA. PERFORM FUNCTIONS-3-7-8.
058     EB-rep.
059         PERFORM EC UNTIL LegalCode.
060     EC. PERFORM FUNCTIONS-3-7-8.
061
062     G-seq.
063         PERFORM GA THROUGH GC-rep.
064     GA. MOVE 'FLEXISAVER' TO AccountName.
065         MOVE BasicRate to rate.
066
067     GB. PERFORM FUNCTIONS-3-9-10-11.
068     GC-rep.
069         PERFORM GD UNTIL investment >= 10.
```

Handwritten annotations:

- NO PERIOD AFTER STOP, BETTER TO USE STOP RUN. (pointing to line 024 STOP)
- MENUCODE NOT DECLARED IN WORKING-STORAGE (pointing to MenuCode)
- DELIMITERS MISSING SHOULD BE 'F' 'S'
- NO PERIOD AT END OF SENTENCE (pointing to line 039)
- COMPUTE MISSING (pointing to line 041)
- PROMPT NOT DECLARED IN WORKING-STORAGE (pointing to line 054 prompt)

```
070     GD. PERFORM FUNCTIONS-3-9-10-11.
071
072     H-seq.
073         PERFORM HA THROUGH HC-rep.
074     HA. MOVE 'SUPERSAVER' TO AccountName.
075         ADD 1.75, BasicRate GIVING rate.
076     HB. PERFORM FUNCTIONS-3-14-10-11.
077     HC-rep.
078         PERFORM HD UNTIL investment >=1000 AND term >= 3.
079     HD. PERFORM FUNCTIONS-3-14-10-11.
080
081     I-seq.
082         PERFORM IA THROUGH IC-rep.
083     IA. MOVE 'MONEYMISER' TO AccountName.
084         ADD 2.5, BasicRate GIVING rate.
085     IB. PERFORM FUNCTIONS-3-17-10-11.
086     IC-rep.
087         PERFORM IE UNTIL investment >= 5000 AND term >= 5.
088     IE.
089         PERFORM FUNCTIONS-3-17-10-11.
090
091
092     * ---------------------- subroutines --------------------
093
094     FUNCTIONS-3-7-8.
095         DISPLAY ClearScreen.
096         DISPLAY 'Welcome to the XYZ Building Society'.
097         DISPLAY SPACE.
098         DISPLAY ' S A V I N G S   A C C O U N T S'.
099         DISPLAY SPACE.
100         DISPLAY 'Do you want information on:'.
101         DISPLAY SPACE.
102         DISPLAY '[F]lexisaver,'.
103         DISPLAY '[S]upersaver, or'.
104         DISPLAY '[M]oneymiser'.
105         DISPLAY SPACE.
106         DISPLAY 'Type F, S or M ' WITH NO ADVANCING.
107         ACCEPT code.
108
109     FUNCTIONS-3-9-10-11.
110         DISPLAY ClearScreen.
111         DISPLAY 'F L E X I S A V E R   A C C O U N T'
112         DISPLAY SPACE.
113         DISPLAY '* Rate of interest 9.5%'.
114         DISPLAY '* Minimum investment  10'.
115         DISPLAY '* Immediate access to your money'.
116         DISPLAY SPACE.
117         DISPLAY 'How much money do you want to save (6 digits) ?'.
```

RESERVED WORD USED AS A VARIABLE

```
118          ACCEPT investment.
119          DISPLAY 'and for how many years (2 digits) ?'.
120          ACCEPT term.
121
122      FUNCTIONS-3-14-10-11.
123          DISPLAY ClearScreen.
124          DISPLAY 'S U P E R S A V E R   A C C O U N T'
125          DISPLAY SPACE.
126          DISPLAY '* Rate of interest 11.25%'.
127          DISPLAY '* Minimum investment  1000'.
128          DISPLAY '* Minimum investment term 3 years'.
129          DISPLAY SPACE.
130          DISPLAY 'How much money do you want to save (6 digits) ?'.
131          ACCEPT investment.
132          DISPLAY 'and for how many years (2 digits) ?'.
133          ACCEPT term.
134
135      FUNCTIONS-3-17-10-11.
136          DISPLAY ClearScreen.
137          DISPLAY 'M O N E Y M I S E R   A C C O U N T'
138          DISPLAY SPACE.
139          DISPLAY '* Rate of interest 12%'.
140          DISPLAY '* Minimum investment  5000'.
141          DISPLAY '* Minimum investment term 5 years'.
142          DISPLAY SPACE.
143          DISPLAY 'How much money do you want to save (6 digits) ?'.
144          ACCEPT investment.
145          DISPLAY 'and for how many years (2 digits) ?'.
146          ACCEPT term.
```

The original source program is then edited using the information from the annotated source listing and then re-compiled. The details relating to editing a source program are specific to the particular editor being used, and for this reason will not be considered here. The reader is again recommended to consult the guide to the editor for the machine being used.

If having compiled the program for the second time there are still syntax errors, then the process of annotating corrections, editing, and compiling must continue until the source program is free from syntax errors and warnings.

The following computer-generated listing contains all the amendments to the source code and compiled without any errors. But is the program error free?

```
          IDENTIFICATION DIVISION.
          PROGRAM-ID. BuildingSoc.

          DATA DIVISION.
          WORKING-STORAGE SECTION.
          77 BasicRate PIC V9999 VALUE IS 0.0950.
```

```
77 growth PIC 9(8).
77 MenuCode PIC A.
   88 LegalCode VALUES 'F', 'S', 'M'.
77 investment PIC 9(6).
77 term PIC 99.
77 rate PIC V9999.
77 AccountName PIC A(10).
77 TimeOfDay PIC 9(8).
77 CloseDown PIC 9(8) VALUE IS 17000000.
77 ClearScreen PIC X(4) VALUE ''.
77 prompt PIC X.


PROCEDURE DIVISION.
A-seq.
    PERFORM B THROUGH L.
B.  ACCEPT TimeOfDay FROM TIME.
C-rep.
    PERFORM D-seq UNTIL TimeOfDay > CloseDown.
L.  STOP RUN.


D-seq.
    PERFORM E-seq THROUGH K.


E-seq
    PERFORM EA THROUGH EB-rep.


F-sel.
    IF MenuCode = 'F'
       PERFORM G-seq
    ELSE
       IF MenuCode = 'S'
          PERFORM H-seq
       ELSE
          PERFORM I-seq.


J.  COMPUTE growth = investment * (1 + rate) ** term.


K.  DISPLAY ClearScreen.
    DISPLAY 'X Y Z    B U I L D I N G    S O C I E T Y'.
    DISPLAY SPACE.
    DISPLAY 'name of account ', AccountName.
    DISPLAY 'amount saved ', investment.
    DISPLAY 'period (years) ', term.
    DISPLAY SPACE.
    DISPLAY 'amount saved at end of period ', growth.
    DISPLAY 'based upon the current rate of interest'.
    DISPLAY SPACE
```

```
            DISPLAY 'press the return key to continue ' WITH NO ADVANCING.
            ACCEPT prompt.
            ACCEPT TimeOfDay FROM TIME.


    EA. PERFORM FUNCTIONS-3-7-8.
    EB-rep.
            PERFORM EC UNTIL LegalCode.
    EC. PERFORM FUNCTIONS-3-7-8.


    G-seq.
            PERFORM GA THROUGH GC-rep.
    GA. MOVE 'FLEXISAVER' TO AccountName.
            MOVE BasicRate to rate.
    GB. PERFORM FUNCTIONS-3-9-10-11.
    GC-rep.
            PERFORM GD UNTIL investment >= 10.
    GD. PERFORM FUNCTIONS-3-9-10-11.


    H-seq.                                        VALUE SHOULD BE
            PERFORM HA THROUGH HC-rep.            0.0175
    HA. MOVE 'SUPERSAVER' TO AccountName.
            ADD 1.75, BasicRate GIVING rate.
    HB. PERFORM FUNCTIONS-3-14-10-11.
    HC-rep.
            PERFORM HD UNTIL investment >=1000 AND term >= 3.
    HD. PERFORM FUNCTIONS-3-14-10-11.


    I-seq.                                        VALUE SHOULD BE
            PERFORM IA THROUGH IC-rep.            0.0250
    IA. MOVE 'MONEYMISER' TO AccountName.
            ADD 2.5, BasicRate GIVING rate.
    IB. PERFORM FUNCTIONS-3-17-10-11.
    IC-rep.
            PERFORM IE UNTIL investment >= 5000 AND term >= 5.
    IE.
            PERFORM FUNCTIONS-3-17-10-11.



    * ---------------------- subroutines --------------------


    FUNCTIONS-3-7-8.
            DISPLAY ClearScreen.
            DISPLAY 'Welcome to the XYZ Building Society'.
            DISPLAY SPACE.
            DISPLAY ' S A V I N G S   A C C O U N T S'.
            DISPLAY SPACE.
            DISPLAY 'Do you want information on:'.
```

```
            DISPLAY SPACE.
            DISPLAY '[F]lexisaver,'.
            DISPLAY '[S]upersaver, or'.
            DISPLAY '[M]oneymiser'.
            DISPLAY SPACE.
            DISPLAY 'Type F, S or M ' WITH NO ADVANCING.
            ACCEPT MenuCode.


        FUNCTIONS-3-9-10-11.
            DISPLAY ClearScreen.
            DISPLAY 'F L E X I S A V E R   A C O U N T'
            DISPLAY SPACE.
            DISPLAY '* Rate of interest 9.5%'.
            DISPLAY '* Minimum investment  10'.
            DISPLAY '* Immediate access to your money'.
            DISPLAY SPACE.
            DISPLAY 'How much money do you want to save (6 digits) ?'.
            ACCEPT investment.
            DISPLAY 'and for how many years (2 digits) ?'.
            ACCEPT term.


        FUNCTIONS-3-14-10-11.
            DISPLAY ClearScreen.
            DISPLAY 'S U P E R S A V E R   A C O U N T'
            DISPLAY SPACE.
            DISPLAY '* Rate of interest 11.25%'.
            DISPLAY '* Minimum investment  1000'.
            DISPLAY '* Minimum investment term 3 years'.
            DISPLAY SPACE.
            DISPLAY 'How much money do you want to save (6 digits) ?'.
            ACCEPT investment.
            DISPLAY 'and for how many years (2 digits) ?'.
            ACCEPT term.


        FUNCTIONS-3-17-10-11.
            DISPLAY ClearScreen.
            DISPLAY 'M O N E Y M I S E R   A C O U N T'
            DISPLAY SPACE.
            DISPLAY '* Rate of interest 12%'.
            DISPLAY '* Minimum investment  5000'.
            DISPLAY '* Minimum investment term 5 years'.
            DISPLAY SPACE.
            DISPLAY 'How much money do you want to save (6 digits) ?'.
            ACCEPT investment.
            DISPLAY 'and for how many years (2 digits) ?'.
            ACCEPT term.
```

The next phase is to load the object program (machine-code program generated by the compiler from the COBOL source program) into the memory of the computer, and run or execute the program on the computer. Once again the commands to perform these functions are computer-specific, and the reader is recommended to consult the appropriate manual for the computer being used.

This phase can be prone to the following errors.

Link/Loading Error. The machine code programs necessary for the running of the COBOL program have not been specified or are not available at the time of linking. For example, the COBOL input/output library may be missing from the systems disc, preventing the program from being linked and eventually loaded.

Logical Error. The program may run to completion, however, the program does not do what you had intended it to do. If you have tested your program design and coded the design correctly, then this type of error can be minimal. In fact the JSP methodology helps to reduce this type of error. In the event of logical errors the programmer should consider the following courses of action.

Perform another desk-check, using the data that caused the error, on the design of the program.

Trace through the source code using the test data that caused the error. This is essentially a desk-check or dry-run on the source code.

Check the sizes of the PICTURES for each item of data. The picture sizes may not be large enough for the results being generated.

If these techniques are methodically carried out then the error will be detected. This statement is not one of blind faith but years of experience.

Readers must avoid, at all costs, the temptation of sitting at a terminal of a computer, editing lines of source code in a haphazard manner in the vague hope that they might fix the errors. Such attempts can only too often result in other errors creeping undetected into the program, and the programmer has wasted time, money and computer resources.

The current program still contains errors. If the reader checks the results on the next three pages, with the test of the design, it is clear to see that a logical errors exist.

When the source program is given a desk-check, using the test data from the test of the design, it becomes obvious that the value for the rate of interest is incorrect for both the Supersaver and Moneymiser accounts.

Program lines 075 and 084 have been wrongly coded as ADD 1.75, BasicRate GIVING rate and ADD 2.5, BasicRate GIVING rate repectively. These lines should be amended to:

ADD 0.0175, BasicRate GIVING rate and ADD 0.025, BasicRate GIVING rate.

```
COBOL85 ERROR2
[COBOL85 Rev. 1.0-22.0 Copyright (c) 1988, Prime Computer, Inc.]
[Serial £S033-1RQH8L-NW62 (Oxford Polytechnic)]
[0 ERRORS IN PROGRAM: <SYSF02>U10>PS0054610>DPCOBOL2>ERROR2.COBOL85]
BIND ERROR2 -LO ERROR2 -LI COBOL85LIB -LI
[BIND Rev. T2.1-22.1 Copyright (c) 1990, Prime Computer, Inc.]
[Serial £S03S-WCQQ1K-2PF6 (Oxford Polytechnic)]
BIND COMPLETE
R ERROR2


Welcome to the XYZ Building Society

  S A V I N G S   A C C O U N T S

Do you want information on:

[F]lexisaver,
[S]upersaver, or
[M]oneymiser


Type F, S or M F

F L E X I S A V E R   A C O U N T

* Rate of interest 9.5%
* Minimum investment  10
* Immediate access to your money

How much money do you want to save (6 digits) ?
001000
and for how many years (2 digits) ?
02


X Y Z   B U I L D I N G   S O C I E T Y

name of account FLEXISAVER
amount saved      1000
period (years)    2

amount saved at end of period      1199
based upon the current rate of interest

press the return key to continue
```

```
Welcome to the XYZ Building Society

   S A V I N G S   A C C O U N T S

Do you want information on:

[F]lexisaver,
[S]upersaver, or
[M]oneymiser

Type F, S or M s

Welcome to the XYZ Building Society

   S A V I N G S   A C C O U N T S

Do you want information on:

[F]lexisaver,
[S]upersaver, or
[M]oneymiser

Type F, S or M S

S U P E R S A V E R   A C O U N T

* Rate of interest 11.25%
* Minimum investment  1000
* Minimum investment term 3 years

How much money do you want to save (6 digits) ?
000100
and for how many years (2 digits) ?
03

S U P E R S A V E R   A C O U N T

* Rate of interest 11.25%
* Minimum investment  1000
* Minimum investment term 3 years

How much money do you want to save (6 digits) ?
001000
and for how many years (2 digits) ?
03
```

```
X Y Z    B U I L D I N G    S O C I E T Y

name of account SUPERSAVER
amount saved        1000
period (years)        3                           RESULT WRONG

amount saved at end of period        6280
based upon the current rate of interest


press the return key to continue

Welcome to the XYZ Building Society

  S A V I N G S   A C C O U N T S

Do you want information on:

[F]lexisaver,
[S]upersaver, or
[M]oneymiser

Type F, S or M M

M O N E Y M I S E R   A C O U N T

* Rate of interest 12%
* Minimum investment  5000
* Minimum investment term 5 years

How much money do you want to save (6 digits) ?
005000
and for how many years (2 digits) ?
05

X Y Z    B U I L D I N G    S O C I E T Y

name of account MONEYMISER
amount saved        5000
period (years)        5                    RESULT WRONG

amount saved at end of period        51614
based upon the current rate of interest


press the return key to continue
```

The correct results from the amended program being run follow.

```
COBOL85 PROGRAM
[COBOL85 Rev. 1.0-22.0 Copyright (c) 1988, Prime Computer, Inc.]
[Serial £S033-1RQH8L-NW62 (Oxford Polytechnic)]
[0 ERRORS IN PROGRAM: <SYSF02>U10>PS0054610>DPCOBOL2>PROGRAM.COBOL85]
BIND PROGRAM -LO PROGRAM -LI COBOL85LIB -LI
[BIND Rev. T2.1-22.1 Copyright (c) 1990, Prime Computer, Inc.]
[Serial £S03S-WCQQ1K-2PF6 (Oxford Polytechnic)]
BIND COMPLETE
R PROGRAM


Welcome to the XYZ Building Society

   S A V I N G S   A C C O U N T S

Do you want information on:

[F]lexisaver,
[S]upersaver, or
[M]oneymiser


Type F, S or M F

F L E X I S A V E R   A C C O U N T

* Rate of interest 9.5%
* Minimum investment  10
* Immediate access to your money

How much money do you want to save (6 digits) ?
001000
and for how many years (2 digits) ?
02


X Y Z    B U I L D I N G    S O C I E T Y

name of account FLEXISAVER
amount saved       1000
period (years)     2

amount saved at end of period     1199
based upon the current rate of interest

press the return key to continue
```

Welcome to the XYZ Building Society

S A V I N G S   A C C O U N T S

Do you want information on:

[F]lexisaver,
[S]upersaver, or
[M]oneymiser

Type F, S or M s

Welcome to the XYZ Building Society

S A V I N G S   A C C O U N T S

Do you want information on:

[F]lexisaver,
[S]upersaver, or
[M]oneymiser

Type F, S or M S

S U P E R S A V E R   A C C O U N T

* Rate of interest 11.25%
* Minimum investment 1000
* Minimum investment term 3 years

How much money do you want to save (6 digits) ?
000100
and for how many years (2 digits) ?
03

S U P E R S A V E R   A C C O U N T

* Rate of interest 11.25%
* Minimum investment 1000
* Minimum investment term 3 years

How much money do you want to save (6 digits) ?
001000
and for how many years (2 digits) ?
03

X Y Z   B U I L D I N G   S O C I E T Y

name of account SUPERSAVER
amount saved   1000
period (years)   3

amount saved at end of period   1376
based upon the current rate of interest

press the return key to continue

Welcome to the XYZ Building Society

  S A V I N G S   A C C O U N T S

Do you want information on:

[F]lexisaver,
[S]upersaver, or
[M]oneymiser

Type F, S or M M

M O N E Y M I S E R   A C C O U N T

* Rate of interest 12%
* Minimum investment   5000
* Minimum investment term 5 years

How much money do you want to save (6 digits) ?
005000
and for how many years (2 digits) ?
05

X Y Z   B U I L D I N G   S O C I E T Y

name of account MONEYMISER
amount saved   5000
period (years)   5

amount saved at end of period   8811
based upon the current rate of interest

 press the return key to continue

5.7 Discussion.

When designing the validation routine for data, input in response to a menu, it is possible to use an alternative approach that avoids the duplication of code, and thus reduces the need to identify groups of code that could be treated as subroutines. The PERFORM .. UNTIL statement tests the value of the loop condition BEFORE executing the statements to be repeated. This TEST BEFORE is taken by default and does not have to be explicitly stated. However, the syntax of the statement does allow for WITH TEST BEFORE to be included in the statement. The syntax of the PERFORM .. UNTIL statement also allows for the test on the condition to exit the loop, to be carried out after the statements within the loop have been executed once, by including the phrase WITH TEST AFTER.

If the reader considers the design for, say, the validation on data input to menu 0, shown earlier in the sub-structure diagram for box E, it should be clear that if the PERFORM .. WITH TEST AFTER .. statement is to be used in the coding of the design then the design can be simplified as follows.

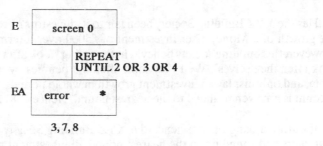

Functions	Conditions
3. clear screen	2. code = F
7. write menu 0	3. code = S
8. read/ write code	4. code = M

For those readers who have programmed in other high-level languages that support *while ..
do* and *repeat..until* control structures for repetition, it should be evident that PERFORM .. WITH TEST BEFORE .. is the COBOL equivalent to the while structure and the PERFORM .. WITH TEST AFTER is the COBOL equivalent to the repeat .. until structure. However, PERFORM statements have been used in a hierarchical manner (out-of-line), only true equivalence can be obtained by using the PERFORM statements in a flat (in-line) manner, which will be fully explained in chapter 14 on the COBOL-85 language.

In selecting the sizes of the PICTURES for the variables in the WORKING-STORAGE SECTION the largest possible value for each variable is taken as a measure for the size of the associated PICTURE. For example if the investment on a Moneymiser account was £500,000 for a term of 10 years then the growth of the investment would be £1,552,924. A six-digit input has produced a 7-digit result. By inspecting the PICTURE for the variable growth an extra digit PIC 9(8) has been included to allow for a margin of error. But what if interest rates went through the roof and the Moneymiser account started to pay interest at 25%. If half a million pounds was invested over say a twenty-five year period then the growth of the account would exceed one hundred million pounds. This figure would require a PICTURE of 9(9) and not 9(8).

When the programmer has allocated PICTURE character strings that are of adequate size for the storage of data, yet wishes to report on an abnormal event when the data becomes too large to fit into the storage allocated the ON SIZE ERROR option should be appended to the arithmetic statements that are likely to cause the overflow error. In this example line 041 can be amended to include:

J.   COMPUTE growth = investment * (1 + rate) ** term
      ON SIZE ERROR MOVE ZERO TO growth.

which would display a growth of zero from screen 4. This is hardly a user friendly approach but it does prevent the system from crashing!

The reader should remember to ensure that PICTURE character- strings are large enough to represent all the data, and that the range of test data is sufficient to detect any discrepancies in the PICTURE clauses as well as the logic of the computer program.

Has the XYZ Building Society been fair to its investors? From the desk-check of the design the growth of a Moneymiser investment of £5000 over a term of 5 years would be £8811.71. However, this building society believes in the saying "look after the pennies and the pounds will look after themselves". Well they look after the pennies by not crediting your account with them, and only display an investment growth in whole pounds. The figure for the growth of the account is not even rounded to the nearest pound. Hence £8811.71 was displayed as £8811.

If during a pang of conscience the XYZ Building Society wanted to be generous with its customers and round up to the nearest pound all investment accounts that were calculated as having attracted fifty or more pennies in addition to the pounds in the account then the ROUNDED option would be appended to the arithmetic expression for calculating growth.

COMPUTE growth ROUNDED = investment * (1 + rate) ** term.

All five of the arithmetic statements may use the ROUNDED option by including the word ROUNDED immediately following the name of the result field. This means that the rightmost remaining digit is increased by one if the leftmost truncated digit is five or greater. If rounded is not specified the value is simply truncated.

Thus £8811.71 becomes £8812 if the ROUNDED option is used otherwise the figure is displayed as £8811.

The method used to clear the screen was to display a non-printing control character that caused the contents of the screen to be erased and the cursor moved to the home position (top left-hand corner of the screen). The visual display unit used for the development of the program was a Televideo TVI 925, which required the control characters ^232 to be sent to the screen in order to clear it. If the reader inspects line 016, the printer has not output the control characters: 77 ClearScreen PIC X(4) VALUE ". Incidentally the control characters ^232 were inserted into the text using a line editor and not the window editor that was used to prepare the rest of the program. Obviously the control characters used to clear a screen are device dependent, therefore, the reader is recommended to refer to the visual display or monitor manual for the system they are using, in order to achieve the same result.

The reader can be excused for thinking that the output from this example program leaves something to be desired! The author would agree with these sentiments as well. However, the example has been chosen to illustrate several points regarding the format of data input to the computer and the output of information from the computer.

The input of numeric data through a keyboard must conform in format to the PICTURE clause for that item of data. It is for this reason that the screen prompts to the user, informing of the size of the PICTURE clause have been used. In order for the datum to conform to the PICTURE clause extra leading and trailing zeros have to be inserted into the data. For example the investment is input as 001000 and not 1000 and term as 05 and not 5, otherwise the investment would have been accepted as 100000 and the term as 50.

On the output of information large gaps have appeared in front of the numbers and the currency symbol does not appear against the amounts. The topic of formatting reports so that the information is presented in a business-like manner is dealt with in the next chapter.

5.8 Summary.
From a functional specification of a system, the input and output screens will form the basis of the input / output structures in the program design.

Perform appropriate validation on data input to the system. Further validation techniques will be explained later in the text.

The availability of language statements may dictate how a particular program structure will be designed. For example the constraint of only having available a WITH TEST BEFORE in a PERFORM .. UNTIL statement prevented the author from using a simpler program structure for validating input data.

Having derived a detailed program structure, invent suitable test data and check the validity of the design. This will help minimise logical errors. If you detect errors in the design then make amendments to the design now. This will save time in the development of the system, since changes made later to the source code should always be accompanied by retrospective changes to the design, if the program documentation is to be kept up-to-date.

The decision to optimise source code must be made on the strength of the program design. Functions that are repeated many times throughout a design must be identified, and perhaps coded as separate subroutines.

Using the hierarchical strategy for coding the Procedure Division it is possible to obtain a one-to-one correspondence between the detailed program structure and the Procedure Division source code.

Use a value clause to initialise a variable or constant.

Use a value clause in conjunction with a level 88 condition identifier to specify legal or illegal values of variables.

Use the short form of expressing a compound condition when testing for values that apply to a particular variable.

If after compilation a program contains errors then obtain a computer print-out of all the syntax errors and check these off against a computer print-out of the source program. This can be a pencil-and-paper exercise away from the computer.

Always ensure that PICTURE clauses are large enough to accommodate all data that is likely to be used in the system.

Use ON SIZE ERROR to report on abnormal sizes of data.

Data input through a keyboard must contain the same number of characters as indicated by the PICTURE clause. Zero fill numbers and space fill characters-strings.

Numeric data can be ROUNDED.

> **Keywords**
>
> *interactive computing, screen, menu;*
> *data validation;*
> *VALUE clause;*
> *level 88*
> *editor, compiler, loader;*
> *syntax errors, logical errors, run-time errors;*
> *ON SIZE ERROR, ROUNDED;*
> *PERFORM .. WITH TEST AFTER UNTIL ..*

5.9 Questions.

1. Compile, load and execute the programs developed as answers to the questions 1 - 6 inclusive at the end of chapter 4. The answers to questions 5 and 6 are available in the Answer Supplement. Use the test data given in the corresponding questions at the end of chapter 2.

Warning. When a numeric item of data is input to a computer, the number of digits must correspond with the PICTURE clause for the variable. For example when the computer executes ACCEPT item, and item has a PICTURE of 99, a value of say, 03 should be input and not 3.

[2]. Using the worked example in this chapter as a template for program development, design, test, code, compile, execute and re- test the interactive insurance system described.

The RISKPLAN insurance company require an interactive computer system to inform potential customers of the insurance premiums they are likely to pay for three types of insurance policy.

The system is only operative from 9.00 am to 4.30 pm.

The system will invite customers to input details relating to the following insurance policies displayed on screen 0.

```
      RISKPLAN INSURANCE

Do you want information on:

1. Building insurance
2. Household contents insurance
3. Holiday insurance

Type 1, 2 or 3
```

After the correct response has been made by a customer the system will display one of the following three screens.

```
              BUILDING
What is the present market value of your property
(6 digits)?
Do you want to pay an excess on a claim ?

          0. NO excess
          1. £100 excess
          2. £500 excess
   Type 0, 1 or 2
```

With the buildings insurance calculate 65% of the market value of the property giving the price to re-build the property in the event of total destruction. To calculate the buildings insurance premium, if there is no excess take 0.25% of the rebuilding cost; if the excess is £100 take 0.2% of the rebuilding cost, otherwise assuming a £500 excess take 0.15% of the re-building cost.

```
              DOMESTIC
What is the current market value of the contents
of your home (6 digits) ?
Do you want to pay an excess on a claim ?

          0. NO excess
          1. £50
          2. £100

Type 0, 1 or 2
```

To calculate the domestic contents premium take 2% of the value of the goods when no excess is specified; take 1.875% of the value of the goods for a £50 excess, otherwise take 1.75% of the value of the goods for a £100 excess.

```
HOLIDAY
How many weeks are you on holiday - for a part week
round up to the nearest whole week (2 digits)?
Are you on holiday in the
                        1. EEC,
                        2. USA, or
                        3. Worldwide
Type 1, 2 or 3
```

To calculate the holiday premium the standard insurance is £10 per week for any EEC country. This charge is increased by 50% of the standard premium, per week for travel to the USA, and increased by 75% of the standard premium, per week for worldwide travel. The concept of paying an excess charge in the event of a claim is not applicable to holiday insurance.

After a particular insurance has been chosen and the correct data has been entered into the system, the following information is displayed to the customer.

```
RISKPLAN INSURANCE

    Type of insurance policy
    Premium
    Excess to pay in the event of a claim

    Press return key to continue
```

6

Picture Editing

The aim of this chapter is to present the reader with the tools of picture editing, so that the DATA DIVISIONS of future programs can be coded to give a much improved output.

6.1 The Purpose of Editing Pictures.

Picture editing is used in the output of numerical information. If the reader considers the specimen statement of account below, all the information under the headings of debit, credit, balance and final balance are printed from edited pictures. The different forms of picture edit in the statement have been circled.

Upon inspecting the specimen statement of account it should reveal that picture editing involves such features as suppressing leading zeros, inserting decimal points, + or - signs, commas, a currency symbol ($) and extra characters (DB).

The Universal Bank

Statement of account: 04973128 1726493

Date	Description	Debit	Credit	Balance
May 1	Balance			+103.98
May 3	Salary		1,076.42	+1,180.40
May 5	Domestic Charge	423.45		+756.95
May 8	Mortgage	932.84		-175.89
May 10	Credit Transfer		2,100.00	+1,924.11
May 12	General Stores	376.29		+1,547.82
May 13	Universal B.S.	1,900.00		-352.18
May 17	Insurance	50.75		-402.93
May 21	Petrol A/C	103.84		-506.77
May 30	General Stores	147.50		-654.27
May 31	Credit Transfer		550.00	-104.27
	Final Balance			$104.27DB

These edits take place as a result of an item of data being transferred using either a MOVE statement or an arithmetic statement, from a source area, where the picture is not edited, to a destination area where the picture is edited . Although the destination identifier in an arithmetic statement can be edited, you must never perform arithmetic upon items of data that have been described using edited pictures.

6.2 Edited Pictures.

In the examples that follow the symbol b represents the space character.

Suppression of Leading Zeros. The position of each leading digit in a number is represented by Z. If this digit happens to be a zero then a space will be output.

Source	Picture	Edited Result
003456	999999	003456
003456	ZZ9999	bb3456
000074	ZZ9999	bb0074
000074	ZZZZ99	bbbb74
001001	ZZZZZ9	bb1001
000000	ZZZZZZ	bbbbbb

Insertion of a currency symbol. A single currency symbol ($) as the leftmost character of a picture, indicates that the character ($) or equivalent, is to be printed in that position. It is possible to change the currency symbol from the dollar to one that is applicable to the application program being constructed. This change of currency symbol will be explained in the next chapter.

Source	Picture	Edited Result
4567	$9999	$4567
006235	$ZZZZZ9	$bb6235
000000	$ZZZZZZ	bbbbbbb

A floating currency symbol can also be used to suppress leading zeros as well as generating a currency symbol immediately to the left of the most significant non-zero digit.

Source	Picture	Edited Result
0004874	$$$$$$9	bb$4874
2300004	$$$$$$$$	$2300004
0000000	$$$$$$$$	bbbbbbbb
0000000	$$$$$$$9	bbbbbb$0

Insertion of a decimal point. If a decimal point is inserted into a picture then it will be output in the required position of the edited numerical item of data. An alignment is performed between the implied decimal point of the source item, indicated by a lower-case v in the examples that follow, and the decimal point of the edited item.

Source	Picture	Edited Result	Comment
376v56	999.99	376.56	
1v4598	999.99999	001.45980	leading and trailing zeros inserted
000v045	ZZZ.ZZZ	bbb.045	Z only suppresses leading zeros
1274v593	99.99	74.59	since alignment is about the implied point (v) and edited point (.), leading and trailing digits are lost when the destination field is smaller

Insertion of commas, blanks and zeros. These characters can be inserted into the picture and will be printed in the position indicated in the edited picture.

Source	Picture	Edited Result	Comment
478935	999,999	478,935	
000593	ZZZ,ZZ9	bbbb593	if the digit(s) to the left of the comma(s) are zeros, and zero suppression is used the comma(s) are replaced by spaces
4567234	Z,ZZZ,ZZZ	4,567,234	
7245v56	9,999.99	7,245.56	
00942v70	ZZ,ZZZ.99	bbb942.70	
589346v	$ZZZ,ZZZ.ZZ	$589,346.00	trailing zeros have been inserted despite the zero suppression
180348	99BB99BB99	18bb03bb48	the use of B in the picture will print a space in the stated position - useful for formatting dates of birth
7839v	Z,ZZZ.000	7,839.000	zeros can be inserted in a picture in the same way as spaces
3459	999900000	345900000	

Insertion of a display sign. A single + (plus) or - (minus) sign inserted into a picture as the first or last character will be printed in the position indicated. If the item of data is negative and a + sign is used, a - sign will be printed. If the item of data is positive and a - sign is used a space will be printed. If neither of these conditions apply the same sign will be printed that appears in the picture.

Source	Operational sign	Picture	Edited Picture
4563	-	-9999	-4563
376	-	999-	376-
27834	-	+99999	-27834
90045	+	-99999	b90045
7398	+	9999+	7398+
18965	-	-9.9999	-1.8965

Zero suppression can be achieved by using either a floating + or floating - sign in the same way as a floating currency symbol was used.

Source	Operational sign	Picture	Edited Picture
00036	-	- - - - 9	bbb - 36
00528	+	+ + +999	bb+528
00000	+	- - - - - -	bbbbbb

Insertion of special characters. Either CR or DB may appear as the rightmost two characters in a picture. If the source item of data is negative then the respective credit CR or debit DB characters will be printed.

Source	Operational sign	Picture	Edited Picture
1456348	-	$$$,$$9.99DB	$14,563.48DB
4784	+	$$$$9CR	$4784bb

In the printing of bank cheques leading spaces are undesirable. An asterisk (*) can be used in the same way as a (Z) for zero suppression. The difference being that the asterisk is printed instead of the space.

Source	Picture	Edited Picture
00045673	*****9.99	***456.73
0003489	$***,**9.99	$*****34.89

Blank when zero. Ths clause BLANK WHEN ZERO can be appended to numeric or numeric edited pictures if it is preferred to represent the item of data as spaces and not zero.

6.3 The effects of Data Movement.

Editing is performed on numeric data as the result of either a MOVE statement or arithmetic statement being executed, provided the destination of the item of data conforms to the edited picture.

When transferring data, the following points should be kept in mind.

The items of data are aligned by decimal points, with either the generation of zeros to fill the field, or the truncation of digits from the numeric item of data, so that the item will fit into the field.

When the data types of the source field and destination field differ, conversion to the type of the receiving field takes place under the following circumstances.

Source	Destination		
	numeric	alphabetic	alphanumeric
numeric	legal	illegal	legal
alphabetic	illegal	legal	legal
alphanumeric	legal *	legal **	legal

* indicates a legal move provided the alphanumeric characters are composed from the numeric character set;

** indicates a legal move provided the alphanumeric characters are composed from the alphabetic character set.

When the data being transferred is non-numeric then the following rules will apply.

The characters are LEFT justified in the receiving or destination field.

If the receiving field is larger than the source field it is filled with spaces to the right.

If the source field is larger that the receiving field the string of characters are truncated from the right.

Source	Picture of receiving field	Receiving field
6v7	9999V99	0006v70
649v472	999V999	649v472
23467v392467	999V999	467v392
78v	999V999	078v000
63v93	X(6)	6393bb
"45628967"	X(6)	456289
1234567890	9(6)V99	567890v00
"ABC"	X(12)	ABCbbbbbbbbb
"ABCDEFGHIJ"	X(4)	ABCD

When using non-numeric data if the:

$$\left\{\begin{matrix} \text{JUSTIFIED} \\ \text{JUST} \end{matrix}\right\} \quad \text{RIGHT}$$

clause is appended to the picture clause then the string of characters is moved to the right of the receiving field if this is larger than the source field. If, however, the receiving field is smaller than the source field then the string of characters is truncated from the left.

Source	Picture of receiving field JUSTIFIED RIGHT	Receiving field
"ABCD"	X(10)	bbbbbbABCD
"ABCDEFGHIJ"	X(5)	FGHIJ

6.4 Worked Example.

The gross annual expenditure of a county council can be broken down into the following areas.

Staff 53%; Goods and services 15%; Premises 8%; Capital charges 7%; Educational grants and contributions 8% and miscellaneous items 9%.

Design and implement a program to output to the screen of a vdu, a report showing the breakdown of expenditure based upon the following layout.

The annual gross expenditure is $210,881,916.00 and should be declared using a VALUE clause. The total, in the report, is intended as check against machine truncation errors.

REPORT ON COUNTY COUNCIL EXPENDITURE 1983/84	
ITEM	AMOUNT
STAFF	$111,767,415.48
GOODS AND SERVICES	$31,632,287.40
PREMISES	$16,870,553.28
CAPITAL CHARGES	$14,761,734.12
EDUCATION GRANTS AND CONTRIB.	$16,870,553.28
MISCELLANEOUS	$18,979,372.44
TOTAL	$210,881,916.00

The detailed program structure for the solution to this problem is no more than a simple sequence of instructions.

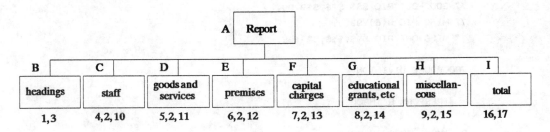

Functions

1. initialise total expenditure to zero
2. increase total expenditure by respective item
3. write headings
4. calculate staff expenditure
5. calculate goods and services expenditure
6. calculate premises expenditure
7. calculate capital charges expenditure
8. calculate educational grants and contributions expenditure
9. calculate miscellaneous expenditure
10. write edited staff expenditure
11. write edited goods and services expenditure
12. write edited premises expenditure
13. write edited capital charges expenditure
14. write edited educational grants and contributions expenditure
15. write edited miscellaneous expenditure
16. write edited total expenditure
17. finish

The following program has been coded directly from the detailed program structure. The results obtained from compiling and running the program are also printed.

```
        IDENTIFICATION DIVISION.
        PROGRAM-ID. Expenditure.

        DATA DIVISION.
        WORKING-STORAGE SECTION.
        77 GROSS-EXP PIC 9(9) VALUE IS 210881916.
        77 TOT-EXP PIC 9(9)V99.
        77 TOT-EXP-OUT PIC $$$$,$$$,$$9.99.
        77 STAFF PIC 9(9)V99.
        77 STAFF-OUT PIC $$$$,$$$,$$9.99.
        77 GOODS PIC 9(9)V99.
        77 GOODS-OUT PIC $$$$,$$$,$$9.99.
        77 PREM PIC 9(8)V99.
        77 PREM-OUT PIC $$$,$$$,$$9.99.
        77 CAPITAL PIC 9(8)V99.
        77 CAPITAL-OUT PIC $$$,$$$,$$9.99.
        77 EDUC PIC 9(8)V99.
        77 EDUC-OUT PIC $$$,$$$,$$9.99.
        77 MISC PIC 9(8)V99.
        77 MISC-OUT PIC $$$,$$$,$$9.99.

        PROCEDURE DIVISION.
        A-seq.
            PERFORM B THROUGH I.

        B.   MOVE ZERO TO TOT-EXP.
             DISPLAY "REPORT ON COUNTY COUNCIL ANNUAL EXPENDITURE 1983/84"
             DISPLAY " ".
             DISPLAY "ITEM                              AMOUNT"
             DISPLAY " ".
        C.   MULTIPLY 0.53 BY GROSS-EXP GIVING STAFF.
             ADD STAFF TO TOT-EXP.
             MOVE STAFF TO STAFF-OUT.
             DISPLAY "STAFF                              " STAFF-OUT.
        D.   MULTIPLY 0.15 BY GROSS-EXP GIVING GOODS.
             ADD GOODS TO TOT-EXP.
             MOVE GOODS TO GOODS-OUT.
             DISPLAY "GOODS AND SERVICES                 " GOODS-OUT.
        E.   MULTIPLY 0.08 BY GROSS-EXP GIVING PREM.
             ADD PREM TO TOT-EXP.
             MOVE PREM TO PREM-OUT.
             DISPLAY "PREMISES                           " PREM-OUT.
        F.   MULTIPLY 0.07 BY GROSS-EXP GIVING CAPITAL.
             ADD CAPITAL TO TOT-EXP.
             MOVE CAPITAL TO CAPITAL-OUT.
             DISPLAY "CAPITAL CHARGES                    " CAPITAL-OUT.
        G.   MULTIPLY 0.08 BY GROSS-EXP GIVING EDUC.
```

```
            ADD EDUC TO TOT-EXP.
            MOVE EDUC TO EDUC-OUT.
            DISPLAY "EDUCATION GRANTS AND CONTRIB.        " EDUC-OUT.
       H.   MULTIPLY 0.09 BY GROSS-EXP GIVING MISC.
            ADD MISC TO TOT-EXP.
            MOVE MISC TO MISC-OUT.
            DISPLAY "MISCELLANEOUS                        " MISC-OUT.
            DISPLAY " ".
       I.   MOVE TOT-EXP TO TOT-EXP-OUT.
            DISPLAY "TOTAL                                " TOT-EXP-OUT.
            STOP RUN.


       REPORT ON COUNTY COUNCIL ANNUAL EXPENDITURE 1983/84


          ITEM                               AMOUNT


          STAFF                              $111,767,415.48
          GOODS AND SERVICES                  $31,632,287.40
          PREMISES                            $16,870,553.28
          CAPITAL CHARGES                     $14,761,734.12
          EDUCATION GRANTS AND CONTRIB.       $16,870,553.28
          MISCELLANEOUS                       $18,979,372.44

          TOTAL                              $210,881,916.00
```

6.5 Summary

A numeric item can be edited, prior to being written, by using the symbols Z $, . - + B CR DB *
0 in a picture clause for the receiving or destination field.

Numeric data is aligned by decimal points, resulting in either the receiving field being zero
filled, or source data digits being truncated.

If an item of data is zero then a blank field can be printed if the picture of the receiving
field is appended with the clause BLANK WHEN ZERO.

Non-numeric items of data can be aligned, either to the left (by default) or to the right of a
receiving field by appending the clause JUSTIFIED RIGHT to the receiving field. Note the
absence of this clause will result in default alignment to the left of the receiving field.

Keywords

Edited Picture
*Edit symbols Z $. , - + B CR DB * 0*
BLANK WHEN ZERO
JUSTIFIED RIGHT.

6.6 Questions

1. What are the edited results when the following items of data are moved from the source field to the edited destination or receiving field?

Picture	Source Data	Op. sign	Receiving area picture
9(5)	00067		ZZ,ZZ9
9(7)V99	004527745		Z,ZZZ,ZZZ.99
9(3)V99	25489		ZZZ.ZZ
9(5)V99	0045734		$$$$$$.99
9(6)V99	00009589		$***,***.99
S9(4)V99	029456	-	$$,$$$.99CR
S9(3)	835	+	**9DB
S9999	4573	-	9999-
S9999	0528	+	-Z999
S9999	0067	+	ZZZZ+
S9(5)	00023	-	----9
S9(6)V99	00004578	-	---,---.99
S9(6)V99	26784590	+	+++,++9.99
9(6)	145623		BBBB9999BB99
9(6)	000345		ZZZ,ZZZ.00

2. What are the edited results when the following items of data are moved from the source field to the edited destination or receiving field?

Picture	Source Data	Op. sign	Receiving area picture
9(5)	46389		$$$,$$9.99
9(5)	00467		$$$,$$9.99
9(5)	00000		$$$,$$9.99
9(4)V9	12345		$$$,$$9.99
V9(5)	93764		$$$,$$9.99
S9(5)	00423	+	-------.99
S9(5)	00004	-	+++++++.99
S9(5)	00543	+	+++++++.99
S9(5)	00003	-	-------.99
9(5)	00832		-------.99
9(5)	00382		-------.99
S9(5)	04127	+	*******.99CR
S999V99	00008	-	ZZZVZZ
S999V99	00067	-	ZZZVZZ
S9(5)	65489	-	*******.99CR
9999V99	001234		9(4).99 BLANK WHEN ZERO
9999V99	000000		****.99 BLANK WHEN ZERO
9999V99	000000		****.99
9999V99	000000		ZZZZ.ZZ BLANK WHEN ZERO
9999V99	004573		****.99 BLANK WHEN ZERO

[3]. The gross income for a district council can be broken down into the following areas.

Rents 39%; Block grants 12%; Housing subsidies 6%; Other Government grants 11%; Community charge 10%; Fees, charges and mortgagors 12%; Interest and balances 10%.

Using the worked example as a model, design a report on the income for the district council. Design and implement a computer program to input at the keyboard of a vdu, the gross annual income for the district council and output to the screen of the vdu the details of the report. Design the program so that it will cater for variable percentages in each area of income.

[4]. A sales invoice for the purchase of a motor-car may contain the following information.

Name and address of the dealer who has sold the vehicle.
Name and address of the purchaser of the vehicle.
Vehicle details
Part-exchange vehicle details (if any)
New vehicle price
Factory fitted accessories
Car tax
Dealer fitted accessories
Delivery charge
Petrol
Number plates
Value added tax
Total
Road Fund Licence
Invoice total
Part-exchange price
Deposit
Balance Due

Car tax is levied at 8.3% on the new vehicle price and the cost of factory fitted accessories. The costs of the new vehicle price, factory fitted accessories and car tax are added together to form sub-total-1.

The costs of dealer fitted accessories, delivery charges, petrol and number plates are added to sub-total-1 to give sub-total-2.

Value added tax is levied at 15% on sub-total-2, and this amount is then added to sub-total-2 to give the total purchase price.

Added to the total purchase price is the road fund licence at, say, £100, to form the invoice total.

Any part-exchange allowance, on a vehicle that has been traded-in, and the deposit on the new vehicle is deducted from the invoice total to form the balance due.

An example of the format of the sales invoice is given over the page.

Brum Brum Car Sales Ltd
The Raceway,
Birmingham B1 0W

Invoiced to:

Mr. J. Stewart
2141 Silverstone Ave
Selly Oak
Birmingham B2 0K

Invoice Number: 5680
Date: 30.07.90

Vehicle Details

Make/Model BMW 316i
Colour/Trim Calypso/Anthracite
Reg. No. H 007 JS
Chassis No. XX123456
Stock No. 1001

Part Exchange vehicle details

Make/Model BMW 318
Colour/Trim Lapis/Anthracite
Reg. No. G 001 SPR
Chassis No. BB65789
Date first registered August 1989

New Vehicle Price	9973.25
Factory Fitted Accessories	
Metallic Paint	301.01
Manual Sunroof	458.33
Car Tax	894.38
Sub-total-1	11626.97
Dealer fitted accessories	
mud flaps	57.47
floor mats	55.91
delivery	256.52
petrol	20.33
number plates	27.50
sub-total-2	12044.70
vat	1806.71
total	13851.41
Road Fund licence	100.00
Invoice Total	13951.41
Part-exchange allowance	4055.00
Deposit	500.00
BALANCE DUE	**$9396.41**

Design and write a program to input the necessary data at the keyboard of a *vdu*, and output the sales invoice in the format shown. Pay particular attention to the use of edited picture fields. You are **not** expected to produce letters of different sizes, shading or highlighted areas of the report.

7

Coding Data Files and Reports

The purpose of this chapter is to demonstrate how to code the records of a data file in the DATA DIVISION. The chapter also deals with the necessary entries in the ENVIRONMENT DIVISION when using data files.

7.1 Elements of a Data File.

A file is a collection of information, stored on either magnetic tape or magnetic disc. Files can also be stored on punched cards and punched paper-tape, however, these storage media are fast becoming obsolete and will not be considered any further in this text.

The reader has already come across the concept of a file when storing a computer program on either magnetic disc or magnetic tape. The program file was composed of a line-by-line collection of COBOL statements stored under a name given to the file.

Data files are similar in concept. Each line of data (or multiple lines) is known as a logical record and is subdivided into smaller areas of information known as fields. Each field is composed from a series of characters. The number of characters grouped into a field can vary from field to field in a record. The records in a file can be either fixed-length or variable-length. For example figure 7.1 illustrates the format of a fixed-length record used to store the details of a factory employee.

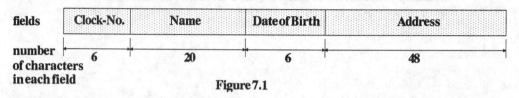

Figure 7.1

Each record in figure 7.1 has a fixed-length of 80 characters, however, although such fields as name and address have fixed lengths of 20 and 48 characters respectively, their contents will not always fill the size of the fields. Each field that is not completely filled will be padded with spaces and the contents of the field will be left justified unless otherwise stated. The result will be an accumulated waste of space between the records in the file. For this reason the fields of a record can be allowed to vary according to the size of the data contained in them. This in turn will bring about records of varying length throughout the file, however, the amount of space that is wasted will be reduced. The records of such a file are said to be variable-length records.

Notice from figure 7.1 that the information contained in the file is related to a specific application, in this example, personnel in a factory. Different files are used for different applications, for example, stock records, airline flight reservations, customer details, etc.

One field of a record is normally specified as a primary key to that record. For example, in figure 7.1, the field clock-number contains a value that is unique to an employee in a factory and could be used as the key (method of identification) to that specific record. If information is needed about an employee, and the clock-number is known in advance, the file of records on employees could be searched, comparing the clock-number of each record with the known clock-number of the employee. When a match between clock-numbers was found the information contained in the record for the employee could be read.

A sequential file is one in which the records are positioned one after another and the keys do not form any specific order. By contrast a sorted sequential file contains records whose positions, relative to the other records in the file, are determined by the values of the keys. The keys of the records, and by implication the entire records, are sorted into either ascending or descending order.

7.2 Coding Records in the Data Division.
Figure 7.2 illustrates the hierarchical nature of the record described in figure 7.1.

Each level of the record has been assigned a level number. Level numbers range from 01 to

01	Employee Record								
02	Clock-No.	Name		Date of Birth			Address		
03		initial	surname	day	month	year	street	town	postcode

Figure 7.2

49, with 01 always being used to denote the highest level or record level. Subordinate fields within the record are assigned larger level numbers in increments that the programmer may choose. At the second level, in figure 7.2, assigned the level number 02, the only field that has not been subdivided further , at a lower-level, is that of the clock number. Because clock number cannot be subdivided any further it is known as an elementary item.

Name, date of birth and address have been subdivided into fields at a lower level and assigned the level number 03. These fields, initial, surname, day, month, year, street, town and postcode have not been subdivided any further and are, therefore, elementary items.

When a record is represented in the Data Division, picture clauses can only be appended to elementary items.

When coding into COBOL statements, the record described in figure 7.2, the reader should be aware that some of the field descriptors are in fact reserved words. Such words must be changed to avoid compilation errors.

The Data Division coding for the record described in figure 7.2 follows. The 01 level is coded in zone A. The other levels must appear in zone B. The indented code signifies the hierarchical relationship between the elements of the record.

```
01   EmployeeRecord.
     02 ClockNumber PIC 9(6).
     02 name.
        03 FirstInitial PIC A.
        03 surname PIC x(19).
     02 DateOfBirth.
        03 DD PIC 99.
        03 MM PIC 99.
        03 YY PIC 99.
     02 address.
        03 street PIC X(20).
        03 town PIC X(20).
        03 postcode PIC X(8).
```

7.3 Coding Reports.

The design of a report is made considerably easier if the reader adopts the habit of planning the layout of the report on a record/report layout sheet, similar to the one shown in figure 7.3. If such a document cannot be obtained then paper pre-ruled into squares with numbered columns can be used. Such a document is an aid towards the Data Division coding of the respective records that will eventually form the report.

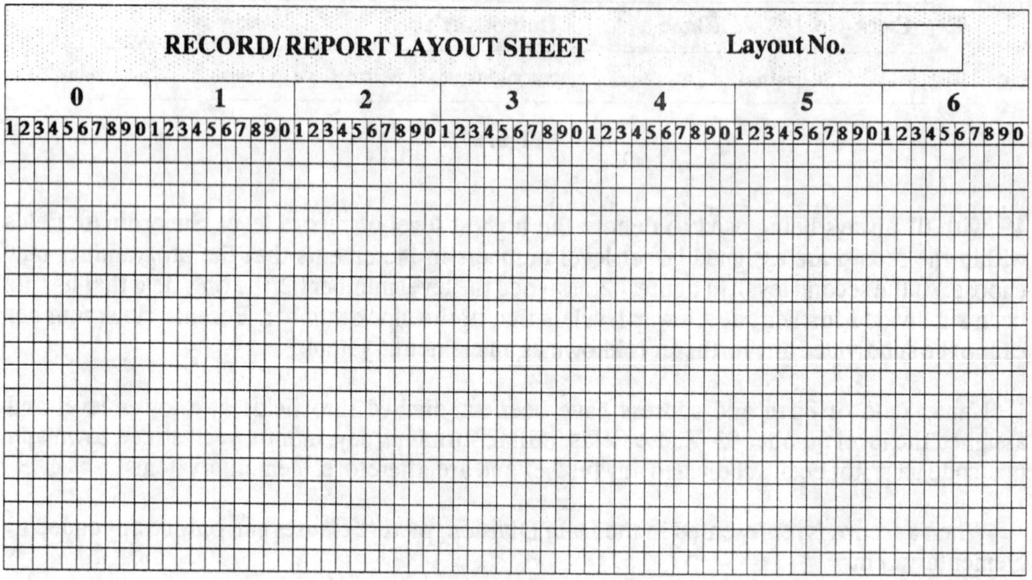

Figure 7.3

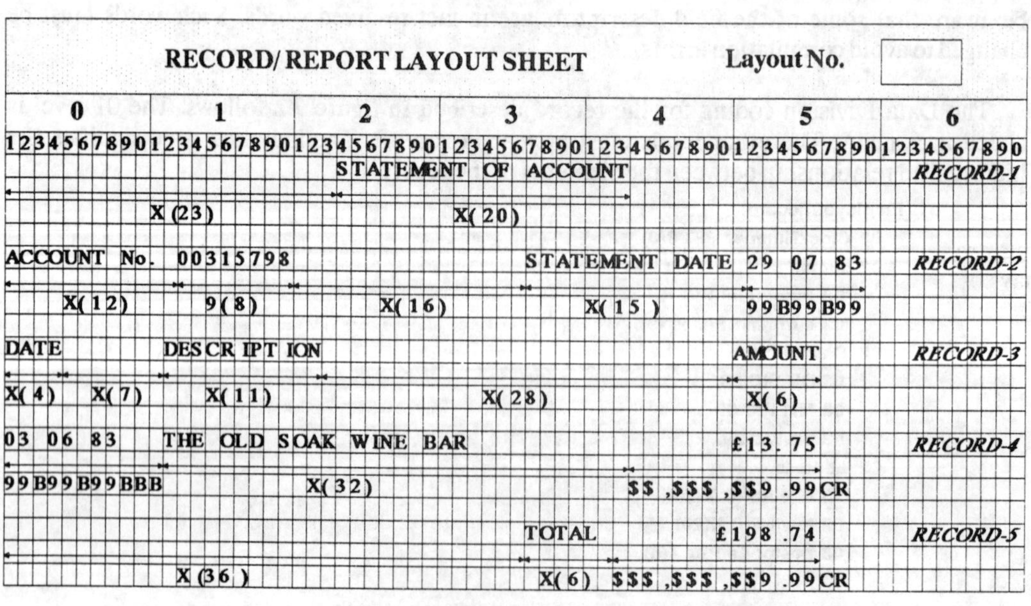

Figure 7.4

Figure 7.4 illustrates a typical layout of a credit card statement of account. The design document illustrates lines of the report that represent records to be coded. Beneath each record are arrowed lines showing the size of the respective fields, and beneath this is the COBOL description for the format of each field. From figure 7.4, many of the fields that have been described using picture clause character-strings do not need an identifier since they will never be referenced. When describing such fields in the Data Division the reserved word FILLER is used to replace the identifier. For example the Data Division coding to represent the first record of the report in figure 7.4 is:

```
01 Record-1.
    02 FILLER PIC X(23).
    02 Heading-1 PIC X(20).
```

The FILLER is to contain 23 spaces and Heading-1 is to contain the 20 characters of STATEMENT OF ACCOUNT. Both can be initialised to their respective values by using a VALUE clause.

```
01 Record-1.
    02 FILLER PIC X(23) VALUE IS SPACES.
    02 Heading-1 PIC X(20) VALUE IS 'STATEMENT OF ACCOUNT'.
```

Because the record will be referenced through the identifier Record-1, identifier Heading-1 will never be used. For this reason it too, can be replaced by a FILLER. The modified form of the record description becomes:

```
01 Record-1.
    02 FILLER PIC X(23) VALUE IS SPACES.
    02 FILLER PIC X(20) VALUE IS 'STATEMENT OF ACCOUNT'.
```

The observant reader will realise that there is a shorter, alternative way of describing this record by using the JUSTIFIED RIGHT clause as:

```
01 Record-1.
    02 FILLER PIC X(43) JUSTIFIED RIGHT VALUE 'STATEMENT OF ACCOUNT'.
```

The heading STATEMENT OF ACCOUNT is stored in the right-hand end of the record with the left-hand portion automatically filled with spaces.

Since there are five different records that make up the report illustrated in figure 7.4, there will be five separate 01 entries, one for each record, in the Working-Storage Section. Notice in this example, that where possible, fields containing spaces and fields containing text literals have been combined into one entry. This is a deliberate attempt to reduce the amount of Data Division coding.

```
WORKING-STORAGE   SECTION.
01 Record-1-WS.
    02 FILLER PIC X(43) VALUE IS 'STATEMENT OF ACCOUNT' JUSTIFIED RIGHT.
01 Record-2-WS.
    02 FILLER PIC X(12) VALUE IS 'ACCOUNT NO.'.
    02 AccountNumber PIC 9(8).
    02 FILLER PIC X(31) VALUE IS 'STATEMENT DATE' JUSTIFIED RIGHT.
    02 StatementDate PIC 99BB99B99.
01 Record-3-WS.
    02 FILLER PIC X(11) VALUE IS 'DATE'.
```

```
      02 FILLER PIC X(39) VALUE IS 'DESCRIPTION'.
      02 FILLER PIC X(6) VALUE IS 'AMOUNT'.
   01 Record-4-WS.
      02 TransactionDate PIC 99B99B99BBB.
      02 TransactionItem PIC X(32).
      02 TransactionAmount PIC $$,$$$,$$9.99CR.
   01 Record-5-WS.
      02 FILLER PIC X(42) VALUE IS 'TOTAL' JUSTIFIED RIGHT.
      02 TotalAmount PIC $$$,$$$,$$9.99CR.
```

7.4 The File Section.

The File section defines the structure of data files. Each file is described by a file description entry (FD), followed by one or more record description entries.

A simplified format for the File Section is:

FILE SECTION.
FD file-name-1
[BLOCK CONTAINS [integer-1 TO]integer-2 {RECORDS / CHARACTERS}]
[RECORD   CONTAINS [integer-3 TO] integer-4 CHARACTERS]
           IS VARYING IN SIZE [[FROM integer-5] [TO integer-6] CHARACTERS]
                    [DEPENDING UPON data-name-1]
[LABEL RECORD[S] {IS / ARE} {STANDARD / OMITTED}
[VALUE OF implementor-name IS {data-name-1 / literal}   ].
[DATA   RECORD[S] {IS / ARE} {data-name-2} ...]
01 record-name-1.
[01 record-name-2] ...

A physical record is defined as one or more logical records read into or written from main memory as a unit of information. Records are not usually transferred to and from main memory as single logical records but grouped together and stored in an area of memory known as a buffer. When information is transferred to a buffer it is transferred as a block of logical records from the storage medium. Similarly when information is transferred from the buffer to the storage medium it is transferred as a block of logical records.

The BLOCK clause specifies the number of logical records contained in a physical record. The clause can be omitted if the size of the block is one logical record.

The RECORD clause specifies the number of characters in a fixed-length record or the range of characters in a variable-length record. If the number of character positions does vary then the clause specifies the number of minimum and maximum characters in a variable-length record. Since the number of characters is specified in the description of each field of a fixed length record this entry is not essential for fixed-length records.

In order to identify different magnetic tape files each file will have a unique machine readable label. Labels contain such information as the external name of the file, the volume number, the date the file was written and perhaps the date after which the data will no longer be valid (purge date). The clause LABEL RECORDS ARE STANDARD is reserved for files stored on magnetic tape.

The VALUE OF clause is used to specify the external name of the file, this is the filename stored in the directory in disc-based systems, and labels in tape-based systems. The clause serves the purpose of linking the external name of the file with the internal name of the file (file-name-1 used in FD entry).

The DATA RECORD clause specifies the name(s) of the record(s) described at the 01 level.

In the 1985 Standard for COBOL the LABEL RECORDS, VALUE OF and DATA RECORDS clauses are defined as being obsolete. This implies that they have been left unchanged in COBOL-85 and are expected to be deleted from the next revision. All obsolete elements should be avoided unless they are required by your compiler or installation.

In defining files the following FD format will be used throughout the text.

FD file-name-1, COMPRESSED.

Since all the programs in this text have been compiled and run on a PRIME computer it has been necessary to include a PRIME extension to the FD entry. All data files that are produced using a PRIME system editor are stored in a compressed format. For this reason the word COMPRESSED must appear after the name of the file in the FD entry.

The file description entry may need to be modified, depending upon the type of compiler and computer system that you are using. This will apply to all the programs found in the remainder of the book. You are advised to consult you COBOL manual for the necessary amendments.

Pre COBOL-85 compilers may generate an error message if the LABEL clause is missing. The PRIME system only requires a LABEL RECORDS ARE STANDARD clause to be inserted when the data files are stored on magnetic tape. For other media the LABEL clause can be omitted or the clause can be inserted as LABEL RECORDS ARE OMITTED.

If the VALUE OF clause is omitted the external name of the file is taken to be the same as the COBOL program name of the file described in the FD entry (file-name-1).

7.5 The Environment Division.
This Division describes the physical environment in which the COBOL program will be executed.

A simplified format for the Division follows.

```
ENVIRONMENT DIVISION.
[CONFIGURATION SECTION.
[SOURCE-COMPUTER. computer-name.]
[OBJECT-COMPUTER. computer-name.]
```

```
[SPECIAL-NAMES. paragraph]]
[INPUT-OUTPUT SECTION.
FILE-CONTROL.
{SELECT file-name-1 ASSIGN TO device-name
[ORGANIZATION IS SEQUENTIAL]
[ACCESS MODE IS SEQUENTIAL]
[FILE STATUS IS data-name-1.]} ...]
```

The programmer may document the name of the computer used to compile and execute the COBOL program under the paragraph names of SOURCE-COMPUTER and OBJECT-COMPUTER respectively.

For example:
```
ENVIRONMENT DIVISION.
CONFIGURATION SECTION.
SOURCE-COMPUTER. PRIME 750.
OBJECT-COMPUTER. PRIME 750.
```

The SPECIAL-NAMES paragraph can contain the following entries.

```
[SPECIAL-NAMES.
[implementor-name IS mnemonic-name.]
[CURRENCY SIGN IS literal.]
[DECIMAL-POINT IS COMMA.]]
```

The ACCEPT and DISPLAY verbs can be written using the alternative syntax of:

```
ACCEPT    identifier-1 FROM mnemonic-name, and
DISPLAY  {identifier-1}  ... UPON mnemonic-name
         {literal-1    }
```

respectively, where mnemonic-name is invented by the programmer and specified as part of the SPECIAL-NAMES paragraph. The implementor-name is a specific name assigned to a hardware device.

For example:
```
ENVIRONMENT DIVISION.
CONFIGURATION SECTION.
SPECIAL-NAMES.
      CONSOLE IS TTY.
      PRINTER IS PRT.
PROCEDURE DIVISION.

      ACCEPT alpha FROM TTY.
      DISPLAY beta UPON PRT.
```

A value of alpha will be entered through the keyboard of the console (terminal) and the value of beta will be output to the printer.

The implementor-name CONSOLE and PRINTER, used in this example, are machine specific. For this reason the reader is advised to refer to the COBOL manual for the computer being used.

The second entry in the SPECIAL-NAMES paragraph, CURRENCY SIGN IS literal, will allow a programmer to specify a single character currency symbol for the country the application program is written for.

For example:
```
ENVIRONMENT  DIVISION.
CONFIGURATION  SECTION.
    CURRENCY SIGN IS '£'.
DATA  DIVISION.
    02 TotalCommission PIC £££,££9.99.
```

The third entry in the SPECIAL-NAMES paragraph is the sentence DECIMAL-POINT IS COMMA. This will allow a programmer to inter-change the functions of the comma and decimal-point. This conforms to the European representation of decimal values. The functions of the comma and the decimal-point are exchanged in the character string of the picture clause and in the numeric literals.

For example, 345,987.45 output using a picture of ZZZ,ZZ9.99 can be changed to 345.897,45 using a picture of ZZZ.ZZ9,99.

The Input-Output Section is used when there are external data files to be accessed from within the computer program. It allows the specification of peripheral devices and the information required to transmit and handle data between the devices and the program.

The SELECT clause enables a file to be assigned to a hardware device. The file-name must be described under the FD for that file in the Data Division. The name of the device is machine specific, therefore, the reader is advised to consult the COBOL manual for the computer being used. Examples of the use of the SELECT clause follow.
```
SELECT EmployeeFile ASSIGN TO PFMS.
SELECT ReportFile ASSIGN TO PRINTER.
SELECT WagesFile ASSIGN TO MT9.
```

In this example PFMS implies disc storage, PRINTER implies a lineprinter and MT9 a nine-track magnetic tape unit. These names are created by the implementor of the COBOL compiler for a specific make of computer.

The clauses for ORGANIZATION and ACCESS describe respectively, the type of file being processed and the manner in which the records in the file are to be referenced. This entry, for sequential files, serves no purpose other than being documentary. The relevance of these two entries with respect to other file organisations will be described in context in a later chapter.

The File-Status clause describes an identifier in the Working- Storage Section that has specific values moved to it after the execution of file-processing statements. The value of the identifier is a code to such information as successful compilation, end of file, permanent I/O error, and can be used in detecting run-time errors. The file-status codes and their meanings are implementation specific.

In order to reduce the amount of coding, so that the reader can write complete COBOL programs as quickly as possible, the following Environment Division will be used throughout the book when using sequential files.

```
ENVIRONMENT  DIVISION.
INPUT-OUTPUT  SECTION.
FILE-CONTROL.
      SELECT file-name ASSIGN TO PFMS.
      SELECT ...
```

7.6 Worked Examples.
Problem 1.

Two files stored on magnetic disc are to be used in a COBOL program. The first file has a filename of MembersFile, the organisation of the file is sequential, with fixed-length records containing the following details about members of a squash club.

name	30 alphanumeric characters
sex	1 alphabetic character
league division	1 numeric character
box	1 alphabetic character
telephone	15 alphanumeric characters

The second file has a filename of ClubNotice, the organisation of this file is also sequential with fixed-length records. The records contain details taken from the first file and the format of a record is a line of information composed from up to 80 alphanumeric characters.

Code COBOL Environment and Data Divisions that fully describe these files.

Solution 1.
```
ENVIRONMENT  DIVISION.
INPUT-OUTPUT  SECTION.
FILE-CONTROL.
      SELECT MembersFile ASSIGN TO PFMS.
      SELECT ClubNotice ASSIGN TO PFMS.
DATA  DIVISION.
FILE SECTION.
FD MembersFile, COMPRESSED.
01 Record-1.
      02 name PIC X(30).
      02 sex PIC A.
      02 league.
            03 div PIC 9.
            03 box PIC A.
      02 TeleNo PIC X(15).
FD ClubNotice, COMPRESSED.
01 Record-2 PIC X(80).
```

Problem 2.

A design for the report on the members of the squash club is illustrated in figure 7.5. Code a Working-Storage entry to represent the four different records that make up the report.

RECORD/REPORT LAYOUT SHEET   Layout No.

0	1	2	3	4	5	6
		SQUASH CLUB MEMBERSHIP				*RECORD -1*
	X (24)		X (22)			
NAME		LEAGUE			TELEPHONE	*RECORD -2*
X (4)	X (27)		X (6)	X (12)	X (9)	
		DIVISION BOX				*RECORD -3*
	X (31)		X (12)			
JOHNSON-SMITH,W.H.		2	C		ASHDOWN 1479	*RECORD -4*
	X (31)	9	X(8)	A	X (8)	X (15)

Figure 7.5

Solution 2.

```
WORKING-STORAGE SECTION.
01 Record-1-WS.
    02 FILLER PIC X(24) VALUE IS SPACES.
    02 FILLER PIC X(22) VALUE IS 'SQUASH CLUB MEMBERSHIP'.
01 Record-2-WS.
    02 FILLER PIC X(4) VALUE IS 'NAME'.
    02 FILLER PIC X(27) VALUE IS SPACES.
    02 FILLER PIC X(6) VALUE IS 'LEAGUE'.
    02 FILLER PIC X(12) VALUE IS SPACES.
    02 FILLER PIC X(9) VALUE IS 'TELEPHONE'.
01 Record-3-WS.
    02 FILLER PIC X(31) VALUE IS SPACES.
    02 FILLER PIC X(12) VALUE 'DIVISION BOX'.
01 Record-4-WS.
    02 name-WS PIC X(31).
    02 div-WS PIC 9.
    02 FILLER PIC X(8) VALUE IS SPACES.
    02 box-WS PIC A.
    02 FILLER PIC X(8) VALUE IS SPACES.
    02 TeleNo-WS PIC X(15).
```

It is possible to re-code this entry and reduce several lines of code by combining the fillers with spaces and text literals, and modifying the sizes of the picture clauses, for example.

```
WORKING-STORAGE  SECTION.
01  Record-1-WS.
      02 FILLER PIC X(46) VALUE IS 'SQUASH CLUB MEMBERSHIP' JUSTIFIED RIGHT.
01  Record-2-WS.
      02 FILLER PIC X(31) VALUE IS 'NAME'.
      02 FILLER PIC X(18) VALUE IS 'LEAGUE'.
      02 FILLER PIC X(9) VALUE IS 'TELEPHONE'.
01  Record-3-WS.
      02 FILLER PIC X(43) VALUE IS 'DIVISION BOX' JUSTIFIED RIGHT.
01  Record-4-WS.
      02 name-WS PIC X(31).
      02 div-WS PIC 9B(8).
      02 box-WS PIC A.
      02 TeleNo-WS PIC X(23) JUSTIFIED RIGHT.
```

When coding from a design document the first approach is probably simpler and requires less mental effort. However, the second method is more succinct. Both methods will compile correctly. The choice is left to the reader.

The records coded in the Working-Storage Section can be moved to the output record, Record-2, described in the File Section of solution 1. The format of the output record is always coded to represent any line of the output report. The individual records that describe the report cannot be coded in the File Section since the VALUE clause used to assign headings and spaces cannot be used in the File Section.

7.7 Summary.
Data files are stored on either magnetic tape or magnetic disc.

A data file is composed from records that can be either fixed or variable length.

A record is composed from individual items of information stored in fields. Fields will vary in size, and can have a hierarchical structure. The hierarchical nature of fields is represented by different level numbers in the range 02 - 49. The level number 01 is reserved for the record level.

The format of records and reports should be planned on squared- paper before coded into a Data Division.

The File Section is used to describe the structure of data files. Each file is defined by a file description entry FD, and one or more record description entries.

The Working-Storage Section describes records and subordinate data items which are not part of the external data files but are developed and processed internally.

The Environment Division consists of two sections, The Configuration Section and the Input-Output Section. The latter section provides a File-Control paragraph that explicitly names and associates files with specific media.

Keywords

Data files, fixed length, variable-length records, fields;
Level numbers 01 - 49, FILLER;
FILE SECTION, FD, BLOCK, LABEL RECORDS, STANDARD, OMITTED,
VALUE OF, DATA RECORD;
ENVIRONMENT DIVISION, CONFIGURATION SECTION,
SOURCE-COMPUTER, OBJECT-COMPUTER, SPECIAL-NAMES;
INPUT-OUTPUT SECTION, FILE-CONTROL, SELECT, ASSIGN,
ORGANIZATION, ACCESS, STATUS;
CURRENCY, DECIMAL-POINT.

7.8 Questions.

1. Code a File Section entry that describes a customer account record held on magnetic disc file. A block contains one logical record. The name of the file is custom. The format of a record is given in the following information.

Identifier	Meaning	Type	Size of datum
CustomerRec	name of record	-	-
AccountNo	account number	numeric	8 digits
name	name of customer	-	-
surname	surname of customer	alphanumeric	20 characters
forename	first name	alphabetic	15 characters
address	address of customer	-	-
street	street address	alphanumeric	20 characters
town	town address	alphanumeric	20 characters
postcode	postcode	alphanumeric	8 characters
CreditLimit	credit limit	numeric	5 digits
balance	credit balance	numeric	6 digits inc 2 decimal places

[2]. Code a File Section entry that describes a stock record held on a magnetic tape file. There are 64 records to a block, standard labels are used and the name of the file is stock. The format of a record is given by the following information.

Identifier	Meaning	Type	Size of datum
StockRecord	name of record	-	-
StockNo	stock number	numeric	8 digits
description	stock name	alphanumeric	20 characters
quantity	stock amount	numeric	3 digits
ReOrder	re order level	numeric	3 digits
cost	price of stock	numeric	5 digits inc 2 decimal places
location	location of stock	-	-
Factory	factory code	alphabetic	2 characters
bin	bin number	numeric	2 digits

[3]. Code a File Section entry that describes a payroll record held on a magnetic tape file. There are 128 records to a block, standard labels are used and the name of the file is payroll. The format of a record is given by the following information.

Identifier	Meaning	Type	Size of datum
PayRecord	name of record	-	-
EmployeeNo	employee number	numeric	8 digits
EmployeeName	name	alphanumeric	20 characters
NatIns	N.I. number	alphanumeric	9 characters
TaxCode	income tax code	alphanumeric	3 characters
GrossPay	gross income	numeric	6 digits inc 2 decimal places
tax	income tax	numeric	6 digits inc 2 decimal places
superan	superannuation	numeric	5 digits inc 2 decimal places
NatInsCont	N.I. contributions	numeric	5 digits inc 2 decimal places
payment	credit transfer	-	-
bank	bank code	numeric	6 digits
AccountNo	number of account	numeric	10 digits
AccountName	name of account	alphanumeric	20 characters

4. Code a Working-Storage Section entry that describes each of the four records in figure 7.6. The identifiers used to store the county, town, model of car and total sales should be coded as county-WS, town-WS, model-WS and sale-WS respectively.

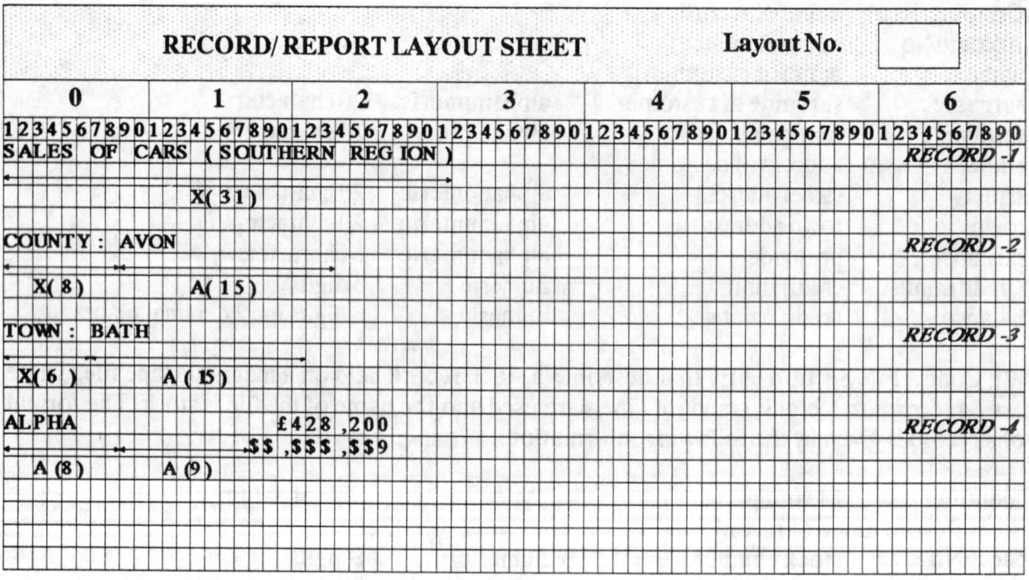

Figure 7.6

[5]. Code a Working-Storage section entry that describes each of the four records in figure 7.7. The identifiers used to store the type of cassette, stock number, and quantity should be coded as music-WS, StockNumber-WS and quantity-WS respectively.

RECORD/ REPORT LAYOUT SHEET   Layout No.

```
        0            1            2            3            4            5            6
123456789012345678901234567890123456789012345678901234567890123456789012345678901234567890
                            CASSETTE  DISTRIBUTION                                  RECORD -1
            X (20)                      X (21)
                            TYPE :  POPULAR                                         RECORD -2
            X (20)             X (6)    X (9)
                            STOCK -NUMBER  QUANTITY                                 RECORD -3
            X (20)                      X (21)
                            0015              100                                   RECORD -4
            X (20)          9999    X (11)    999
```

Figure 7.7

6. Code a Working-Storage Section entry that describes the report in figure 7.8. The following identifiers should be used in the coding.

AccountNo-WS   15 digits in two groups of 8 and 7 digits
date-WS   5 characters
description-WS   11 characters
debit-WS   9 characters including commas and decimal point
credit-WS   9 characters including commas and decimal point
balance-WS   9 characters including commas and decimal point
FinalBalance-WS 12 characters including currency symbol, commas, decimal point and DB.

RECORD/ REPORT LAYOUT SHEET   Layout No.

```
        0            1            2            3            4            5            6
123456789012345678901234567890123456789012345678901234567890123456789012345678901234567890
THE  UNIVERSAL  BANK
STATEMENT  OF  ACCOUNT :  04971328  1726493
DATE    DESCRIPTION       DEBIT        CREDIT       BALANCE
MAY  1  BALANCE                                     103 .9 8
MAY  3  SALARY                         1 ,076 .42   1,180 .4 0
MAY  5  DOMESTIC          423 .45                   756 .9 5
                                                         .
                                                         .
                         FINAL  BALANCE             £104 .27 DB
```

Figure 7.8

[7]. Code a Working-Storage Section entry that describes the report in figure 7.9. The following identifiers should be used in coding.

name-WS	25 characters
road-WS	20 characters
town-WS	20 characters
postcode-WS	8 characters
TelephoneNo-WS	20 characters
PreviousReading-WS	6 digits with zero suppression
PresentReading-WS	6 digits with zero suppression
UnitPrice-WS	5 characters including currency symbol and decimal point
UnitsUsed-WS	6 digits with zero suppression
CallsCost-WS	9 characters including decimal point
rental-WS	7 characters including decimal point
SubTotal-WS	10 characters including decimal point
VatPercent-WS	2 digits
vat-WS	9 characters including decimal point
total-WS	11 characters including currency symbol and decimal point

Figure 7.9

8. A COBOL program is compiled on a PRIME 750 computer and executed on a PRIME 550 computer. Throughout the Procedure Division the computer CONSOLE is referred to as a TTY and the system PRINTER is referred to as PRT. The currency symbol used in the printed reports is F for French Francs and the decimal point must be changed to a comma. The computer uses four data files in conjunction with four different hardware devices. Code a complete Environment Division to express these facts.

Filename	Device	System Code	File Organisation
alpha	card reader	CR0	sequential
beta	line printer	LP0	sequential
delta	magnetic tape	MT9	sequential
epsilon	magnetic disc	PFMS	sequential

8

Introduction to File Processing

The purpose of this chapter is to introduce the reader to the fundamental concepts of file processing. The chapter is divided into three parts.

The first part covers a selection of the Procedure Division statements that are used in file processing. The second part looks at the creation of a sequential file and the production of a report. The final part investigates the use of the SORT statement.

8.1 Why use files?

The only method described up to now for inputting data to a computer has been through a keyboard in conjunction with the ACCEPT statement. This form of input, although useful, is not adequate for coping with large volumes of data and suffers from the following disadvantages.

In using a keyboard for the input of data the advantage of using a high-speed computer to process work becomes irrelevant since the speed of the computer system becomes dependent upon the typing speed of the user.

Data that is input via a keyboard to the main memory of a computer is not permanently stored. Switch the power off from the computer and the data stored in the main memory is destroyed. Switch the power on again and the user must re-load and run the program before entering the data again!

To avoid these disadvantages data should be stored on magnetic tape or disc in the form of a data file. Such storage has the following advantages.

Peripheral units such as magnetic tape and disc units can transfer data from the medium on which it is stored to the main memory of the computer at hundreds of thousands of characters per second. Thus the speed of data input/output becomes more realistic in terms of the power of the computer.

Data can be stored permanently on both magnetic tape and disc. Switch the power off and the data remains intact on the magnetic medium. Magnetic tapes and disc packs are portable, so not only can data be moved from one computer to another but libraries of data can also be kept. Data stored on magnetic tape or disc can be duplicated for security.

Changes to data held on peripheral media (tape or disc) will not involve changes to the program that uses the data. In fact a program can and will bring about changes to the data and not the reverse.

8.2 File Processing Statements.

Opening a file.

Before a file can be used it must be opened. A simplified format for the OPEN statement is:

$$\text{OPEN} \quad \left\{ \begin{array}{ll} \textbf{INPUT} & \text{\{file-name\} ..} \\ \textbf{OUTPUT} & \text{\{file-name\} ..} \end{array} \right\} ...$$

A file is opened in the INPUT mode when records are to be read from it, and opened in the OUTPUT mode when records are to be written to it.

For example, OPEN INPUT MembersFile, OUTPUT ClubNotice.

Closing a file.

When all the processing activities are completed on a file it must be closed. The activity of closing a file will cause the contents of a buffer (sequence of logical records), which may be partially full, to be written to the file if the mode was set to OUTPUT, and an end of file marker appended after the last record in the file.

A file must also be closed before it can be opened for a different mode of processing. A file that has been opened for OUTPUT, could be closed and then re-opened in the INPUT mode ready for reading. The format of the close statement is:

CLOSE {file-name} ...

For example CLOSE MembersFile, ClubNotice.

Reading a file.
The READ statement makes available the next logical record from a file. The execution of subsequent read statements will cause successive records to be accessed in sequence from the file buffer. When all the logical records from the buffer have been accessed, the buffer will be replenished with the next physical record. A simplified format for reading a sequential file that is stored on either magnetic tape or disc is:

READ file-name-1 RECORD [**INTO** identifier-1] [**AT END** imperative-statement]

If the MembersFile described in the worked example in section 7.6 was read using the statement READ MembersFile, then the values for name, sex, league and telephone number would be moved into the respective fields name, sex, div, box and TeleNo described under Record-1 in the File Section. Reading a record from a file will always result in the associated field identifiers being assigned respective values from the record.

When the INTO option is used the values of the fields are also moved into a data area in the Working-Storage Section described by identifier-1.

The repeated execution of a READ file statement will eventually cause the last record in the file to be read. After this event, the next time a READ file statement is executed, will result in an attempt to read beyond the end of file marker. To prevent this happening the AT END option should normally be present, so that when the end of file is reached the computer can be directed to execute further instructions. However, it is a desirable feature to be able to test for the end of a file anywhere in the program, and not simply through a READ .. AT END statement. The imperative statement associated with the AT END option, therefore, takes the form of setting the identifier EOF to T for [T]RUE to show that the end of file has been reached.

The declaration for EOF in the Working-Storage Section can take advantage of the VALUE statement to initialise EOF to 'F' for [F]ALSE and stipulate the condition name EndOfFile that is true when EOF is assigned the value 'T'.

> 77 EOF PIC A VALUE IS 'F'.
> 88 EndOfFile VALUE IS 'T'.

In the Procedure Division the read statement would be coded as:

READ filename AT END MOVE 'T' TO EOF.

A test for the end of the file could be made anywhere in the Procedure Division by using the condition name EndOfFile. For example:

PERFORM E UNTIL EndOfFile.

In order to preserve the structure of a computer program it is necessary to introduce at least TWO read statements when processing a file. The technique, known as reading ahead, can be summarised by two rules for allocating the read operation.

Rule 1: Read the first record immediately following the OPEN statement.

Rule 2: Read again at the end of each program component which processes an input record.

Writing to a file.
The WRITE statement releases a logical record to an output file. It can also be used for the positioning of lines within a logical page. The format of a logical record would be specified in a program and the fields used to represent that format would be assigned values before writing a record. The use of successive WRITE statements will cause the output buffer to be filled by logical records. The physical record is then written on to the magnetic medium. The output buffer is then ready to receive further logical records. A simplified format for writing a record to a sequential file stored on either magnetic tape or disc is:

$$\textbf{WRITE}\ \text{record-name-1}\ [\textbf{FROM}\ \text{identifier-1}]$$
$$\begin{Bmatrix}\textbf{BEFORE}\\\textbf{AFTER}\end{Bmatrix}\ \text{ADVANCING}\ \begin{Bmatrix}\text{identifier-2}\\\text{integer-1}\\\textbf{PAGE}\end{Bmatrix}\ \begin{Bmatrix}\text{LINE}\\\text{LINES}\end{Bmatrix}$$

For example:

WRITE Record-1.
WRITE Record-2 AFTER ADVANCING 2 LINES.

The first example illustrates the correct format for creating a file that when complete can be re-opened in the INPUT mode for reading. Note the absence of paper-control commands.

The second example illustrates the correct format for creating a report file. Such a file contains paper-control characters (codes to advance the paper in the lineprinter a specific number of lines or to advance to the top of a page) and should never be re- opened in the INPUT mode for reading.

If the FROM option is used the contents of identifier-1 in the Working-Storage Section is moved to record-name-1 prior to the WRITE operation.

Notice from the formats of the read and write statements that files are read and records are written.

8.3 Creating a sequential File.
There are three methods of creating a sequential file. The first is by invoking the system editor and typing each record as a line- by-line entry at the keyboard of a terminal. This is no different than using the editor to input a COBOL program and save the program on either disc or tape.

The second method involves reading an existing file and writing the information, perhaps in a modified format, to a new file. This method will be covered later in the chapter.

Finally the third method involves writing a program to input the details of each record at the keyboard of a terminal, and writing each complete record to a file. This method will now be explored in greater depth.

The following detailed program structure is used to create the squash club members file described in section 7.6.

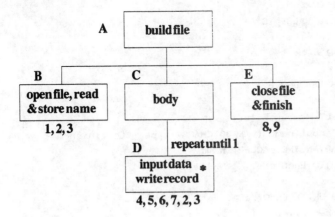

Functions

1. open file for output
2. input name
3. store name in temporary store
4. input sex
5. input league
6. input telephone number
7. write record to file
8. close file
9 stop

Condition

1. first character of name = !

The COBOL program, with Procedure Division derived from this detailed program structure diagram follows.

```
IDENTIFICATION DIVISION.
PROGRAM-ID. BuildFile.
ENVIRONMENT DIVISION.
INPUT-OUTPUT SECTION.
FILE-CONTROL.
    SELECT MembersFile ASSIGN TO PFMS.
DATA DIVISION.
FILE SECTION.
FD MembersFile, COMPRESSED.
01 Record-1.
    02 FILLER PIC X(48).
```

```
WORKING-STORAGE SECTION.
01 Record-1-WS.
    02 name PIC X(30).
    02 sex PIC A.
    02 league.
        03 div PIC 9.
        03 box PIC A.
    02 TeleNo PIC X(15).

77 EndStore PIC X.
    88 EndOfData VALUE IS '!'.

PROCEDURE DIVISION.
A-seq.
    PERFORM B THROUGH E.

B.  OPEN OUTPUT MembersFile.
    DISPLAY "input name (MAX 30 CHARS) type ! to finish "
    WITH NO ADVANCING, ACCEPT name.
    MOVE name TO EndStore.
C-rep.
    PERFORM D UNTIL EndOfData.
E.  CLOSE MembersFile.
    STOP RUN.

D.      DISPLAY "input sex (M OR F) " WITH NO ADVANCING.
        ACCEPT sex.
        DISPLAY "input league 1 DIGIT 1 LETTER " WITH NO ADVANCING.
        ACCEPT league.
        DISPLAY "input telephone number (MAX 15 CHARS) "
        WITH NO ADVANCING, ACCEPT TeleNo.
        WRITE Record-1 FROM Record-1-WS.
        DISPLAY "input name (MAX 30 CHARS) TYPE ! to finish "
        WITH NO ADVANCING, ACCEPT name.
        MOVE name TO EndStore.
```

Discussion.

The format of a record in the MembersFile has been coded in the Working-Storage Section. This reflects the fact that the records are to be created by running the program and using local data (data that is not already part of the file). When a record is complete and is to be written to the file, the contents of the record is transferred from the Working-Storage Section to the File Section. Notice that the specific names of the fields are not required for the output file in the File Section, and therefore, the description of a record has been replaced by the reserved word FILLER. The total number of characters that form one record must be inserted into the picture clause after the reserved word FILLER. This figure, 48, is calculated by adding together the number of characters in each field of Record-1-WS.

The function of EndStore is to duplicate and truncate, to the first character only, the value stored in the identifier name. This value is then compared with the character used to denote the end of the data from the keyboard, i.e. EndOfData = '!'. If both characters match then the MembersFile is closed and the program terminates.

The following part-listing is the result of running the program to create the file of squash club members and is an extract from the session at the terminal to input the data.

```
input name (MAX 30 CHARS) type ! to finish Stevenson,G.R
input sex (M OR F) M
input league 1 DIGIT 1 LETTER 3A
input telephone number (MAX 15 CHARS) Lechlade 194
input name (MAX 30 CHARS) TYPE ! to finish O'Flinn,P
input sex (M OR F) M
input league 1 DIGIT 1 LETTER 4B
input telephone number (MAX 15 CHARS) Cholsey 3259
input name (MAX 30 CHARS) TYPE ! to finish Lowe,J.C
input sex (M OR F) F
input league 1 DIGIT 1 LETTER 1C
input telephone number (MAX 15 CHARS) Bicester 4264
input name (MAX 30 CHARS) TYPE ! to finish Stott,P.A
input sex (M OR F) M
input league 1 DIGIT 1 LETTER 1A
input telephone number (MAX 15 CHARS) Wallingford 837
input name (MAX 30 CHARS) TYPE ! to finish Barrett,G.C
input sex (M OR F) F
input league 1 DIGIT 1 LETTER 1B
input telephone number (MAX 15 CHARS) Standlake 87936
input name (MAX 30 CHARS) TYPE ! to finish Allen,D.J
input sex (M OR F) M
input league 1 DIGIT 1 LETTER 2B
input telephone number (MAX 15 CHARS) Ickford 947361
input name (MAX 30 CHARS) TYPE ! to finish Ostle,D.M
input sex (M OR F) M
input league 1 DIGIT 1 LETTER 2C
input telephone number (MAX 15 CHARS) Clanfield 4932
input name (MAX 30 CHARS) TYPE ! to finish Tilbury,C
input sex (M OR F) M
input league 1 DIGIT 1 LETTER 3C
input telephone number (MAX 15 CHARS) Didcot 9873
input name (MAX 30 CHARS) TYPE ! to finish Fox,F.M
input sex (M OR F) M
input league 1 DIGIT 1 LETTER 1C
input telephone number (MAX 15 CHARS) Freeland 93412

input name (MAX 30 CHARS) TYPE ! to finish !
```

The contents of the file that was just created follows.

Stevenson,G.R	M3ALechlade 194
O'Flinn,P	M4BCholsey 3259
Lowe,J.C	F1CBicester 4264
Stott,P.A	M1AWallingford 837
Barrett,G.C	F1BStandlake 87936
Allen,D.J	M2BIckford 947361
Ostle,D.M	M2CClanfield 4932
Tilbury,C	M3CDidcot 9873
Fox,F.M	M1CFreeland 93412
Jones,N.L	F4AWitney 192
Collins,P	F3BThame 94287
Gillot,D	F1CHarwell 6829
Long,C	M1ACumnor 863
McDougall,G	F3BAbingdon 81773
Dimitriou,B	M3COxford 235
Elwin,J	F1APortway 14732
Pepper,D	M2ALongworth 6498
Gunnasekara,A	M1AHarwell 2124
Rodriguez-Bachiller,A	F2BFritwell 916
Thomas,K	F1CDidcot 48973
Ward,S	M3CDidcot 27918
Anderson,T	M3CWitney 817963
Hill,L	M3CUffington 36782
Walton,B	M1BTackley 1134
Winter,M	M2ABurford 223
Keable,R	F2ACholsey 1414
Goddard,P	M1ACrowmarsh 81793
May,N	F1CDidcot 98149
Edwards,E	M2CWoodstock 932
Priscott,M	F2CWitney 419523
Allen,P	M3BWantage 9696
Jackson,J	M3BThame 8137
Winslet,M.J	M3BLechlade 2130
Clayton,A	M4CIckford 326
Black,A	M4CFilkins 159
East,W	F4AChildrey 4267
Lyle,S	M1BGt. Milford 714
Sanders,M.A	M4CWoodstock 1136
Daniels,J	M3COxford 713
Robbins,H	M2CWitney 219597
Harrison,C	F1AAbingdon 2123
Brown,M.L	M4BWantage 416

8.4 Generating a Report.
There are two methods for producing printed reports from a COBOL program. The first method uses an optional feature of the COBOL language known as Report Writer, and will **not** be covered in this book.

The second method uses the techniques already discussed. To illustrate this method the MembersFile and ClubNotice files described in section 7.6 will be used. The MembersFile has already been created in the last section. The format of the ClubNotice file is shown below.

SQUASH CLUB MEMBERSHIP			
NAME	**LEAGUE** **DIVISION BOX**		**TELEPHONE**
Stevenson,G.R	3	A	Lechlade 194
O'Flinn P	4	B	Cholsey 3259
Lowe J.C	1	C	Bicester 4264
Stott,P.A	1	A	Wallingford 837
Barrett,G.C	1	B	Standlake 87936

The initial data structures show that the MembersFile can be regarded as an iteration of members records and the report file contains a number of headings, as detailed in figure 7.5, followed by an iteration of lines made up from members records. Where one line of the report corresponds to one record. The three criteria for correspondence between the input and output data structures are satisfied. In both structures the records occur in the same order, the same number of times and under the same circumstances.

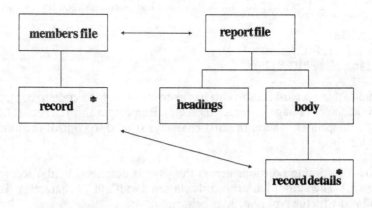

The basic program structure is similar to the output structure for the report. This can be expanded to form the detailed program structure shown over the page. Notice that *function 3, Read Record from MembersFile,* has been emphasised on the diagram to illustrate the two rules for reading ahead in a sequential file.

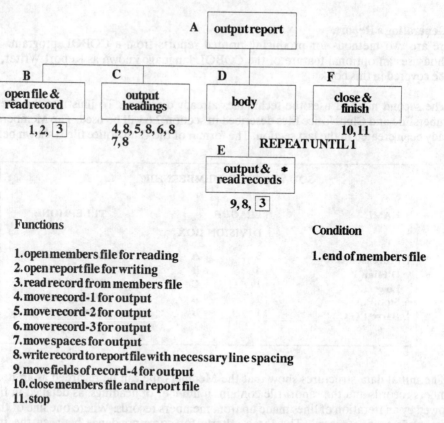

Functions

1. open members file for reading
2. open report file for writing
3. read record from members file
4. move record-1 for output
5. move record-2 for output
6. move record-3 for output
7. move spaces for output
8. write record to report file with necessary line spacing
9. move fields of record-4 for output
10. close members file and report file
11. stop

Condition

1. end of members file

The Procedure Division of the following program has been derived from this detailed structure diagram. The reader's attention is drawn to a change in the File Section description for ClubNotice. In section 7.6 the record for ClubNotice had been described as 01 Record-2 PIC X(80). However, in this program the description has been changed to:

```
01 ReportOut.
   02 FILLER PIC X.
   02 LineImage PIC X(79).
```

The first field of the record ReportOut has been set aside for a code to control the vertical movement of the paper (1 page, 1 line, 2 lines, etc). Remember this is a report file that can be printed using a lineprinter, where, the first character is used to control the number of blank lines in the report.

The number of printing positions across the page is described by the second field of the record ReportOut. The author has arbitrarily chosen a width of 79 characters. The number of characters will vary with the type of printer being used.

In the design of this program the MembersFile is assumed to contain at least one record. If the file was empty then when the program was executed it would print the headings for the report and then terminate. If the reader finds this style offensive then the author would recommend amending the program structure to contain a selection after the initial read statement and before the first heading is output. The selection might be coded as:

```
IF NOT EndOfFile
    PERFORM C THROUGH F.
```

In printing the various report headings it has been necessary to use both a MOVE statement and a WRITE statement. The FROM option associated with the WRITE statement has not been used here, since it would have the effect of moving, say, Record-1-WS to ReportOut and storing the first character of the line, in the FILLER reserved for the paper control character.

The output of a blank line is possible by moving spaces to the output record prior to writing the record.

Since the program is meant to produce a report the reader may be puzzled by the select clause SELECT ClubNotice ASSIGN TO PFMS. Here the report is assigned to a disc as a sequential file. The reason for this statement is because the system used to develop the program is a multi-user system, with no one user being allowed total control of the printer. The user can obtain a printed copy of the report by spooling the file. The print spooler will then place the file in a queue with other files to be printed. When the job reaches the head of the queue the associated file will be printed on the system printer. This way no one person has control over the system printer.

In a batch processing system the SELECT clause would be modified to:

```
SELECT ClubNotice ASSIGN TO PRINTER.
```

This is acceptable since the batch jobs are queued, and under normal circumstances a batch job would relinquish control over the printer when the job had ended.

```
        IDENTIFICATION DIVISION.
        PROGRAM-ID. ReportGeneration.

        ENVIRONMENT DIVISION.
        INPUT-OUTPUT SECTION.
        FILE-CONTROL.
            SELECT MembersFile ASSIGN TO PFMS.
            SELECT ClubNotice ASSIGN TO PFMS.

        DATA DIVISION.
        FILE SECTION.
        FD MembersFile, COMPRESSED.
        01 Record-1.
            02 name PIC X(30).
            02 sex PIC A.
            02 league.
              03 div PIC 9.
              03 box PIC A.
            02 TeleNo PIC X(15).
```

```
FD ClubNotice, COMPRESSED.
01 ReportOut.
    02 FILLER PIC X.
    02 LineImage PIC X(79).


WORKING-STORAGE SECTION.
01 Record-1-WS.
    02 FILLER PIC X(24) VALUE IS SPACES.
    02 FILLER PIC X(22) VALUE IS "SQUASH CLUB MEMBERSHIP".
01 Record-2-WS.
    02 FILLER PIC X(4) VALUE IS "NAME".
    02 FILLER PIC X(27) VALUE IS SPACES.
    02 FILLER PIC X(6) VALUE IS "LEAGUE".
    02 FILLER PIC X(12) VALUE IS SPACES.
    02 FILLER PIC X(9) VALUE IS "TELEPHONE".
01 Record-3-WS.
    02 FILLER PIC X(31) VALUE IS SPACES.
    02 FILLER PIC X(12) VALUE IS "DIVISION BOX".
01 Record-4-WS.
    02 name-WS PIC X(30).
    02 FILLER PIC X VALUE IS SPACE.
    02 div-WS PIC 9.
    02 FILLER PIC X(8) VALUE IS SPACES.
    02 box-WS PIC A.
    02 FILLER PIC X(8) VALUE IS SPACES.
    02 TeleNo-WS PIC X(15).


77 EOF PIC A VALUE IS 'F'.
    88 EndOfFile VALUE 'T'.


PROCEDURE DIVISION.
A-seq.
    PERFORM B THROUGH F.


B.  OPEN INPUT MembersFile
        OUTPUT ClubNotice.
    READ MembersFile AT END MOVE 'T' TO EOF.
C.  MOVE Record-1-WS TO LineImage.
    WRITE ReportOut AFTER ADVANCING PAGE.
    MOVE Record-2-WS TO LineImage.
    WRITE ReportOut AFTER ADVANCING 2 LINES.
    MOVE Record-3-WS TO LineImage.
    WRITE ReportOut AFTER ADVANCING 1 LINE.
    MOVE SPACES TO LineImage.
    WRITE ReportOut AFTER ADVANCING 1 LINE.
D-rep.
```

```
        PERFORM E UNTIL EndOfFile.
    F.  CLOSE MembersFile, ClubNotice.
        STOP RUN.


    E.  MOVE name TO name-WS.
        MOVE div TO div-WS.
        MOVE box TO box-WS.
        MOVE TeleNo TO TeleNo-WS.
        MOVE Record-4-WS TO LineImage.
        WRITE ReportOut AFTER ADVANCING 1 LINE.
        READ MembersFile AT END MOVE 'T' TO EOF.
```

The results from spooling the ClubNotice file are printed on the next page.

8.5 The SORT Statement.

The information given in the last report was not very well presented. This was due to the data on the sequential file not being sorted into any predetermined order. It is possible to use the same program, with minor modifications, to produce two reports on the members of the squash club. The first report would contain a list of members split into two groups - male and female members, and have the members names listed alphabetically within each group. The second report would contain a list of members split into their respective league divisions and boxes. Within each box the members' names would be listed alphabetically.

To produce the first report the original MembersFile would need to be sorted on sex as the primary key, and name as secondary key.

The second report requires that the original MembersFile is sorted again, this time on division as the primary key, and within division on box as the secondary key, and within box on name as the tertiary key.

The COBOL language contains a statement to sort the contents of a sequential file. A simplified format for the SORT statement is:

> **SORT** file-name-1 ON $\left\{ \begin{array}{l} \textbf{ASCENDING} \\ \textbf{DESCENDING} \end{array} \right\}$ KEY {data-name-1} ... ...
> **USING** file-name-2
> **GIVING** file-name-3.

Where the file to be sorted is file-name-2, the sorted file is file-name-3 and file-name-1 is an intermediate work-file used by the sorting routine. This work-file must be described using an SD entry in the File Section. The SD entry does not contain any of the options available in an FD entry. The format of the three files, file-name-1, file-name-2 and file-name-3 must be identical. The keys used in sorting the file must be described under the SD entry of file-name-1. Before the SORT statement can be used file-name-1, file-name-2 and file-name-3 must be closed. The SORT statement will perform all the necessary opening and closing of

SQUASH CLUB MEMBERSHIP

NAME	LEAGUE		TELEPHONE
	DIVISION	BOX	
Stevenson,G.R	3	A	Lechlade 194
O'Flinn,P	4	B	Cholsey 3259
Lowe,J.C	1	C	Bicester 4264
Stott,P.A	1	A	Wallingford 837
Barrett,G.C	1	B	Standlake 87936
Allen,D.J	2	B	Ickford 947361
Ostle,D.M	2	C	Clanfield 4932
Tilbury,C	3	C	Didcot 9873
Fox,F.M	1	C	Freeland 93412
Jones,N.L	4	A	Witney 192
Collins,P	3	B	Thame 94287
Gillot,D	1	C	Harwell 6829
Long,C	1	A	Cumnor 863
McDougall,G	3	B	Abingdon 81773
Dimitriou,B	3	C	Oxford 235
Elwin,J	1	A	Portway 14732
Pepper,D	2	A	Longworth 6498
Gunnasekara,A	1	A	Harwell 2124
Rodriguez-Bachiller,A	2	B	Fritwell 916
Thomas,K	1	C	Didcot 48973
Ward,S	3	C	Didcot 27918
Anderson,T	3	C	Witney 817963
Hill,L	3	C	Uffington 36782
Walton,B	1	B	Tackley 1134
Winter,M	2	A	Burford 223
Keable,R	2	A	Cholsey 1414
Goddard,P	1	B	Crowmarsh 81793
May,N	1	C	Didcot 98149
Edwards,E	2	C	Woodstock 932
Priscott,M	2	C	Witney 419523
Allen,P	3	B	Wantage 9696
Jackson,J	3	B	Thame 8137
Winslet,M.J	3	B	Lechlade 2130
Clayton,A	4	C	Ickford 326
Black,A	4	C	Filkins 159
East,W	4	A	Childrey 4267
Lyle,S	1	B	Gt. Milford 714
Sanders,M.A	4	C	Woodstock 1136
Daniels,J	3	C	Oxford 713
Robbins,H	2	C	Witney 219597
Harrison,C	1	A	Abingdon 2123
Brown,M.L	4	B	Wantage 416

these files during its execution.

The following skeletal COBOL code illustrates how the last program can be modified so that the original MembersFile can be sorted and suitable reports printed.

```
IDENTIFICATION DIVISION.
ENVIRONMENT DIVISION.
        SELECT MembersFile-SD ASSIGN TO PFMS.
        SELECT MembersFile ASSIGN TO PFMS.
        SELECT MembersFile-sorted ASSIGN TO PFMS.
DATA DIVISION.
FILE SECTION.
SD MembersFile-SD.
01 Record-SD.
        02 name-SD PIC X(30).
        02 sex-SD PIC A.
        02 league-SD.
            03 div-SD PIC 9.
            03 box-SD PIC A.
        02 FILLER PIC X(15).
    FD MembersFile, COMPRESSED.
    01 Record-1.
        02 FILLER PIC X(48).
    FD MembersFile-sorted, COMPRESSED.
    01 Record-3.
        02 name PIC X(30).
        02 sex PIC A.
        02 league.
            03 div PIC 9.
            03 box PIC A.
        02 TeleNo PIC X(15).
WORKING-STORAGE  SECTION.
PROCEDURE DIVISION.
B.  SORT MembersFile-SD
        ON DESCENDING KEY sex-SD
        ON ASCENDING KEY name-SD
        USING MembersFile
        GIVING  MembersFile-sorted.
```

The complete program follows.

```
IDENTIFICATION DIVISION.
PROGRAM-ID. FileSort.

ENVIRONMENT DIVISION.
INPUT-OUTPUT SECTION.
FILE-CONTROL.
        SELECT MembersFile-SD ASSIGN TO PFMS.
        SELECT MembersFile ASSIGN TO PFMS.
        SELECT MembersFile-sorted ASSIGN TO PFMS.
        SELECT ClubNotice ASSIGN TO PFMS.
```

```
DATA DIVISION.
FILE SECTION.
SD MembersFile-SD.
01 Record-SD.
    02 name-SD PIC X(30).
    02 sex-SD PIC A.
    02 league-SD.
        03 div-SD PIC 9.
        03 box-SD PIC A.
    02 FILLER PIC X(15).


FD MembersFile, COMPRESSED.
01 Record-1.
    02 FILLER PIC X(48).


FD MembersFile-sorted, COMPRESSED.
01 Record-3.
    02 name PIC X(30).
    02 sex PIC A.
    02 league.
        03 div PIC 9.
        03 box PIC A.
    02 TeleNo PIC X(15).


FD ClubNotice, COMPRESSED.
01 ReportOut.
    02 FILLER PIC X.
    02 LineImage PIC X(79).


WORKING-STORAGE SECTION.
01 Record-1-WS.
    02 FILLER PIC X(24) VALUE IS SPACES.
    02 FILLER PIC X(22) VALUE IS "SQUASH CLUB MEMBERSHIP".
01 Record-2-WS.
    02 FILLER PIC X(4) VALUE IS "NAME".
    02 FILLER PIC X(27) VALUE IS SPACES.
    02 FILLER PIC X(6) VALUE IS "LEAGUE".
    02 FILLER PIC X(12) VALUE IS SPACES.
    02 FILLER PIC X(9) VALUE IS "TELEPHONE".
01 Record-3-WS.
    02 FILLER PIC X(31) VALUE IS SPACES.
    02 FILLER PIC X(12) VALUE IS "DIVISION BOX".
01 Record-4-WS.
    02 name-WS PIC X(30).
    02 FILLER PIC X VALUE IS SPACE.
    02 div-WS PIC 9.
    02 FILLER PIC X(8) VALUE IS SPACES.
```

```
    02 box-WS PIC A.
    02 FILLER PIC X(8) VALUE IS SPACES.
    02 TeleNo-WS PIC X(15).

  77 EOF PIC A VALUE IS 'F'.
    88 EndOfFile VALUE 'T'.

PROCEDURE DIVISION.
A-seq.
    PERFORM B THROUGH F.

B.  SORT MembersFile-SD
        ON DESCENDING KEY sex-SD
        ON ASCENDING KEY name-SD
    USING MembersFile
    GIVING MembersFile-sorted.

    OPEN INPUT MembersFile-sorted,
        OUTPUT ClubNotice.
    READ MembersFile-sorted AT END MOVE 'T' TO EOF.

C.  MOVE Record-1-WS TO LineImage.
    WRITE ReportOut AFTER ADVANCING PAGE.
    MOVE Record-2-WS TO LineImage.
    WRITE ReportOut AFTER ADVANCING 2 LINES.
    MOVE Record-3-WS TO LineImage.
    WRITE ReportOut AFTER ADVANCING 1 LINE.
    MOVE SPACES TO LineImage.
    WRITE ReportOut AFTER ADVANCING 1 LINE.

D-rep.
    PERFORM E UNTIL EndOfFile.

F.  CLOSE MembersFile-sorted, ClubNotice.
    STOP RUN.

E.  MOVE name TO name-WS.
    MOVE div TO div-WS.
    MOVE box TO box-WS.
    MOVE TeleNo TO TeleNo-WS.
    MOVE Record-4-WS TO LineImage.
    WRITE ReportOut AFTER ADVANCING 1 LINE.
    READ MembersFile-sorted AT END MOVE 'T' TO EOF.
```

The results obtained by listing the ClubNotice file follows.

SQUASH CLUB MEMBERSHIP

NAME	LEAGUE		TELEPHONE
	DIVISION	BOX	
Allen,D.J	2	B	Ickford 947361
Allen,P	3	B	Wantage 9696
Anderson,T	3	C	Witney 817963
Black,A	4	C	Filkins 159
Brown,M.L	4	B	Wantage 416
Clayton,A	4	C	Ickford 326
Daniels,J	3	C	Oxford 713
Dimitriou,B	3	C	Oxford 235
Edwards,E	2	C	Woodstock 932
Fox,F.M	1	C	Freeland 93412
Goddard,P	1	A	Crowmarsh 81793
Gunnasekara,A	1	A	Harwell 2124
Hill,L	3	C	Uffington 36782
Jackson,J	3	B	Thame 8137
Long,C	1	A	Cumnor 863
Lyle,S	1	B	Gt. Milford 714
O'Flinn,P	4	B	Cholsey 3259
Ostle,D.M	2	C	Clanfield 4932
Pepper,D	2	A	Longworth 6498
Robbins,H	2	C	Witney 219597
Sanders,M.A	4	C	Woodstock 1136
Stevenson,G.R	3	A	Lechlade 194
Stott,P.A	1	A	Wallingford 837
Tilbury,C	3	C	Didcot 9873
Walton,B	1	B	Tackley 1134
Ward,S	3	C	Didcot 27918
Winslet,M.J	3	B	Lechlade 2130
Winter,M	2	A	Burford 223
Barrett,G.C	1	B	Standlake 87936
Collins,P	3	B	Thame 94287
East,W	4	A	Childrey 4267
Elwin,J	1	A	Portway 14732
Gillot,D	1	C	Harwell 6829
Harrison,C	1	A	Abingdon 2123
Jones,N.L	4	A	Witney 192
Keable,R	2	A	Cholsey 1414
Lowe,J.C	1	C	Bicester 4264
May,N	1	C	Didcot 98149
McDougall,G	3	B	Abingdon 81773
Priscott,M	2	C	Witney 419523
Rodriguez-Bachiller,A	2	B	Fritwell 916
Thomas,K	1	C	Didcot 48973

To produce the second report described, only the SORT statement needs to be changed, the program re-compiled and executed. The modification to the SORT statement would be:

SORT MembersFile-SD ON ASCENDING KEY div-SD, box-SD, name-SD
USING MembersFile GIVING MembersFile-sorted.

The results obtained by listing the ClubNotice file again, using the re-sorted MembersFile follows.

SQUASH CLUB MEMBERSHIP

NAME	LEAGUE		TELEPHONE
	DIVISION	BOX	
Elwin,J	1	A	Portway 14732
Goddard,P	1	A	Crowmarsh 81793
Gunnasekara,A	1	A	Harwell 2124
Harrison,C	1	A	Abingdon 2123
Long,C	1	A	Cumnor 863
Stott,P.A	1	A	Wallingford 837
Barrett,G.C	1	B	Standlake 87936
Lyle,S	1	B	Gt. Milford 714
Walton,B	1	B	Tackley 1134
Fox,F.M	1	C	Freeland 93412
Gillot,D	1	C	Harwell 6829
Lowe,J.C	1	C	Bicester 4264
May,N	1	C	Didcot 98149
Thomas,K	1	C	Didcot 48973
Keable,R	2	A	Cholsey 1414
Pepper,D	2	A	Longworth 6498
Winter,M	2	A	Burford 223
Allen,D.J	2	B	Ickford 947361
Rodriguez-Bachiller,A	2	B	Fritwell 916
Edwards,E	2	C	Woodstock 932
Ostle,D.M	2	C	Clanfield 4932
Priscott,M	2	C	Witney 419523
Robbins,H	2	C	Witney 219597
Stevenson,G.R	3	A	Lechlade 194
Allen,P	3	B	Wantage 9696
Collins,P	3	B	Thame 94287
Jackson,J	3	B	Thame 8137
McDougall,G	3	B	Abingdon 81773
Winslet,M.J	3	B	Lechlade 2130
Anderson,T	3	C	Witney 817963
Daniels,J	3	C	Oxford 713
Dimitriou,B	3	C	Oxford 235
Hill,L	3	C	Uffington 36782
Tilbury,C	3	C	Didcot 9873
Ward,S	3	C	Didcot 27918
East,W	4	A	Childrey 4267
Jones,N.L	4	A	Witney 192
Brown,M.L	4	B	Wantage 416
O'Flinn,P	4	B	Cholsey 3259
Black,A	4	C	Filkins 159
Clayton,A	4	C	Ickford 326
Sanders,M.A	4	C	Woodstock 1136

8.6 Summary.

Data Files are a means of storing large amounts of information permanently on either magnetic tape or disc.

The rate of transferring data between files and main memory is fast.

Files can be duplicated for security back-up.

COBOL provides for sequential file storage and retrieval of information both from magnetic tape and disc.

Sequential files can be created by either an editor (line-editor, or window editor) or through a computer program.

The records in sequential files can be sorted on any key fields within a record.

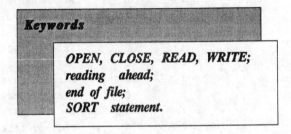

Keywords

OPEN, CLOSE, READ, WRITE;
reading   ahead;
end of file;
SORT   statement.

8.7 Questions.

1. If the first three fields of a record for a factory employee are:

FullName PIC X(30);
sex PIC A;
DateOfBirth PIC 9(6) presented as DDMMYY; comment upon the following SORT statements.

SORT EmployeeFile ON ASCENDING KEY FullName, sex
USING DataFile-1 GIVING DataFile-2.

SORT EmployeeFile ON ASCENDING KEY DateOfBirth
USING DataFile-1 GIVING DataFile-3.

[2]. Create a sequential file that contains the details of items of stock in a brewery. Records are of fixed-length and contain the following details.

StockNumber PIC X(5)
description PIC X(20)
StockQuantity PIC 999.
UnitPrice PIC 99V99.

Assume that the records are not sorted in StockNumber order when they are input into the computer system. Limit the number of test data records to no more than twenty in this question. Write a complete COBOL program to input and store the test data. Use a program design similar to that given in section 8.3 as a basis of the Procedure Division code.

Write a second COBOL program to sort, on the ascending primary key StockNumber, the contents of the stock file created.

In the second part of this program read the sorted file and output the report shown in figure 8.1. Use a program design similar to that given in section 8.4 as a basis of the Procedure Division code.

STOCK NO	DESCRIPTION	QUANTITY	PRICE
STOCK REPORT			
91189	BEST BITTER BRLS	200	3,158.20
92258	MASTER BREW MILD	40	120.50
9238X	STOCK ALE	125	1,320.80
	TOTAL VALUE		£4,599.50

Figure 8.1

3. A sequential file is to be created containing the details of telephone subscribers. Records are of fixed-length and contain the following details.

```
FullName.
        surname PIC X(19).
        initials.
            initial-1 PIC A.
            initial-2 PIC A.
        title PIC A(4).
TeleNo.
        exchange PIC X(15).
        number PIC 9(8).
PreviousReading PIC 9(6).
PresentReading PIC 9(6).
```

Invent a minimum of twenty test data records containing the fields described.

Assume that the present reading is always greater than the previous reading. Create a sequential file using an editor. Write a complete COBOL program to sort this file on telephone exchange and number as primary key, and surname and initials as secondary key, both in ascending order and output the report shown in figure 8.2. Note: since telephone numbers are unique sorting on the secondary key will have little or no affect.

RECORD/ REPORT LAYOUT SHEET				Layout No.		
0	**1**	**2**	**3**	**4**	**5**	**6**
1234567890	1234567890	1234567890	1234567890	1234567890	1234567890	1234567890
		SUBSCRIBERS				
NAME		TELEPHONE NUMBER			UNITS USED	
MISS J.	BROWN	ABINGDON 21483			645	
MR F. G. BLOGGS		ABINGDON 41937			2,719	
MRS P. S. ALLEN		BLADEN 413			384	

Figure 8.2

[4]. A sequential file is to be created containing the details of invoice payments against customer orders. Records are of fixed-length and contain the following details.

```
CustomerAccount PIC X(6).
InvoiceNumber PIC X(6).
DateOfInvoice.
    DD PIC 99.
    MM PIC 99.
    YY PIC 99.
AmountReceived PIC 9(6)V99.
InvoiceAmount PIC 9(6)V99.
```

Invent a minimum of twenty test data records containing the fields described. Assume that there is only one invoice payment per customer. Input this data using an editor.

Write a COBOL program to sort the file on DateOfInvoice, using YY as the primary key, MM the secondary key and DD as the tertiary key. The three keys are sorted into ascending order. The sorted file is called AccountDate.

Within the same program sort the original file again on CustomerAccount as primary key in ascending order. The sorted file is called AccountCustomer.

In the second part of the program output two reports taken from the files AccountDate and AccountCustomer. The format of the two reports is shown in figures 8.3 and 8.4 respectively.

RECORD/REPORT LAYOUT SHEET				Layout No.	

```
            0         1         2         3         4         5         6
1234567890123456789012345678901234567890123456789012345678901234567890
              INVOICE REPORT

DATE          INVOICE  NO        INVOICE  AMOUNT

13  03  80    147386               1,923.40
14  04  80    156921              17,018.50
01  05  80    159326                 746.00
```

Figure 8.3

RECORD/REPORT LAYOUT SHEET				Layout No.	

```
            0         1         2         3         4         5         6
1234567890123456789012345678901234567890123456789012345678901234567890
              DEBTORS  LIST

CUSTOMER AC   DATE OF INVOICE   INVOICE NO  BALANCE OWING

319874        19  07  81        351176        100.00
492113        11  12  80        129712         50.00
500618        21  03  81        219799        450.00
```

Figure 8.4

9

Program Structures from File Structures

The essence of the JSP method is to derive the structure of a program from the input and output structures of the data used in the program. This chapter continues the work of chapter 2, by applying structured design to file structures.

Within the chapter two worked examples involving sequential files and reports will be discussed in detail.

9.1 Problem One Specification.

A vehicle manufacturer keeps on file the value of the sales of cars to authorised motor agents in the South of England, excluding the London area. The file is organised so that it is categorised alphabetically into counties, within each county alphabetically into towns, and within each town alphabetically by model of car. The format of a record on this sequential file is:

County - 15 alphabetic characters
Town - 15 alphanumeric characters
Model - 8 alphabetic characters
Sales - 7 digits with no decimal places.

For example, a typical set of records might contain the following data.

Avon	Bath	Alpha	0036100
Avon	Bath	Beta	0147900
Avon	Bristol	Alpha	1376580
Berks	Newbury	Beta	2100500

Design, test and write a computer program to read the file and print the following report.

```
SALES OF CARS (SOUTHERN REGION)

COUNTY: Avon

TOWN: Bath

Alpha                              £36,100
Beta                              £147,900
Gamma                             £294,875

TOWN: Bristol

Alpha                           £1,376,580
.                                        .
.                                        .

COUNTY: Berks

TOWN: Newbury

.
.
```

The spacing of details on this report is given in the report/layout form over the page.

RECORD/ REPORT LAYOUT SHEET   Layout No. ☐

```
        0              1               2              3              4              5              6
1234567890 1234567890 1234567890 1234567890 1234567890 1234567890 1234567890
SALES  OF  CARS   ( SOUTHERN  REGION )                                              RECORD -1
                    X( 31 )

COUNTY :  Avon                                                                       RECORD -2
   X( 8 )           A( 15 )

TOWN :  Bath                                                                         RECORD -3
  X( 6 )            A ( 15 )

Alpha               £36 ,100                                                         RECORD -4
                   ££ ,£££ ,££9
        X ( 17 )
```

9.2 Program One Design and Test.

From the description of the problem it is possible to construct the initial structure diagrams to represent the file (input structure) and the report (output structure).

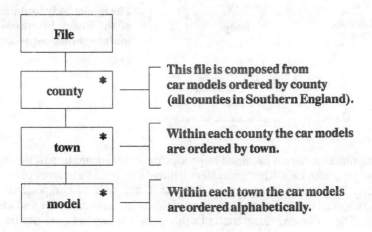

File

county * ⎯ This file is composed from car models ordered by county (all counties in Southern England).

town * ⎯ Within each county the car models are ordered by town.

model * ⎯ Within each town the car models are ordered alphabetically.

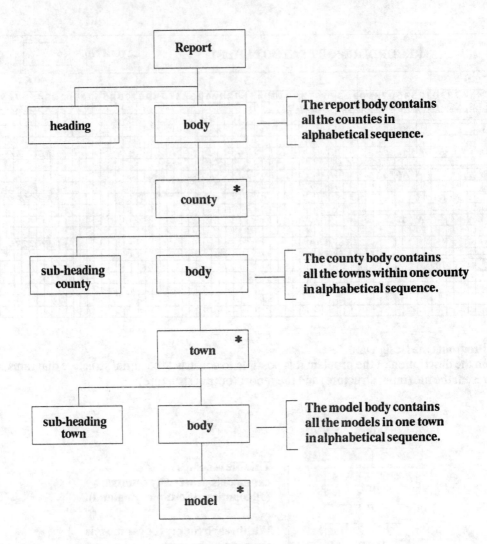

A basic program structure is obtained by producing an amalgamation of the input structure and the output structure only when each item common to both structures obeys the rules for correspondence. To reiterate, these rules state that any pair of components in an initial structure diagram must occur the same number of times, in the same order and under the same circumstances. The following diagram indicates that correspondence occurs at all levels between the input and output structures.

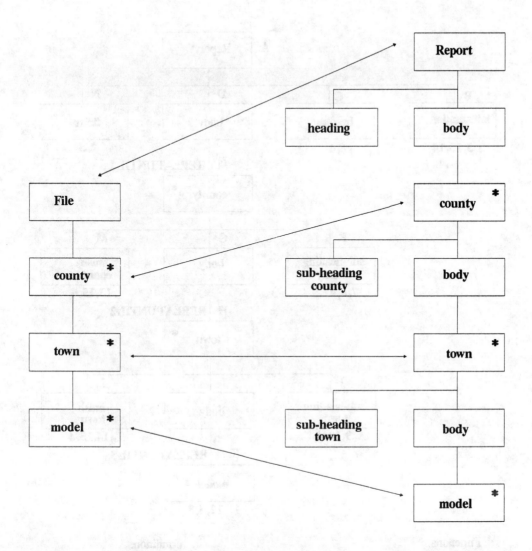

The basic program structure is a fusing together of both the input and output structures and is, therefore, similar to the initial output structure.

The detailed program structure is produced from the basic program structure, with extra boxes being added to the basic program structure, so as to accommodate all of the functions. Those boxes that have been added to the basic program structure are shaded in the following detailed program structure diagram, complete with the necessary functions and conditions necessary to solve the problem.

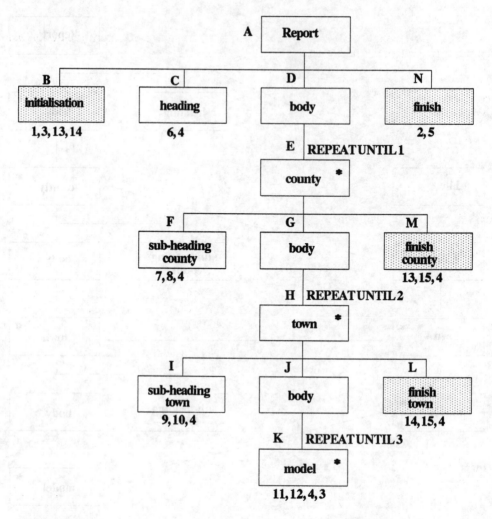

Functions.
1. open files
2. close files
3. read file
4. write line of report
5. stop
6. move record-1 for output
7. move county to record-2
8. move record-2 for output
9. move town to record-3
10. move record-3 for output
11. move model of car and sales total to record-4
12. move record-4 for output
13. store county
14. store town
15. move spaces for output

Conditions.
1. end of file
2. not same county or (1)
3. not same town or (2)

Using the following test data it is possible to perform a desk-check on the design before attempting to implement the design as a COBOL program.

Each record in the test data will contain the following values in the respective fields of each record. Enough test data should be invented to test every pathway through the detailed program structure.

Avon	Bath	Alpha	0036100
Avon	Bath	Beta	0147900
Avon	Bristol	Alpha	1376580
Berks	Newbury	Beta	2100500

Box	Function	Condition	Result from function being executed
A			
B	1,3		county=Avon
			town=Bath
			model=Alpha
			sales=36100
	13,14		CountyStore=Avon
			TownStore=Bath
C	6,4		*SALES OF CARS (SOUTHERN REGION)*
D		1 false	
E			
F	7,8,4		*COUNTY: Avon*
G		2,1 false	
H			
I	9,10,4		*TOWN: Bath*
J		3,2,1 false	
K	11,12,4		*Alpha* *36,100*
	3		county=Avon
			town=Bath
			model=Beta
			sales=147900
J		3,2,1 false	
K	11,12,4		*Beta* *147,900*
	3		county=Avon
			town=Bristol
			model=Alpha
			sales=1376580
J		3 true	
		2,1 false	
L	14,15,4		TownStore=Bristol
I	9,10,4		*TOWN: Bristol*
J		3,2,1 false	
K	11,12,4		*Alpha* *1,376,580*
	3		county=Berks
			town=Newbury
			model=Beta
			sales=2100500

Box	Function	Condition	Result from function being executed
J		3,2 true	
		1 false	
L	14,15,4		TownStore=Newbury
M	13,15,4		CountyStore=Berks
F	7,8,4		*COUNTY: Berks*
G			
H		2,1 false	
I	9,10,4		*TOWN: Newbury*
J		3,2,1 false	
K	11,12,4		*Beta* *2,100,500*
	3		county=?
			town=?
			model=?
			sales=?
J		3,2 ?	
		1 true	
L	14,15,4		TownStore=?
M	13,15,3		CountyStore=?
N	2,5		

When the end of file has been reached and there is an attempt to read beyond the end of the file, the EOF flag will be set to [T]rue. Since a test within a loop then specifically tests for the EOF flag being set at EndOfFile, it is not possible to say what the values for *county*, *town*, *model* and *sales* will be. The author has assumed that these values are non-determinant, yet in practise the PRIME computer system set strings to null and numbers to zero.

9.3 Program One Implementation.
The complete COBOL implementation of the design follows, together with the test data and results from running the program. Notice that the test data used in the desk check is also used in the testing of the program. Both sets of results agree, and it may be assumed that the program implementation is error-free in the context of this problem.

```
IDENTIFICATION DIVISION.
PROGRAM-ID. CarSales.

ENVIRONMENT DIVISION.
CONFIGURATION SECTION.
SPECIAL-NAMES.
    CURRENCY SIGN IS '£'.
INPUT-OUTPUT SECTION.
FILE-CONTROL.
    SELECT SalesData ASSIGN TO PFMS.
    SELECT SalesReport ASSIGN TO PFMS.

DATA DIVISION.
FILE SECTION.
FD SalesData, COMPRESSED.
```

```
01 RecordLayout.
    02 county PIC A(15).
    02 town PIC X(15).
    02 model PIC A(8).
    02 sale PIC 9(7).
FD SalesReport, COMPRESSED.
01 ReportOut.
    02 FILLER PIC X.
    02 LineImage PIC X(79).

WORKING-STORAGE SECTION.
01 Record-1-WS.
    02 FILLER PIC X(31) VALUE 'SALES OF CARS (SOUTHERN REGION)'.
01 Record-2-WS.
    02 FILLER PIC X(8) VALUE 'COUNTY: '.
    02 county-WS PIC A(15).
01 Record-3-WS.
    02 FILLER PIC X(6) VALUE 'TOWN: '.
    02 town-WS PIC A(15).
01 Record-4-WS.
    02 model-WS PIC A(8).
    02 FILLER PIC X(9) VALUE SPACES.
    02 sale-WS PIC ££,£££,££9.

77 EOF PIC A VALUE IS 'F'.
    88 EndOfFile VALUE IS 'T'.
77 CountyStore PIC A(15).
77 TownStore PIC X(15).

PROCEDURE DIVISION.
A-seq.
    PERFORM B THROUGH N.

B.  OPEN INPUT SalesData
         OUTPUT Salesreport.
    READ SalesData AT END MOVE 'T' TO EOF.
    MOVE county TO CountyStore.
    MOVE town TO TownStore.
C.  MOVE Record-1-WS TO LineImage.
    WRITE ReportOut AFTER ADVANCING PAGE.
D-rep.
    PERFORM E-seq UNTIL EndOfFile.
N.  CLOSE Salesdata, SalesReport.
    STOP RUN.


E-seq.
    PERFORM F THROUGH M.
```

```
F.   MOVE county TO county-WS.
     MOVE Record-2-WS TO LineImage.

     WRITE ReportOut AFTER ADVANCING 2 LINES.
G-rep.
     PERFORM H-seq UNTIL county NOT = CountyStore
                        OR EndOfFile.
M.   MOVE county TO CountyStore.
     MOVE SPACES TO LineImage.
     WRITE ReportOut AFTER ADVANCING 2 LINES.


H-seq.
     PERFORM I THROUGH L.


I.   MOVE town TO town-WS.
     MOVE record-3-WS TO LineImage.
     WRITE ReportOut AFTER ADVANCING 2 LINES.
     MOVE SPACES TO LineImage.
     WRITE ReportOut AFTER ADVANCING 1 LINE.
J-rep.
     PERFORM K UNTIL town NOT = TownStore
                   OR county NOT = CountyStore
                   OR EndOfFile.
L.   MOVE town TO TownStore.
     MOVE SPACES TO LineImage.
     WRITE ReportOut AFTER ADVANCING 2 LINES.
K.   MOVE model TO model-WS.
     MOVE sale TO sale-WS.
     MOVE record-4-WS TO LineImage.
     WRITE ReportOut AFTER ADVANCING 1 LINE.
     READ SalesData AT END MOVE 'T' TO EOF.
```

Contents of the data file SalesData.

Avon	Bath	Alpha	0036100
Avon	Bath	Beta	0147900
Avon	Bath	Gamma	0294875
Avon	Bristol	Alpha	1376580
Avon	Bristol	Beta	0829640
Avon	Bristol	Epsilon	0507300
Avon	Bristol	Gamma	0428550
Berks	Newbury	Beta	2100500
Berks	Newbury	Gamma	1701600
Berks	Reading	Alpha	0335970
Berks	Reading	Beta	0015730
Berks	Reading	Epsilon	0008950

Contents of the report file SalesReport.

```
SALES OF CARS (SOUTHERN REGION)

COUNTY: Avon

TOWN: Bath

Alpha                £36,100
Beta                £147,900
Gamma               £294,875


TOWN: Bristol

Alpha             £1,376,580
Beta                £829,640
Epsilon             £507,300
Gamma               £428,550


COUNTY: Berks

TOWN: Newbury

Beta              £2,100,500
Gamma             £1,701,600

TOWN: Reading

Alpha               £335,970
Beta                 £15,730
Epsilon               £8,950
```

9.4 Problem Two Specification.

A distributor for a chain of music shops receives music cassettes from the manufacturer and distributes the cassettes to individual music shops. Each distribution of a batch of cassettes is entered as a record on a sequential file. The format of each record on the file is:

> Music code - 1 character (A-popular, B-jazz, C-classical)
> Stock Number - 4 digits
> Quantity - 4 digits.

At the end of each month the records in the file are sorted on music code, in ascending order, as primary key and on stock number, in ascending order, as secondary key. For example, a file might contain the following records.

```
A01400020
A01400100
A01750150
A02030070
A02030150
A02030250
  .
  .

B14900500
B16300130
B16300140
  .
  .

C09040010
C09050015
  .
  .
```

Notice from this example of the data, that within a music category the same stock number can appear more than once.

Design, test and implement a COBOL program to read the file and print the following report. The report contains the total monthly distribution for every different stock number that is stored on the file. Although the same stock number can appear many times on the input file it must only appear once on the report. For this reason it will be necessary to keep a running total of the stock for each group of cassettes classified by the same stock number.

```
          CASSETTE DISTRIBUTION

          TYPE: POPULAR

          STOCK-NUMBER          QUANTITY

          0140                  120
          0175                  150
          0203                  470
            .                     .

          TYPE: JAZZ

          STOCK-NUMBER          QUANTITY

            .                     .
            .                     .
```

The spacing of details on this report is given on the following report/layout form.

RECORD/ REPORT LAYOUT SHEET   Layout No. [ ]

```
        0         1         2         3         4         5         6
1234567890123456789012345678901234567890123456789012345678901234567890
                        CASSETTE DISTRIBUTION                  RECORD -1
          X (20)                      X (21)

                        TYPE : POPULAR                        RECORD -2
          X (20)        X (6)   X (9)

                        STOCK -NUMBER  QUANTITY               RECORD -3
          X (20)                    X (21)

                        0140              120                 RECORD -4
          X (20)        9999    X (11)    999
```

9.5 Program Two Design and Test.

From the problem specification and example of the organisation of records on the input file, it should be clear that the file is classified into groups of records having the same music code, within each group there is a further classification of records into groups with each group having the same stock number. Within a group having the same stock number there is a further number of records showing the number of cassettes, with the same stock number, that have been distributed. The initial structure diagram for the input file can be drawn as;

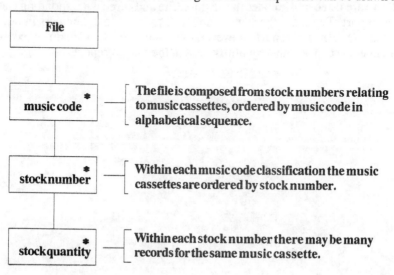

From the physical format of the layout of the report the initial output structure for the report can be drawn as:

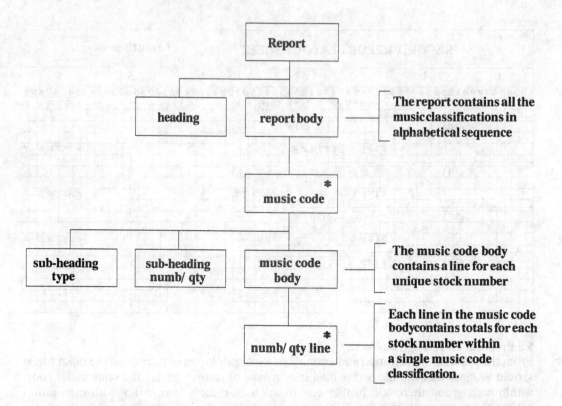

When both structure diagrams are inspected for correspondence between components, see the diagram on the next page, it is clear that the order of the components is the same for both diagrams. There are three music codes in the input file and three corresponding classifications in the output report. There are the same number of unique stock numbers in both the input file and printed on the output report. However, the number of stock/quantity records does not match the number of stock number/quantity lines in the output report.

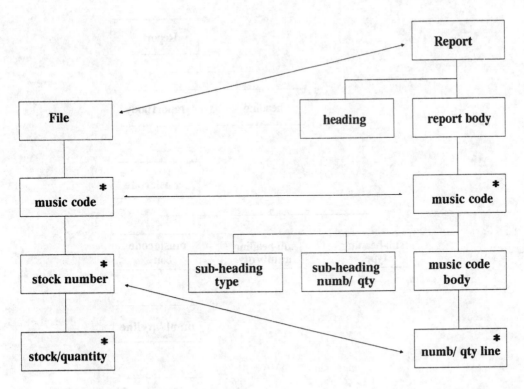

The stock number/ quantity line in the report is made up from a unique stock number, for which correspondence exits, and the sum of the stock/quantity records having the same unique stock number, in the input file. The repetitive component for the stock/quantity having the same stock number cannot be seen in the report structure, however, this repetitive component must appear in the detailed program structure. The amalgamation of the two structures is possible, as shown in the basic program structure on the next page, provided the repetitive component for stock/quantity is not neglected.

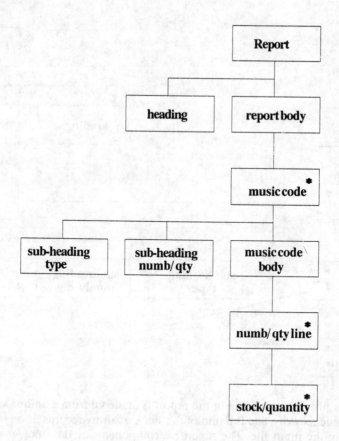

In determining suitable functions and conditions it becomes clear that the basic program structure must have more boxes added to it if the functions and conditions are to be dispersed over the structure. These extra boxes have been shaded in the detailed program structure shown over the page.

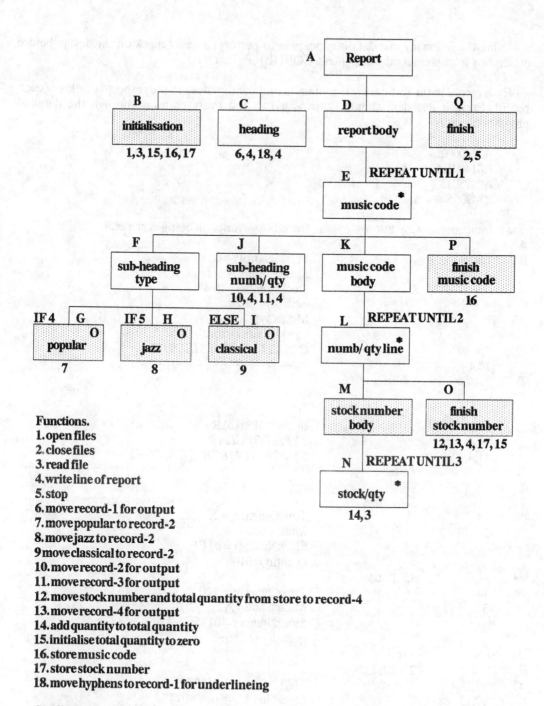

Functions.
1. open files
2. close files
3. read file
4. write line of report
5. stop
6. move record-1 for output
7. move popular to record-2
8. move jazz to record-2
9 move classical to record-2
10. move record-2 for output
11. move record-3 for output
12. move stock number and total quantity from store to record-4
13. move record-4 for output
14. add quantity to total quantity
15. initialise total quantity to zero
16. store music code
17. store stock number
18. move hyphens to record-1 for underlineing

Conditions.
1. end of file
2. not same music code or (1)
3. not same stock number or (2)
4. music code = A
5. music code = B

Using the following test data it is possible to perform a desk- check on the design before attempting to implement the design as a COBOL program.

Each record in the test data will contain the following values in the respective fields of each record. Enough test data should be invented to test every pathway through the detailed program structure.

```
A01400020
A01400100
A01750150
B14900500
```

Box	Function	Condition	Result from function being executed
A			
B	1,3,15,16,17		TotalQuantity=0
			MusicCode=A
			StockNumber=0140
			quantity=0020
			MusicCode-store=A
			StockNumber-store=0140
C	6,4		*CASSETTE DISTRIBUTION*
	18,4		--
D		1 false	
E			
F		4 true	
G	7		title=POPULAR
J	10,4		*TYPE:POPULAR*
	11,4		*STOCK-NUMBER QUANTITY*
K		2,1 false	
L			
M		3,2,1 false	
N	14		TotalQuantity=20
	3		MusicCode=A
			StockNumber=0140
			quantity=0100
M		3,2,1 false	
N	14		TotalQuantity=120
	3		MusicCode=A
			StockNumber=0175
			quantity=0150
M		3 true	
		2,1 false	
O	12,13,4		*0140 120*
	17,15		StockNumber-store=0175
			TotalQuantity=0
M		3,2,1 false	
N	14		TotalQuantity=150
	3		MusicCode=B
			StockNumber=1490

Box	Function	Condition	Result from function being executed
			quantity=0500
M		3,2 true	
		1 false	
O	12,13,4		*0175* *150*
	17,15		StockNumber-store=1490
			TotalQuantity=0
P	16		MusicCode-store=B
F		5 true	
H	8		title=JAZZ
J	10,4		*TYPE:JAZZ*
	11,4		*STOCK-NUMBER QUANTITY*
K		2,1 false	
L			
M		3,2,1 false	
N	14		TotalQuantity=500
	3		MusicCode=?
			StockNumber=?
			quantity=?
M		1 true	
		2,3 ?	
O	12,13,4		*1490* *500*
	17		StockNumber-store=?
	15		TotalQuantity=0
P	16		MusicCode-store=?
Q	2,5		

9.6 Program Two Implementation.

The complete COBOL implementation of the design follows, together with the test data and results from running the program. Notice that the test data used in the desk check is also used in the testing of the program. Both sets of results agree, and it may be assumed that the program implementation is error-free in the context of this problem.

```
IDENTIFICATION DIVISION.
PROGRAM-ID. Music.

ENVIRONMENT DIVISION.
INPUT-OUTPUT SECTION.
FILE-CONTROL.
    SELECT MusicData ASSIGN TO PFMS.
    SELECT MusicReport ASSIGN TO PFMS.

DATA DIVISION.
FILE SECTION.
FD MusicData, COMPRESSED.
01 Record-FS.
    02 MusicCode PIC A.
```

```
        02 StockNumber PIC 9(4).
        02 quantity PIC 9999.
    FD MusicReport, COMPRESSED.
    01 ReportOut.
        02 FILLER PIC X.
        02 LineImage PIC X(79).

    WORKING-STORAGE SECTION.
    01 Record-1-WS.
        02 FILLER PIC X(20) VALUE IS SPACES.
        02 title-1 PIC X(21) VALUE IS 'CASSETTE DISTRIBUTION'.
    01 Record-2-WS.
        02 FILLER PIC X(20) VALUE IS SPACES.
        02 FILLER PIC X(6) VALUE IS 'TYPE: '.
        02 title-2 PIC A(9).
    01 Record-3-WS.
        02 FILLER PIC X(20) VALUE IS SPACES.
        02 FILLER PIC X(21) VALUE IS 'STOCK-NUMBER QUANTITY'.
    01 Record-4-WS.
        02 FILLER PIC X(20) VALUE IS SPACES.
        02 StockNumber-WS PIC 9(4).
        02 FILLER PIC X(10) VALUE IS SPACES.
        02 Quantity-WS PIC ZZZ9.

    77 StockNumber-Store PIC 9(4).
    77 MusicCode-Store PIC A.
    77 EOF PIC A VALUE IS 'F'.
        88 EndOfFile VALUE 'T'.
    77 TotalQuantity PIC 9999 VALUE IS ZERO.


    PROCEDURE DIVISION.
    A-seq.
        PERFORM B THROUGH Q.


    B.  OPEN INPUT MusicData
             OUTPUT MusicReport.
        READ MusicData AT END MOVE 'T' TO EOF.
        MOVE ZERO TO TotalQuantity.
        MOVE MusicCode TO MusicCode-Store.
        MOVE StockNumber TO StockNumber-Store.
    C.  MOVE Record-1-WS TO LineImage.
        WRITE ReportOut AFTER ADVANCING PAGE.
        MOVE ALL '-' TO Title-1.
        MOVE Record-1-WS TO LineImage.
        WRITE ReportOut AFTER ADVANCING 1 LINE.
```

```
D-rep.
    PERFORM E-seq UNTIL EndOfFile.
Q.  CLOSE MusicData, MusicReport.
    STOP RUN.


E-seq.
    PERFORM F-sel THROUGH P.


F-sel.
    IF MusicCode = 'A'
       PERFORM G
    ELSE
       IF MusicCode = 'B'
          PERFORM H
       ELSE
          PERFORM I.
J.  MOVE Record-2-WS TO LineImage.
    WRITE ReportOut AFTER ADVANCING 2 LINES.
    MOVE Record-3-WS TO LineImage.
    WRITE ReportOut AFTER ADVANCING 2 LINES.
K-rep.
    PERFORM L-seq UNTIL MusicCode NOT = MusicCode-store
                   OR EndOfFile.
P.  MOVE MusicCode TO MusicCode-Store.
G.  MOVE "POPULAR" TO Title-2.
H.  MOVE "JAZZ" TO Title-2.
I.  MOVE "CLASSICAL" TO Title-2.


L-seq.
    PERFORM M-rep THROUGH O.


M-rep.
    PERFORM N UNTIL StockNumber NOT = StockNumber-Store
                OR MusicCode NOT = MusicCode-Store
                OR EndOfFile.
O.  MOVE StockNumber-Store TO StockNumber-WS.
    MOVE TotalQuantity TO quantity-WS.
    MOVE record-4-WS TO LineImage.
    WRITE ReportOut AFTER ADVANCING 1 LINE.
    MOVE StockNumber TO StockNumber-Store.
    MOVE ZERO TO TotalQuantity.
N.  ADD quantity TO TotalQuantity.
    READ MusicData AT END MOVE 'T' TO EOF.
```

Contents of data file MusicData and report file MusicReport.

```
A01400020
A01400100
A01750150
A02030070
A02030150
A02030250
A05140010
A05140075
A06380105
A07490250
B14900500
B16300130
B16300140
B16300150
B17400070
C09040010
C09050015
C09060010
C09860040
C09860050
C09870030
```

```
CASSETTE DISTRIBUTION
---------------------

TYPE: POPULAR

STOCK-NUMBER QUANTITY
0140          120
0175          150
0203          470
0514           85
0638          105
0749          250


TYPE: JAZZ

STOCK-NUMBER QUANTITY
1490          500
1630          420
1740           70


TYPE: CLASSICAL

STOCK-NUMBER QUANTITY
0904           10
0905           15
0906           10
0986           90
0987           30
```

9.7 Summary

The diagrammatic structure of the input and output files corresponds with the format of the data file and report respectively.

The components of selection and repetition between the two structure diagrams must correspond before the two diagrams can be fused together to form a basic program structure.

Functions and conditions are identified and distributed over the basic program structure. Where the basic program structure does not contain sufficient boxes to allow for the dispersion of the functions and conditions extra boxes must be added to the diagram. The presence of the extra boxes must not violate the fundamental basic program structure. The modified diagram containing all the components of the solution or algorithm is known as the detailed program structure.

When the detailed program structure has been completed it must be desk checked or tested with suitable data to ensure that the design is logically sound. To implement a COBOL program on the basis of a faulty design would prove to be a waste of time, and often lead to fixes being made on the COBOL code without further consideration of amendments to the design.

When the complete COBOL program has been coded and compiled it should be run using the same data that was used in the desk check and both sets of results checked for consistency.

9.8 Questions.

Design, test and implement COBOL programs as answers to the following questions. You will need to plan the exact spacing of items in each report, using a record/layout sheet, before attempting to code the Data Division.

1. Return to the data for the squash club members file described in section 8.5 of the last chapter. If the data is sorted on division as primary key, box as secondary key and name as tertiary key, with all the keys being sorted in ascending order, then develop a program to produce the *Squash Club membership Report* shown on the next page.

[2]. The XYZ Building Society keeps on file the details of all its customers holding ordinary share accounts. A record contains the following fields.

> Branch - 20 alphanumeric characters
> Account number - 6 digits
> Number of £1 shares - 5 digits with no decimal places.

The file is sorted on branch as primary key, in ascending order, and account number as secondary key, also in ascending order. It is required to print a report on the contents of the file using the same format as the *XYZ Building Society* report shown on the next page.

SQUASH CLUB MEMBERSHIP

DIVISION 1
BOX A

Ms Elwin, J	Portway 14732
Mr Goddard, P	Crowmarsh 81793
Mr Gunnasekara, A	Harwell 2124
Ms Harrison, C	Abingdon 2123
Mr Long, C	Cumnor 863
Mr Stott, P.A	Wallingford 837
.	.
.	.

BOX B

Ms Barrett, G.C	Standlake 87936
.	.
.	.

DIVISION 2
BOX A

.	.
.	.

The XYZ Building Society

Details by branch of ordinary share account customers

Branch Bournemouth

Account No.	£1 shares
112345	1,000
121456	550
131000	670
.	.
.	.
Total £235,643	

Branch Cardiff

Account No.	£1 shares
101456	2,578
111598	1,234
113789	10,900

3. A sequential file is used to store the details of library books. The format of a record on the file is:

> Book title - 30 alphanumeric characters
> Author(s) - 20 alphanumeric characters
> Publisher - 15 alphanumeric characters
> Status code - 1 character [A]ctive, [D]amaged, [E]xternal, [L]ost
> Price - 4 digits with 2 decimal places.

The file is sorted on status code as primary key, in ascending order, and author as secondary key, in descending order. It is required to print a report on the contents of the library file using the format shown below.

```
LIBRARY BOOK INDEX

Status: Active
Author              Title                   Publisher         Price
Bellinger,C         The Art of Sculpture    Moore-Hill        £18.75
Bragg,L             Diffraction Physics     Hall              £15.50
  .                   .                       .                 .
  .                   .                       .                 .
  .                                                          

                                            Total  £123,786.50

Status: Damaged
Author              Title                   Publisher         Price
Collins,J           The Vampire Catchers    Minster-Bell      £3.75
  .                   .                       .                 .
  .                   .                       .                 .
```

[4]. An estate agents wants to keep on file the following details about properties.

> Vendor's name - 20 alphanumeric characters
> Address of property - 40 alphanumeric characters
> Price of property - 6 digits with no decimal places
> Type of dwelling - 1 character coded as:
> > > A - detached
> > > B - semi-detached
> > > C - terraced
> > > D - bungalow
> > > E - maisonette or flat
> Number of bedrooms - 2 digits
> Tenure - 1 character [F]reehold, [L]easehold.

The file is sorted on type of dwelling as primary key, in ascending order, and price of property as secondary key, in descending order. It is required to print a report on the contents of the file using the following format.

QUICK & FIDDLE ESTATE AGENTS Established 1991

Property type Detached

Vendor	Address	Price	Beds	Tenure
Smith,C	2 Liberal Walk	£45,675	4	freehold
Bowyer,F	69 Church View	£44,350	4	leasehold
Sumner,S	3 Hope Street	£43,000	4	freehold
.	.	.	.	.
.	.	.	.	.

Total number of properties 23

Property type Semi-detached

Vendor	Address	Price	Beds	Tenure
Jones,M	145 River View	£36,750	4	freehold
Evans,M	27 Ridge Bank	£35,500	3	freehold
.	.	.	.	.
.	.	.	.	.

10

File Maintenance

In the first part of this chapter the JSP method is used to define two basic algorithms for file maintenance - merging and updating. The latter part of the chapter explains the errors that can arise when updating files, and defines a general algorithm for file maintenance. Throughout the chapter worked examples are used to develop and implement the algorithms.

10.1 Two-way File Merge.

Two sequential files, File-A and File-B, contain records of the names, departments and telephone extension numbers of staff based on two sites of a college. A third file, File-C, is to be produced that combines the details of the staff from both sites into one file. The format of a record for the three files is:

Name (key field) - 20 alphanumeric characters.
Department - 4 alphabetic characters.
Extension number 3 digits.

The following records illustrate the contents of File-A and File- B, ordered alphabetically on the name field as key, and also illustrates how the two files are combined or merged to produce File-C.

File-A

Appleton,J.N	CPS 446
Bainbridge,R	EDUC210
Beaumont,J.E	CATR415
Butler,N.J	COMP422
Daindridge,J	LIB 552
Dunford,C	ARCI512

File-B

Axford,B	LPE 397
Ayers,C.A	COMP305
Barrett,D.A	CONS579
Elliot,M.J	GPS 447

File-C

Appleton,J.N	CPS 446
Axford,B	LPE 397
Ayers,C.A	COMP305
Bainbridge,R	EDUC210
Barrett,D.A	CONS579
Beaumont,J.E	CATR415
Butler,N.J	COMP422
Daindridge,J	LIB 552
Dunford,C	ARCI512
Elliot,M.J	GPS 447

File-C is shown to be an amalgamation of all the records of File- A and File-B, combined together such that the names of the members of staff are kept in strict alphabetical sequence.

The following data structures can be drawn for the three files. For correspondence to exist between the components of the files, the components involved must occur the same number of times, in the same order, and under the same circumstances. The only correspondence exists at the first level, since there is only one file in each case. Correspondence does not exist at lower levels since the number of records in each file is not the same, and the records are not in the same order.

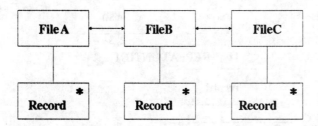

File-C is an amalgam of the contents of both input files, File-A and File-B. Since both files are processed together to produce File-C, the data structure diagram can be modified to:

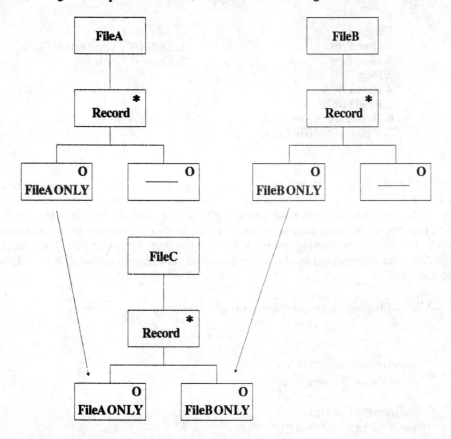

From this diagram the basic program structure for the two-way merge is identical to the structure depicted for File-C, and for this reason will not be re-drawn again. The detailed program structure for the two-way merge follows.

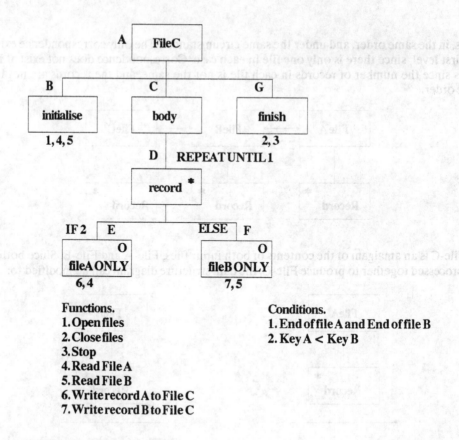

Functions.
1. Open files
2. Close files
3. Stop
4. Read File A
5. Read File B
6. Write record A to File C
7. Write record B to File C

Conditions.
1. End of file A and End of file B
2. Key A < Key B

In the following program to merge two files, it is necessary to compare a key from File-A with a key from File-B. However, when the end of either file is reached it is necessary to set the key field, of the file that has ended, to a higher value than all the other keys in the two files. The purpose of this practice is to force the remainder of the records in the remaining file to be copied to File-C. By moving HIGH-VALUES to either Key-A or Key-B will fill the key with the character represented by the highest ordinal value in either the ASCII or EBCDIC character sets.

The COBOL program to merge the two files follows.

```
IDENTIFICATION DIVISION.
PROGRAM-ID. TwoWayMerge.


ENVIRONMENT DIVISION.
INPUT-OUTPUT SECTION.
```

```
FILE-CONTROL.
    SELECT File-A ASSIGN TO PFMS.
    SELECT File-B ASSIGN TO PFMS.
    SELECT File-C ASSIGN TO PFMS.


DATA DIVISION.
FILE SECTION.
FD File-A, COMPRESSED.
01 Record-A.
    02 Key-A PIC X(20).
    02 Details-A PIC X(7).
FD File-B, COMPRESSED.
01 Record-B.
    02 Key-B PIC X(20).
    02 Details-B PIC X(7).
FD File-C, COMPRESSED.
01 Record-C.
    02 FILLER PIC X(27).

WORKING-STORAGE SECTION.
77 EOF-A PIC A VALUE 'F'.
    88 EndOfFile-A VALUE IS 'T'.
77 EOF-B PIC A VALUE 'F'.
    88 EndOfFile-B VALUE IS 'T'.


PROCEDURE DIVISION.
A-seq.
    PERFORM B THROUGH G.


B.  OPEN INPUT File-A, File-B
         OUTPUT File-C.
    READ File-A AT END MOVE 'T' TO  EOF-A,
                    MOVE HIGH-VALUES TO Key-A.
    READ FILE-B AT END MOVE 'T' TO EOF-B,
                    MOVE HIGH-VALUES TO Key-B.
C-rep.
    PERFORM D-sel UNTIL EndOfFile-A AND EndOfFile-B.
G.  CLOSE File-A, File-B, File-C.
    STOP RUN.


D-sel.
    IF Key-A NOT > Key-B
        PERFORM E
    ELSE
        PERFORM F.
```

```
E.  WRITE Record-C FROM Record-A.
    READ File-A AT END MOVE 'T' TO EOF-A,
                    MOVE HIGH-VALUES TO Key-A.
F.  WRITE Record-C FROM Record-B.
    READ File-B AT END MOVE 'T' TO EOF-B,
                    MOVE HIGH-VALUES TO Key-B.
```

10.2 File Updating.

Information that is contained in data files is not always static, it can be subject to changes. Such changes to the information will come about through the insertion, amendment and deletion of records. The process of changing the information held on data files is known as updating.

The most common types of files used in an updating situation are the master file and transaction file.

Master files are files of a permanent nature. For example, a stock file, a personnel file, a customer file. A feature to note is the regular updating of these files to show a current position. For example, when orders are processed the amount of stock should be decreased in the stock file. It is seen, therefore, that master records will contain data of a static nature, for example a stock number, description of stock, minimum re-order level, and data which by its nature will change each time a transaction occurs, for example the depletion of a stock level.

A transaction file is made up from the various transactions created from source documents, for example sales invoices. In a stock control application the file will contain a list of stock items that have been sold. This file will be used to update the master file. As soon as it has been used for this purpose it is no longer required. It will, therefore, have a very short life because it will be replaced by another transaction file containing the next list of stock items that have been sold.

In the last problem File-C can be regarded as a master file, created from merging the two files, File-A and File-B together. This master file will eventually require updating. New staff may enter the college, current staff may change either their department telephone extension number or both, and staff may leave the college.

A transaction file of staff movement could have the following records.

```
Axford,B
Bailey,S.K        SOC 832
Beswick,K.P       MEDI654
Butler,N.J        MATH342
Dunford,C
Elliot,M.J        COMP422
Harris,P.T        CATR416
```

From this file the new members to be inserted into the master file are Bailey,S.K, Beswick,K.P and Harris,P.T. Those members of file who already exist on the master file, yet require to have their records amended owing to a change of department are Butler,N.J and Elliott,M.J. The records of Axford,B and Dunford,C are to be deleted since they have left the college.

To distinguish between those records that are to be deleted and those that are to amended, records that contain only the key field, name, and the remainder of the fields blank will be deleted in this example.

If the transaction file is processed against the master file

```
Appleton,J.N        CPS 446
Axford,B            LPE 397
Ayers,C.A           COMP305
Bainbridge,R        EDUC210
Barrett,D.A         CONS579
Beaumont,J.E        CATR415
Butler,N.J          COMP422
Daindridge,J        LIB 552
Dunford,C           ARCI512
Elliot,M.J          GPS 447
```

then the following updated master file will be the result.

```
Appleton,J.N        CPS 446
Ayers,C.A           COMP305
Bailey,S.K          SOC 832
Bainbridge,R        EDUC210
Barrett,D.A         CONS579
Beaumont,J.E        CATR415
Beswick,K.P         MEDI654
Butler,N.J          MATH342
Daindridge,J        LIB 552
Elliot,M.J          COMP422
Harris,P.T          CATR416
```

The design of an algorithm to update a master file from a transaction file follows. The initial structure diagrams for the input files, transaction and master, and the output file, the updated master file, are shown on the next page.

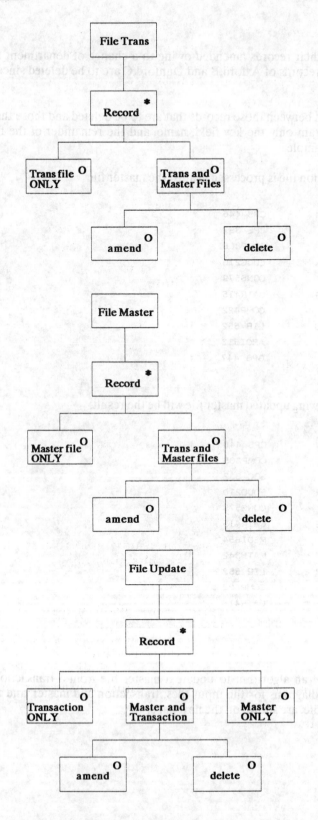

The basic program structure is identical to the data structure for the updated master file and for this reason will not be included here. However, the basic program structure is modified to take into account the functions and conditions and a detailed program structure drawn.

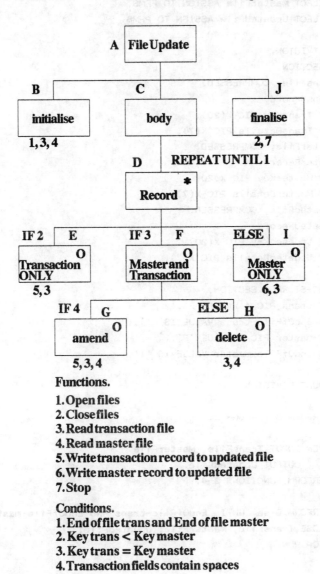

Functions.

1. Open files
2. Close files
3. Read transaction file
4. Read master file
5. Write transaction record to updated file
6. Write master record to updated file
7. Stop

Conditions.

1. End of file trans and End of file master
2. Key trans < Key master
3. Key trans = Key master
4. Transaction fields contain spaces

The COBOL program to update the master file from the transaction file follows.

```
IDENTIFICATION DIVISION.
PROGRAM-ID. FileUpdate-1.
```

```
ENVIRONMENT DIVISION.
INPUT-OUTPUT SECTION.
FILE-CONTROL.
    SELECT TransFile ASSIGN TO PFMS.
    SELECT MasterFile ASSIGN TO PFMS.
    SELECT UpdatedFile ASSIGN TO PFMS.


DATA DIVISION.
FILE SECTION.
FD TransFile, COMPRESSED.
01 TransRecord.
    02 TransKey PIC X(20).
    02 TransDetails PIC X(7).
FD MasterFile, COMPRESSED.
01 MasterRecord.
    02 MasterKey PIC X(20).
    02 MasterDetails PIC X(7).
FD UpdatedFile, COMPRESSED.
01 UpdatedRecord.
    02 UpdatedKey PIC X(20).
    02 UpdatedDetails PIC X(7).


WORKING-STORAGE SECTION.
77 EOF-trans PIC A VALUE 'F'.
    88 EndOfFile-trans VALUE IS 'T'.
77 EOF-master PIC A VALUE 'F'.
    88 EndOfFile-master VALUE IS 'T'.


PROCEDURE DIVISION.
A-seq.
    PERFORM B THROUGH J.


B.  OPEN INPUT TransFile, MasterFile
        OUTPUT UpdatedFile.
    PERFORM FUNCTIONS-3-4.
C-rep.
    PERFORM D-sel UNTIL EndOfFile-trans AND EndOfFile-master.
J.  CLOSE TransFile, MasterFile, UpdatedFile.
    STOP RUN.


D-sel.
    IF TransKey < MasterKey
        PERFORM E
    ELSE
        IF TransKey = MasterKey
            PERFORM F-sel
        ELSE
            PERFORM I.
```

```
E.   WRITE UpdatedRecord FROM TransRecord.
     READ TransFile AT END MOVE 'T' TO EOF-trans,
                          MOVE HIGH-VALUES TO TransKey.
F-sel.
     IF TransDetails NOT = SPACES
         PERFORM G
     ELSE
         PERFORM H.
I.   WRITE UpdatedRecord FROM MasterRecord.
     READ MasterFile AT END MOVE 'T' TO EOF-master,
                          MOVE HIGH-VALUES TO MasterKey.


G.   WRITE UpdatedRecord FROM TransRecord.
     PERFORM FUNCTIONS-3-4.

H.   PERFORM FUNCTIONS-3-4.


*   ----------------------- subroutines -------------------------


FUNCTIONS-3-4.
     READ TransFile AT END MOVE 'T' TO EOF-trans,
                          MOVE HIGH-VALUES TO TransKey.
     READ MasterFile AT END MOVE 'T' TO EOF-master,
                          MOVE HIGH-VALUES TO MasterKey.
```

10.3 Update Algorithm with Validation.

A transaction file from a customer accounts system contains records with the following format.

> Account number (key) - 4 digits.
> Transaction code 1 digit -   (1) amend a record
>   (2) delete a record
>   (3) insert a new record
> Name - 20 alphanumeric characters.
> Address - 30 alphanumeric characters
> Amount - 6 digits including 2 decimal places, with the number being prefixed by a sign
>   (-) for payment and (+) for purchase.

A sample of records on the transaction file might appear as:

12461	26 Avon Cr. Bath	+013000
12533Davies,J	4 Queen Mary Walk, Swindon	+050050
12542		
12871		+031475
12871		-017850
12871		-005000
13461	16 Hook St. Wallingford	+005070
13493Jones,P.T	49 Brook St. Abingdon	+010000
13491		-005000
13571Evans,P.V		+035070
13873Vaughan,L.S	8 Hilltop View, Oxford	+100050
13942		
14821		-007575
15031		+010070
15103Smith,P	4 Watford Road, Luton	+000000
15101		+010050
15101	3 Junction Road, Aylesbury	-010050
15102		
16321		+175436
16321		+219321
16321	14 Haymarket, Oxford	-300000
16433Spencer,S	184 Palace Road, Witney	+005000

Notice from the transaction code that records can be inserted, amended or deleted from the master file, and the transaction file may contain multiple records having an identical key. In an extreme case it is possible for a record to be inserted into the master file (new account customer), amendments made to this record in the master file (payments, purchases, change of name, change of address) and the record to be deleted from the master file (account closed). From the sample records it can be seen that when a record is to be amended the key and the fields to be changed are included, however, when a record is to be deleted only the key is specified in the transaction record, and the remaining fields are left blank. New records to be inserted into the updated master file contain the record key and information about the customer that is available at the time.

The format of the master file is similar to that of the transaction file, however, the exceptions are that the transaction code is missing and multiple records sharing the same key do not appear. A sample of records on the master file might appear as:

1245Joseph,S	14 Harcourt Cr. Bath	+014000
1246Hamilton,P	2 Pump St. Bath	+013000
1254Maskins,M	18 Oxford Rd, Watford	+000000
1277Trent,P	1 Vicarage Cr. Oxford	+100000

```
1278Vicars,M        28 Row Walk, Stratford       +001000
1287Billings,P      18 Knoll St. Watford         +010050
1300Jones,T         29 Park Rd. Witney           +001075
1346Tyrer           2 Cottage St. Didcot         +015870
1357Evans,P.V       2 Church Rd. Didcot          +000000
1387Vaughan,L.S     8 Hilltop View, Oxford       +000000
1482Andrews,A       29 High Rd. Watford          +030050
1503Gaynor,M        2 Lux Lane, Didcot           +000000
1612Lord,V          77 River St. Abingdon        +015720
1632Mellor,N        64 Hoe St. Watford           +000000
```

The insertion, amendment and deletion of records on the master file can appear on the transaction file in any combination, however, some of the combinations are illegal. For example, a record cannot be amended or deleted if it has not first been inserted into the master file. A record cannot be inserted more than once into the master file. Error situations arise when the record to be amended or deleted does not exist on the master file, or the record to be inserted already exists on the master file.

Such errors in the records of the transaction file cannot be detected before the transaction file is processed against the master file, and it is for this reason that the procedure to update the master file should contain a record validation routine.

If the transaction file is processed against the master file the following updated master file will be produced.

```
1245Joseph,S        14 Harcourt Cr. Bath          +014000
1246Hamilton,P      26 Avon Cr. Bath              +026000
1253Davies,J        4 Queen Mary Walk, Swindon    +050050
1277Trent,P         1 Vicarage Cr. Oxford         +100000
1278Vicars,M        28 Row Walk, Stratford        +001000
1287Billings,P      18 Knoll St. Watford          +018675
1300Jones,T         29 Park Rd. Witney            +001075
1346Tyrer           16 Hook St. Wallingford       +020940
1349Jones,P.T       49 Brook St. Abingdon         +005000
1357Evans,P.V       2 Church Rd. Didcot           +035070
1387Vaughan,L.S     8 Hilltop View, Oxford        +000000
1482Andrews,A       29 High Rd. Watford           +022475
1503Gaynor,M        2 Lux Lane, Didcot            +010070
1612Lord,V          77 River St. Abingdon         +015720
1632Mellor,N        14 Haymarket, Oxford          +094757
1643Spencer,S       184 Palace Road, Witney       +005000
```

The program used to produce these results also displayed upon the screen of the vdu, at run-time, the following error messages about the records in the transaction file.

ERROR - ATTEMPT TO INSERT A RECORD THAT EXISTS
13873Vaughan,L.S   8 Hilltop View, Oxford   +100050
ERROR - ATTEMPT TO AMEND/DELETE A NON-EXISTENT RECORD
13942

Notice also from the updated master file that the system does not check for a customer opening an account, purchasing goods and then closing the account without payment. Customer 1510 Smith,P opened an account, purchased goods worth £100.50, changed his address and made the payment in full for the goods, then closed the account. If the transaction of changing the address had not been accompanied by a payment the account would have been closed and the loss of payment gone without notice!

To prevent this from happening a simple modification can be made to the final program listed in this chapter. Whenever, there is a request to delete a record and the balance of the account is not zero, the request will be denied and the customer record containing the outstanding balance will then remain on file.

The algorithm to update the master file with a validation on the records of the transaction file is developed as follows.

The records on both the transaction and master files are in key sequence. In considering the data structures for both files it is necessary to consider the procedures associated with records that have a key match between the two files and those that do not have a key match between the two files.

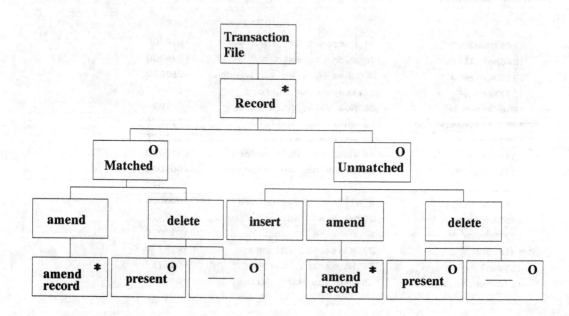

Notice in the unmatched case, a record must be inserted before it can be amended or deleted, hence the sequence insert, amend and delete.

In both the matched and unmatched cases, since the amended record can be repeated zero or more times, and the deletion is either present or absent, the combinations of insertion, amendment and deletion are all possible in this data structure.

The unmatched branch of this structure could be modified to cater for error conditions. If the record is not matched with a record in the master file, the file update must be an insertion, otherwise, an error exists in the transaction record key.

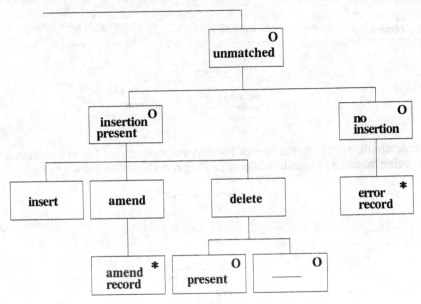

In this last structure diagram error record has been described as an iteration since more than one record might be at fault.

In a similar manner the matched branch, in the original structure diagram, can cater for errors when an attempt is made to insert a record into the master file when it already exists in the master file.

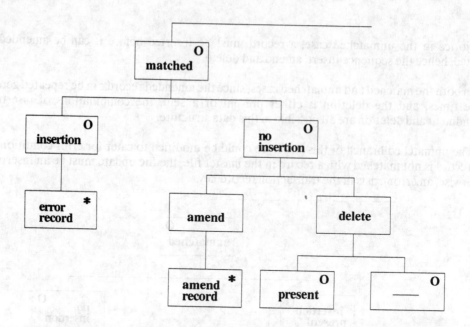

The structure diagrams for the master file and updated master file are expressed in terms of records being matched or unmatched between the transaction and master files.

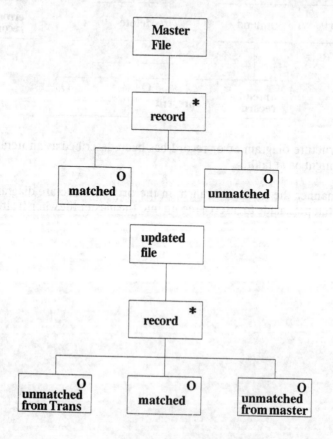

The basic program structure follows.

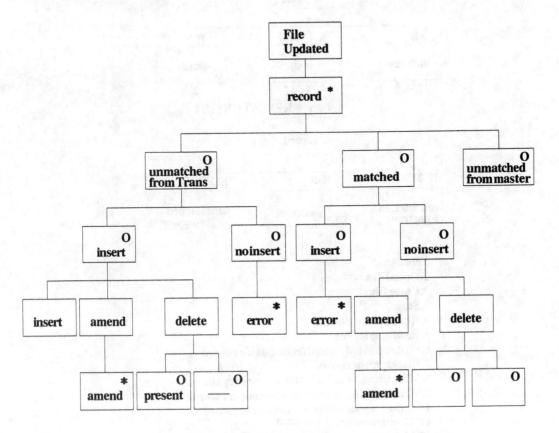

The detailed program structure follows over the next four pages.

From an examination of the detailed program structure, all the components of EG-seq and FG-seq are the same and, therefore, will be treated as a subroutine. The structures for E-sel and F-sel have been re-drawn, replacing the components for EG-seq and FG- seq by a single subroutine component SRA.

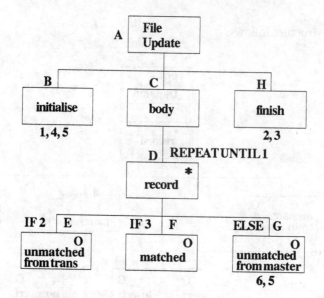

Functions.
1. Open files
2. Close files
3. Stop
4. Read transaction file
5. Read master file
6. Write updated record from master record
7. Display error record
8. Move transaction record to temporary store
9. Write updated record from temporary store
10. Move transaction key to temporary store
11. Move transaction name field to temporary store
12. Move transaction address field to temporary store
13. Increase amount in temporary store by transaction amount
14. Move master record to temporary store

Conditions.

1. End of Transaction file and End of master file
2. Transaction key < Master key
3. Transaction key = Master key
4. Transaction code = 1
5. Transaction code = 2
6. Transaction code = 3
7. Transaction key = value of key in temporary store
8. Transaction name field not blank
9. Transaction address field not blank

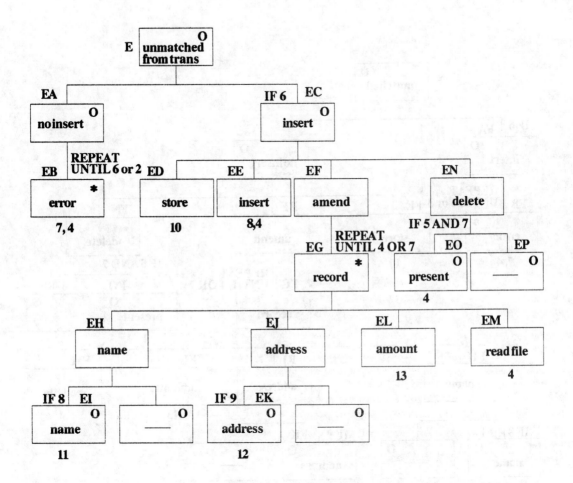

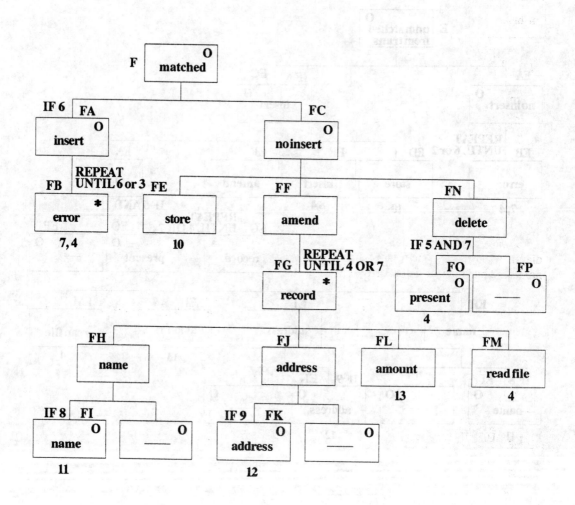

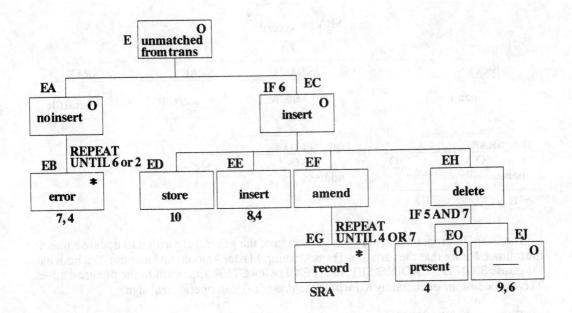

Beware of inadvertently using COBOL reserved words as component names. In this last diagram FD has not been used since it would have ultimately been coded into a paragraph name and produced a syntax error!

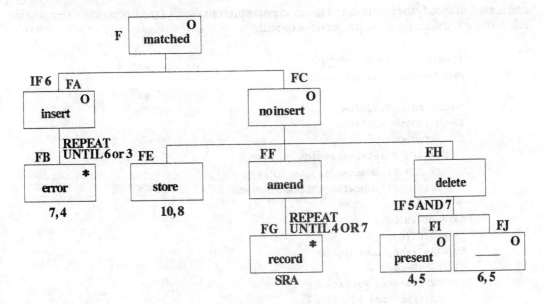

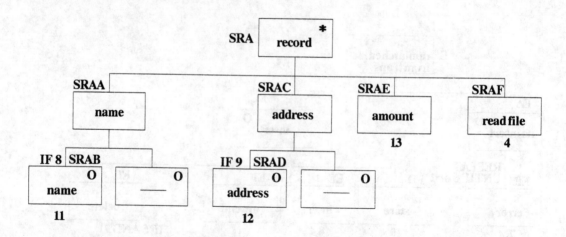

The COBOL program derived from the design of the general algorithm to update a master file follows. Notice that the variables TransAmount, MasterAmount and amount-WS have had the clause SIGN IS LEADING SEPARATE CHARACTER appended to the picture clauses. This has been done deliberately to include the presence of an operational sign.

The format of the SIGN clause is:

$$[\text{SIGN IS}] \quad \begin{Bmatrix} \textbf{LEADING} \\ \textbf{TRAILING} \end{Bmatrix} \quad [\textbf{SEPARATE } \text{CHARACTER}]$$

and is used to specify the position and the mode of representation of the operational sign when it is necessary to describe these properties explicitly.

```
IDENTIFICATION DIVISION.
PROGRAM-ID. FileUpdate-2.

ENVIRONMENT DIVISION.
INPUT-OUTPUT SECTION.
FILE-CONTROL.
    SELECT FileTrans ASSIGN TO PFMS.
    SELECT FileMaster ASSIGN TO PFMS.
    SELECT FileUpdated ASSIGN TO PFMS.

DATA DIVISION.
FILE SECTION.
FD FileTrans, COMPRESSED.
01 TransRecord.
    02 TransKey PIC X(4).
    02 TransCode PIC 9.
    02 TransName PIC X(20).
    02 TransAddress PIC X(30).
    02 TransAmount PIC S9(4)V99 SIGN LEADING SEPARATE CHARACTER.
```

```
FD FileMaster, COMPRESSED.
01 MasterRecord.
    02 MasterKey PIC X(4).
    02 MasterName PIC X(20).
    02 MasterAddress PIC X(30).
    02 MasterAmount PIC S9(4)V99 SIGN LEADING SEPARATE CHARACTER.
FD FileUpdated, COMPRESSED.
01 UpdatedRecord.
    02 FILLER PIC X(61).


WORKING-STORAGE SECTION.
01 Record-WS.
    02 key-WS PIC X(4).
    02 name-WS PIC X(20).
    02 address-WS PIC X(30).
    02 amount-WS PIC S9(4)V99 SIGN IS LEADING SEPARATE CHARACTER.
77 EOF-trans PIC A VALUE IS 'F'.
    88 EndOfFile-trans VALUE IS 'T'.
77 EOF-master PIC A VALUE IS 'F'.
    88 EndOfFile-master VALUE IS 'T'.
77 TempStore PIC 9(4).


PROCEDURE DIVISION.
A-seq.
    PERFORM B THROUGH H.


B.
    OPEN INPUT FileTrans, FileMaster, OUTPUT FileUpdated.
    PERFORM FUNCTION-4. PERFORM FUNCTION-5.
C-rep.
    PERFORM D-sel UNTIL EndOfFile-trans AND EndOfFile-master.
H.  CLOSE FileTrans, FileMaster, FileUpdated.
    STOP RUN.


D-sel.
    IF TransKey < MasterKey
        PERFORM E-sel
    ELSE
        IF TransKey = MasterKey
            PERFORM F-sel
        ELSE
            PERFORM G.


E-sel.
    IF TransCode NOT = 3
        PERFORM EA-rep
    ELSE
```

```
                    PERFORM EC-seq.


    EA-rep.
        PERFORM EB UNTIL TransCode = 3 OR TransKey NOT < MasterKey.
    EC-seq.
        PERFORM ED THROUGH EH-sel.


    EB.
        DISPLAY "ERROR-ATTEMPT TO AMEND/DELETE NON-EXISTENT RECORD".
        DISPLAY TransRecord.
        PERFORM FUNCTION-4.
    ED. MOVE TransKey TO TempStore.
    EE. MOVE TransKey TO key-WS.
        MOVE TransName TO name-WS.
        MOVE TransAddress TO address-WS.
        MOVE TransAmount TO amount-WS.
        PERFORM FUNCTION-4.
    EF-rep.
        PERFORM EG UNTIL TransCode NOT = 1 OR
                        TransKey NOT = TempStore.
    EH-sel.
        IF TransCode = 2 AND TransKey = TempStore
            PERFORM EI
        ELSE
            PERFORM EJ.


    EG. PERFORM SRA-seq.
    EI. PERFORM FUNCTION-4.
    EJ. WRITE UpdatedRecord FROM Record-WS.


    F-sel.
        IF TransCode = 3
            PERFORM FA-rep
        ELSE
            PERFORM FC-seq.


    FA-rep.
        PERFORM FB UNTIL TransCode NOT = 3 OR
                        TransKey NOT = MasterKey.
    FC-seq.
        PERFORM FE THROUGH FH-sel.


    FB. DISPLAY "ERROR-ATTEMPT TO INSERT A RECORD THAT EXISTS".
        DISPLAY TransRecord.
        PERFORM FUNCTION-4.
    FE. MOVE TransKey TO TempStore, key-WS.
        MOVE MasterName TO name-WS.
        MOVE MasterAddress TO address-WS.
```

```
                MOVE MasterAmount TO amount-WS.
        FF-rep.
            PERFORM FG UNTIL TransCode NOT = 1 OR
                              TransKey NOT = TempStore.
        FH-sel.
            IF TransCode = 2 AND TransKey = TempStore
                PERFORM FI
            ELSE
                PERFORM FJ.

        FG. PERFORM SRA-seq
        FI. PERFORM FUNCTION-4.
            PERFORM FUNCTION-5.
        FJ. WRITE UpdatedRecord FROM Record-WS.
            PERFORM FUNCTION-5.

        G.  WRITE UpdatedRecord FROM MasterRecord.
            PERFORM FUNCTION-5.


    * --------------------- subroutines ---------------------


        FUNCTION-4.
            READ FileTrans AT END MOVE 'T' TO EOF-trans,
                                    MOVE HIGH-VALUES TO TransKey.
        FUNCTION-5.
            READ FileMaster AT END MOVE 'T' TO EOF-master,
                                MOVE HIGH-VALUES TO MasterKey.


        SRA-seq.
            PERFORM SRAA-sel THROUGH SRAF.

        SRAA-sel.
            IF TransName NOT = ALL SPACES
                PERFORM SRAB.
        SRAC-sel.
            IF TransAddress NOT = ALL SPACES
                PERFORM SRAD.
        SRAE.
            ADD TransAmount TO amount-WS.
        SRAF.
            PERFORM FUNCTION-4.


        SRAB.
            MOVE TransName TO name-WS.
        SRAD.
            MOVE TransAddress TO address-WS.
```

10.4 Summary.

The contents of data files very rarely remain unchanged. The contents of data files must frequently be changed to reflect the changes in the information that they represent.

The updating of a data file will bring about the insertion of new records into a file, the amendment of existing records and the deletion of records that are no longer required.

Merging of records from two or more files is no more than the insertion of records into a file, where one file is regarded as the master file and the remaining files as transaction files.

In comparing key fields from different files, it is necessary to set the key field of each file, that has been read to the end of file, to a value higher than all the other keys. This is achieved by moving HIGH-VALUES to the key field of the file whose end has been reached. The purpose behind this practice is to force the remaining records from the remaining files to be written to the new, updated, master file.

Irrespective of whether the fields of a transaction file have been validated before being used to update a master file, the order in which records are presented for processing can still lead to errors.

Attempting to insert a record into a master file that already exits in the file is an error, and attempting to amend or delete a record from the master file that does not exist in the file is another error.

Such errors can only be detected at the time of updating the files.

> **Keywords**
>
> *Merge, two-way and multi-way;*
> *Transaction and Master files;*
> *File update, insert, amend and delete;*
> *Updating errors;*
> *HIGH-VALUES, SIGN.*

10.5 Questions.

[1]. Three files contain lists of English words, as keys in alphabetical sequence, and their meanings. Each word and meaning occupies one fixed-length record. Design and write a program to merge the three files into a fourth file and output the contents of the new file. Assume that the format of a record is:

    Word - 10 characters.
    Meaning - 70 characters.

2. In a simplified weekly wage system, factory employees are allocated one fixed-length record per employee, on a wages master file. The format of a record on this file is:

Employee number - 10 characters
Hourly rate of pay - 4 digits including 2 decimal places
Fixed allowance against pay - 5 digits including 2 decimal places
Total gross income to date - 7 digits including 2 decimal places
Total tax paid to date - 7 digits including 2 decimal places
Total pension contributions to date - 6 digits including 2 decimal places
Total National Insurance contributions to date - 6 digits including 2 decimal places

For every employee the pension contribution is 6% of the gross income. National Insurance is £10.50 and income tax is levied at 30% of taxable income.

Taxable income is calculated as the difference between gross income, pension contributions and fixed allowances.

A transaction file contains fixed-length records with the format.

Employee number - 10 characters
Hours worked in week (including overtime) - 3 digits

Design and write a program to process the transaction file against the employee master file and produce both an updated master file and pay-slips for each employee on the transaction file.

Assume that both files are sequential and ordered by employee number. The number of employees on the transaction file is less than those on the master file and only amendments to the master file are required (no deletions or insertions).

The format of a pay-slip is:

Employee Number: X342567SMI
Gross Wage: £307.69

                              Pension: £18.46
                              NatIns: £10.50
                              Tax: £77.77

Nett Wage: £200.96

[3]. A small college keeps on file a description of the use of all its rooms. The format of a record on the master file is:

Room number (key) - 2 digits
Description of use - 20 alphanumeric characters

The records on the master room file are stored in ascending key order. Over the period of a year the use each room is put to may change. The records on the master room file will, therefore, have to be updated. Such changes that exist will be:

Change of use of room (amendment to the description).

Room demolished (deletion).

New room built (insertion).

These changes are described in a transaction file, the format of which is:

Room number (key) - 2 digits.
Transaction code - 1 digit [1] amend, [2] delete, [3] insert.
Description of use - 20 alphanumeric characters   (this field is blank when a record is to be deleted).

The records on the transaction file are stored in ascending key order, and each record has a unique key.

Design with validation an algorithm to process the transaction file against the master file and produce an updated master file.

11

Tables

A table is a data structure that enables data to be stored in the main memory of the computer. By specifying a unique location within the structure it is possible to access the data in a direct manner without having to search through the data structure.

Within this chapter the methods of defining tables, storing and accessing data within tables is explained. The latter part of the chapter explores the methods available in COBOL for searching tables.

11.1 One-dimensional Tables.

The main memory of a computer is divided into many storage areas, each of which has a unique memory address. The size of a computer's memory is dependent upon the model of computer, and varies in size from hundreds of thousands, to millions of bytes or words. A computer word is normally a multiple number of bytes. A table uses part of the main memory to store data. The construction of a table is such, that the data is accessed by the position of the data in the table. The programmer is not aware of which part of the computer's memory is being used, since the mapping of this position into a memory address is a function of the computer system and is seldom of any concern to the programmer.

A one-dimensional table can be represented diagramatically as a linear set of storage areas. Each storage area is designated a position number or subscript, to enable the programmer to make reference to the position of the data in the table. Figure 11.1 depicts a one-dimensional area containing five storage areas. The subscript to each storage area is a positive integer, and represents the position in the table of each item of data.

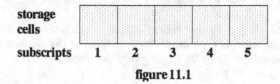

figure 11.1

If the table shown in figure 11.1 is to contain five integers in the range 1 to 99, and the table structure is given the name IntegerTable, then the declaration in the Data Division for the one-dimensional table would be:

```
01 IntegerTable.
   02 integer PIC 99 OCCURS 5 TIMES.
```

and the subscript would be defined as:

```
77 subscript-1 PIC 9.
```

From this example, it should be clear that the name of the one-dimensional table has been represented at level *01 IntegerTable*, and the individual items of data have been represented at level *02 integer*, together with a picture clause, *PIC 99*, describing the format of a single item of data. Since the one-dimensional table is to contain 5 items of data, the clause *OCCURS 5 TIMES* has been appended to the level 02 entry.

The function of the OCCURS clause is to eliminate the need for separate entries for repeated items of data. The general format of the OCCURS clause is:

```
OCCURS integer-1 TIMES
⎧ASCENDING ⎫ KEY IS {data-name-1} ...
⎩DESCENDING⎭
[INDEXED BY {index-name-1} ...].
```

Clearly the format used to define the one-dimensional table, in figure 11.1, does not contain the options. The relevance of these will be explained later in the chapter.

The OCCURS clause must not be specified in a data description entry that has a level number of 66, 77 or 88, and must not have a VALUE clause associated with it.

Tables can be defined in either the File Section or Working-Storage Section of the Data Division.

At the same time as defining the table it is also important to define the subscript(s) that are to be used in accessing the storage locations of the table. Subscripts are normally defined in the Working-Storage Section as unsigned whole numbers. The number of subscripts defined must be the same as the number of dimensions.

Data is input into a table in one of three ways.

(i)   Data being typed at a keyboard.
(ii)   Direct assignment using the VALUE and REDEFINES clauses.
(iii)   Reading records from a file.

The example that follows uses the first method. The other methods will be explained later in the chapter.

An alternative format of the PERFORM statement is extremely useful when dealing with tables. The format allows for the subscript to be initialised to any position in the table (normally FROM 1, the first position); incremented to another position in the table (normally BY 1, the next position) and tested to see if an end point in the table has been reached (normally UNTIL > size of the table). The syntax of the PERFORM statement is:

```
PERFORM   procedure-name-1 [THROUGH procedure-name-2]
VARYING   identifier-1
FROM      {identifier-2}
          {literal-1   }
BY        {identifier-3}
          {literal-2   }
UNTIL     condition-1
```

The Procedure Division code necessary to fill the table described in figure 11.1 with five non-zero positive integers input via a keyboard is:

```
BB-rep.
     PERFORM BC VARYING subscript-1 FROM 1 BY 1
     UNTIL subscript-1 > 5.
BC.
     DISPLAY "cell " subscript-1, SPACE WITH NO ADVANCING
     ACCEPT integer (subscript-1).
```

If the values 18, 07, 15, 08 and 13 are used as test data, input at the keyboard, then the following desk check can be made on the code.

Box	Condition subscript-1 > 5	subscript-1	integer (subscript-1)
BB	false	1	
BC		1	cell 1 18
BB	false	2	
BC		2	cell 2 07
BB	false	3	
BC		3	cell 3 15
BB	false	4	
BC		4	cell 4 08
BB	false	5	
BC		5	cell 5 13
BB	true	6	

The data is stored in each of the cells of the table as depicted in figure 11.2

storage cells	18	07	15	08	13
subscripts	1	2	3	4	5

figure 11.2

The contents of the table can be displayed on the screen of a visual display unit by using the PERFORM statement in a similar manner. The following code can be used to display the contents of the table shown in figure 11.2.

```
DB-rep.
        PERFORM DC VARYING subscript-1 FROM 1 BY 1
        UNTIL subscript-1 > 5.
DC.
        MOVE integer (subscript-1) TO integer-ED.
        DISPLAY integer-ED WITH NO ADVANCING.
```

Where *integer-ED* is defined as *77 integer-ED PIC ZZZ9,* and is deliberately used to suppress leading zeros and space the numbers out along one line. If this code is given a desk check the reader should notice how the contents of the table can be displayed.

Box	Condition subscript-1 > 5	subscript-1	integer (subscript-1)	integer-ED
DB	false	1		
DC		1	18	bb18
DB	false	2		
DC		2	07	bbb7
DB	false	3		
DC		3	15	bb15
DB	false	4		
DC		4	08	bbb8
DB	false	5		
DC		5	13	bb13
DB	true	6		

11.2 Selection Sort.

The only method of sorting records, that has been explained so far in the text, used the SORT statement. This was ideal for ordering records held in a file, but what if the records are stored in a table, can the SORT statement be used? The answer is no. An alternative method of ordering the contents of the table must be found. There are numerous methods for sorting data stored in tables. Only one method will be considered here. The method is known as the selection sort, it is simple to comprehend and reasonably efficient in execution time.

Figure 11.3 illustrates how the integers stored in the table IntegerTable, described in the last section, can be sorted into ascending order. In the first pass through the table the largest integer (18) is found and swapped with integer (13) from cell 5; in the second pass through the table the next largest integer (15) is found and swapped with integer (8) in cell 4; in the third pass through the table the next largest integer (13) is found and swapped with integer (8) in cell 3; and finally on the fourth pass through the table the next largest integer (8) is found and swapped with the integer (7) in cell 2.

A pass through the table means that the contents of consecutive cells are inspected and compared. Notice that the number of comparisons for the next largest key will diminish by one after each pass through the table, since the largest numbers will be at the right-hand end of the table. Notice also that only one swap of a pair of integers is made on each pass through the table.

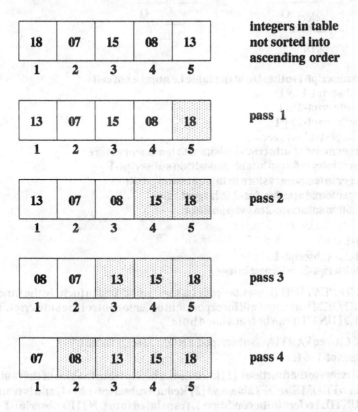

Figure 11.3

The algorithm to perform a selection sort can be represented by the following detailed program structure.

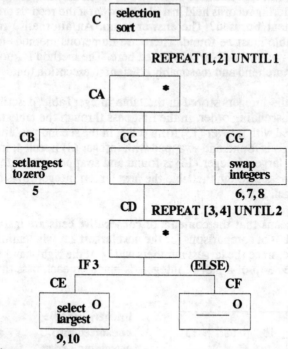

Functions.
1. Initialise subscript-1 to the size of the table i.e number of cells
2. Reduce subscript-1 by 1
3. Initialise subscript-2 to 1
4. Increase subscript-2 by 1
5. Initialise largest value to zero
6. Move integer found at subscript-1 position to temporary store
7. Move largest integer found to table at position subscript-1
8. Move integer in temporary store to table at swap position
9. Move integer found at subscript-2 to largest value
10. Move position subscript-2 to swap position.

Conditions.
1. subscript-1 < 1
2. subscript-2 > subscript-1
3. integer (subscript-2) > largest integer

NOTE. The REPEAT UNTIL pseudo-code has been modified to include the functions that the PERFORM statement will incorporate in order to control the subscript. Thus REPEAT [1, 2] UNTIL 1 can be translated into:

PERFORM CA-seq VARYING subscript-1 FROM SizeOfTable BY -1
UNTIL subscript-1 < 1.

Where [1, 2] refers to the functions [1] initialise subscript-1 to the size of the table, and is translated into FROM SizeOFTable, and [2] Reduce subscript-1 by -1, and is translated into BY -1. UNTIL 1 refers to the condition 1, translated into UNTIL subscript-1 < 1.

A similar translation exists for the pseudocode REPEAT [3, 4] UNTIL 2.

It is now possible to piece together the work of the last section and this section by devising a program to input and store in a one-dimensional table, five non-zero positive integers, sort the integers into ascending order using a Selection Sort, and display the contents of the sorted integers on the screen of a visual display unit.

The design for the solution to this problem falls into four areas B through E, depicted by the sequence shown below, where boxes B, C (already given) and D will be expanded into further structure diagrams.

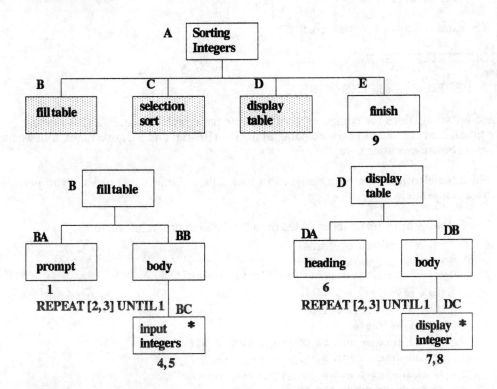

Functions.

1. Display prompt to input five integers
2. Initialise subscript-1 to 1
3. Increase subscript-1 by 1
4. Display cell number
5. Input integer and store in cell
6. Display heading 'contents of table sorted into ascending order'
7. Edit integer
8. Display integer from respective cell
9. Stop

Condition.

1. subscript-1 > 5

The coding of the Procedure Division from the structure diagram must be modified very slightly to:

PROCEDURE DIVISION.
A-seq.
      PERFORM B-seq.
      PERFORM C-rep.
      PERFORM D-seq.
      PERFORM E.

The usual coding of a sequence as:

PROCEDURE DIVISION.
A-seq.
      PERFORM B-seq THROUGH E.

would be wrong, since the computer would execute paragraphs B-seq, BA, (BB-rep and BC) five times, then continue to execute paragraphs BA, (BB-rep and BC) five times, followed by BC again before executing C-rep!

Since the algorithm has been designed in four separate stages it is necessary to perform each stage separately.

The following program has been coded from the detailed program structures.

```
IDENTIFICATION DIVISION.
PROGRAM-ID. SelectionSort.

DATA DIVISION.
WORKING-STORAGE SECTION.
01 IntegerTable.
    02 integer PIC 99 OCCURS 5 TIMES.
77 subscript-1 PIC 9.
77 subscript-2 PIC 9.
77 TemporaryStore PIC 99.
77 SwapPosition PIC 9.
77 integer-ED PIC ZZZ9.
77 largest PIC 99.

PROCEDURE DIVISION.
A-seq.
    PERFORM B-seq.
    PERFORM C-rep.
    PERFORM D-seq.
    PERFORM E.

B-seq.
    PERFORM BA THROUGH BB-rep.
```

```
BA.
    DISPLAY "input five non-zero positive integers".
    DISPLAY SPACE.
BB-rep.
    PERFORM BC VARYING subscript-1 FROM 1 BY 1
    UNTIL subscript-1 > 5.


BC.
    DISPLAY "cell " subscript-1, SPACE WITH NO ADVANCING
    ACCEPT integer (subscript-1).


* --------------- Selection Sort Routine --------------


C-rep.
    PERFORM CA-seq VARYING subscript-1 FROM 5 BY -1
    UNTIL subscript-1 < 1.


CA-seq.
    PERFORM CB THROUGH CG.


CB.
    MOVE ZERO TO largest.
CC-rep.
    PERFORM CD-sel VARYING subscript-2 FROM 1 BY 1
    UNTIL subscript-2 > subscript-1.
CG.
    MOVE integer (subscript-1) TO TemporaryStore.
    MOVE largest TO integer (subscript-1).
    MOVE TemporaryStore TO integer (SwapPosition).


CD-sel.
    IF integer (subscript-2) > largest
        PERFORM CE.


CE.
    MOVE integer (subscript-2) TO largest.
    MOVE subscript-2 TO SwapPosition.

* -------------- End Of Selection Sort Routine ---------


D-seq.
    PERFORM DA THROUGH DB-rep.


DA.
    DISPLAY "contents of table sorted into ascending order"
    DISPLAY SPACE
```

```
DB-rep.
    PERFORM DC VARYING subscript-1 FROM 1 BY 1
    UNTIL subscript-1 > 5.

DC.
    MOVE integer (subscript-1) TO integer-ED.
    DISPLAY integer-ED WITH NO ADVANCING.

E.  DISPLAY SPACE.
    STOP RUN.
```

The results from running this program follow.

```
input five non-zero positive integers

cell    1 18
cell    2 07
cell    3 15
cell    4 08
cell    5 13
contents of table sorted into ascending order

   7   8  13  15  18
```

The size of the table used in this last example was defined during the coding of the program. COBOL, however, does permit the use of variable length tables by using an alternative form of OCCURS clause. This is a useful feature when the number of entries in a table is known to vary and the programmer does not want to invoke the overhead of using memory space to store an empty part of the table.

For example, the contents of a table might vary between 5 and 50 entries, depending upon the amount of data that needs to be stored. In the previous example if the number of integers to be stored and sorted was only known at run-time then the declaration of the table is modified to:

```
01 IntegerTable.
    02 integer PIC 99 OCCURS 5 TO 50 TIMES DEPENDING ON SizeOfTable.
77 SizeOfTable PIC 99.
```

Where a value for the SizeOfTable, between 5 and 50, would be input during the execution of the program.

The last program has been modified to cater for the variable length table. Notice from the listing that the size of *subscript-1* and *subscript-2* has been changed to *PIC 99*, and that all references to the previous size of the table as the numeric literal 5 have been replaced by the variable *SizeOfTable*. A value for the variable *SizeOfTable* is input through the statements.

BA.
  DISPLAY "input size of table " WITH NO ADVANCING.
  ACCEPT SizeOfTable.

```
IDENTIFICATION DIVISION.
PROGRAM-ID. SelectionSort.

DATA DIVISION.
WORKING-STORAGE SECTION.
01 IntegerTable.
    02 integer PIC 99 OCCURS 5 TO 50 TIMES
    DEPENDING ON SizeOfTable.

77 SizeOfTable PIC 99.
77 subscript-1 PIC 99.
77 subscript-2 PIC 99.
77 TemporaryStore PIC 99.
77 SwapPosition PIC 99.
77 integer-ED PIC ZZZ9.
77 largest PIC 99.

PROCEDURE DIVISION.
A-seq.
    PERFORM B-seq.
    PERFORM C-rep.
    PERFORM D-seq.
    PERFORM E.

B-seq.
    PERFORM BA THROUGH BB-rep.

BA.
    DISPLAY "input the size of the table " WITH NO ADVANCING
    ACCEPT SizeOfTable.
    DISPLAY "input " SizeOfTable " non-zero positive integers"
    DISPLAY SPACE.
BB-rep.
    PERFORM BC VARYING subscript-1 FROM 1 BY 1
    UNTIL subscript-1 > SizeOfTable.
```

```
     BC.
         DISPLAY "cell " subscript-1, SPACE WITH NO ADVANCING
         ACCEPT integer (subscript-1).


* --------------- Selection Sort Routine --------------


   C-rep.
       PERFORM CA-seq VARYING subscript-1 FROM SizeOfTable BY -1
       UNTIL subscript-1 < 1.


   CA-seq.
       PERFORM CB THROUGH CG.


   CB.
       MOVE ZERO TO largest.
   CC-rep.
       PERFORM CD-sel VARYING subscript-2 FROM 1 BY 1
       UNTIL subscript-2 > subscript-1.
   CG.
       MOVE integer (subscript-1) TO TemporaryStore.
       MOVE largest TO integer (subscript-1).
       MOVE TemporaryStore TO integer (SwapPosition).


   CD-sel.
       IF integer (subscript-2) > largest
           PERFORM CE.


   CE.
       MOVE integer (subscript-2) TO largest.
       MOVE subscript-2 TO SwapPosition.


* --------------- End Of Selection Sort Routine ---------


   D-seq.
       PERFORM DA THROUGH DB-rep.


   DA.
       DISPLAY "contents of table sorted into ascending order"
       DISPLAY SPACE


   DB-rep.
       PERFORM DC VARYING subscript-1 FROM 1 BY 1
       UNTIL subscript-1 > SizeOfTable.
```

```
DC.
        MOVE integer (subscript-1) TO integer-ED.
        DISPLAY integer-ED WITH NO ADVANCING.

    E.  DISPLAY SPACE.
        STOP RUN.
```

The results from this program being run are:

```
input the size of the table 15
input      15 non-zero positive integers

cell     1 56
cell     2 62
cell     3 21
cell     4 03
cell     5 89
cell     6 99
cell     7 45
cell     8 31
cell     9 99
cell    10 05
cell    11 07
cell    12 44
cell    13 33
cell    14 22
cell    15 11
contents of table sorted into ascending order

    3   5   7  11  21  22  31  33  44  45  56  62  89  99  99
```

Before leaving the topic of one-dimensional tables it is worth exploring the second method of filling the table with data. This method uses the VALUE and REDEFINES clause, and will also be used in the next section.

Returning to the first program, it is possible to define the five integers, in a concatenated string using a value clause, for example.

```
01 IntegerString PIC X(10) VALUE IS "1807150813".
01 IntegerTable REDEFINES IntegerString.
   02 integer PIC 99 OCCURS 5 TIMES.
```

An area of memory, IntegerString, contains the alphanumeric literal "1807150813". However, this data can be viewed by the programmer in a different way by using the REDEFINES clause. The constant IntegerString can be regarded as consisting of five, two digit integers, contained within the one-dimensional table IntegerTable.

IntegerTable 18 | 07 | 15 | 08 | 13

The original alphanumeric literal has not been destroyed. The REDEFINES clause allows a programmer to view an area of memory using a different classification for the data. Thus the function of the REDEFINES clause is to allow the same computer storage area (main memory) to be described by different data description entries.

The general format for this clause is:

level number $\begin{Bmatrix} \text{data-name-1} \\ \text{FILLER} \end{Bmatrix}$ **REDEFINES** data-name-2

The REDEFINES clause, when specified, must immediately follow the subject of the entry. The level-numbers of data-name-2 and the subject of the entry must be identical, and must not be level 66 or level 88. This clause must not be used in level 01 entries in the File Section. The data description entry for data-name-2 cannot contain an OCCURS clause. The entries giving the new description of the character positions must not contain any value clauses, except in condition-name entries.

11.3 Two-dimensional Tables.

A two-dimensional table should be thought of as a number of one-dimensional tables, with each one-dimensional table being given a subscript value. A two-dimensional table is illustrated in figure 11.4.

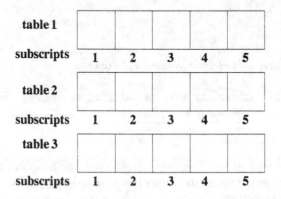

Figure 11.4 Two-dimensional table

This type of structure can be thought of as a matrix, in which the one-dimensional tables form rows, and the respective cells between the different one-dimensional tables, form columns. Access to a particular cell in a two-dimensional table is first by row subscript, and then by column subscript.

The Data Division coding used to describe this two-dimensional table, assuming the table is to store 2-digit integers, is:

```
01 IntegerMatrix.
    02 IntegerTable OCCURS 3 TIMES.
        03 integer PIC 99 OCCURS 5 TIMES.
77 RowSubscript PIC 9.
77 ColumnSubscript PIC 9.
```

The last method described for filling a one-dimensional table with numbers is also applicable to tables of higher dimensions.

The two-dimensional table described can be filled with integers using the following code.

```
01 IntegerNumbers.
    02 FILLER PIC X(10) VALUE IS "1807150813".
    02 FILLER PIC X(10) VALUE IS "1011030226".
    02 FILLER PIC X(10) VALUE IS "5601679245".
01 IntegerMatrix REDEFINES IntegerNumbers.
    02 IntegerTable OCCURS 3 TIMES.
        03 integer PIC 99 OCCURS 5 TIMES.
```

The data name IntegerNumbers still contains a string of numbers as: "180715081310110302265601679245", yet the data name IntegerMatrix refers to the numbers stored as shown in figure 11.5.

row 1	18	07	15	08	13
column	1	2	3	4	5

row 2	10	11	03	02	26
column	1	2	3	4	5

row 3	56	01	67	92	45
column	1	2	3	4	5

Figure 11.5 Two-dimensional table filled with integers

Where access to any number is through the name of the field, in this case *integer*, and a row subscript followed by a column subscript.

For example integer $(1, 3) = 15$; integer $(2, 5) = 26$; integer $(3, 2) = 01$, etc.

The PERFORM statement can be extended to cater for more than one subscript by appending the following option to the previously defined format.

```
[AFTER  identifier-4
FROM  ⌠identifier-5⌡
       ⌡literal-3  ⌠
BY     ⌠identifier-6⌡
       ⌡literal-4  ⌠
UNTIL  condition-2]...
```

The integers from the two dimensional table can be output using the PERFORM statement as follows.

A-rep.
```
PERFORM B    VARYING RowSubscript FROM 1 BY 1
             UNTIL RowSubscript > 3
             AFTER ColumnSubscript FROM 1 BY 1
             UNTIL ColumnSubscript > 5.
B.    DISPLAY integer (RowSubscript, ColumnSubscript).
```

A desk check of this code indicates how the values of the subscripts are controlled by the PERFORM statement. In the desk check RowSubscript > 3 is represented as condition 1, and ColumnSubscript > 5 is represented by condition 2.

Box	Condition	RowSubscript	ColumnSubscript	integer
A	1, 2 false	1	1	
B				18
A	1, 2 false	1	2	
B				07
A	1, 2 false	1	3	
B				15
A	1, 2 false	1	4	
B				08
A	1, 2 false	1	5	
B				13
A	2 true	1	6	
A	1, 2 false	2	1	
B				10
A	1, 2 false	2	2	
B				11
A	1, 2 false	2	3	
B				03
A	1, 2 false	2	4	
B				02
A	1, 2 false	2	5	
B				26
A	2 true	2	6	
A	1, 2 false	3	1	
B				56
A	1, 2 false	3	2	
B				01
A	1, 2 false	3	3	

Box	Condition	RowSubscript	ColumnSubscript	integer
B				67
A	1, 2 false	3	4	
B				92
A	1, 2 false	3	5	
B				45
A	1, 2 true	4	6	

Notice from this desk check that the last subscript, ColumnSubscript, to be described in the PERFORM statement is always incremented first until such time that the condition on this subscript becomes true. The first subscript, RowSubscript, described in the PERFORM statement is then incremented, and the last subscript is re-initialised. This pattern continues until the condition on the first subscript becomes true.

Tables are not confined to storing numbers they can also be used to store strings of alphanumeric characters. A two- dimensional table called PopularCars contains six ten-character strings as illustrated in figure 11.6.

Fordbbbbbb	Roverbbbbb	Vauxhallbb
Renaultbbb	Volkswagen	Fiatbbbbbb

figure 11.6

To initialise this table with these values in the Working- Storage Section would require the following coding.

```
01 CarManufacturer.
   02 FILLER PIC X(30) VALUE IS "FordbbbbbbRoverbbbbbVauxhallbb".
   02 FILLER PIC X(30) VALUE IS "RenaultbbbVolkswagenFiatbbbbbb".
01 PopularCars REDEFINES CarManufacturer.
   02 BritishForeign OCCURS 2 TIMES.
      03 manufacturer PIC X(10) OCCURS 3 TIMES.
77 RowSubscript PIC 9.
77 ColumnSubscript PIC 9.
```

An alternative coding for CarManufacturer is:

```
01 CarManufacturer PIC X(60) VALUE is "FordbbbbbbRoverbbbbbVauxhallbb
"RenaultbbbVolkswagenFiatbbbbbb".
```

Notice the use of the hyphen in column 7 to indicate the continuation of an alphanumeric string from the previous line. The area of memory CarManufacturer contains the alphanumeric string

"FordbbbbbbRoverbbbbbVauxhallbbRenaultbbbVolkswagenFiatbbbbbb"

This data string can be split up into two components using the statement 02 BritishForeign OCCURS 2 TIMES giving the one-dimensional table shown in figure 11.7.

1	FordbbbbbbRoverbbbbb Vauxhallbb
2	Renaultbbb Volkswagen Fiatbbbbbb

figure 11.7

Each of the one-dimensional tables that has been formed is split up into three components using the statement: 03 manufacturer PIC X(10) OCCURS 3 TIMES.

1	Fordbbbbbb	Roverbbbbb	Vauxhallbb
2	Renaultbbb	Volkswagen	Fiatbbbbbb
	1	2	3

figure 11.8

Access to any component in the table will be through the name of the component manufacturer and a row subscript followed by a column subscript. Therefore, manufacturer (1, 2) = Roverbbbbb; manufacturer (2, 1) = Renaultbbb; manufacturer (2 3) = Fiatbbbbbb, etc

11.4 Worked Example.
A sporting league is divided into four divisions, and within each division there are eight teams with each team being named after its home town.

Division 1	Division 2	Division 3	Division 4
Southampton	Portsmouth	Basingstoke	Newbury
Winchester	Reading	Banbury	Witney
Oxford	Bicester	Gloucester	Cheltenham
Thame	Swindon	Cirencester	Salisbury
Poole	Bournemouth	Dorchester	Aylesbury
Bristol	Bath	Exeter	Torquay
St. Albans	Colchester	Chelmsford	Ipswich
Cambridge	Birmingham	Coventry	Leicester

Design and implement a COBOL program to store the names of the teams in a two-dimensional table.

Code a menu-driven Procedure Division to interrogate the table and display the following information.

Input a division number and output a list of the teams in that division.

Input a division number and team position, taking the top team as position 1, second down as position 2, etc, and output the name of the team.

Input a team position and output all the teams in the same position in the four divisions.

The detailed program structure for this solution follows.

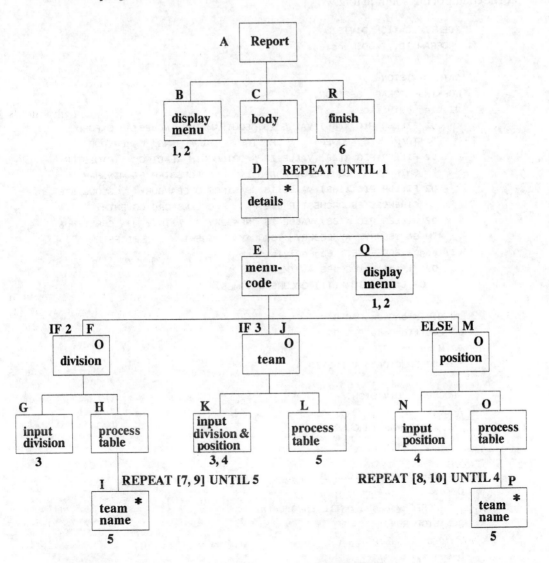

Functions.
1. Display menu
2. Input menu-code
3. Input division code
4. Input position code
5. Display team from table
6. Stop
7. Initialise position code to 1
8. Initialise division code to 1
9. Increase position code by 1
10. Increase division code by 1

Conditions.
1. Menu-code = 4
2. Menu-code = 1
3. Menu-code = 2
4. Division > 4
5. Position > 8

The coding of this solution follows.

```
IDENTIFICATION DIVISION.
PROGRAM-ID. TwoDimensions.

DATA DIVISION.
WORKING-STORAGE SECTION.
01 LeagueDivisions.
    02 FILLER PIC X(88) VALUE IS "SOUTHAMPTONWINCHESTER OXFORD
-   "  THAME     POOLE      BRISTOL    ST.ALBANS  CAMBRIDGE  ".
    02 FILLER PIC X(88) VALUE IS "PORTSMOUTH READING    BICESTER
-   "  SWINDON    BOURNEMOUTHBATH      COLCHESTER BIRMINGHAM ".
    02 FILLER PIC X(88) VALUE IS "BASINGSTOKEBANBURY    GLOUCESTE
-   "R CIRENCESTERDORCHESTER EXETER     CHELMSFORD COVENTRY   ".
    02 FILLER PIC X(88) VALUE IS "NEWBURY    WITNEY     CHELTENHA
-   "M SALISBURY AYLESBURY  TORQUAY    IPSWICH    LEICESTER  ".
 01 league REDEFINES LeagueDivisions.
    02 divisions OCCURS 4 TIMES.
       03 teams PIC X(11) OCCURS 8 TIMES.


 77 DivisionCode PIC 9.
 77 PositionCode PIC 9.
 77 MenuCode PIC 9.
    88 EndOfData VALUE IS 4.

 PROCEDURE DIVISION.
 A-seq.
    PERFORM B THROUGH R.

 B.
    PERFORM FUNCTIONS-1-2.
 C-rep.
    PERFORM D-seq UNTIL EndOfData.
 R.   STOP RUN.

 D-seq.
    PERFORM E-sel THROUGH Q.

 E-sel.
    IF MenuCode = 1
       PERFORM F-seq
    ELSE
       IF MenuCode = 2
          PERFORM J-seq
       ELSE
          PERFORM M-seq.
 Q.   PERFORM FUNCTIONS-1-2.
```

```
F-seq.
    PERFORM G THROUGH H-rep.
J-seq.
    PERFORM K THROUGH L.
M-seq.
    PERFORM N THROUGH O-rep.


G.        DISPLAY "Enter Division Number " WITH NO ADVANCING.
          ACCEPT DivisionCode
H-rep.
          PERFORM I VARYING PositionCode FROM 1 BY 1
                  UNTIL PositionCode > 8.


I.        DISPLAY teams (DivisionCode, PositionCode)


K.        DISPLAY "Enter Division Number " WITH NO ADVANCING.
          ACCEPT DivisionCode.
          DISPLAY "Enter Position Number " WITH NO ADVANCING.
          ACCEPT PositionCode.

L.        DISPLAY teams (DivisionCode, PositionCode).


N.        DISPLAY "Enter Position Number " WITH NO ADVANCING.
          ACCEPT PositionCode.

O-rep.
          PERFORM P VARYING DivisionCode FROM 1 BY 1
                  UNTIL DivisionCode > 4.


P.        DISPLAY teams (DivisionCode, PositionCode).



* --------------------- subroutine ---------------------


FUNCTIONS-1-2.
        DISPLAY SPACE
        DISPLAY "Do you require".
        DISPLAY SPACE
        DISPLAY "1 teams in specified division".
        DISPLAY "2 team in a specified division and position".
        DISPLAY "3 teams in a specified position".
        DISPLAY "4 EXIT FROM SYSTEM".
        DISPLAY SPACE
        DISPLAY "Enter code " WITH NO ADVANCING.
        ACCEPT MenuCode.
        DISPLAY SPACE.
```

The results from the execution of the program follow.

```
Do you require

1 teams in specified division
2 team in a specified division and position
3 teams in a specified position
4 EXIT FROM SYSTEM

Enter code 1

Enter Division Number 3
BASINGSTOKE
BANBURY
GLOUCESTER
CIRENCESTER
DORCHESTER
EXETER
CHELMSFORD
COVENTRY

Do you require

1 teams in specified division
2 team in a specified division and position
3 teams in a specified position
4 EXIT FROM SYSTEM

Enter code 2

Enter Division Number 2
Enter Position Number 5
BOURNEMOUTH

Do you require

1 teams in specified division
2 team in a specified division and position
3 teams in a specified position
4 EXIT FROM SYSTEM

Enter code 3

Enter Position Number 8
CAMBRIDGE
BIRMINGHAM
COVENTRY
LEICESTER
```

```
Do you require

1 teams in specified division
2 team in a specified division and position
3 teams in a specified position
4 EXIT FROM SYSTEM

Enter code 4
```

11.5 Three-dimensional Tables.

A three-dimensional table should be though of as a number of two-dimensional tables, with each two-dimensional table given a subscript value. A three-dimensional table is illustrated in figure 11.9.

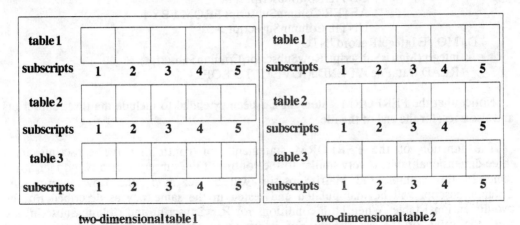

two-dimensional table 1   two-dimensional table 2

Figure 11.9 Three-dimensional table

Access to a specific location in the three-dimensional table is by the two-dimensional table subscript, and within the respective two-dimensional table by row and column subscripts.

If the three dimensional table illustrated in figure 11.9 is used to store two-digit integers, then the table would be declared as:

```
01 ThreeDTable.
    02 IntegerMatrix OCCURS 2 TIMES.
        03 IntegerTable OCCURS 3 TIMES.
            04 integer PIC 99 OCCURS 5 TIMES.
77 MatrixSubscript PIC 9.
77 RowSubscript PIC 9.
77 ColumnSubscript PIC 9.
```

The third method of filling a table, by reading records from a file and storing them in a table, could be used to fill the three-dimensional table with integers. However, it must be said that the first two methods for filling a table are equally as applicable to three-dimensional tables, as one or two dimensional tables.

The following code fills the three-dimensional table with integers stored on a sequential file.

```
A-seq.
    PERFORM B THROUGH C-rep.
B.
    OPEN INPUT DataFile.
    READ DataFile AT END MOVE 'T' TO EOF.
C-rep.
    PERFORM D   VARYING MatrixSubscript FROM 1 BY 1
                UNTIL EndOfFile OR MatrixSubscript > 2
                AFTER RowSubscript FROM 1 BY 1
                UNTIL RowSubscript > 3
                AFTER ColumnSubscript FROM 1 BY 1
                UNTIL ColumnSubscript > 5.
D.  MOVE IntegerRecord INTO
    integer (MatrixSubscript, RowSubscript, ColumnSubscript).
    READ DataFile AT END MOVE 'T' TO EOF.
```

Notice that the PERFORM statement has been extended to include the three subscripts and also a test for the end of the file.

The function of the PERFORM statement, for controlling the subscripts in a three-dimensional table, is very similar to the control of the subscripts in a two-dimensional table. In this example the MatrixSubscript will be set at 1, and RowSubscript and ColumnSubscript will be manipulated and tested in the same way as described for the two-dimensional table. When both conditions for RowSubscript and ColumnSubscript are true, the value of the MatrixSubscript is increased by 1, and the RowSubscript and ColumnSubscript are both re-initialised to 1. This pattern continues until all three conditions on the three subscripts are true.

11.6 Worked Example.
A national union of workers is divided into four regions. Within each region there are two branches. In a national ballot to elect a union president every worker is allowed to vote for one of the four candidates. The votes for the candidates are to be read from a sequential file and stored by region and by branch in a three- dimensional table.

The names of the four candidates are Bloggs, Davies, Jones and Smith, and are stored in a separate one-dimensional table, which is accessed on candidate number as subscript.

Design and write a COBOL program to execute the following procedures.

Fill a three-dimensional table, from a sequential file, with the votes for every candidate, sorted on region as primary key, branch as secondary key and name of candidate as tertiary key.

Process and output the following information.

The total number of votes cast for all candidates.

The total number of votes cast for each candidate in each region.

The percentage number of votes cast for each candidate.

The winner of the election.

Where a result applies to an individual candidate, the name of the candidate should be printed and not the candidate's number.

The three-dimensional table required to store the votes is illustrated in figure 11.10.

Region 1

Branch 1	86	91	82	70
Branch 2	101	67	92	35
Candidate	1	2	3	4

Region 2

Branch 1	40	70	53	18
Branch 2	21	52	34	21
Candidate	1	2	3	4

Region 3

Branch 1	53	37	48	36
Branch 2	86	97	84	98
Candidate	1	2	3	4

Region 4

Branch 1	84	31	66	23
Branch 2	98	21	49	36
Candidate	1	2	3	4

Figure 11.10 A three-dimensional table used to store votes

The detailed program structures follow on the next page.

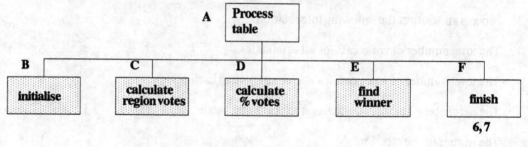

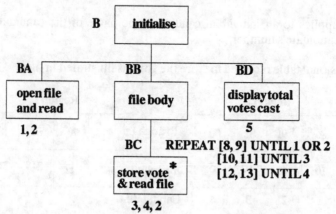

REPEAT [8, 9] UNTIL 1 OR 2
[10, 11] UNTIL 3
[12, 13] UNTIL 4

Functions.	Conditions.
1. Open file	1. End of file
2. Read file	2. Region > 4
3. Move candidate vote to table	3. Branch > 2
4. Increase total votes cast by candidate vote	4. Candidate > 4
5. Display total number of votes cast	
6. Close file	
7. Stop	
8. Initialise region to 1	
9. Increase region by 1	
10. Initialise branch to 1	
11. Increase branch by 1	
12. Initialise candidate to 1	
13. Increase candidate by 1	

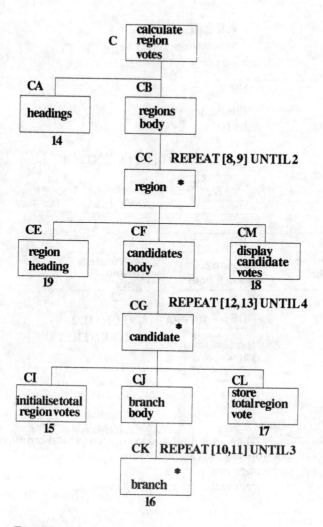

Functions.
14. Display headings
15. Move zero to total regional votes
16. Add candidate vote to total regional vote
17. Store total regional vote in candidate vote table
18. Display candidates regional votes
19. Move region to regional votes output line

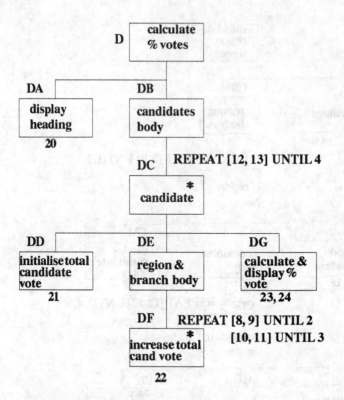

Functions.
20. Display headings
21. Move candidate name for output and move zero to total candidate total
22. Add candidate vote to total candidate vote
23. Calculate percentage vote
24. Display name of candidate and percentage vote

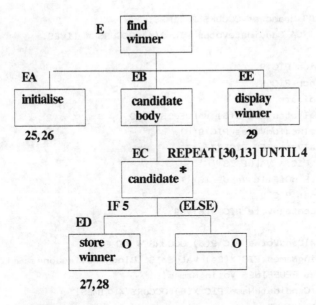

Functions.
25. Initialise winning votes to first candidates's votes
26. Initialise winner to first candidate
27. Move candidate's votes to winning votes
28. Move candidate to winner
29. Display winning candidate with number of votes
30. Initialise candidate to 2.

Condition.
5. Next candidate's votes > votes of winner

The COBOL program derived from the detailed program structures follows.

```
IDENTIFICATION DIVISION.
PROGRAM-ID. UnionVote.

ENVIRONMENT DIVISION.
INPUT-OUTPUT SECTION.
FILE-CONTROL.
    SELECT VotingFile ASSIGN TO PFMS.

DATA DIVISION.
FILE SECTION.
FD VotingFile, COMPRESSED.
01 Record-1.
    02 vote PIC 9(4).

WORKING-STORAGE SECTION.
01 VotingTable.
    02 regions OCCURS 4 TIMES.
```

```
      03 branches OCCURS 2 TIMES.
         04 CandidateVotes PIC 9(4) OCCURS 4 TIMES.


77 region PIC 9.
77 branch PIC 9.
77 candidate PIC 9.
77 TotalVotes PIC 9(6) VALUE IS ZERO.
77 TotalRegionVotes PIC 9(6).
77 TotalVotes-ED PIC ZZZ,ZZ9.
77 EOF PIC A VALUE IS 'F'.
   88 EndOfFile VALUE IS 'T'.
77 winner PIC 9.
77 PercentageVote PIC 9(6)V99.


01 TotalCandVotes PIC 9(6) OCCURS 4 TIMES.
01 VotingNames PIC X(24) VALUE IS "BloggsDaviesJones Smith ".
01 names REDEFINES VotingNames.
   02 CandidateName PIC X(6) OCCURS 4 TIMES.
01 Record-1-WS.
   02 FILLER PIC X(17) VALUE IS "Candidates".
   02 Candidate-1 PIC X(15).
   02 Candidate-2 PIC X(15).
   02 Candidate-3 PIC X(15).
   02 Candidate-4 PIC X(15).


01 Record-2-WS.
   02 FILLER PIC X(7) VALUE IS "Regions".
01 Record-3-WS.
   02 Region-WS PIC 9.
   02 FILLER PIC X(14) VALUE IS SPACES.
   02 VotesCast OCCURS 4 TIMES.
      03 Vote-ED PIC ZZZ,ZZ9.
      03 FILLER PIC X(8) VALUE IS SPACES.
01 Record-4-WS.
   02 FILLER PIC X(23) VALUE IS "Candidate  % Total Vote".
01 Record-5-WS.
   02 Candidate-WS PIC X(13).
   02 Vote-WS PIC Z9.


PROCEDURE DIVISION.
A-seq.
    PERFORM B-seq.
    PERFORM C-seq.
    PERFORM D-seq.
    PERFORM E-seq.
    PERFORM F.
```

```
  B-seq.
      PERFORM BA THROUGH BD.

  BA.
      OPEN INPUT VotingFile.
      READ VotingFile AT END MOVE 'T' TO EOF.
  BB-rep.
      PERFORM BC VARYING region FROM 1 BY 1
                 UNTIL EndOfFile OR region > 4
                 AFTER branch FROM 1 BY 1 UNTIL branch > 2
                 AFTER candidate FROM 1 BY 1 UNTIL candidate > 4.
  BD.
      MOVE TotalVotes TO TotalVotes-ED.
      DISPLAY "Total number of votes cast for all candidates ",
      TotalVotes-ED.


  BC.
      MOVE vote TO CandidateVotes (region, branch, candidate)
      ADD CandidateVotes (region, branch, candidate) TO TotalVotes.
      READ VotingFile AT END MOVE 'T' TO EOF.



  C-seq.
      PERFORM CA THROUGH CB-rep.
  CA.
      MOVE CandidateName (1) TO Candidate-1.
      MOVE CandidateName (2) TO Candidate-2.
      MOVE CandidateName (3) TO Candidate-3.
      MOVE CandidateName (4) TO Candidate-4.
      DISPLAY SPACE.
      DISPLAY Record-1-WS.
      DISPLAY Record-2-WS.
  CB-rep.
      PERFORM CC-seq VARYING region
                  FROM 1 BY 1 UNTIL region > 4.


  CC-seq.
      PERFORM CE THROUGH CM.


  CE.
      MOVE region TO Region-WS.
  CF-rep.
      PERFORM CG-seq VARYING candidate FROM 1 BY 1
                  UNTIL candidate > 4.
  CM.
      DISPLAY Record-3-WS.
```

```
CG-seq.
    PERFORM CI THROUGH CL.


CI.
    MOVE ZERO TO TotalRegionVotes.
CJ-rep.
    PERFORM CK VARYING branch
              FROM 1 BY 1 UNTIL branch > 2.
CL.
    MOVE TotalRegionVotes TO Vote-ED (candidate).


CK.
    ADD CandidateVotes (region, branch, candidate)
    TO TotalRegionVotes.


D-seq.
    PERFORM DA THROUGH DB-rep.

DA.
    DISPLAY SPACE.
    DISPLAY Record-4-WS.
DB-rep.
    PERFORM DC-seq VARYING candidate
                FROM 1 BY 1 UNTIL candidate > 4.


DC-seq.
    PERFORM DD THROUGH DG.

DD.
    MOVE CandidateName (candidate) TO Candidate-WS.
    MOVE ZERO TO TotalCandVotes (candidate).
DE-rep.
    PERFORM DF VARYING region
               FROM 1 BY 1 UNTIL region > 4
               AFTER branch
               FROM 1 BY 1 UNTIL branch > 2.


DG.
    DIVIDE TotalVotes INTO TotalCandVotes (candidate)
    GIVING PercentageVote ROUNDED.
    MULTIPLY 100 BY PercentageVote GIVING Vote-WS.
    DISPLAY Record-5-WS.


DF.
    ADD CandidateVotes (region, branch, candidate)
    TO TotalCandVotes (candidate).
```

```
E-seq.
    PERFORM EA THROUGH EE.

EA.
    MOVE TotalCandVotes (1) TO TotalVotes.
    MOVE 1 TO winner.
EB-rep.
    PERFORM EC-sel VARYING candidate
                   FROM 2 BY 1 UNTIL candidate > 4.
EE.
    MOVE TotalVotes TO TotalVotes-ED.
    DISPLAY SPACE.
    DISPLAY "Elected President of Union is Mr. "
    CandidateName (winner) " with " TotalVotes-ED " votes".

EC-sel.
    IF TotalCandVotes (candidate) > TotalVotes
        PERFORM ED.

ED.
    MOVE TotalCandVotes (candidate) TO TotalVotes.
    MOVE candidate TO winner.

F.
    CLOSE VotingFile.
    STOP RUN.
```

The contents of the voting file and the results from this program being run follows.

0086	0021	0084
0091	0052	0031
0082	0034	0066
0070	0021	0023
0101	0053	0098
0067	0037	0021
0092	0048	0049
0035	0036	0036
0040	0086	
0070	0097	
0053	0084	
0018	0098	

```
Total number of votes cast for all candidates    1,880
```

Candidates Regions	Bloggs	Davies	Jones	Smith
1	187	158	174	105
2	61	122	87	39
3	139	134	132	134
4	182	52	115	59

Candidate	% Total Vote
Bloggs	30
Davies	25
Jones	27
Smith	18

```
Elected President of Union is Mr. Bloggs with     569 votes
```

11.7 Indices.

An index serves the same purpose as a subscript. However, there are advantages of using indices compared with subscripts.

The name of the index is defined within the declaration of a table.

A picture clause is not required when defining an index since an index is stored within a fixed number of bytes or words in the memory of a computer.

The use of indices, in declaring a table, will permit the SEARCH and SEARCH ALL statements to be used.

An index is defined by using an option of the OCCURS clause. One format of the OCCURS clause that is used to describe an index is:

OCCURS integer-1 TIMES **INDEXED** BY index-name-1

The examples of table declarations given in earlier sections can be re-stated to include indices and not separate subscripts.

The one-dimensional table for storing two-digit integers would be declared as:

```
01 IntegerTable.
   02 integer PIC 99 OCCURS 5 TIMES INDEXED BY column.
```

Access to the data in this table would be through integer (column).

The two-dimensional table would be declared as:

```
01 IntegerMatrix.
   02 IntegerTable OCCURS 3 TIMES INDEXED BY row.
      03 integer PIC 99 OCCURS 5 TIMES INDEXED BY column.
```

Access to data in the table would be through integer (row, column).

Finally the three dimensional table would be declared as:

    01 ThreeDTable.
        02 IntegerMatrix OCCURS 2 TIMES INDEXED BY matrix.
            03 IntegerTable OCCURS 3 TIMES INDEXED BY row.
                04 integer PIC 99 OCCURS 5 TIMES INDEXED BY column.

Access to the table would be through integer (matrix, row, column).

There is a minor limitation in the use of indices, in so far as arithmetic can only be performed on an index by using PERFORM, SEARCH, SEARCH ALL and SET statements. If the reader refers to the format of PERFORM in Appendix II, the inclusion of the index names in format 4 shows how the statement can be used to manipulate indices.

The SET statement has two formats.

$$\text{SET} \begin{Bmatrix} \text{index-name-1} \dots \\ \text{identifier-1} \end{Bmatrix} \text{TO} \begin{Bmatrix} \text{index-name-2} \\ \text{identifier-2} \\ \text{integer-1} \end{Bmatrix}$$

which is equivalent to the MOVE statement in respect of initialising either an index name or an identifier, and

$$\text{SET} \{\text{index-name-3}\} \dots \begin{Bmatrix} \text{UP BY} \\ \text{DOWN BY} \end{Bmatrix} \begin{Bmatrix} \text{identifier-3} \\ \text{integer-2} \end{Bmatrix}$$

which is equivalent to the ADD and SUBTRACT statements in respect of modifying a subscript.

For example the index *Index-1* can be initialised to the value 1 by using the statement *SET Index-1 TO 1*, or initialised to the value of *Index-2* by using *SET Index-1 TO Index-2*, or initialised to the value of the identifier *counter* by using *SET Index-1 TO counter*.

The index *Index-1* can be increased by the value of 1 by using the statement *SET Index-1 UP BY 1*, or increased by the identifier *StepValue* (assuming StepValue > 0) by using *SET Index-1 UP BY StepValue*.

In a similar manner *Index-1* may be decreased by using *SET Index-1 DOWN BY 1* or *SET Index-1 DOWN BY StepValue*.

An index can be increased or decreased by a fixed amount by appending a positive or negative integer to the index name (the same technique also applies to subscripts). For example:

    SET column TO 5.
    ADD IntegerTable (column + 3) TO TotalValue.
    IF IntegerTable (column) > IntegerTable (column + 1) PERFORM KJ.

11.8 Searching.

In processing a table it is often necessary to search a table until a particular item of data can be found. COBOL provides a facility for searching tables.

The SEARCH statement provides a method of performing a serial search through a table when the keys to the items within the table are not sorted. Whereas the SEARCH ALL statement performs a binary search through a table provided the keys to the items within the table are sorted into either ascending or descending order. The general formats for the SEARCH and SEARCH ALL statements are found in Appendix II.

Imagine that a one-dimensional table contains the costs for the replacement of major components of a bicycle.

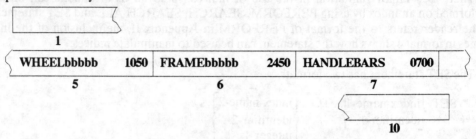

If the table contains ten records, with each record containing two fields, then the data can be accessed through the index PositionIndex, and the table declared as:

```
01 BicycleComponents.
    02 parts OCCURS 10 TIMES INDEXED BY PositionIndex.
        03 component PIC X(10).
        03 cost PIC 99V99.
```

If a description of a bicycle component, DescriptionComp, is input to a computer system, the table can be searched using component as a key, and when a match is found the cost of the component can be output.

To search the BicycleComponents table the following statements would be necessary.

```
SET PositionIndex TO 1.
SEARCH parts VARYING PositionIndex
AT END DISPLAY "component not found"
WHEN DescriptionComp = component (PositionIndex)
MOVE cost (PositionIndex) TO cost-ED,
DISPLAY "cost of component ", cost-ED.
```

Notice that it is the responsibility of the programmer to initialise the index to the first storage location in the table. After this initialisation the SEARCH statement automatically increases the value of the index by 1, so that each location in turn can be can be examined and tested. If a key match is not made then the end of table will have been reached and the programmer should provide a notification of this. In this example the message *component not found* is displayed.

When a key match is made the programmer must state what action is to be taken. In this example the cost of the bicycle component is displayed.

A one-dimensional table contains the first four characters of a post code as a key, and the name of the postal district as the remainder of the entry. There are 984 entries in the table, and the keys are sorted into ascending order. A selection of typical entries might appear as:

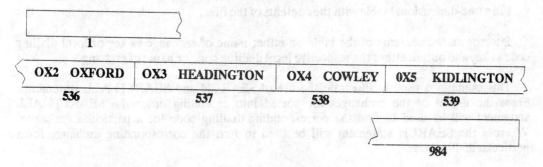

OX2 OXFORD	OX3 HEADINGTON	OX4 COWLEY	OX5 KIDLINGTON
536	537	538	539

984

If each entry in the table can be located by the index PositionIndex, then the table can be declared by the following statements.

```
01 PostCodeTable.
    02 districts OCCURS 984 TIMES INDEXED BY PositionIndex
                        ASCENDING KEY IS PostCode.
        03 PostCode PIC X(4).
        03 PostalDistrict PIC X(15).
```

If the SEARCH ALL statement is to be used then it is necessary to state in the declaration the name of the key and the mode in which the keys are sorted.

When the first four characters of the post code, PostalCode are input to the computer, the table is searched, using a binary search algorithm, with PostCode as key. If a match is found between PostCode and PostalCode then the name of the PostalDistrict can be output. If no match is found then the message post code not listed is displayed.

To search the PostCodeTable the following statements are used.

```
SEARCH ALL districts
AT END DISPLAY "post code not listed"
WHEN PostalCode = PostCode (PositionIndex)
DISPLAY "name of district is ", PostalDistrict (PositionIndex).
```

When a binary search begins, the system locates the mid-point of the table and checks to see if the required entry is in the upper or lower half of the table. The system then locates the mid-point of the appropriate half in the sub-table, and checks to see if the required entry is in the upper half or lower half of the new sub-table. The process of dividing the sub-table into half is repeated until a match for the key is found or no match is possible.

11.9 Worked Example.

A sequential file contains the names of telephone exchanges in a particular area of Oxfordshire and their respective local dialling codes. The format of a record on the file is name of exchange (key) 25 alphanumeric characters; local dialling code 7 alphanumeric characters and the file is sorted into ascending key sequence. If the file contains 25 entries, write a COBOL program to execute the following procedures.

Fill a one-dimensional table with the contents of the file.

Interrogate the contents of the table on either name of exchange as key or local dialling code as key and output either the respective local dialling code or name of exchange.

This example is used to illustrate the use of SEARCH and SEARCH ALL statements. Since the names of the exchanges are sorted into ascending order the SEARCH ALL statement will be used to find the corresponding dialling code for a particular exchange. Whereas the SEARCH statement will be used to find the corresponding exchange for a particular dialling code.

The detailed program structures follow.

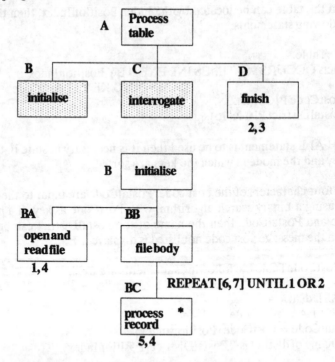

Functions.	Conditions.
1. Open file	1. End of file
2. Close file	2. index > 25
3. Stop	
4. Read file	
5. Move record to table	
6. Initialise index to 1	
7. Increase index by 1	

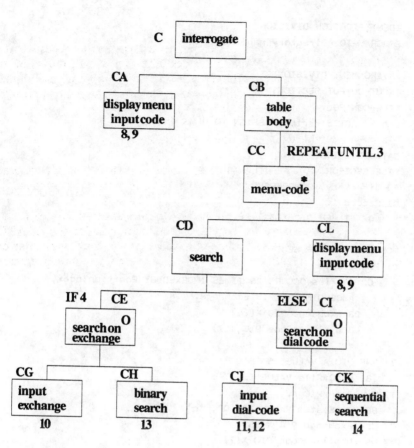

Functions.
8. Display menu
9. Input menu-code
10. Input name of exchange
11. Input dialling code
12. Set index to 1
13. Perform binary search and display result
14. Perform sequential serach and display result

Conditions
3. Menu-code = 'Q' or 'q'
4. Menu-code = 'D' or 'd'

The program derived from the detailed program structure follows on the next page.

```
       IDENTIFICATION DIVISION.
       PROGRAM-ID. DirectoryEnquiries.

       ENVIRONMENT DIVISION.
       INPUT-OUTPUT SECTION.
       FILE-CONTROL.
           SELECT directory ASSIGN TO PFMS.

       DATA DIVISION.
       FILE SECTION.
       FD directory, COMPRESSED.
       01 Record-1.
           02 FILLER PIC X(32).

       WORKING-STORAGE SECTION.
       01 PhoneTable.
           02 entries OCCURS 25 TIMES INDEXED BY PositionIndex,
               ASCENDING KEY IS exchange.
               03 exchange PIC X(25).
               03 DiallingCode PIC X(7).

       77 EOF PIC A VALUE IS 'F'.
           88 EndOfFile VALUE IS 'T'.
       77 MenuCode PIC A.
           88 QuitSystem VALUE IS 'Q', 'q'.
       77 UserExchange PIC X(25).
       77 UserDiallingCode PIC X(7).

       PROCEDURE DIVISION.
       A-seq.
           PERFORM B-seq.
           PERFORM C-seq.
           PERFORM D.

       B-seq.
           PERFORM BA THROUGH BB-rep.

       BA.
           OPEN INPUT directory.
           READ directory AT END MOVE 'T' TO EOF.
       BB-rep.
           PERFORM BC VARYING PositionIndex FROM 1 BY 1
                       UNTIL EndOfFile OR PositionIndex > 25.

       BC.
           MOVE Record-1 TO entries (PositionIndex).
           READ directory AT END MOVE 'T' TO EOF.
```

```
C-seq.
    PERFORM CA THROUGH CB-rep.


CA.
    PERFORM FUNCTIONS-8-9.
CB-rep.
    PERFORM CC-seq UNTIL QuitSystem.


CC-seq.
    PERFORM CD-sel THROUGH CL.


CD-sel.
    IF MenuCode = 'D' OR 'd'
        PERFORM CE-seq
    ELSE
        PERFORM CI-seq.
CL.
    PERFORM FUNCTIONS-8-9.


CE-seq.
    PERFORM CG THROUGH CH.
CI-seq.
    PERFORM CJ THROUGH CK.


CG.
    DISPLAY "input exchange name " WITH NO ADVANCING.
    ACCEPT UserExchange.
CH.
    SEARCH ALL entries
    AT END DISPLAY "EXCHANGE NOT LISTED"
    WHEN UserExchange = exchange (PositionIndex)
    DISPLAY "local dialling code is "
    DiallingCode (PositionIndex).
CJ.
    DISPLAY "input dialling code " WITH NO ADVANCING.
    ACCEPT UserDiallingCode.
    SET PositionIndex TO 1.
CK.
    SEARCH entries VARYING PositionIndex
    AT END DISPLAY "DIALLING CODE NOT LISTED"
    WHEN UserDiallingCode = DiallingCode (PositionIndex)
    DISPLAY "name of exchange is " exchange (PositionIndex).


D.  CLOSE directory.
    STOP RUN.
```

```
*  ----------------------- subroutine -----------------------

    FUNCTIONS-8-9.
        DISPLAY "Do you require"
        DISPLAY SPACE
        DISPLAY "[D]ialling code"
        DISPLAY "[E]xchange name"
        DISPLAY "[Q]uit from system ?".
        DISPLAY SPACE.
        ACCEPT MenuCode.
```

The contents of the directory file and the results from running the program follow.

```
Abingdon                92
Asthall Leigh           9787
Bampton Castle          97
Bicester                91
Buckland                036 787
Charlton-on-Otmoor      833
Checkendon              0491
Clanfield               036 781
Faringdon               0367
Filkins                 036 786
Goring-on-Thames        0491
Kidlington              85
Long Crendon            94
Middleton Stoney        9189
Princes Risborough      944
Southrop                036 785
Stanford-in-the-Vale    036 77
Steeple Aston           91
Stonesfield             9789
Stratton Audley         917
Tetsworth               9428
Turville Heath          049 163
Uffington               036 782
Upper Heyford           9182
Watlington              049 161
```

```
Do you require

[D]ialling code
[E]xchange name
[Q]uit from system ?


D
input exchange name Goring-on-Thames
local dialling code is 0491
Do you require

[D]ialling code
[E]xchange name
[Q]uit from system ?


d
input exchange name Charlton-on-Otmoor
local dialling code is 833
Do you require

[D]ialling code
[E]xchange name
[Q]uit from system ?


D
input exchange name Woodstock
EXCHANGE NOT LISTED
Do you require

[D]ialling code
[E]xchange name
[Q]uit from system ?


E
input dialling code 036 786
name of exchange is Filkins
Do you require

[D]ialling code
[E]xchange name
[Q]uit from system ?


E
input dialling code 97
name of exchange is Bampton Castle
Do you require
```

```
[D]ialling code
[E]xchange name
[Q]uit from system ?


e
input dialling code 999
DIALLING CODE NOT LISTED
Do you require

[D]ialling code
[E]xchange name
[Q]uit from system ?


Q
```

11.10 Summary

Tables are lists of data items in the same format.

Tables are defined in the Data Division using the OCCURS clause.

The PERFORM statement can be used to control the subscripts or indices to a table and any conditions associated with the subscripts or indices.

Access to an item of data in a table is through the name of the datum followed by the position of the datum in the table. The position is indicated by the value of a subscript(s). There are normally the same number of subscripts present as there are dimensions in a table.

A table can be loaded by either inputting data at the keyboard, initialising the table in the Working-Storage Section using VALUE and REDEFINES clauses or reading data from a sequential file.

In COBOL-85 tables can have up to seven dimensions.

An item in a table can be searched for either sequentially using a SEARCH statement, or if the keys of the table are ordered, by a binary search using SEARCH ALL.

Keywords

Table, subscript, OCCURS;
PERFORM VARYING..AFTER..
Selection sort;
Dimensions of a table;
REDEFINES;
Indices, SET, SEARCH, SEARCH ALL;

11.11 Questions.
1. Use the descriptions of the OCCURS and REDEFINES clauses to identify the errors in the following lines of code.

(a)   01 item PIC X(10) OCCURS 50 TIMES.

(b)   01 Table-1.
           02 DataValue PIC 99 OCCURS 6 TIMES VALUE IS 30.

(c)   01 Table-2.
           02 DataX PIC X(20) OCCURS 6 TIMES.
              03 DataY PIC X(20) OCCURS 10 TIMES.

(d)   77 DataValue PIC X(20) OCCURS 5 TIMES.

(e)   FILE SECTION.
        01 Record-1.
        01 Record-2 REDEFINES record-1.

(f)   WORKING-STORAGE SECTION.
        01 alpha.
           02 beta REDEFINES alpha.

(g)   01 Record-1-WS.
           02 alpha PIC X(6).
           02 beta PIC X(6).
        01 Record-2-WS.
           02 delta REDEFINES alpha.
              03 gamma PIC X OCCURS 12 TIMES.

2. Code WORKING-STORAGE SECTION entries to define the following tables.

   (a) A one-dimensional table containing 50 entries, each entry represents a three-digit integer *alpha*.

   (b) A two-dimensional table containing 10 rows and 3 columns, each entry represents a real number *beta* having 7 digits, including 2 decimal places.

   (c) A two-dimensional table containing 10 rows and 50 columns, each entry represents a 20 character string *gamma* followed by a three-digit code *delta*.

   (d) A three-dimensional table represents 5 two-dimensional tables, each two-dimensional table represents 10 one-dimensional tables, each one-dimensional table has 8 entries and each entry represents a 3 digit integer *epsilon*.

3. A selection of towns in three counties in the South of England have the following populations.

county	town	population
Cornwall	Penzance	19210
	Truro	18557
	Newquay	15209
Dorset	Poole	124974
	Dorchester	14225
	Shaftesbury	4951
Hampshire	Southampton	214802
	Basingstoke	73492
	Winchester	35664

Write segments of code to initialise the following tables.

(a) A one-dimensional table containing the names of the counties.

(b) A two-dimensional table containing the names of the towns, where each row represents a different county, in the order given in the first table.

(c) A second two-dimensional table containing the population of each town, where each row represents a different county and each column a different town, in the order given in the first two- dimensional table.

4. Using the tables defined in the last question write a procedure to input the name of a county and the name of a town, and perform a serial search on the one-dimensional table to match the county and obtain a row subscript, then perform a serial search on the first two-dimensional table, to match the town, and obtain a column subscript. Using the row and column subscripts, access the second two-dimensional table and display the value for the population of the chosen town.

Write a second procedure to input the name of a county and output the total population for the towns listed in the county. Re- express this figure as a percentage of the population of all the towns defined in the table.

5. The surnames of friends and their respective telephone numbers are stored in a one-dimensional table.

JONES 0296-41573	COLLINS 128-273	SMYTHE 01-111-9147

The following code is used to define the table and search the table for a telephone number given a surname. The coding, however, contains 12 deliberate errors. Identify the errors then re-write the code correctly.

```
WORKING-STORAGE SECTION.
01 TeleTable.
   02 RECORD OCCURS 50 TIMES INDEXED BY I.
      ASCENDING-KEY IS name (I).
      03 name PIC X(12).
         04 TeleNumber PIC 9(12).
77 I PIC 99.

PROCEDURE DIVISION.
   MOVE 1 TO I.
   ACCEPT InputName (I).
   SEARCH ALL TeleTable CHANGING name
   WHEN InputName (I) = name (I)
   DISPLAY TeleNumber (I).
```

[6]. Using the file, directory, from the worked example in section 11.9 write a program to input the name of an exchange, search the one-dimensional table containing records from the directory and output the exchange number if a match is found. DO NOT USE THE SEARCH or SEARCH ALL statements.

Since the contents of the table is ordered on name of exchange pay particular attention to what happens when:

Search key is less than the key being compared in the table.

Search key is greater than the key being compared in the table.

Search key is equal to the key being compared in the table.

[7]. Each team in the sporting league, described in 11.4, plays a weekly home or away match with another member of the same division, and is awarded points on the following basis.

	HOME	AWAY
WIN	2	3
DRAW	1	2
LOSE	0	1

A sequential file, ordered on primary key division number and secondary key, points awarded to date in the season, contains records with the following format.

Division number - 1 digit
Team name - 11 characters
Points - 3 digits.

A second sequential file ordered on the primary key Division number only, contains details of current fixtures and the results of those matches played. The format of records on this file is:

Division number - 1 digit
Team name (home) - 11 characters
Score (home team) - 2 digits
Team name (away) - 11 characters
Score (away team) - 2 digits.

Write a COBOL program to execute the following procedures.

Fill a two-dimensional table with the contents of the first sequential file.

Use the second sequential file to update the table with the latest results, thus increasing the points awarded to date, for all the teams in the league who have played matches.

Using the updated table sort each division on the number of points awarded to each team, and output the position of each team in each league. Hint: Use the selection sort given in the text. Produce a report according to the following design.

DIVISION 1		DIVISION 2		DIVISION 3		DIVISION 4	
TEAM	POINTS	TEAM	POINTS	TEAM	POINTS	TEAM	POINTS
POOLE	58	BATH	67	BANBURY	45	WITNEY	54
OXFORD	56	COLCHESTER	63	EXETER	44	IPSWICH	50
.	.	.	.	.	.	.	.
.	.	.	.	.	.	.	.

Write a separate procedure to overwrite the contents of the original sequential file, with the contents of the sorted updated table.

[8]. A secondhand car dealer uses a computer file to store descriptions of his stock of cars. Each car is allocated a fixed- length record with the following format.

Manufacturer - 2 characters (coded)
Model - 3 characters (coded)
Year of registration - 2 digits
Current mileage - 6 digits
Number of doors - 1 digit
Type - 1 character (coded)
Engine size - 4 digits
Colour of paintwork - 2 characters (coded)
Registration number - 7 characters
Engine number - 12 characters
Chassis number - 12 characters
Sale price - 5 digits.

The organisation of the file is sequential, records being ordered on manufacturer code as primary key, model code as secondary key, and type of car code as tertiary key.

The car dealer requires a comprehensive report on his stock. The report must not contain the codes used for manufacturer, model, type and colour of paintwork, but be replaced by a full description for each of the codes.

The descriptions for each of the codes are stored in four, one- dimensional tables, for example.

BL BRITISH LEYLAND	CH CHRYSLER	DA DATSUN	FO FORD UK

ALL ALLEGRO	CAP CAPRI	GRA GRANADA

E ESTATE	H HATCHBACK	S SALOON

BE BEIGE	BL BLUE	BR BROWN

Invent suitable data for the four, one-dimensional tables and the sequential file.

Design the layout of a comprehensive report.

Design and write a complete COBOL program to read the sequential file, translate all the coded fields into full descriptions and output the information found in every record to the report.

12
Random Access Files

The organisation of files, discussed so far in the text, have been sequential. If a record was required from such a file, it was necessary to search the file comparing keys until either a match was found or the end of file was reached.

Random access files provide a facility for locating a particular record without the need for searching through part of a file. The term random implies processing in no particular order. There are two commonly used methods for organising files for random access - Indexed Sequential and Relative file organisations. Both methods will be discussed in this chapter, together with worked examples showing how the files can be used.

12.1 Indexed Sequential Files.

Files organised in this manner are stored on magnetic disc to allow for random access, as well as sequential access, to records on the file. The file organisation uses three areas on the disc for data storage. An index area, a main record storage area and a record overflow area. The index to the file contains a list of sorted record keys. Not every key to a record is stored in the index, but only those necessary to reference a physical record. Associated with each key in the index is an address that corresponds to a position on the surface of the disc where the record belonging to that key is stored. A record may contain a primary key and possibly, alternative secondary keys. Therefore, by specifying either the primary key or a secondary key it is possible to access a record directly from the disc.

Records stored in the main storage area are not necessarily in sequential order, however, this is dependent upon the system being used, and does not change the sequential access to the file, since it the index that is organised in a sequential manner. Records in the main and overflow storage areas can be amended, deleted and inserted into the file without having to create a separate updated master file. However, as a matter of security, it is recommended to create a separate sequential file that logs all the changes to the master file.

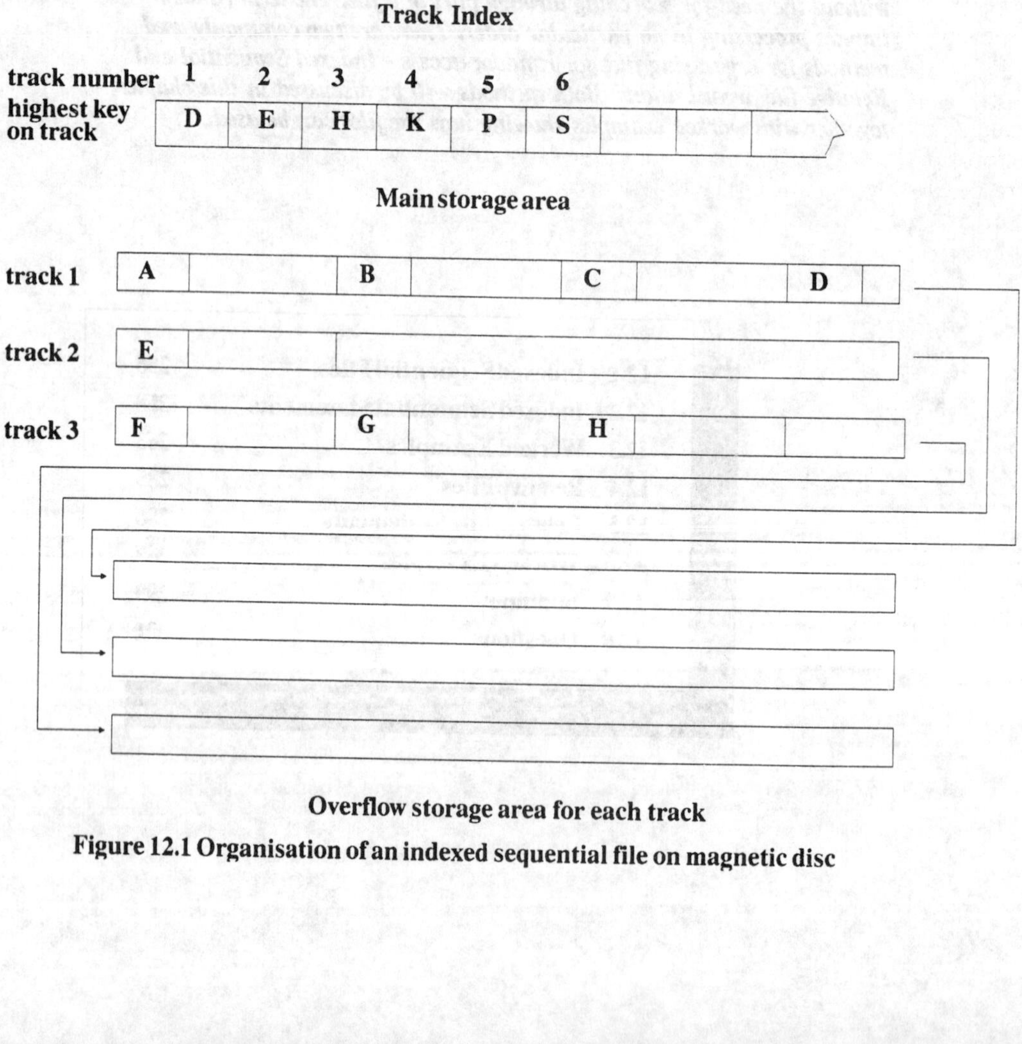

Track Index

track number	1	2	3	4	5	6			
highest key on track	D	E	H	K	P	S			

Main storage area

track 1	A		B		C		D	

track 2	E	

track 3	F		G		H	

Overflow storage area for each track

Figure 12.1 Organisation of an indexed sequential file on magnetic disc

The highest key found on each track of the disc is stored in the track index. If a record has a key of G, the index is searched until either a match for G is found, or G is less than the next highest key in the index. In the example shown in figure 12.1, the next highest key is H, which has a track number of 3. Track 3 is read into an input buffer (temporary storage area) and the record keys are searched until a match for the key G can be found. The record having key G has then been accessed.

Each track can have an overflow storage area, so that when a track becomes full the overflowed records can be written to the appropriate overflow track. The system must also change the value for the highest key for that track in the index, since an insertion of records into a track will result in the original highest key value changing.

When records are deleted from an indexed sequential file, gaps appear between records in the file and storage space becomes wasted. However, if records are inserted into the file there will eventually be no more room in the main storage area and records are then stored in an overflow area. After a considerable number of changes to the file the main storage area may contain an unacceptable amount of wasted space and the utilisation of the overflow area becomes too great. This imbalance in the storage of records is of little concern to the COBOL programmer since the computer systems provide utility programs to condense indexed sequential files, closing the gaps in the main file and emptying the overflow area.

Figure 12.2 illustrates a conceptual format for storing the names of friends and their addresses on an indexed sequential file. The primary index is the name of the friend and is stored in sequential order in an index file. The primary key and address that forms a complete record is stored on disc in a record file area. Notice that the contents of the record file area is not ordered on the primary key. Information held in the index file points to the correct location on the surface of the disc where the name and address of the respective friends are stored.

Record File

Index File	Primary Key	Contents of other fields
Adams	Moon	14 Finch Close, Basildon, Essex
Bateman	Davy	108 West Way, Bournemouth, Dorset
Collins	Nichols	93 Balfour Road, Anfield, Liverpool
Davy	Adams	33 Courtlands Road, Poole, Dorset
Edwards	Quayle	26 Stowford Road, Winchester, hants
Holbrook	Edwards	16 Kennedy Close, Abingdon, Oxon
Jenkins	Jenkins	31 New Road, Southend-on-Sea, Essex
Moon	Bateman	42 High Street, Brighton, Sussex
Nichols	Peters	4 Little Clarendon Street, York
Peters	Stevens	5 Victoria Cross St, Southport
Quayle	Collins	92 The Broadway, Stratford-upon-Avon
Stevens	Holbrook	74 The Avenue, Woodstock, Oxon

Figure 12.2 Indexed Record File and File of Indices

12.2 Indexed Sequential Statements.

File Control

The general format for FILE CONTROL in the ENVIRONMENT DIVISION is:

        SELECT file-name ASSIGN TO device-name
        ORGANIZATION IS INDEXED
        [ACCESS MODE IS ⎡SEQUENTIAL⎤]
                         ⎨RANDOM   ⎬
                         ⎣DYNAMIC   ⎦
        RECORD KEY IS data-name-1
        [ALTERNATE RECORD KEY IS data-name-2 [WITH DUPLICATES]] ...
        [FILE STATUS IS data-name-3]

The SELECT clause specifies the name of the indexed sequential file in the COBOL program and assigns the file to a hardware device (e.g. PFMS for the PRIME disc system).

The ORGANIZATION clause, note the spelling, specifies that the file-name in the SELECT clause contains data organised by indices.

The ACCESS clause specifies how an indexed file is written or retrieved.

If the ACCESS mode is not specified, then the default mode is taken to be sequential. The sequential mode specifies that records will be written or retrieved sequentially. When a WRITE statement is used the record must be submitted in ascending sequence by RECORD KEY value. A READ statement retrieves a record sequentially.

When the random mode is specified a record will be written or retrieved randomly based upon the value stored in the RECORD KEY field prior to the READ or WRITE. The random mode precludes a sequential READ or WRITE.

When the dynamic mode is specified an indexed file can be written to, or retrieved from, in either a random or sequential mode.

The RECORD KEY clause specifies the field within each record that is used as the primary index.

The field must be defined in the record description for the file, and must be the first field in the record. The value of the primary index must be unique for each record.

The primary index cannot be subscripted (i.e. defined using an OCCURS clause).

The ALTERNATE RECORD KEY clause specifies secondary keys that may be present in a record. A secondary key cannot be embedded within the primary key. Secondary keys can have values in the file that are not unique, in which case WITH DUPLICATES should be appended to the ALTERNATE RECORD KEY clause.

The FILE STATUS clause specifies a two-digit unsigned integer described in the

Working-Storage Section, that is used to store a code signifying either a successful or an unsuccessful operation on the file.

Open and Close

The general format for the OPEN statement is:

OPEN $\begin{bmatrix} \text{I-O} \\ \text{INPUT} \\ \text{OUTPUT} \end{bmatrix}$ {index-file-name} ... ...

A file opened for INPUT can be read, opened for OUTPUT can be written to, and opened for I-O (INPUT and OUTPUT) can be either read or written to.

The general format for the CLOSE statement is:

CLOSE {index-file-name} ...

Read and Start

The READ statement has two formats.

Format 1 - for sequential or dynamic access

READ file-name NEXT RECORD INTO data-name-1
[AT END {imperative statement} ...]

Format 2 - for sequential, random or dynamic access.

READ file-name INTO data-name-1
[KEY IS data-name-2]
[INVALID KEY {imperative statement} ...]

When format 1 is used for sequential access the continuous execution of READ will cause the successive records in the file to be accessed until the end of the file is reached. Since the primary keys are stored in sequence they ensure that access to the records in the file will be sequential even if the records themselves are not stored sequentially. The NEXT RECORD clause is not required for a file described as having sequential access, therefore, the statement becomes identical to the format that the reader has already used. If, however, the dynamic mode of access is specified and sequential access is required then the NEXT RECORD clause must be present when using format 1.

When format 2 is used for either random or dynamic access, a record will be retrieved directly, based upon the value found in data-name-2 of the KEY IS clause. If the key cannot be matched with a key in the file then the imperative statement INVALID KEY clause, if present, will be executed. If the INVALID KEY clause is not present and a key match is not possible then the outcome will be a run-time error. The value of data-name-2 can be that of a primary or secondary key. Since the primary key is unique, the READ statement will access a unique record, however, if a secondary key is used a READ statement will access the first record in a sequence of records with that secondary key. If the dynamic mode has been specified then further access to those records with the same secondary key is possible by using the format - 1 READ statement.

The START statement allows an indexed organised file to be positioned for reading at a specified key value. This is permitted for files opened in either the sequential or dynamic modes. The START statement is not allowed with random access.

The general format of the START statement is:

START file-name [KEY IS $\left\{ \begin{array}{l} \text{GREATER THAN} \\ \text{NOT LESS THAN} \\ \text{EQUAL TO} \end{array} \right\}$ data-name]

INVALID KEY {imperative-statement} ...]

START file-name positions the file to the value contained in the primary key.

START file-name KEY IS data-name positions the file to the value contained in either the primary key or secondary key data-name.

When the full format of the START statement contains either of the options GREATER THAN or NOT LESS THAN the file is positioned for the next access to be greater than or less than the value specified in data-name. This option allows the keys to contain partial values.

The START statement only positions the file ready for access it does not read the file.

If the INVALID KEY clause is absent and either a key match or key positioning is impossible then the outcome will be a run-time error.

Examples.

An indexed sequential file is described in the following manner.

```
ENVIRONMENT  DIVISION.
INPUT-OUTPUT  SECTION.
FILE-CONTROL.
      SELECT staff ASSIGN TO PFMS,
      ORGANIZATION IS INDEXED,
      ACCESS MODE IS DYNAMIC,
      RECORD KEY IS surname,
      ALTERNATIVE RECORD KEY IS TeleNo WITH DUPLICATES.
DATA DIVISION.
FILE SECTION.
FD staff.
01  Record-1.
      02 surname PIC X(20).
      02 TeleNo PIC AAA.
      02 StatusSubject PIC X(20).
```

From the COBOL description of the file it can be seen that the name of the primary key is surname and the name of the secondary key is TeleNo for which duplicate values are allowed. A typical selection of records from the file could be:

> Blanchard　328Head-Science
> Collins　　397Lecturer-Maths
> Evans　　　397Lecturer-Computing
> Houghton　397Lecturer-Physics
> Jeffries　　405Technician-Science
> .　　　.
> .　　　.
> .　　　.

The following segments of code will produce the output described.

```
PROCEDURE  DIVISION.
A-seq.
        PERFORM B THROUGH H.
B.      OPEN staff INPUT.
        MOVE "Evans" TO surname.
        READ staff KEY IS surname.
        DISPLAY TeleNo, SPACE, StatusSubject.
```

The value Evans has been provided as the primary key, retrieval from the file will be direct and the values 397 Lecturer- Computing will be output.

```
C.      MOVE "397" TO TeleNo, TeleStore.
        START staff KEY IS TeleNo.
        READ staff NEXT RECORD.
D-rep.
        PERFORM E UNTIL TeleNo NOT = TeleStore.
```

The value "397" has been provided as a secondary key that also has duplicate values in the file. The START statement positions the file for access to the first record with the secondary key TeleNo of 397, the file is then READ and the surname of the member of staff with that telephone number is output. The records in the file with the same secondary key value are accessed in sequence and output. The result would be:

> Collins
> Evans
> Houghton

```
E.      MOVE "H" TO surname.
        START staff KEY IS NOT LESS THAN surname.
        READ staff NEXT RECORD AT END MOVE 'T' TO EOF.
G-rep.
        PERFORM I UNTIL EndOfFile.
H.      CLOSE staff.
        STOP RUN.
```

The value of "H" has been provided as a partially complete primary key. The file is positioned such that the first record to be accessed will have a key value that is greater than the value "H" found in the surname. The file is READ at this position and the surname displayed. The file is read sequentially until the end of file is encountered. The output using the specimen data is:

> Houghton
> Jeffries

.
.

```
E.      DISPLAY  surname.
        READ staff NEXT RECORD.
I.      DISPLAY  surname.
        READ staff NEXT RECORD AT END MOVE 'T' TO EOF.
```

Write and ReWrite.

The WRITE statement releases a logical record for an OUTPUT or I- O file. The general format of the statement is:

WRITE record-name [**FROM** data-name-1]
[**INVALID KEY** {imperative-statement} ...]

Prior to the WRITE statement being executed a valid, unique value must be stored in the primary record key data-name. If the FROM option is used the unique value in the primary key data-name must be stored in the relative location of data-name-1. If the primary key is not unique the imperative statement in the INVALID KEY clause, if present, will be executed.

The REWRITE statement is used to amend a record in an indexed sequential file. The format of the REWRITE statement is:

REWRITE record-name [**FROM** data-name-1]
[**INVALID KEY** {imperative-statement} ...]

The REWRITE statement physically replaces an existing record, and is used to change any or all of the data fields in a record except the primary key value. The file must be opened in an I-O mode, and must have been read successfully prior to the execution of the REWRITE.

If the FROM data-name-1 option is used the primary record key must have the same value as the key from the previous READ statement otherwise an INVALID KEY condition will occur, and the imperative statements in the INVALID KEY clause, if present, will be executed, since the value of the primary key had been changed.

Delete

The DELETE statement logically removes a data record from the indexed file, together with all the indices.

The format of the DELETE statement is:

DELETE file-name [**INVALID KEY** {imperative-statement} ...]

When this statement is used in either random or dynamic access modes only a value of the key for the record to be deleted need be placed in the primary record key field prior to the execution of the DELETE. If the record does not exist in the file the INVALID KEY clause will be invoked, if present.

In sequential access the record to be deleted must have been successfully read before a delete can be executed. Should the value of the primary key be changed between the operations of READ and DELETE the INVALID KEY clause will be invoked, if present.

Figure 12.3 summarises the types of OPEN statements which are permissible with the different access modes and procedural statements.

Access Mode	Procedural Statements	Open option being used		
		INPUT	OUTPUT	I-O
SEQUENTIAL	READ	yes		yes
	WRITE		yes	
	REWRITE			yes
	START	yes		yes
	DELETE			yes
RANDOM	READ	yes		yes
	WRITE		yes	yes
	REWRITE			yes
	START			
	DELETE			yes
DYNAMIC	READ	yes		yes
	WRITE		yes	yes
	REWRITE			yes
	START	yes		yes
	DELETE			yes

Figure 12.3 Summary of OPEN statements applicable to access modes

12.3 Worked Examples.

An indexed sequential file contains details about staff in a college. The format of a record on the file follows.

Department code - 1 character   B - Business Studies
                                          E - Engineering
                                          G - General Studies
                                          S - Science
Surname of member of staff - 20 characters
note the department code and surname concatenated together form the primary key
Telephone extension number - 3 digits
Status of member of staff - 1 character   H - Head of department
                                          L - Lecturer
                                          S - Secretary
                                          T - Technician
note the telephone extension number and status of a member of staff both represent secondary (alternate) keys and can have duplicate entries
Qualifications of staff member - 10 characters
Academic subjects member of staff teaches - 20 characters.

Design and write a program to maintain the file, catering for the amendment, deletion and insertion of records. Since the maintenance is to take place on a master file you should assume that a copy of this file is made each day and that every change made to a record is stored on a sequential log file. In the event of a disc head-crash or the file being accidently erased the file can be re-built using the copy of the master and the transactions stored on the sequential log file.

The program is menu-driven and access to a record will be through the primary key only.

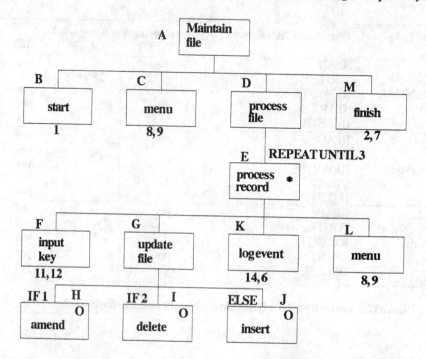

Functions
1. Open files
2. Close files
3. Read ISAM file
4. Write ISAM file
5. ReWrite ISAM file
6. Write log file
7. Stop
8. Display menu
9. Input menu-code
10. Input fields of record
11. Input key
12. Initialise error flag to false (F)
13. Delete record
14. Format record for output
15. Display error message
16. Space fill fields of record

Conditions
1. menu-code = Amend (A) or (a)
2. menu-code = Delete (D) or (d)
3. menu-code = Exit (E) or (e)
4. Error flag = false (F)

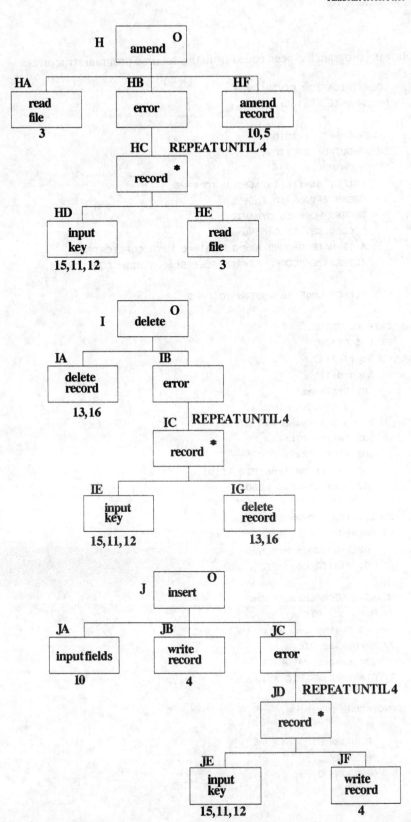

The following program has been coded from the detailed program structures.

```
IDENTIFICATION DIVISION.
PROGRAM-ID. FileCreation.

ENVIRONMENT DIVISION.
INPUT-OUTPUT SECTION.
FILE-CONTROL.
    SELECT StaffFile ASSIGN TO PFMS,
    ORGANIZATION IS INDEXED,
    ACCESS MODE IS DYNAMIC
    RECORD KEY IS DeptName,
    ALTERNATE RECORD KEY IS TeleNo WITH DUPLICATES,
    ALTERNATE RECORD KEY IS StaffStatus WITH DUPLICATES.

    SELECT LogFile ASSIGN TO PFMS.

DATA DIVISION.
FILE SECTION.
FD StaffFile.
01 Record-1.
    02 DeptName.
        03 DeptCode PIC A.
        03 StaffName PIC X(20).
    02 TeleNo PIC AAA.
    02 StaffStatus PIC A.
    02 qualifications PIC X(10).
    02 subjects PIC X(20).

FD LogFile, COMPRESSED.
01 Record-2.
    02 TransCode PIC A.
    02 StaffRecord PIC X(60).

WORKING-STORAGE SECTION.
77 MenuCode PIC A.
    88 QuitSystem VALUE 'E', 'e'.
77 ErrorFlag PIC A.
    88 errors VALUE 'T'.
77 ClearScreen PIC X VALUE ''.

PROCEDURE DIVISION.
A-seq.
    PERFORM B.
    PERFORM C.
    PERFORM D-rep.
    PERFORM M.
```

```
B.   OPEN I-O StaffFile, OUTPUT LogFile.
C.   PERFORM FUNCTIONS-8-9.
D-rep.
     PERFORM E-seq UNTIL QuitSystem.
M.   CLOSE StaffFile, LogFile.
     STOP RUN.


E-seq.
     PERFORM F THROUGH L.


F.   PERFORM FUNCTIONS-11-12.
G-sel.
     IF MenuCode = 'A' OR 'a'
        PERFORM H-seq
     ELSE IF MenuCode = 'D' OR 'd'
             PERFORM I-seq
          ELSE
             PERFORM J-seq.
K.   MOVE MenuCode TO TransCode.

     MOVE Record-1 TO StaffRecord.
     WRITE Record-2.
L.   PERFORM FUNCTIONS-8-9.


H-seq.
     PERFORM HA THROUGH HF.


HA.  READ StaffFile KEY IS DeptName
     INVALID KEY MOVE 'T' TO ErrorFlag.
HB-rep.
     PERFORM HC-seq UNTIL NOT errors.
HF.  PERFORM FUNCTION-10.
     REWRITE Record-1 INVALID KEY MOVE 'T' TO ErrorFlag.


HC-seq.
     PERFORM HD THROUGH HE.


HD.  DISPLAY "ERROR - INVALID KEY"
     PERFORM FUNCTIONS-11-12.
HE.  READ StaffFile KEY IS DeptName
     INVALID KEY MOVE 'T' TO ErrorFlag.


I-seq.
     PERFORM IA THROUGH IB-rep.


IA.  DELETE StaffFile
     INVALID KEY MOVE 'T' TO ErrorFlag.
```

```
            MOVE SPACES TO TeleNo, StaffStatus, qualifications,
                          subjects.
    IB-rep.
        PERFORM IC-seq UNTIL NOT errors.


    IC-seq.
        PERFORM IE THROUGH IG.


    IE. DISPLAY "ERROR - INVALID KEY"
        PERFORM FUNCTIONS-11-12.
    IG. DELETE StaffFile
        INVALID KEY MOVE 'T' TO ErrorFlag.
        MOVE SPACES TO TeleNo, StaffStatus, qualifications,
                          subjects.
    J-seq.
        PERFORM JA THROUGH JC-rep.


    JA. PERFORM FUNCTION-10.
    JB. WRITE Record-1
        INVALID KEY MOVE 'T' TO ErrorFlag.
    JC-rep.
        PERFORM JD-seq UNTIL NOT errors.


    JD-seq.
        PERFORM JE THROUGH JF.


    JE. DISPLAY "ERROR - INVALID KEY"
        PERFORM FUNCTIONS-11-12.
    JF. WRITE Record-1
        INVALID KEY MOVE 'T' TO ErrorFlag.


*  ------------------------- subroutines -------------------


FUNCTIONS-8-9.
        DISPLAY ClearScreen.
        DISPLAY "Do you require to:"
        DISPLAY " "
        DISPLAY "[A]mend record"
        DISPLAY "[D]elete record"
        DISPLAY "[I]nsert record"
        DISPLAY "[E]xit from system".
        DISPLAY SPACE.
        DISPLAY "input code A,D,I or E " WITH NO ADVANCING.
        ACCEPT MenuCode.
```

```
FUNCTIONS-11-12.
    DISPLAY "Names of departments are:"
    DISPLAY SPACE.
    DISPLAY "[B]usiness Studies"
    DISPLAY "[E]ngineering"
    DISPLAY "[G]eneral Studies"
    DISPLAY "[S]cience".
    DISPLAY SPACE.
    DISPLAY "input department code B, E, G or S "
    WITH NO ADVANCING. ACCEPT DeptCode.
    DISPLAY SPACE.
    DISPLAY "input surname " WITH NO ADVANCING.
    ACCEPT StaffName.
    MOVE 'F' TO ErrorFlag.

FUNCTION-10.
    DISPLAY "input the following details"
    DISPLAY SPACE.
    DISPLAY "telephone number " WITH NO ADVANCING.
    ACCEPT TeleNo.
    DISPLAY SPACE.
    DISPLAY "status of staff [H]ead"
    DISPLAY "              [L]ecturer"
    DISPLAY "              [S]ecretary"
    DISPLAY "              [T]echnician"
    DISPLAY "input status code H, L, S or T "
    WITH NO ADVANCING. ACCEPT StaffStatus.
    DISPLAY SPACE.
    DISPLAY "qualifications " WITH NO ADVANCING.
    ACCEPT qualifications.
    DISPLAY "subject specialisms " WITH NO ADVANCING.
    ACCEPT subjects.
```

The results from running the program follow. Only an extract has been printed since the menu-driven dialogue is repetitive. The listing of the log file at the end of the results is intended to show all the changes that were made to the file and not only the small extract given here.

```
Do you require to:

[A]mend record
[D]elete record
[I]nsert record
[E]xit from system

input code A,D,I or E I
```

Names of departments are:

[B]usiness Studies
[E]ngineering
[G]eneral Studies
[S]cience

input department code B, E, G or S S

input surname Houghton
input the following details

telephone number 397

status of staff [H]ead
                [L]ecturer
                [S]ecretary
                [T]echnician
input status code H, L, S or T L

qualifications Ph.D
subject specialisms Chemistry

Do you require to:

[A]mend record
[D]elete record
[I]nsert record
[E]xit from system

input code A,D,I or E I
Names of departments are:

[B]usiness Studies
[E]ngineering
[G]eneral Studies
[S]cience

input department code B, E, G or S S

input surname Jeffries
input the following details

telephone number 405

status of staff [H]ead
                [L]ecturer

                    [S]ecretary
                    [T]echnician
input status code H, L, S or T T

qualifications HNC
subject specialisms Laboratory skills

Do you require to:

[A]mend record
[D]elete record
[I]nsert record
[E]xit from system

input code A,D,I or E A
Names of departments are:

[B]usiness Studies
[E]ngineering
[G]eneral Studies
[S]cience

input department code B, E, G or S S

input surname Houghton
input the following details

telephone number 397

status of staff [H]ead
               [L]ecturer
               [S]ecretary
               [T]echnician
input status code H, L, S or T L

qualifications Ph.D
subject specialisms Physics

Do you require to:

[A]mend record
[D]elete record
[I]nsert record
[E]xit from system

input code A,D,I or E D
Names of departments are:

```
[B]usiness Studies
[E]ngineering
[G]eneral Studies
[S]cience

input department code B, E, G or S S

input surname Evans

Do you require to:

[A]mend record
[D]elete record
[I]nsert record
[E]xit from system

input code A,D,I or E e

logfile

IBCross          201HB.A       English
IBHayward        223LM.A       Marketing
IBBarnett        202SHND       Office skills
IGBeadle         324HPh.D      Sociology
IGThurling       325LPh.D      Philosophy
ISBlanchard      328HB.Sc      Physics
ISCollins        397LM.A       Mathematics
ISEvans          397LM.Sc      Computing
ISHoughton       397LPh.D      Chemistry
ISJeffries       405THNC       Laboratory skills
ASHoughton       397LPh.D      Physics
DSEvans
```

Having created a program to maintain the staff file it is possible to design and write a second program to interrogate the file. A menu driven program should allow for interrogation on the following information.

> 1 - department and staff name
> 2 - department only
> 3 - staff name only
> 4 - telephone extension number
> 5 - department and staff status

When the appropriate record has been accessed the information should be displayed on a screen. The design for the program to interrogate the indexed sequential file follows on the next page.

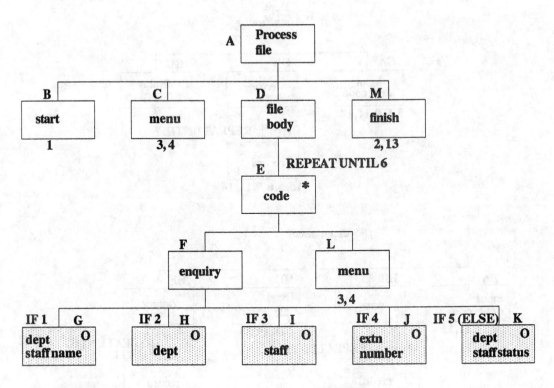

Functions
1. Open file
2. Close file
3. Display procedure menu
4. Input procedure code
5. Display department menu
6. Input department code
7. Display staff-status menu
8. Input staff-status code
9. Input surname
10. Input telephone extension number
11. Initialise error flag to false (F)
12. Position record ready for access
13. Stop
14. Read file using key
15. Display error message
16. Display record
17. Fill staff name with spaces
18. Store department code
19. Initialise end of file flag to false (F)
20. Read file sequentially
21. Set table index to 1
22. Move element in table to department code
23. Increase table index by 1
24. Store telephone number
25. Store status code

Conditions
1. Menu-code = 1
2. Menu-code = 2
3. Menu-code = 3
4. Menu-code = 4
5. Menu-code = 5
6. Menu-code = 6
7. Error flag = false (F)
8. End of file
9. Not same telephone extension number
10. Not same staff status code
11. Not same department code
12. Table index > 4
13. Same status AND department

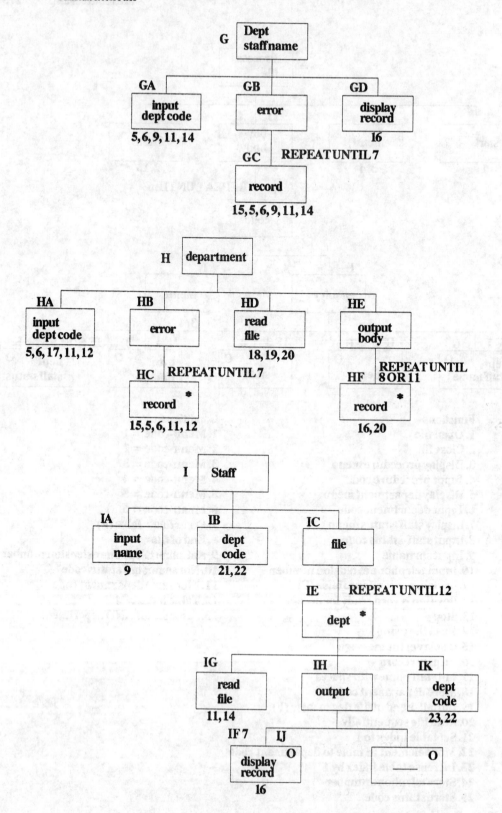

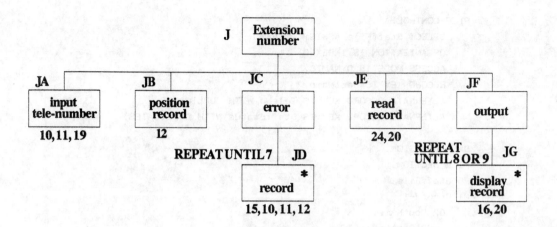

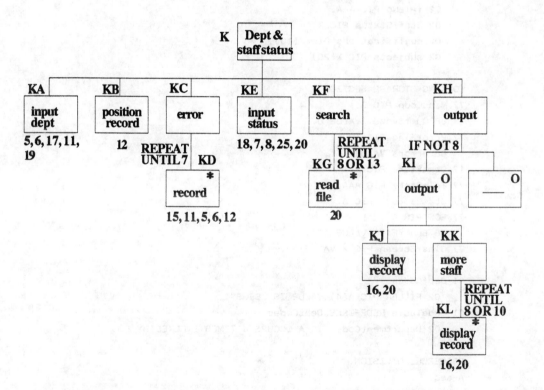

The following program has been coded from the detailed program structures.

```
IDENTIFICATION DIVISION.
PROGRAM-ID. Interrogation.

ENVIRONMENT DIVISION.
INPUT-OUTPUT SECTION.
```

```
FILE-CONTROL.
    SELECT StaffFile ASSIGN TO PFMS,
    ORGANIZATION IS INDEXED,
    ACCESS MODE IS DYNAMIC,
    RECORD KEY IS DeptName,
    ALTERNATE RECORD KEY IS TeleNo WITH DUPLICATES,
    ALTERNATE RECORD KEY IS StaffStatus WITH DUPLICATES.

DATA DIVISION.
FILE SECTION.
FD StaffFile.
01 Record-1.
    02 DeptName.
      03 DeptCode PIC X.
      03 StaffName PIC X(20).
    02 TeleNo PIC AAA.
    02 StaffStatus PIC X.
    02 qualifications PIC X(10).
    02 subjects PIC X(20).

WORKING-STORAGE SECTION.
77 MenuCode PIC 9.
    88 QuitSystem VALUE 6.
77 ErrorFlag PIC A.
    88 errors VALUE 'T'.
77 DeptStore PIC A.
77 TeleStore PIC AAA.
77 StatusStore PIC A.
77 EOF PIC A.
    88 EndOfFile VALUE 'T'.
77 ClearScreen PIC X VALUE ''.

01 DeptCodes.
    02 FILLER PIC A(4) VALUE IS "BEGS".
01 CodeTable REDEFINES DeptCodes.
    02 DepartmentCode PIC A OCCURS 4 TIMES INDEXED BY POS.

PROCEDURE DIVISION.
A-seq.
    PERFORM B THROUGH M.

B.  OPEN INPUT StaffFile.
C.  PERFORM FUNCTIONS-3-4.
D-rep.
    PERFORM E-seq UNTIL QuitSystem.
M.  CLOSE StaffFile.
    STOP RUN.
```

```
E-seq.
    PERFORM F-sel THROUGH L.


F-sel.
    IF MenuCode = 1
       PERFORM G-seq
    ELSE IF MenuCode = 2
       PERFORM H-seq
    ELSE IF MenuCode = 3
       PERFORM I-seq
    ELSE IF menuCode = 4
       PERFORM J-seq
    ELSE
       PERFORM K-seq.
 L. PERFORM FUNCTIONS-3-4.


G-seq.
    PERFORM GA THROUGH GD.


GA. PERFORM FUNCTIONS-5-6.
    PERFORM FUNCTION-9.
    MOVE 'F' TO ErrorFlag.
    READ StaffFile KEY IS DeptName,
    INVALID KEY MOVE 'T' TO ErrorFlag.
GB-rep.
    PERFORM GC UNTIL NOT errors.
GD. PERFORM FUNCTION-16.


GC. DISPLAY "ERROR - INVALID KEY".
    PERFORM FUNCTIONS-5-6.
    PERFORM FUNCTION-9.
    MOVE 'F' TO ErrorFlag.
    READ StaffFile KEY IS DeptName,
    INVALID KEY MOVE 'T' TO ErrorFlag.


H-seq.
    PERFORM HA THROUGH HE-rep.


HA. PERFORM FUNCTIONS-5-6.
    MOVE SPACES TO StaffName.
    MOVE 'F' TO ErrorFlag.
    START StaffFile KEY IS NOT LESS THAN DeptName,
    INVALID KEY MOVE 'T' TO ErrorFlag.
HB-rep.
    PERFORM HC UNTIL NOT errors.
HD. MOVE DeptCode TO DeptStore.
```

```
            MOVE 'F' TO EOF.
            READ StaffFile NEXT RECORD AT END MOVE 'T' TO EOF.
      HE-rep.
            PERFORM HF UNTIL EndOfFile OR DeptCode NOT = DeptStore.

      HC. DISPLAY "ERROR - INVALID KEY"
            PERFORM FUNCTIONS-5-6.
            MOVE 'F' TO ErrorFlag.
            START StaffFile KEY IS NOT LESS THAN DeptName,
            INVALID KEY MOVE 'T' TO ErrorFlag.
      HF. PERFORM FUNCTION-16.
            READ StaffFile NEXT RECORD AT END MOVE 'T' TO EOF.


      I-seq.
            PERFORM IA THROUGH IC-rep.


      IA. PERFORM FUNCTION-9.
      IB. SET POS TO 1.
            MOVE DepartmentCode (POS) TO DeptCode.
      IC-rep.
            PERFORM IE-seq UNTIL POS > 4.


      IE-seq.
            PERFORM IG THROUGH IK.


      IG. MOVE 'F' TO ErrorFlag.
            READ StaffFile KEY IS DeptName,
            INVALID KEY MOVE 'T' TO ErrorFlag.
      IH-sel.
            IF NOT errors
                  PERFORM IJ.
      IK. SET POS UP BY 1.
            MOVE DepartmentCode (POS) TO DeptCode.
      IJ. PERFORM FUNCTION-16.


      J-seq.
            PERFORM JA THROUGH JF-rep.


      JA. PERFORM FUNCTION-10.
            MOVE 'F' TO ErrorFlag, EOF.
      JB. START StaffFile KEY IS NOT LESS THAN TeleNo,
            INVALID KEY MOVE 'T' TO ErrorFlag.
      JC-rep.
            PERFORM JD UNTIL NOT errors.
      JE. MOVE TeleNo TO TeleStore.
            READ StaffFile NEXT RECORD AT END MOVE 'T' TO EOF.
```

```
JF-rep.
    PERFORM JG UNTIL EndOfFile OR TeleNo NOT = TeleStore.


JD. DISPLAY "ERROR - INVALID KEY"
    PERFORM FUNCTION-10.
    MOVE 'F' TO ErrorFlag.
    START StaffFile KEY IS NOT LESS THAN TeleNo,
    INVALID KEY MOVE 'T' TO ErrorFlag.
JG.
    PERFORM FUNCTION-16.
    READ StaffFile NEXT RECORD AT END MOVE 'T' TO EOF.


K-seq.
    PERFORM KA THROUGH KH-sel.


KA. PERFORM FUNCTIONS-5-6.
    MOVE SPACES TO StaffName.
    MOVE 'F' TO ErrorFlag, EOF.
KB. START StaffFile KEY IS NOT LESS THAN DeptName,
    INVALID KEY MOVE 'T' TO ErrorFlag.
KC-rep.
    PERFORM KD UNTIL NOT errors.
KE. MOVE DeptCode TO DeptStore.
    PERFORM FUNCTIONS-7-8.
    MOVE StaffStatus TO StatusStore.
    READ StaffFile NEXT RECORD AT END MOVE 'T' TO EOF.
KF-rep.
    PERFORM KG UNTIL EndOfFile OR
    (StaffStatus = StatusStore AND DeptCode = DeptStore).
KH-sel.
    IF NOT EndOfFile
        PERFORM KI-seq.


KD. DISPLAY "ERROR - INVALID KEY DEPARTMENT" DeptCode.
    PERFORM FUNCTIONS-5-6.
    MOVE 'F' TO ErrorFlag.
    START StaffFile KEY IS NOT LESS THAN DeptName,
    INVALID KEY MOVE 'T' TO ErrorFlag.
KE.
    MOVE DeptCode TO DeptStore.
    PERFORM FUNCTIONS-7-8.
    MOVE StaffStatus TO StatusStore.
    READ StaffFile NEXT RECORD AT END MOVE 'T' TO EOF.
KG. READ StaffFile NEXT RECORD AT END MOVE 'T' TO EOF.


KI-seq.
    PERFORM KJ THROUGH KK-rep.
```

```
KJ. PERFORM FUNCTION-16.
    READ StaffFile NEXT RECORD AT END MOVE 'T' TO EOF.
KK-rep.
    PERFORM KL UNTIL EndOfFile OR StaffStatus
                                 NOT = StatusStore.

KL. PERFORM FUNCTION-16.
    READ StaffFile NEXT RECORD AT END MOVE 'T' TO EOF.




* -------------------- subroutines -------------------

FUNCTIONS-3-4.
    DISPLAY "Do you require record access on:"
    DISPLAY " "
    DISPLAY "1. Department and staff name".
    DISPLAY "2. Department only".
    DISPLAY "3. Staff name only".
    DISPLAY "4. Telephone extension number".
    DISPLAY "5. Department and staff status".
    DISPLAY "6. EXIT from system".
    DISPLAY " "
    DISPLAY "input numeric code 1-6 " WITH NO ADVANCING.
    ACCEPT MenuCode.
    DISPLAY ClearScreen.

FUNCTIONS-5-6.
    DISPLAY "input department code"
    DISPLAY "[B]usiness Studies"
    DISPLAY "[E]ngineering"
    DISPLAY "[G]eneral Studies"
    DISPLAY "[S]cience"
    ACCEPT DeptCode.

FUNCTION-9.
    DISPLAY "input surname ", WITH NO ADVANCING.
    ACCEPT StaffName.

FUNCTION-10.
    DISPLAY "input telephone extension number "
    WITH NO ADVANCING. ACCEPT TeleNo.
```

```
FUNCTION-16.
    DISPLAY "DEPARTMENT CODE: " DeptCode.
    DISPLAY "SURNAME:         " StaffName.
    DISPLAY "EXTENSION:       " TeleNo.
    DISPLAY "STAFF STATUS:    " StaffStatus.
    DISPLAY "QUALIFICATIONS:  " qualifications.
    DISPLAY "SUBJECT(S):      " subjects
    DISPLAY SPACE.

FUNCTIONS-7-8.
    DISPLAY "input staff status code"
    DISPLAY "[H]ead of department"
    DISPLAY "[L]ecturer"
    DISPLAY "[S]ecretary"
    DISPLAY "[T]echnician".
    ACCEPT StaffStatus.
```

The results from running the program follow.

```
Do you require record access on:

1. Department and staff name
2. Department only
3. Staff name only
4. Telephone extension number
5. Department and staff status
6. EXIT from system


input numeric code 1-6 1

input department code
[B]usiness Studies
[E]ngineering
[G]eneral Studies
[S]cience
B
input surname Hayward
DEPARTMENT CODE: B
SURNAME:         Hayward
EXTENSION:       223
STAFF STATUS:    L
QUALIFICATIONS:  M.A
SUBJECT(S):      Marketing


Do you require record access on:
```

1. Department and staff name
2. Department only
3. Staff name only
4. Telephone extension number
5. Department and staff status
6. EXIT from system

input numeric code 1-6 2

input department code
[B]usiness Studies
[E]ngineering
[G]eneral Studies
[S]cience
B
DEPARTMENT CODE: B
SURNAME: Barnett
EXTENSION: 202
STAFF STATUS: S
QUALIFICATIONS: HND
SUBJECT(S):   Office skills

DEPARTMENT CODE: B
SURNAME: Cross
EXTENSION: 201
STAFF STATUS: H
QUALIFICATIONS: B.A
SUBJECT(S):   English

DEPARTMENT CODE: B
SURNAME: Hayward
EXTENSION: 223
STAFF STATUS: L
QUALIFICATIONS: M.A
SUBJECT(S):   Marketing

Do you require record access on:

1. Department and staff name
2. Department only
3. Staff name only
4. Telephone extension number
5. Department and staff status
6. EXIT from system

input numeric code 1-6 3

```
input surname Beadle
DEPARTMENT CODE: G
SURNAME:        Beadle
EXTENSION:      324
STAFF STATUS:   H
QUALIFICATIONS: Ph.D
SUBJECT(S):     Sociology


Do you require record access on:

1. Department and staff name
2. Department only
3. Staff name only
4. Telephone extension number
5. Department and staff status
6. EXIT from system

input numeric code 1-6 4

input telephone extension number 405
DEPARTMENT CODE: S
SURNAME:        Jeffries
EXTENSION:      405
STAFF STATUS:   T
QUALIFICATIONS: HNC
SUBJECT(S):     Laboratory skills


Do you require record access on:

1. Department and staff name
2. Department only
3. Staff name only
4. Telephone extension number
5. Department and staff status
6. EXIT from system

input numeric code 1-6 4

input telephone extension number 397
DEPARTMENT CODE: S
SURNAME:        Collins
EXTENSION:      397
STAFF STATUS:   L
QUALIFICATIONS: M.A
SUBJECT(S):     Mathematics
```

```
DEPARTMENT CODE: S
SURNAME:        Houghton
EXTENSION:      397
STAFF STATUS:   L
QUALIFICATIONS: Ph.D
SUBJECT(S):     Physics


Do you require record access on:


1. Department and staff name
2. Department only
3. Staff name only
4. Telephone extension number
5. Department and staff status
6. EXIT from system


input numeric code 1-6 5


input department code
[B]usiness Studies
[E]ngineering
[G]eneral Studies
[S]cience
G
input staff status code
[H]ead of department
[L]ecturer
[S]ecretary
[T]echnician
H
DEPARTMENT CODE: G
SURNAME:        Beadle
EXTENSION:      324
STAFF STATUS:   H
QUALIFICATIONS: Ph.D
SUBJECT(S):     Sociology


Do you require record access on:


1. Department and staff name
2. Department only
3. Staff name only
4. Telephone extension number
5. Department and staff status
6. EXIT from system


input numeric code 1-6 5
```

```
input department code
[B]usiness Studies
[E]ngineering
[G]eneral Studies
[S]cience
S
input staff status code
[H]ead of department
[L]ecturer
[S]ecretary
[T]echnician
T
DEPARTMENT CODE: S
SURNAME:          Jeffries
EXTENSION:        405
STAFF STATUS:     T
QUALIFICATIONS:   HNC
SUBJECT(S):       Laboratory skills

Do you require record access on:

1. Department and staff name
2. Department only
3. Staff name only
4. Telephone extension number
5. Department and staff status
6. EXIT from system

input numeric code 1-6 6
```

12.4 Relative Files.

Files organised in this manner are stored on magnetic disc and will allow either sequential or random access to records. A relative record key is a positive numeric integer that represents the relative position of a logical record with respect to the beginning of the file. For example a record with key of value 10, represents a record occupying the tenth logical record area in the file, irrespective of whether the relative record areas 1 through to 9 have been filled.

Relative files have the potential of being efficient since records are stored in sequence, access is fast and there are no problems with overflow. However, with record deletions or the fact that the keys are numerically spaced far apart, gaps of wasted space can soon occur in such a file organisation.

Figure 12.4 illustrates records stored in a relative file. The record key represents time slots for patients visiting a doctor. The time slots represent the relative key to each record, however, these keys do not form part of a record. The time slots can be translated into an appropriate time of day. For example time slot 001 could be 10.00 am, time slot 002 10.10 am, time slot 003 10.20 am, etc. The illustration shows that the name and address of a patient is recorded in a patient record and access to that record is through the appropriate time slot.

Relative key not part of relative record		Relative record	
001			
002	→	Jones	124 Leighton Ave
003	→	Smith	1 Towers Ave
004	→	Edwards	44 Sunnyhill Road
005			
006	→	Evans	108 West Way
007	→	Holmes	93 Balfour Road
008	→	Devereux	33 Courtlands Road
009			
010	→	Hordern	16 Kennedy Close
011	→	Brewer	31 New Road
012			
013	→	Goodman	4 Little Clarendon Street
014	→	Crossley	5 Victoria Cross Street
015	→	Sundby	92 The Broadway
016	→	Redfearn	74 The Avenue

Figure 12.4 A Relative File

12.5 Relative File Statements.

File Control

The general format for File Control in the Environment Division is very similar to that for indexed sequential files.

```
SELECT file-name ASSIGN TO PFMS
ORGANIZATION IS RELATIVE
[ACCESS MODE IS  ⎡SEQUENTIAL⎤ ]
                 ⎨RANDOM     ⎬
                 ⎣DYNAMIC    ⎦
RELATIVE KEY IS data-name-1
[FILE STATUS IS data-name-2]
```

The differences in this format and that for indexed sequential files should be apparent to the reader. The organisation of the file has been described as RELATIVE, the record key is described as RELATIVE KEY with the description for data-name-1 being given in the Working-Storage Section, and not as the first field of the record in the File Section. The relative file organisation does not support secondary keys, since they have no meaning here, therefore the ALTERNATE RECORD clause is not included as part of the format for File Control. The value contained within data- name-1 must be a unique positive integer, duplicates are invalid.

Procedure Division Statements.

The statements already described for processing indexed sequential files are identical to those used for processing Relative files, however, the only exception to this statement is the second format of the READ statement. The KEY IS clause is omitted from the format of the statement, however, a value for the Relative key should be stored in the Working-Storage entry prior to the READ statement being executed.

12.6 Worked Examples.
A relative file is used to store the details of aircraft departures from an airport in the U.K. The format of a record on the file follows.

Departure time - 4 digits
Flight number - 6 characters
Destination - 30 characters

The records are organised into departure time order and the relative key is the time of day based on the 24-hour clock.

Design and write a program to maintain the file catering for the amendment, deletion and insertion of records.

The design and structure of this program is identical to the file maintenance program used for updating the indexed sequential file, therefore, the design phase will be omitted and only the source listing of the program and the test run will be given.

```
IDENTIFICATION DIVISION.
PROGRAM-ID. FileMaintenance.

ENVIRONMENT DIVISION.
INPUT-OUTPUT SECTION.
FILE-CONTROL.
    SELECT departures ASSIGN TO PFMS,
    ORGANIZATION IS RELATIVE,
    ACCESS MODE IS RANDOM,
    RELATIVE KEY IS clock.

    SELECT FlightLog ASSIGN TO PFMS.
```

```
DATA DIVISION.
FILE SECTION.
FD departures.
01 Record-1.
    02 DepartureTime PIC 9(4).
    02 FlightNumber PIC X(6).
    02 FlightDestination PIC X(30).


FD FlightLog, COMPRESSED.
01 Record-2.
    02 TransCode PIC A.
    02 FlightRecord PIC X(40).


WORKING-STORAGE SECTION.
77 MenuCode PIC A.
    88 QuitSystem VALUE 'E', 'e'.
77 ErrorFlag PIC A VALUE 'F'.
    88 errors VALUE 'T'.
77 clock PIC 9(4).
77 ClearScreen PIC X VALUE ''.


PROCEDURE DIVISION.
A-seq.
    PERFORM B THROUGH M.


B.  OPEN I-O departures, OUTPUT FlightLog.
C.  PERFORM FUNCTIONS-8-9.
D-rep.
    PERFORM E-seq UNTIL QuitSystem.
M.  CLOSE departures, FlightLog.
    STOP RUN.


E-seq.
    PERFORM F THROUGH L.


F.  PERFORM FUNCTIONS-11-12.
G-sel.
    IF MenuCode = 'A' OR 'a'
       PERFORM H-seq
    ELSE
       IF MenuCode = 'D' OR 'd'
          PERFORM I-seq
       ELSE
          PERFORM J-seq.
K.  MOVE MenuCode TO TransCode.
    MOVE Record-1 TO FlightRecord.
    WRITE Record-2.
```

```
L.  PERFORM FUNCTIONS-8-9.


H-seq.
    PERFORM HA THROUGH HF.


HA. READ departures INVALID KEY MOVE 'T' TO ErrorFlag.
HB-rep.
    PERFORM HC-seq UNTIL NOT errors.
HF. PERFORM FUNCTION-10.
    REWRITE Record-1 INVALID KEY MOVE 'T' TO  ErrorFlag.


HC-seq.
    PERFORM HD THROUGH HE.

HD. DISPLAY "ERROR - INVALID KEY".
    PERFORM FUNCTIONS-11-12.
HE. READ departures INVALID KEY MOVE 'T' TO ErrorFlag.


I-seq.
    PERFORM IA THROUGH IB-rep.


IA. DELETE departures INVALID KEY MOVE 'T' TO ErrorFlag.
    MOVE SPACES TO FlightNumber, FlightDestination.
IB-rep.
    PERFORM IC-seq UNTIL NOT errors.


IC-seq.
    PERFORM IE THROUGH IG.


IE. DISPLAY "ERROR - INVALID KEY"
    PERFORM FUNCTIONS-11-12.
IG. DELETE departures INVALID KEY MOVE 'T' TO ErrorFlag.
    MOVE SPACES TO FlightNumber, FlightDestination.


J-seq.
    PERFORM JA THROUGH JC-rep.


JA. PERFORM FUNCTION-10.
JB. WRITE Record-1 INVALID KEY MOVE 'T' TO ErrorFlag.
JC-rep.
    PERFORM JD-seq UNTIL NOT errors.


JD-seq.
    PERFORM JE THROUGH JF.


JE. DISPLAY "ERROR - INVALID KEY"
    PERFORM FUNCTIONS-11-12.
```

```
JF. WRITE Record-1 INVALID KEY MOVE 'T' TO ErrorFlag.

* ----------------------- subroutines --------------------

FUNCTIONS-8-9.
    DISPLAY ClearScreen.
    DISPLAY "Do you require to:"
    DISPLAY SPACE
    DISPLAY "[A]mend record"
    DISPLAY "[D]elete record"
    DISPLAY "[I]nsert record"
    DISPLAY "[E]xit from system".
    DISPLAY SPACE.
    DISPLAY "input code A,D,I or E " WITH NO ADVANCING.
    ACCEPT MenuCode.

FUNCTIONS-11-12.
    DISPLAY "input time of departure as a four digit number".
    DISPLAY "example 2.15 P.M. AS 1415".
    DISPLAY "         2.15 A.M. AS 0215".
    ACCEPT clock.
    MOVE clock TO DepartureTime.
    MOVE 'F' TO ErrorFlag.

FUNCTION-10.
    DISPLAY "input flight number (MAX 6 CHARACTERS)"
    ACCEPT FlightNumber.
    DISPLAY "input FlightDestination (MAX 30 CHARACTERS)"
    ACCEPT FlightDestination.
```

The results from the program being run follow. Again only an extract of the results will be shown, together with the full log of all the changes made to the relative file.

```
Do you require to:

[A]mend record
[D]elete record
[I]nsert record
[E]xit from system

input code A,D,I or E I
input time of departure as a four digit number
```

```
example 2.15 P.M. AS 1415
        2.15 A.M. AS 0215
1040
input flight number (MAX 6 CHARACTERS)
IB194
input FlightDestination (MAX 30 CHARACTERS)
Nice

Do you require to:

[A]mend record
[D]elete record
[I]nsert record
[E]xit from system

input code A,D,I or E A
input time of departure as a four digit number
example 2.15 P.M. AS 1415
        2.15 A.M. AS 0215
1040
input flight number (MAX 6 CHARACTERS)
IB193
input FlightDestination (MAX 30 CHARACTERS)
Nice (cancelled)

Do you require to:

[A]mend record
[D]elete record
[I]nsert record
[E]xit from system

input code A,D,I or E D
input time of departure as a four digit number
example 2.15 P.M. AS 1415
        2.15 A.M. AS 0215
1015


Do you require to:

[A]mend record
[D]elete record
[I]nsert record
[E]xit from system

input code A,D,I or E I
```

```
input time of departure as a four digit number
example 2.15 P.M. AS 1415
        2.15 A.M. AS 0215
1100
input flight number (MAX 6 CHARACTERS)
PA7461
input FlightDestination (MAX 30 CHARACTERS)
New York

Do you require to:

[A]mend record
[D]elete record
[I]nsert record
[E]xit from system

input code A,D,I or E I
input time of departure as a four digit number
example 2.15 P.M. AS 1415
        2.15 A.M. AS 0215
1105
input flight number (MAX 6 CHARACTERS)
PA7469
input FlightDestination (MAX 30 CHARACTERS)
Chicago


flightlog

I1015BA271 Rome
I1016BA274 Geneva
I1030BC0113Athens Via Rome
I1031LU0777Majorca
I1035IB193 Majorca
I1040IB194 Nice
A1040IB193 Nice (cancelled)
D1015
I1100PA7461New York
I1105PA7469Chicago
I1115BA275 Paris
I1130BA444 Stockholm
I1145BC0197Geneva
A1145BC0197Oslo
I1200BC0203Edinburgh
I1205B181  Guernsey
I1210M76   Madrid
```

Design and write a second program to access the relative file created by the last program. This new program should output a real-time display of the next ten flights that are scheduled to depart from the airport. Using the TIME facility available in COBOL change the departure display every minute. Assume that the departure details are for one 24-hour period and that the system will stop at midnight. The layout of the display is shown below.

```
date 13/03/91
time 10:43

F L I G H T    D E P A R T U R E S

TIME      FLIGHT      DESTINATION

10  45    KLM123      Amsterdam
10  46    MON56       Rimini
10  47    DA171       Glasgow
10  48    BC1090      Liverpool
11  00    PA7461      New York
11  05    PA7469      Chicago
11  15    BA275       Paris
11  30    BA444       Stockholm
11  45    BC0197      Geneva
12  00    BC0203      Edinburgh
```

From the organisation of records on the file and the layout of the display it is possible to construct the input and output structures as follows.

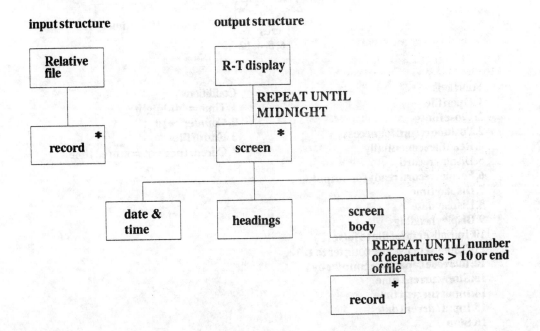

The order in which the records are stored on the relative file, and the order in which the records are displayed is the same. The number of different records that are displayed over a 24-hour period and the number of records stored on the relative file is also the same. There exists correspondence between the components of the input and output structures. The detailed program structure, complete with functions and conditions lists follows. The reserved word DATE can be used to input the current date into Working-Storage identifiers. DATE is a six-digit integer representing YYMMDD. ACCEPT DATE-WS FROM DATE will input the current date to the identifier DATE-WS.

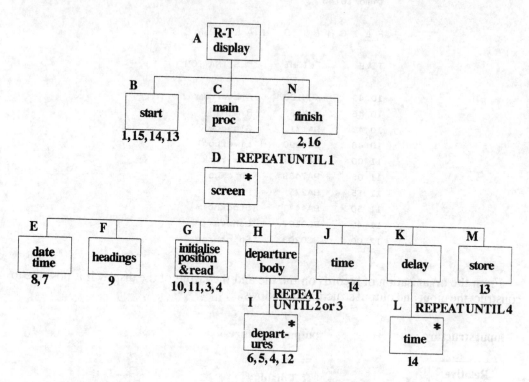

Functions
1. Open file
2. Close file
3. Position record for access
4. Read file sequentially
5. Display record
6. Format record ready for output
7. Display time
8. Display date
9. Display headings
10. Initialise end of file to false (F)
11. Initialise departure counter to 1
12. Increase departure counter by 1
13. Store current time
14. Input current time
15. Input current date
16. Stop

Conditions
1. Time = Midnight
2. Counter > 10
3. End of file
4. Current time not = stored time

The following program has been coded directly from the detailed program structure.

Comment. The reader may notice that a new level number has been introduced into the program. A level 66 entry is used when an existing area of memory is to be referenced by a different name. The RENAMES clause permits alternative, possible overlapping, grouping of elementary items. The format of the RENAMES clause is:

66 data-name-1 RENAMES data-name-2 $\left\{ \begin{array}{l} \text{THROUGH} \\ \text{THRU} \end{array} \right\}$ data-name-3

If in a program the variables HRS and MINS were defined as:

```
02 hrs PIC 99.
02 mins PIC 99.
```

the area of memory that contains a total of four digits can be renamed RTclock by using:

```
66 RTclock RENAMES hrs THROUGH mins.
```

All references to the variable RTclock in the program are references to a 4-digit number composed from hrs and mins.

```
        IDENTIFICATION DIVISION.
        PROGRAM-ID. DepartureBoard.

        ENVIRONMENT DIVISION.
        INPUT-OUTPUT SECTION.
        FILE-CONTROL.
            SELECT departures ASSIGN TO PFMS,
            ORGANIZATION IS RELATIVE,
            ACCESS MODE IS SEQUENTIAL,
            RELATIVE KEY IS clock.

        DATA DIVISION.
        FILE SECTION.
        FD departures.
        01 Record-1.
            02 DepartureTime PIC 9(4).
            02 FlightNumber PIC X(6).
            02 FlightDestination PIC X(30).

        WORKING-STORAGE SECTION.
        01 Record-1-WS.
            02 DepartureTime-WS PIC 99B99.
            02 FILLER PIC X(5) VALUE IS SPACES.
            02 FlightNumber-WS PIC X(6).
            02 FILLER PIC X(5) VALUE IS SPACES.
            02 FlightDestination-WS PIC X(30).
```

```
01 Record-2-WS.
    02 FILLER PIC X(32) VALUE IS "TIME      FLIGHT      DESTINATIO
-   "N".
01 Record-3-WS.
    02 FILLER PIC X(34) VALUE IS "F L I G H T    D E P A R T U R
-   "E S".
01 date-WS.
    02 YY PIC ZZ.
    02 MM PIC ZZ.
    02 DD PIC ZZ.
01 time-WS.
    02 HRS PIC ZZ.
    02 MINS PIC ZZ.
    02 FILLER PIC 9(4).


66 RT-clock RENAMES HRS THRU MINS.


01 time-store.
    02 FILLER PIC 9(4).


77 counter PIC 99.
77 EOF PIC A VALUE 'F'.
    88 EndOfFile VALUE 'T'.
77 clock PIC 9(4).
77 Midnight PIC 9(8) VALUE ZERO.
77 ClearScreen PIC X VALUE ''.



PROCEDURE DIVISION.
A-seq.
    PERFORM B THROUGH N.


B.  OPEN INPUT departures.
    ACCEPT date-WS FROM date.
    ACCEPT time-WS FROM time.
    MOVE RT-clock TO time-store, clock.
C-rep.
    PERFORM D-seq UNTIL time-WS = Midnight.
N.  CLOSE departures.
    STOP RUN.
D-seq.
    PERFORM E THROUGH M.


E.  DISPLAY ClearScreen.
    DISPLAY "date " DD "/" MM "/" YY.
    DISPLAY "time " HRS ":" MINS.
    DISPLAY SPACE.
```

```
    F.   DISPLAY Record-3-WS.
         DISPLAY SPACE.
         DISPLAY Record-2-WS.
         DISPLAY SPACE.
    G.   MOVE 'F' TO EOF.
         MOVE 1 TO counter.
         START departures KEY IS NOT LESS THAN clock
         INVALID KEY DISPLAY ClearScreen,
                     DISPLAY "NO FLIGHTS AVAILABLE",
                     CLOSE departures,
                     STOP RUN.
         READ departures AT END MOVE 'T' TO EOF.
    H-rep.
         PERFORM I UNTIL counter > 10 OR EndOfFile.
    J.   ACCEPT time-WS FROM TIME.
    K-rep.
         PERFORM L UNTIL RT-clock NOT = time-store.
    M.   MOVE RT-clock TO time-store, clock.


    I.   MOVE DepartureTime TO DepartureTime-WS.
         MOVE FlightNumber TO FlightNumber-WS.
         MOVE FlightDestination TO FlightDestination-WS.
         DISPLAY Record-1-WS.
         READ departures AT END MOVE 'T' TO EOF.
         ADD 1 TO counter.
    L.   ACCEPT time-WS FROM time.
```

An extract from running the program follows. The display shows the changes in the departures between 10.44 and 10.49.

```
date 13/03/91
time 10:44


F L I G H T    D E P A R T U R E S


TIME      FLIGHT      DESTINATION


10 45     KLM123      Amsterdam
10 46     MON56       Rimini
10 47     DA171       Glasgow
10 48     BC1090      Liverpool
11 00     PA7461      New York
11 05     PA7469      Chicago
11 15     BA275       Paris
11 30     BA444       Stockholm
```

```
11 45        BC0197       Geneva
12 00        BC0203       Edinburgh
```

date 13/03/91
time 10:45

F L I G H T   D E P A R T U R E S

TIME	FLIGHT	DESTINATION
10 45	KLM123	Amsterdam
10 46	MON56	Rimini
10 47	DA171	Glasgow
10 48	BC1090	Liverpool
11 00	PA7461	New York
11 05	PA7469	Chicago
11 15	BA275	Paris
11 30	BA444	Stockholm
11 45	BC0197	Geneva
12 00	BC0203	Edinburgh

date 13/03/91
time 10:46

F L I G H T   D E P A R T U R E S

TIME	FLIGHT	DESTINATION
10 46	MON56	Rimini
10 47	DA171	Glasgow
10 48	BC1090	Liverpool
11 00	PA7461	New York
11 05	PA7469	Chicago
11 15	BA275	Paris
11 30	BA444	Stockholm
11 45	BC0197	Geneva
12 00	BC0203	Edinburgh
12 05	B181	Guernsey

date 13/03/91
time 10:47

F L I G H T   D E P A R T U R E S

TIME	FLIGHT	DESTINATION
10 47	DA171	Glasgow

```
10 48      BC1090      Liverpool
11 00      PA7461      New York
11 05      PA7469      Chicago
11 15      BA275       Paris
11 30      BA444       Stockholm
11 45      BC0197      Geneva
12 00      BC0203      Edinburgh
12 05      B181        Guernsey
12 10      M76         Madrid

date 13/03/91
time 10:48

F L I G H T    D E P A R T U R E S

TIME       FLIGHT      DESTINATION

10 48      BC1090      Liverpool
11 00      PA7461      New York
11 05      PA7469      Chicago
11 15      BA275       Paris
11 30      BA444       Stockholm
11 45      BC0197      Geneva
12 00      BC0203      Edinburgh
12 05      B181        Guernsey
12 10      M76         Madrid

date 13/03/91
time 10:49

F L I G H T    D E P A R T U R E S

TIME       FLIGHT      DESTINATION

11 00      PA7461      New York
11 05      PA7469      Chicago
11 15      BA275       Paris
11 30      BA444       Stockholm
11 45      BC0197      Geneva
12 00      BC0203      Edinburgh
12 05      B181        Guernsey
12 10      M76         Madrid
```

12.7 Summary

An indexed sequential file is a disc-based file, in which data records can be accessed by the value of a key, or accessed sequentially in the same manner as a sequential file would be read. A record description for such a file must include one or more data items used as keys.

For amending, deleting and inserting records into an indexed sequential file, the value of the record key, which must be unique, identifies each record. The data item named in the RECORD KEY clause of a file-control entry for a file is the primary record key for that file. The ALTERNATE RECORD KEY clause designates secondary keys which may contain duplicate entries.

Relative file organisation is permitted only on disc. A relative file consists of records that are identified by relative record numbers. Think of such a file as a table with each cell capable of holding a logical record. A relative record number identifies the position of each cell in the table. Records are amended, deleted and inserted based on this record number or relative key. The relative key is not described as part of the record entry for the file, but defined in the Working-Storage Section as an unsigned integer large enough to hold the largest relative record number.

File definition requires entries in the Environment Division (Input-Output Section) and the Data Division (File Section) to define the file and specify its attributes. File input/ output achieved through the following Procedure Division statements.

OPEN - make a file available to a program and specify its use (INPUT, OUTPUT I-O).
CLOSE - make a file unavailable to a program, unless opened at a later stage for re-use.
READ - gain access to one record from a file (input).
WRITE - place one record in a file (output).
REWRITE - update one record in a file (i-o).
DELETE - remove one record from an indexed or relative file (i- o).
START - begin sequential access of a Dynamic file (input or i-o).

A level 66 is used with a RENAMES clause. RENAMES allows for a regrouping of fields in a record under a different name. A RENAMES is coded at the end of a record description entry containing the renamed items. RENAMES cannot name items defined at levels 01, 66, 77 or 88.

Keywords

*Random Access, Indexed Sequential File,
track index, main storage area, overflow area
Relative File;
ORGANIZATION, INDEXED, RELATIVE;
ACCESS MODE,
SEQUENTIAL, RANDOM, DYNAMIC;
RECORD KEY, ALTERNATE RECORD KEY,
DUPLICATES; RELATIVE KEY;
FILE STATUS;
OPEN I-O, INPUT, OUTPUT, CLOSE;
INVALID KEY;
START, READ, WRITE, REWRITE, DELETE;
level 66, RENAMES, DATE.*

12.8 Questions

1. A police computer is used to keep records on all registered vehicles. Use an indexed sequential file to create a simplified version of this system. Assume that records in the file are of fixed-length with the following format.

> Vehicle registration number (primary key) - 7 characters
> Date of registration - 4 digits MMYY
> Manufacturer - 10 characters
> Model - 10 characters
> Colour - 8 characters
> *Note - the concatenated fields of manufacturer, model and colour is an alternative key with duplicates*
> Name of registered owner - 25 characters
> Address where vehicle is kept - 30 characters
> Date of expiry of excise licence - 4 digits MMYY

Write a file maintenance program to cater for a change in the owner of a vehicle (amendment), vehicles being scrapped (deletion) and new vehicles being registered (insertion).

2. Using the file created in question (1) write a program to retrieve and output all the information contained in record(s) with access on either a specified primary key, or specified alternative key. The alternative key may have duplicate entries, therefore several records will be output.

Print a report of those vehicle owners who have failed to re-new their vehicle excise licence.

[3]. A doctor requires a computerised appointments system for use in his surgery. He holds a two-hour surgery in the morning (10.00 - 12.00) and a two-hour surgery in the evening (17.00-19.00) each day from Monday to Friday.

The appointments file is a relative file having a key coded as a 3- digit integer. The coding of this key is such that the first digit (0-9) represents the day and session, for example 0 - Monday AM, 1 - Monday PM, 2 - Tuesday AM, 3 -Tuesday PM, etc. The next two digits represents the time slot for the appointment. For example 01 - first time slot, 02 - second time slot, 03 - third time slot, etc, where a time slot is a ten minute period. Therefore, a key coded as 0507 would represent Wednesday at 18.00.

An appointment record consists of the name (25 characters) and address (30 characters) of the patient.

Write a program to allow his patients to make and cancel appointments throughout the week.

[4]. Using the file created in question (3) write a program to output a list of the vacant appointment slots for each day and a list of the names and addresses of the patients the doctor can expect to see.

13

Program Implementation Techniques

This chapter investigates several areas of Jackson Structured Programming where the technique of producing a detailed program structure diagram is complicated by clashes in the input and output initial structure diagrams or complicated by lack of information available when executing a condition in the structure diagram. These complications are respectively known as structure clashes and recognition problems.

Within the chapter methods for modifying the detailed program structures will be discussed together with the methods in COBOL for implementing the modifications.

13.1 Schematic Logic.

A detailed program structure conveys all the information necessary to code the procedural part of a solution in a chosen language. The method adopted in the text has been a translation of the detailed program structures into hierarchically coded Procedure Divisions. This method, however, does have the following disadvantages.

The hierarchical code will run slower because of the need to invoke lower levels of code.

The code is broken-up into very small logical sections.

Owing to the hierarchical nature of the code the techniques of inversion and backtracking will be less straightforward to implement.

A pseudo-code or schematic logic can be derived directly from the detailed program structure. This can be used as a framework for coding a Procedure Division by using flat or in-line coding methods. Such coding methods offer advantages over hierarchical coding in so much as the code is efficient in execution. The code can be used consistently throughout the JSP method, since it permits a relatively simple implementation of program inversion and backtracking.

Figure 13.1 on page 306, illustrates a detailed program structure that was derived as far back as chapter 2. To construct a schematic logic from this detailed program structure it is necessary to traverse the structure starting at component A in level 1, which represents a sequence. Move down to level 2 and to the left to component B, then right to components C, D and E until either a selective or repetitive component is found. Since component E is repetitive it is necessary to move down to level 3 and component F. Component F is a sequence, therefore, it is necessary to move down to level 4 and to the left to component G, then right to component H. Since H is a selective component it is then necessary to move down to level 5, and traverse the components I, J and K. Having met the end of the selection, further traversal of the diagram is possible by moving up to level 4, and from left to right to components L, M and N. This now marks the end of the sequence F, therefore, it is necessary to go back to level 3, and level 2, then move left to right through components O and P. This is then the end of the sequence from component A in level 1.

Notice that the alphabetical lettering of the structure diagram shows the order in which the diagram is traversed. Sequences, repetitions and selections are written in their abbreviated form of *seq*, *rep* and *sel*, preceded by the name of the component, which is the same as for hierarchical coding. However, all sequences, repetitions and selections must be given endings using the the word *end* preceded by the name of the component. Elementary components are represented by their function numbers, preceded by the name of the component and the word *do*. A sequence is coded as:

A-seq

    B do 9
    C do 10
    D do 2

    .

    .

A-end

Conditions are coded into a repetition as:

E-rep until 1
.
.
E-end

and conditions are coded into selections as:

H-sel if 2
        I do 5
H-alt-1 if 3
        J do 6
H-alt-2 (else)
        K do 7
H-end

In writing the schematic logic, each level in the detailed program structure is represented by indenting, to the right, the left-most character of the line. The schematic logic for the detailed program structure given in figure 13.1 follows.

A-seq
        B do 9
        C do 10
        D do 2
        E-rep until 1
            F-seq
                G do 1
                H-sel if 2
                    I do 5
                H-alt-1 if 3
                    J do 6
                H-alt-2 else
                  | K do 7
                H-end
                L do 11
                M do 8
                N do 12
            F-end
        E-end
        O do 4
        P do 3, 13
 A-end

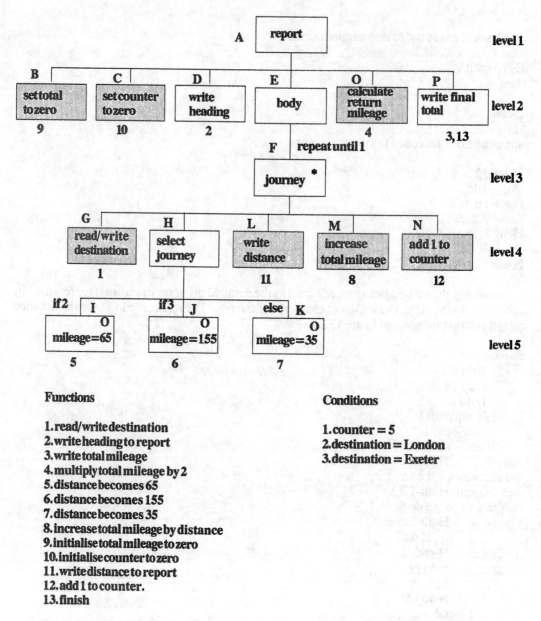

Figure 13.1 Detailed Program Structure taken from section 2.8 in chapter 2

13.2 Flat Code.

Flat code or in-line code can be produced directly from a schematic logic. Prior to the 1985 Standard for COBOL being introduced, the language did not contain in-line statements for repetition, and the programmer was forced to construct an in-line repetition by using an IF statement and a GO TO statement. The IF statement is the same as used throughout the text, however, the GO TO statement is new to the reader and its function will be explained here.

The GO TO (two words) statement causes control to be transferred from one part of the Procedure Division to another.

Format - 1   GO TO paragraph-name-1

The GO TO statement has received much bad press over the last decade. However, the GO TO statement, if used correctly, can aid in the formation of a control structure, or be used to exit from code, that owing to error data, no longer needs to be executed.

To quote from M.A.Jackson's book entitled the Principles of Program Design. "It is vital to distinguish surface appearance from underlying substance. When we write:

        PXITER. IF NOT CONDITION-1 GO TO PXEND.
                .
                .
                .
                GO TO PXITER.
        PXEND.

we are writing an iteration no less well-formed than:

        PX: DO WHILE (CONDITION 1);
                .
                .
                .
                ENDPX;

We are merely forced, because of shortcomings in the language (which it shares with PL/1 and ALGOL), to code our well formed iteration in an unusual manner. We are writing by hand the text which we would prefer our compiler to generate automatically. The true objection to GO TO statements is, of course, that they permit unrestrained branching from one part of a program to another. The two GO TO statements in the example do no such thing: they are an utterly standardised implementation of the schematic logic".

From this information it is clear to see that the repetition (iteration) from the detailed program structure in figure 13.1 can be coded as:

        E-rep.
                IF counter = 5 GO TO E-end.
                .
                .
                .
                GO TO E-rep.
        E-end.

The selection statement can be coded in several ways. However, the first and most obvious method, does not closely follow the schematic logic. The statements:

H-sel.
```
        IF city = 'London'
            MOVE 65 TO distance
        ELSE IF city = 'Exeter'
            MOVE 155 TO distance
        ELSE
            MOVE 35 TO distance.
```

accurately represent the selection given in the detailed program structure diagram and the schematic logic. However, the statements do not offer a direct mapping between the schematic logic and the COBOL code. For instance, what has happened to the labels I, J, K, H-alt-1, H-alt-2 and H-end?

In order to represent a direct mapping between the schematic logic and program it is necessary to code the selection in either of the following two ways.

H-sel.
```
        IF city NOT = 'London' GO TO H-alt-1.
I.          MOVE 65 TO distance.
        GO TO H-end.
H-alt-1.
        IF city NOT = 'Exeter' GO TO H-alt-2.
J.          MOVE 155 TO distance.
        GO TO H-end.
H-alt-2.
K.          MOVE 35 TO distance.
H-end.
```

Alternatively

H-sel.
```
        IF city = 'London' NEXT SENTENCE
        ELSE GO TO H-alt-1.
I.      MOVE 65 TO distance, GO TO H-end.
H-alt-1.
        IF city = 'Exeter' NEXT SENTENCE
        ELSE GO TO H-alt-2.
J.      MOVE 155 TO distance, GO TO H-end.
H-alt-2.
K.      MOVE 35 TO distance.
H-end.
```

The advantage of this last method over the second method is that the conditions for selection do not have to be negated.

To conclude this section, the schematic logic derived from figure 13.1, is now coded into a COBOL Procedure Division using flat or in-line code.

```
PROCEDURE  DIVISION.
A-seq.
B.          MOVE ZERO TO total.
C.          MOVE ZERO TO counter.
D.          DISPLAY "REPORT ON JOURNEYS".
            DISPLAY SPACE.
E-rep.
            IF counter = 5 GO TO E-end.
F-seq.
G.          DISPLAY "destination ? " WITH NO ADVANCING.
            ACCEPT city.
H-sel.
            IF city = 'London' NEXT SENTENCE
            ELSE GO TO H-alt-1.
I.          MOVE 65 TO distance, GO TO H-end.
H-alt-1.
            IF city = 'Exeter' NEXT SENTENCE
            ELSE GO TO H-alt-2.
J.          MOVE 155 TO distance, GO TO H-end.
H-alt-2.
K.          MOVE 35 TO distance.
H-end.
L.          DISPLAY "distance = ", distance, " miles".
M.          ADD distance TO total.
N.          ADD 1 TO counter.
F-end.
            GO TO E-rep.
E-end.
O.          MULTIPLY 2 BY total.
P.          DISPLAY "total mileage for return trips is ", total, " miles".
            STOP RUN.
A-end.
```

13.3 Structure Clashes.

In attempting to form a basic program structure, correspondence must exist between the respective components of the initial data structure diagrams. For a correspondence to exist three conditions must be satisfied. The pairs of components must occur the same number of times, in the same order and under the same circumstances. If one of these conditions is not satisfied then there is likely to be a structure clash between the components of the initial data structure diagrams. Structure clashes can be categorised into either an ordering clash or a boundary clash, depending upon the problem.

The following problem serves to illustrate an *ordering* clash between the components of data structure diagrams.

A file contains records of the names and academic details of staff at a college. The file is sorted by department as primary key, staff status as secondary key and staff name as tertiary key. A report is to be printed on the contents of the file, however, the format of the report is such that only the names of the members of staff are to be printed under the headings of the status of staff for the entire college. The staff names will not be categorised by department.

The initial data structure diagrams for the staff file and the report are shown in figure 13.2.

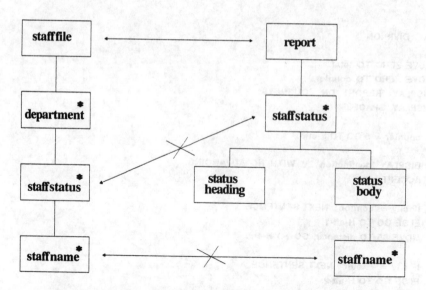

Figure 13.2 An illustration of an ordering structure clash between components in the input and output initial structure diagrams

A structure clash exists between two components in these structures. A staff status will appear a different number of times on each structure, once for each department on the staff file and only once in the report. Staff name will also appear in a different order in each structure.

Since the difference between the staff file and the report is the ordering of the records, this type of structure clash is known as an ordering clash. Such a structure clash is very simply resolved. The staff file (input file) is re-sorted using the staff status as primary key and the staff name as the secondary key. In effect the re-sorted file becomes an intermediate file, and it is this file that is processed to print the report.

In resolving this structure clash it is necessary, in theory, to design two programs. The first program to read the staff file, sort the records into the correct sequence and write to an intermediate file the sorted records. The second program reads the intermediate file and prints the report with the records in the correct order.

In practice, if the function to sort the records in the file appears before the coding to read and print the sorted file, then only one program need be written.

The following problem serves to illustrate a *boundary* clash between the components of data structure diagrams.

A hotel manager keeps a register of all his guests on a computer file. The records on the file are of fixed-length with the format:

    date of end-of-week - 6 digits
    day number - 1 digit
    guest details - 73 characters

For each room occupied in the hotel there is a guest record. At the end of each week the records are stored in a batch, each batch is identified by a batch header record that contains the date of the end of the week, with the remaining fields blank. An example of part of the file is:

```
311283
3112831Mr P.Jones        136 Welsh Way       Watford       British    45
3112831Mrs E.Smythe       24 Anvil Cr         Luton         British    23
3112832Rev S.Evans        7 Church Rd         Tring         British    13
070184
0701841Mr S.Davies        36 Black St         Coventry      British    16
0701841Miss P.Jones       23 West Way          Watford       British    30
0701841Mr S.Spencer       109 High St         Poole         British    31
0701845Mr P.Allen         2 Church Green      Witney        French     32
```

The manager requires a report based on the contents of the sequential register file. The layout of the report is such that the details of the guests for each new week must begin on a new page; the date for the week ending must appear at the top of every page; the total number of guests registered for each day of the week must be printed; the day number must be converted into the day name before printing the name on the report (assume day 1 is Sunday). An example of part of the report is shown in figure 13.3.

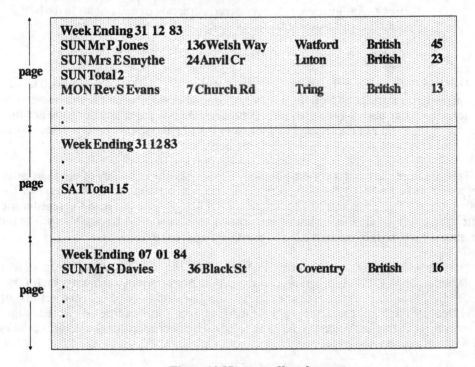

Figure 13.3 Layout of hotel report

The data structure diagrams for the sequential file and the report are shown in figure 13.4.

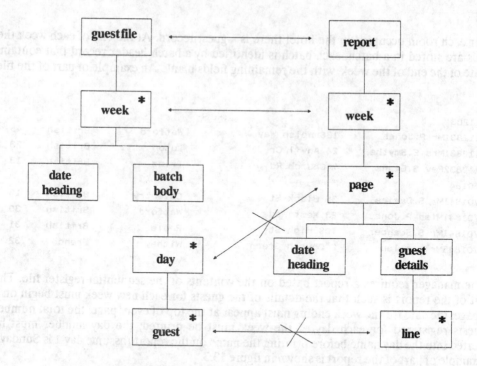

Figure 13.4 An illustration of a boundary clash between components in the initial input and output structure diagrams

There are two structure clashes between the components in the two diagrams. The number of pages will not correspond with the number of days, since one day may require several pages, or more likely, one page may be used for several days. On one page, excluding the heading, the number of lines will not correspond with the number of guests, since an extra line is required for the total number of guests registering at the hotel in one day.

This structure clash is known as a boundary clash, since the boundary of the page is causing the problem. In resolving this structure clash the same technique will be used as for the ordering clash. Two programs will be designed. The first program to read the register file and write to an intermediate file the lines to be printed, including the extra total lines. The second program to read the intermediate file and print the required report.

The detailed program structure diagrams for the two separate programs, their implementation as COBOL programs and the results from running each program follow. The results are based on the extract of the register file given on page 311. In the results for the hotel report file, the character 1, appearing before the heading Week Ending, is a paper-control character. When this file is spooled on a lineprinter this character is used by the printer to generate a new page.

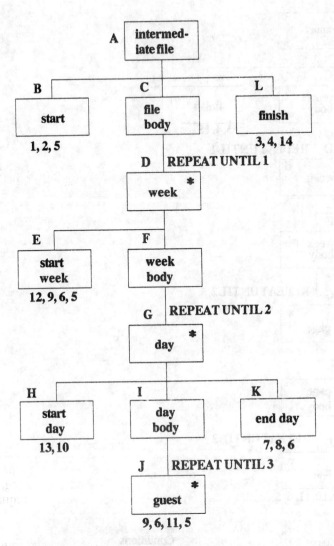

Functions
1. Open input register file
2. Open output intermediate file
3. Close register
4. Close intermediate
5. Read register file
6. Write intermediate file
7. Format registration count for day
8. Format total registrations line
9. Transfer register record for output
10. Initialise registration count to zero
11. Increase registration count by 1
12. Store date in temporary store
13. Store day in temporary store
14. Stop

Conditions
1. End of register file
2. NOT same date OR (1)
3. NOT same day OR (2)

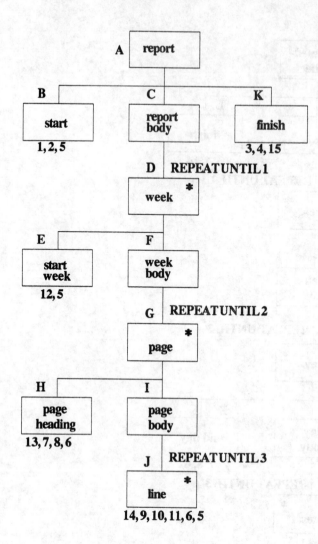

Functions
1. Open input intermediate file
2. Open output report file
3. Close intermediate file
4. Close report file
5. Read intermediate file
6. Write report file
7. Format date for output
8. Format page heading for output
9. Format name of day for output
10. Format guest details for output
11. Move record for output
12. Store date in temporary store
13. Initialise line count to zero
14. Increase line count by 1
15. stop

Conditions
1. End of intermediate file
2. NOT same date OR (1)
3. Line count NOT < 60 OR (2)

```
IDENTIFICATION DIVISION.
PROGRAM-ID. FirstProgram.

ENVIRONMENT DIVISION.
INPUT-OUTPUT SECTION.
FILE-CONTROL.
    SELECT register ASSIGN TO PFMS.
    SELECT intermediate ASSIGN TO PFMS.

DATA DIVISION.
FILE SECTION.
FD register, COMPRESSED.
01 RegisterRecord.
    02 date-RR PIC 9(6).
    02 day-RR PIC 9.
    02 details-RR PIC X(73).

FD intermediate, COMPRESSED.
01 IntermediateRecord.
    02 date-IR PIC 9(6).
    02 day-IR PIC 9.
    02 details-IR PIC X(73).

WORKING-STORAGE SECTION.
01 Record-1-WS.
    02 FILLER PIC X(6) VALUE IS "Total".
    02 RegCount PIC Z9.

77 EOF PIC A VALUE 'F'.
    88 EndOfFile VALUE 'T'.

77 DateStore PIC 9(6).
77 DateStore-RR PIC 9(6).
77 DayStore PIC 9.
77 RegistrationCount PIC 99.

PROCEDURE DIVISION.
A-seq.
B.   OPEN INPUT register.
     OPEN OUTPUT intermediate.
     READ register AT END MOVE 'T' TO EOF.
C-rep.
     IF EndOfFile GO TO C-end.
D-seq.
E.       MOVE date-RR TO DateStore.
         MOVE RegisterRecord TO IntermediateRecord.
         WRITE IntermediateRecord.
```

```
                    READ register AT END MOVE 'T' TO EOF.
        F-rep.

                    IF EndOfFile OR
                    date-RR NOT = DateStore GO TO F-end.
        G-seq.
        H.          MOVE day-RR TO DayStore.
                    MOVE ZERO TO RegistrationCount.
        I-rep.

                    IF EndOfFile OR
                    date-RR NOT = DateStore OR
                    day-RR NOT = DayStore GO TO I-end.
        J.              MOVE RegisterRecord TO IntermediateRecord.
                        WRITE IntermediateRecord.
                        ADD 1 TO RegistrationCount.
                        READ register AT END MOVE 'T' TO EOF.
                    GO TO I-rep.
        I-end.
        K.          MOVE RegistrationCount TO RegCount.

                    MOVE Record-1-WS TO details-IR.
                    WRITE IntermediateRecord.
        G-end.
                    GO TO F-rep.
        F-end.
        D-end.
                GO TO C-rep.
        C-end.
        L.  CLOSE register.
            CLOSE intermediate.
            STOP RUN.
        A-end.
```

Intermediate File

```
311283
3112831Mr P.Jones         136 Welsh Way        Watford      British    45
3112831Mrs E.Smythe       24 Anvil Cr          Luton        British    23
3112831Total  2
3112832Rev S.Evans        7 Church Rd          Tring        British    13
3112832Total  1
070184
0701841Mr S.Davies        36 Black St          Coventry     British    16
0701841Miss P.Jones       23 West Way          Watford      British    30
0701841Mr S.Spencer       109 High St          Poole        British    31
0701841Total  3
0701845Mr P.Allen         2 Church Green       Witney       French     32
0701845Total  1
```

```
IDENTIFICATION DIVISION.
PROGRAM-ID. ProgramTwo.

ENVIRONMENT DIVISION.
INPUT-OUTPUT SECTION.
FILE-CONTROL.
      SELECT intermediate ASSIGN TO PFMS.
      SELECT HotelReport ASSIGN TO PFMS.

DATA DIVISION.
FILE SECTION.
FD intermediate, COMPRESSED.
01 IntermediateRecord.
      02 date-IR PIC 9(6).
      02 day-IR PIC 9.
      02 details-IR PIC X(73).

FD HotelReport, COMPRESSED.
01 ReportRecord.
      02 FILLER PIC X.
      02 LineImage PIC X(79).

WORKING-STORAGE SECTION.
01 Record-1-WS.
      02 FILLER PIC X(13) VALUE IS "Week Ending".
      02 HeaderDate PIC 99BB99BB99.
01 Record-2-WS.
      02 DayName PIC X(4).
      02 Guest-Details-WS-1 PIC X(73).
01 Record-3-WS.
      02 FILLER PIC X(21) VALUE IS "SUNMONTUEWEDTHUFRISAT".
01 Record-4-WS REDEFINES Record-3-WS.
      02 NameOfday PIC X(3) OCCURS 7 TIMES.


77 EOF PIC A VALUE 'F'.
      88 EndOfFile VALUE 'T'.
77 LineCount PIC 99.
77 DateStore PIC 9(6).

PROCEDURE DIVISION.
A-seq.
B.  OPEN INPUT intermediate.
      OPEN OUTPUT HotelReport.
      READ intermediate AT END MOVE 'T' TO EOF.
C-rep.
      IF EndOfFile GO TO C-end.
D-seq.
E.        MOVE date-IR TO DateStore
```

```
                    READ intermediate AT END MOVE 'T' TO EOF.
        F-rep.

                    IF EndOfFile OR date-IR NOT = DateStore
                    GO TO F-end.
        G-seq.
        H.          MOVE ZERO TO LineCount.
                    MOVE date-IR TO HeaderDate.
                    MOVE Record-1-WS TO LineImage.
                    WRITE ReportRecord AFTER ADVANCING PAGE.
        I-rep.

                    IF EndOfFile OR date-IR NOT = DateStore
                    OR LineCount NOT < 60 GO TO I-end.
        J.              ADD 1 TO LineCount.
                        MOVE NameOfday (day-IR) TO DayName.
                        MOVE details-IR TO Guest-Details-WS-1.
                        MOVE Record-2-WS TO LineImage.
                        WRITE ReportRecord AFTER ADVANCING 1 LINE.
                        READ intermediate AT END MOVE 'T' TO EOF.
                    GO TO I-rep.
        I-end.
        G-end.
                    GO TO F-rep.
        F-end.
        D-end.
            GO TO C-rep.
        C-end.
        K.  CLOSE intermediate.
            CLOSE HotelReport.
            STOP RUN.
        A-end.
```

Hotel Report File

```
1Week Ending  31  12  83
   SUN Mr P.Jones          136 Welsh Way           Watford          British      45
   SUN Mrs E.Smythe        24 Anvil Cr             Luton            British      23
   SUN Total  2
   MON Rev S.Evans         7 Church Rd             Tring            British      13
   MON Total  1
1Week Ending  07  01  84
   SUN Mr S.Davies         36 Black St             Coventry         British      16
   SUN Miss P.Jones        23 West Way             Watford          British      30
   SUN Mr S.Spencer        109 High St             Poole            British      31
   SUN Total  3
   THU Mr P.Allen          2 Church Green          Witney           French       32
   THU Total  1
```

13.4 Program Inversion.

Program inversion is a technique, whereby the intermediate file invented at the program design stage, is not created at the program implementation stage. The two separate programs developed at the program design stage are used, however, one program becomes a subprogram of the other, and the main program calls the subprogram every time it would have made reference to the intermediate file had it still existed.

If the second program is chosen as the main control program, all references to the intermediate file are replaced by calls to the first program as a subprogram. The subprogram will have access to the first data file, in this example, the register file. Each call to the subprogram will result in the data file being either, opened, read or closed, depending upon the position of entry into the subprogram. After the appropriate statements have been executed the computer is directed to return to the main program. All references to writing to the intermediate file in the subprogram, reading the intermediate file in the main program and opening and closing the intermediate file in both programs are deleted.

If the first program is chosen as the main control program, then all references to either opening, writing or closing the intermediate file are replaced by calls to the second program as a subprogram. The subprogram either opens, writes a record or closes the report file, depending upon the position of entry into the subprogram. After the appropriate statements have been executed the computer is directed to return to the main program. All references to reading the intermediate file in the subprogram, writing to the intermediate file in the main program and opening and closing the intermediate file in both programs are deleted.

However, before the two COBOL programs listed earlier are converted into a main program and a subprogram, there are several changes that must be made to the schematic logic of the two programs.

From the detailed program structure for the first program the schematic logic can be coded as follows.

```
A-seq
        B do 1,2,5
        C-rep until 1
            D-seq
                E do 12,9,6,5
                F-rep until 2
                    G-seq
                        H do 13,10
                        I-rep until 3
                            J do 9,6,11,5
                        I-end
                        K do 7,8,6
                    G-end
                F-end
            D-end
        C-end
        L do 3,4,14
    A-end
```

The modifications necessary to the schematic logic, if the first program is to be used as a subprogram, follow. Functions 2 (open) and 4 (close) are deleted since they relate to opening and closing the intermediate file. Function 14 (stop) is replaced by exit program, to allow the computer to return to the main program. Function 6 (write) is replaced by a statement to store the re-entry position into the subprogram, when it is next called from the main program, and direct the computer to exit from the subprogram.

```
A-seq
        goto Q1, Q2, Q3, Q4, Q5, Q6 depending on QS
Q1
        B  do 1, 2 move 2 to QS goto QEXIT
Q2         do 5
        C-rep until 1
           D-seq
              E  do 12, 9, 6 move 3 to QS goto QEXIT
Q3            do 5
           F-rep until 2
              G-seq
                 H do 13, 10
                 I-rep until 3
                    J  do 9, 6 move 4 to QS goto QEXIT
Q4                  do 11, 5
                 I-end
                 K do 7, 8, 6   move 5 to QS goto QEXIT
Q5
              G-end
           F-end
        D-end
     C-end
     L  do 3, 4
Q6      move 6 to QS
        do 14
QEXIT   exit program
A-end
```

From the detailed program structure for the second program the schematic logic can be coded as follows.

```
A-seq
        B do 1,2,5
        C-rep until 1
           D-seq
              E do 12,5
           F-rep until 2
              G-seq
                 H do 13,7,8,6
                 I-rep until 3
                    J do 14,9,10,11,6,5
                 I-end
```

```
            G-end
          F-end
        D-end
      C-end
      K do 3,4,15
A-end
```

The modifications necessary to the schematic logic, if the second program is to be used as a main program, follow.

Functions 1 (open) and 3 (close) are deleted since they relate to opening and closing the intermediate file.

Function 5 (read) the intermediate file is replaced by a call to the subprogram. Depending upon the re-entry point in the subprogram, this call causes the register file to be opened, read or closed. When the register file is read a record is passed over to the main program for processing. When there is a change of day in the subprogram a total record is constructed and passed across to the main program.

```
A-seq
      B   do 1 call subprogram
          do 2
          do 5 call subprogram
      C-rep until 1
          D-seq
              E do 12, 5 call subprogram
              F-rep until 2
                  G-seq
                      H do 13, 7, 8, 6
                      I-rep until 3
                          J do 14, 9, 10, 11, 6, 5 call subprogram
                      I-end
                  G-end
              F-end
          D-end
      C-end
      K   do 5 call subprogram
          do 4, 15
A-end
```

13.5 Subprograms.

A subprogram is a self-contained program that has been compiled independently of any other program, yet can be executed from within another program. Although different programs can be compiled independently of each other, they can be link-loaded together and executed as one suite of programs that produce the required solution to the problem. The two programs can be compiled separately on the PRIME system by using the command COBOL85. For example:

OK, COBOL85 MainProgram
[0 errors]

OK, COBOL85 subprogram
[0 errors]

On the PRIME system, both programs can be link/loaded into a single executable program, by using the following commands.

OK, BIND MainProgram
    :LOAD MainProgram
    :LOAD subprogram
    :LI COBOL85LIB
    :LI
BIND COMPLETE
    :FILE
OK,

The single executable program containing the two programs MainProgram and subprogram can be executed, on a PRIME computer, by the command:

OK, R MainProgram

Notice that the single executable program is given the name of the main or controlling program.

In a more general discussion, the use of subprograms for building computer systems offer the following advantages over single programs.

Subprograms can be written to represent specific functions. These programs can be compiled, tested and catalogued to form part of a library of functional units that can be accessed by many different programmers.

Subprograms help to facilitate team projects. By dividing a system into smaller components, each component can be implemented as a subprogram, which can be developed and tested by a single programmer.

When more than one program is used in the same run-time environment, there will be a need to call one program from within another program and also to communicate data between the programs.

Figure 13.5 illustrates how one COBOL program can be used to call another COBOL program. Notice from the diagram that a CALL to the subprogram directs the computer to the first statement of the PROCEDURE DIVISION. The statements in the Procedure Division are processed until the EXIT PROGRAM statement is executed. This causes the computer to branch back to the next executable statement after the CALL statement in the main program. Notice from the diagram that the CALL statement can be used from different positions in the Procedure Division of the main program, and the statements within the Procedure Division of the subprogram are again executed until the EXIT PROGRAM statement is executed. This process of entry and re-entry into a subprogram from a main program is the basis under which program inversion can be implemented.

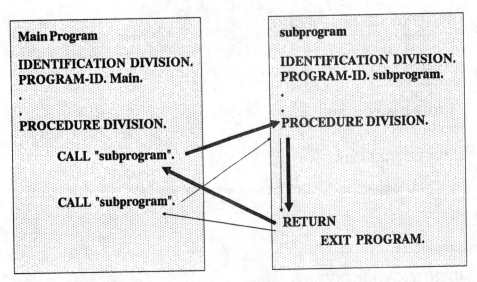

Figure 13.5 An illustration of the CALL and EXIT statements in COBOL programs.

A simplified format of the CALL statement is:

CALL literal-1 [**USING** {data-name-1} ...]

where literal-1 is the name of the program being called. If the subprogram is another COBOL program then literal-1 is the name associated with the PROGRAM-ID statement.

To enable a computer to return from the called program, every subprogram must have an **EXIT PROGRAM** statement as a single sentence in a paragraph.

One subprogram can call another subprogram, however, it must not call the calling program, and since recursion is not allowed in COBOL, a subprogram must not call itself.

In the earlier discussion about program inversion it was made clear that the subprogram would pass a record back to the main program, to enable the main program to process the data. The communication of data between two programs at run-time is achieved through the USING clause in the CALL statement of the main program, the USING clause in the Procedure Division heading of the subprogram and the LINKAGE SECTION of the subprogram. The following skeletal code illustrates data communication between two COBOL programs.

Main Program

    IDENTIFICATION DIVISION.
    PROGRAM-ID. MainProgram.

```
WORKING-STORAGE SECTION.
01 Parameter-1.
    02 alpha PIC 9(4).
    02 beta PIC 99.
01 Parameter-2.
    02 delta PIC X(10).
    02 epsilon PIC X(20).
    .
    .
    .

PROCEDURE DIVISION.

    CALL "subprogram" USING Parameter-1, Parameter-2.
    .
    .
```

Subprogram

```
IDENTIFICATION DIVISION.
PROGRAM-ID. subprogram.
    .
    .
    .
WORKING-STORAGE SECTION.
    .
    .
    .
LINKAGE SECTION.
01 Parameter-1.
    02 a PIC 9(4).
    02 b PIC 99.
01 Parameter-2.
    02 d PIC X(10).
    02 e PIC X(20).
    .
    .
    .

PROCEDURE DIVISION USING Parameter-1, Parameter-2.
    .
    .
    .
RETURN.
EXIT PROGRAM.
```

There must be the same number of data items in the USING clause of the main program as the USING clause of the subprogram. The names of the items of data need not be the same, since it is the positions of the items of data that is important. The picture clauses for the respective items of data between the main program and the subprogram must be the same.

The subprogram contains a LINKAGE SECTION after the Working-Storage Section, where all the identifiers specified in the USING clause of the subprogram are defined. Only level 01 and level 77 entries are permitted in this section, however, level 01 entries may have subordinate entries. The purpose of the Linkage Section is to provide memory addresses where the data items defined by the main program are stored, thereby providing a memory link between the items of data in the main program and items of data in the subprogram.

If there are no items of data to pass between two programs then the USING clauses and LINKAGE SECTION can be omitted.

13.6 Program Inversion Implemented.

From the modified designs of the programs given in section 13.4 and the work on subprograms in the last section, it is possible to implement the first program as a subprogram and the second program as the main program.

```
IDENTIFICATION DIVISION.
PROGRAM-ID. ProgramTwo.

ENVIRONMENT DIVISION.
INPUT-OUTPUT SECTION.
FILE-CONTROL.
      SELECT HotelReport ASSIGN TO PFMS.

DATA DIVISION.
FILE SECTION.
FD HotelReport, COMPRESSED.
01 ReportRecord.
      02 FILLER PIC X.
      02 LineImage PIC X(79).

WORKING-STORAGE SECTION.
01 Record-0-WS.
      02 date-WS PIC 9(6).
      02 day-WS PIC 9.
      02 details-WS PIC X(73).
01 Record-1-WS.
      02 FILLER PIC X(13) VALUE IS "Week Ending".
      02 HeaderDate PIC 99BB99BB99.
01 Record-2-WS.
      02 DayName PIC X(4).
      02 Guest-Details-WS-1 PIC X(73).
01 Record-3-WS.
      02 FILLER PIC X(21) VALUE IS "SUNMONTUEWEDTHUFRISAT".
01 Record-4-WS REDEFINES Record-3-WS.
      02 NameOfday PIC X(3) OCCURS 7 TIMES.

01 EOF PIC A VALUE 'F'.
      88 EndOfFile VALUE 'T'.
77 LineCount PIC 99.
77 DateStore PIC 9(6).
77 DayStore PIC 9.
```

```
PROCEDURE DIVISION.
A-seq.
B.   CALL "FirstProgram" USING Record-0-WS, EOF.
     OPEN OUTPUT HotelReport.
     CALL "FirstProgram" USING Record-0-WS, EOF.
C-rep.
     IF EndOfFile GO TO C-end.
D-seq.
E.       MOVE date-WS TO DateStore.
         CALL "FirstProgram" USING Record-0-WS, EOF.
F-rep.
         IF EndOfFile OR date-WS NOT = DateStore
         GO TO F-end.
G-seq.
H.           MOVE ZERO TO LineCount.
             MOVE date-WS TO HeaderDate.
             MOVE Record-1-WS TO LineImage.
             WRITE ReportRecord AFTER ADVANCING PAGE.
I-rep.
             IF EndOfFile OR date-WS NOT = DateStore
             OR LineCount NOT < 60 GO TO I-end.
J.               ADD 1 TO LineCount.
                 MOVE NameOfday (day-WS) TO DayName.
                 MOVE details-WS TO Guest-Details-WS-1.
                 MOVE Record-2-WS TO LineImage.
                 WRITE ReportRecord AFTER ADVANCING 1 LINE.
                 CALL "FirstProgram" USING Record-0-WS, EOF.
             GO TO I-rep.
I-end.
G-end.
             GO TO F-rep.
F-end.
D-end.
     GO TO C-rep.
C-end.
K.   CALL "FirstProgram" USING Record-0-WS, EOF.
     CLOSE HotelReport.
     STOP RUN.
A-end.
```

In the coding of the inverted subprogram the goto Q1, Q2, Q3, Q4, Q5, Q6 depending on QS, found in the schematic logic, has an equivalent statement in COBOL. This is the second format of the GO TO statement.

Format - 2 **GO** TO {paragraph-name-1} ... **DEPENDING** ON identifier- 1.

In the program the statement has been coded as:

GO TO Q1, Q2, Q3, Q4, Q5, Q6 DEPENDING ON QS.

When QS has the value 1 the computer branches to paragraph Q1, when QS has the value 2 the computer branches to paragraph Q2, when QS is 3 the branch is to Q3, and so on.

```
IDENTIFICATION DIVISION.
PROGRAM-ID. FirstProgram.

ENVIRONMENT DIVISION.
INPUT-OUTPUT SECTION.
FILE-CONTROL.
      SELECT register ASSIGN TO PFMS.

DATA DIVISION.
FILE SECTION.
FD register, COMPRESSED.
01 RegisterRecord.
      02 date-RR PIC 9(6).
      02 day-RR PIC 9.
      02 details-RR PIC X(73).

WORKING-STORAGE SECTION.
01 Record-1-WS.
      02 FILLER PIC X(6) VALUE IS "Total".
      02 RegCount PIC Z9.

77 EOF PIC A VALUE 'F'.
      88 EndOfFile VALUE 'T'.

77 DateStore PIC 9(6).
77 DayStore PIC 9.
77 RegistrationCount PIC 99.
77 QS PIC 9 VALUE 1.

LINKAGE SECTION.
01 Record-1-LS.
      02 date-LS PIC 9(6).
      02 day-LS PIC 9.
      02 details-LS PIC X(73).
01 FileEnd PIC A.
```

```
PROCEDURE DIVISION USING Record-1-LS, FileEnd.
A-seq.
        GO TO Q1, Q2, Q3, Q4, Q5, Q6 DEPENDING ON QS.
Q1.
B.   OPEN INPUT register.
     MOVE 2 TO QS, GO TO QEXIT.
Q2. READ register INTO Record-1-LS
     AT END MOVE 'T' TO EOF, FileEnd.
C-rep.
     IF EndOfFile GO TO C-end.
D-seq.
E.       MOVE date-RR TO DateStore.
         MOVE RegisterRecord TO Record-1-LS.
         MOVE 3 TO QS, GO TO QEXIT.
Q3.      READ register INTO Record-1-LS
         AT END MOVE 'T' TO EOF, FileEnd.
F-rep.
         IF EndOfFile OR
         date-RR NOT = DateStore GO TO F-end.
G-seq.
H.           MOVE day-RR TO DayStore.
             MOVE ZERO TO RegistrationCount.
I-rep.
             IF EndOfFile OR
             date-RR NOT = DateStore OR
             day-RR NOT = DayStore GO TO I-end.
J.               MOVE RegisterRecord TO Record-1-LS.
                 MOVE 4 TO QS, GO TO QEXIT.
Q4.              ADD 1 TO RegistrationCount.
                 READ register INTO Record-1-LS
                     AT END MOVE 'T' TO EOF, FileEnd.
                 GO TO I-rep.
I-end.
K.           MOVE DateStore TO date-LS.
             MOVE DayStore TO day-LS.
             MOVE RegistrationCount TO RegCount.
             MOVE Record-1-WS TO details-LS.
             MOVE 5 TO QS, GO TO QEXIT.
Q5.
G-end.
         GO TO F-rep.
F-end.
D-end.
     GO TO C-rep.
C-end.
```

```
L.  CLOSE register.
Q6. MOVE 1 TO QS.
QEXIT.
     EXIT PROGRAM.
A-end.
```

In the testing of this program it was necessary to introduce a blank record at the end of the register file otherwise the last total record was never written when the end of the register file was detected.

13.7 Interleaving Clashes.

Consider a situation where students at a college have access to a central computer through terminals. In order to use the computer system a student must login through one of the terminals. Having gained access to the computer it is then possible for the student to use different packages on the computer system. A package must be loaded into the memory of the computer, and when it is no longer required, unloaded from the memory. When a student no longer wants to use the computer, the student must logout. An activity log file keeps track of the use of the computer during the course of a day. In a simplified form of this file the time of every student login and logout is recorded, together with the time a package is loaded and unloaded. Figure 13.6 illustrates a typical pattern of activity for just three students who use the computer system over a total time period of 34 minutes.

Student 1	Student 2	Student 3	Time
login start 00			00
	login start 03		03
package 1 load 05			05
		login start 10	10
	package 1 load 12		12
		package 1 load 13	13
	package 1 unload 16		16
	package 2 load 17		17
			20
package 1 unload 20			21
package 2 load 21		package 1 unload 22	22
	package 2 unload 23		23
		package 2 load 24	24
			28
package 2 unload 28			29
logout finish 29		package 2 unload 30	30
		logout finish 31	31
	package 3 load 32		32
	package 3 unload 33		33
	logout finish 34		34

Figure 13.6 An illustration of the activity of three students logged on to a computer over a total time period of 34 minutes.

If each line from figure 13.6 is coded into the activity log file, the contents of the file might appear as follows, where b represents a single blank space.

```
1S00b00
2S00b03
1P01L05
3S00b10
2P01L12
3P01L13
2P01U16
      .
      .
2F00b34
```

The records in this file correspond to the following format.

Student ID - 1 digit
Student activity - 1 character, coded as: S - login [S]TART, P - [P]ACKAGE activity
                                          F - logout [F]INISH
Time of student activity - 2 digits
Package ID - digit
Package activity - 1 character, coded as: L - [L]OAD package, U - [U]NLOAD package
                                          b - blank space when student activity S or F
Time of package activity - 2 digits

The output required from the system is a display of the current usage of the system in the following format.

System Usage Report

shortest student use = 21
longest student use = 31
shortest package use = 1
longest package use = 15

The initial data structure diagrams for the activity log file and the system usage report follow.

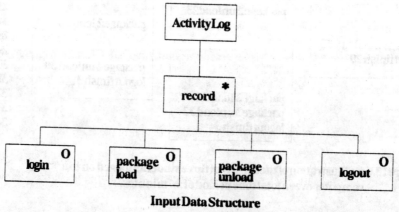

Input Data Structure

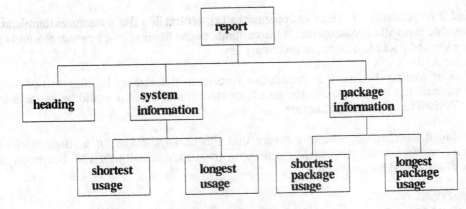

Output Structure Diagram

Consider the problem of identifying correspondences between the two structures. There is only one correspondence and that is at the highest level between activity log and report. However, there are no structure clashes at the other levels and the two structures can be amalgamated to produce the following basic program structure.

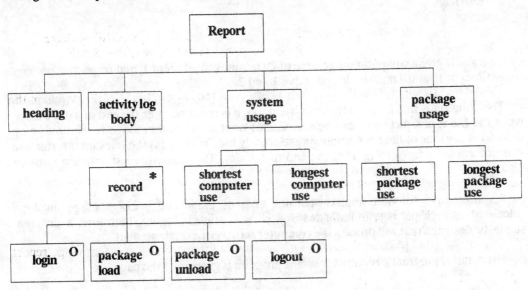

The next phase in JSP is to derive functions and conditions, and distribute them over the basic program structure to form a detailed program structure. Such functions might include:

1. Store login time.
2. Subtract login time from logout time giving student use.
3. Store package load time.
4. Subtract package load time from package unload time giving package use.

These functions could be distributed over the basic program structure so that the elementary components login, package load, package unload and logout contain the functions 1,

3, 4 and 2 respectively. However, in processing the activity log file it becomes immediately obvious that this will only be correct if the contents of the file is sorted by student number as primary key and package number as secondary key.

Without sorting the file, the consecutive records in the activity log file do not form a self-contained unit of information for each respective student, and it would be impossible to use the derived basic program structure.

Sorting the activity log file will ensure that the package usage for a single student is contained within several consecutive records on the sorted activity log file. For example a sample of the sorted file might be:

```
1S00b00
1P01L05
1P01U20
1P02L21
1P02U28
1F00b29
2S00b03
2P01L12
    .
    .
```

This would give a computer usage time of 29 minutes for student 1, and respective package usage times of 15 and 7 minutes for packages 1 and 2.

This solution is fine if an analysis of system usage is required after the end of a day's work, when the file is complete and can be sorted. But what if the system usage is required upon demand at any time of the day? Although the activity log file contains the relevant information it is not available for sorting until the end of the day. Therefore, the last solution must be discounted.

An alternative solution implies that the student usage and package usage must be calculated as each package is unloaded and at each student logout, therefore, a program should be designed that will process the computer activity of a single student.

The detailed program structure for such a program is given over the page.

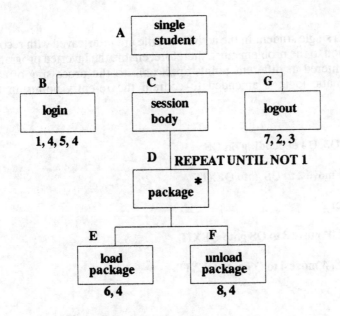

Functions
1. Open activity log file
2. Close activity log file
3. Stop
4. Read activity log file
5. Save login start time
6. Save package load time
7. Subtract login start time from logout finish time
8. Subtract package load time from package unload time

Conditions
1. Package load record

The schematic logic for this program follows.

```
A-seq
      B do 1, 4, 5, 4
      C-rep until not 1
          D-seq
              E do 6, 4
              F do 8, 4
          D-end
      C-end
      G do 7, 2, 3
A-end
```

If this program is inverted with respect to the program that produces the report, then it becomes a re-entrant subprogram of the report program. All references to the activity log file are deleted from this subprogram, since they are accessed by the main program.

The records for a single student in the activity log file are interleaved with records for other students. The solution to the problem must, therefore, enable the inverted program for a single student, to be re-entered at different points applicable to the processing of each students records. The schematic logic is amended to contain the re-entry points in the inverted subprogram.

A-seq

    goto Q1, Q2, Q3, Q4 depending on QS

Q1

    B do 1, 4, 5, 9 move 2 to QS goto QEXIT

Q2

    C-rep until not 1
      D-seq
        E do 6, 9 move 3 to QS goto QEXIT

Q3

        F do 8, 9 move 4 to QS goto QEXIT

Q4

      D-end
    C-end
    G do 7, 2, 3

QEXIT

    exit program

A-end

The position of re-entry in the inverted program, for each student, and the necessary data for each student is stored in a one-dimensional table, known as a state-vector table. This is illustrated in figure 13.7

student number	StateVariable [QS]	Login [S]tart	Logout [F]inish	Package [L]oad	Package [U]nload
1					
2					
3					

The COBOL description of this table is:

```
01 StateVector.
    02 Record-SV OCCURS 3 TIMES.
        03 StateVariable PIC 9.
        03 StartTime PIC 99.
        03 FinishTime PIC 99.
        03 LoadTime PIC 99.
        03 UnloadTime PIC 99.
```

Figure 13.7   A one-dimensional table representing the state vectors for the time spent on the computer and the level of usage of the packages.

The basic program structure for the report program given earlier is the basis for the detailed program structure of the main program. This program is the main or controlling program and calls the inverted subroutine in order to process the data on a single student.

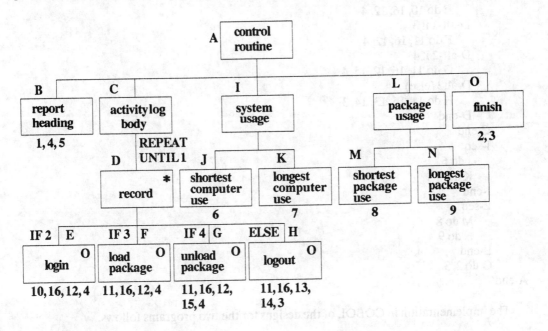

Functions
1. Open activity log file
2. Close activity log file
3. Stop
4. Read activity log file
5. Display heading
6. Display shortest computer use
7. Display longest computer use
8. Display shortest package use
9. Display longest package use
10. Create new state vector
11. Get relevant state vector
12. Store state vector
13. Delete state vector from store
14. Save shortest and longest computer usage so far
15. Save shortest and longest package usage so far
16. Call suprogram

Conditions
1. End of file
2. login record
3. package load record
4. package unload record

The schematic logic for this program follows on the next page.

```
A-seq
    B do 1, 4, 5
    C-rep until 1
        D-sel if 2
            E do 10, 16, 12, 4
        D-alt-1 if 3
            F do 11, 16, 12, 4
        D-alt-2 if 4
            G do 11, 16, 12, 15, 4
        D-alt3 (else)
            H do 11, 16, 13, 14, 3
        D-end
    C-end
    I-seq
        J do 6
        K do 7
    I-end
    L-seq
        M do 8
        N do 9
    L-end
    O do 2, 3
A-end
```

The implementation in COBOL of the designs for the two programs follows.

```
IDENTIFICATION DIVISION.
PROGRAM-ID. MainProgram.

ENVIRONMENT DIVISION.
INPUT-OUTPUT SECTION.
FILE-CONTROL.
    SELECT ActivityLog ASSIGN TO PFMS.

DATA DIVISION.
FILE SECTION.
FD ActivityLog, COMPRESSED.
01 Record-1.
    02 StudentDescription.
        03 StudentID PIC 9.
        03 StudentActivity PIC X.
    02 PackageDescription.
        03 PackageID PIC 99.
        03 PackageActivity PIC X.
    02 clock PIC 99.

WORKING-STORAGE SECTION.
01 ClockTime.
```

```
        02 PackageTime PIC 99.
        02 StudentTime PIC 99.
    01 StateVector.
        02 Record-SV OCCURS 3 TIMES.
            03 StateVariable PIC 9.
            03 StartTime PIC 99.
            03 FinishTime PIC 99.
            03 LoadTime PIC 99.
            03 UnloadTime PIC 99.


    77 EOF PIC A VALUE 'F'.
        88 EndOfFile VALUE 'T'.
    77 PackageShort PIC 99 VALUE 99.
    77 PackageLong PIC 99 VALUE ZERO.
    77 StudentShort PIC 99 VALUE 99.
    77 StudentLong PIC 99 VALUE ZERO.


    PROCEDURE DIVISION.
    A-seq.
    B.  OPEN INPUT ActivityLog.
        READ ActivityLog AT END MOVE 'T' TO EOF.
        DISPLAY "System Usage Report". DISPLAY SPACE.


    C-rep.
        IF EndOfFile GO TO C-end.


    D-sel.
        IF StudentActivity NOT = 'S' GO TO D-alt-1.
    E.      MOVE clock TO StartTime (StudentID).
            MOVE 1 TO StateVariable (StudentID).
            CALL "subprogram" USING StateVector,
                                    Record-1,
                                    ClockTime.
            READ ActivityLog AT END MOVE 'T' TO EOF.
            GO TO D-end.
    D-alt-1.
        IF PackageActivity NOT = 'L' GO TO D-alt-2.
    F.      CALL "subprogram" USING StateVector,
                                    Record-1,
                                    ClockTime.
            READ ActivityLog AT END MOVE 'T' TO EOF.
            GO TO D-end.
    D-alt-2.

        IF PackageActivity NOT = 'U' GO TO D-alt-3.
    G.      CALL "subprogram" USING StateVector,
                                    Record-1,
                                    ClockTime.
```

```
        IF PackageTime < PackageShort
            MOVE PackageTime TO PackageShort
        ELSE IF PackageTime > PackageLong
            MOVE PackageTime TO PackageLong.

        READ ActivityLog AT END MOVE 'T' TO EOF.
        GO TO D-end.
D-alt-3.
H.  CALL "subprogram" USING StateVector,
                            Record-1,
                            ClockTime.
        MOVE 1 TO StateVariable (StudentId).

        IF StudentTime < StudentShort
            MOVE StudentTime TO StudentShort
        ELSE IF StudentTime > StudentLong
            MOVE StudentTime TO StudentLong.

        READ ActivityLog AT END MOVE 'T' TO EOF.
D-end.
    GO TO C-rep.
C-end.
I-seq.
J.  DISPLAY "shortest student use = ", StudentShort.
K.  DISPLAY "longest student use = ", StudentLong.
I-end.


L-seq.
M.  DISPLAY "shortest package use = ", PackageShort.
N.  DISPLAY "longest package use = ", PackageLong.
L-end.


O.  CLOSE ActivityLog.
    STOP RUN.




IDENTIFICATION DIVISION.
PROGRAM-ID. subprogram.

DATA DIVISION.
LINKAGE SECTION.
01 StateVector.
    02 Record-SV OCCURS 3 TIMES.
        03 Statevariable PIC 9.
        03 StartTime PIC 99.
```

```
            03 FinishTime PIC 99.
            03 LoadTime PIC 99.
            03 UnloadTime PIC 99.


     01 Record-1.
         02 StudentDescription.
            03 StudentID PIC 9.
            03 StudentActivity PIC X.
         02 PackageDescription.
            03 PackageID PIC 99.
            03 PackageActivity PIC X.
         02 clock PIC 99.


     01 ClockTime.
         02 PackageTime PIC 99.
         02 StudentTime PIC 99.




PROCEDURE DIVISION USING StateVector, Record-1, ClockTime.
A-seq.
         GO TO Q1, Q2, Q3, Q4 DEPENDING ON StateVariable (StudentID).
     Q1.
     B.  MOVE clock TO StartTime (StudentID).
         MOVE 2 TO StateVariable (StudentID), GO TO QEXIT.
     Q2.
     C-rep.
         IF PackageActivity NOT = "L" GO TO C-end.
     D-seq.
     E.      MOVE clock TO LoadTime (StudentID).
         MOVE 3 TO StateVariable (StudentID), GO TO QEXIT.
     Q3.
             MOVE clock TO UnloadTime (StudentID).
     F.  SUBTRACT LoadTime (StudentID) FROM UnloadTime (StudentID)
             GIVING PackageTime.
         MOVE 4 TO StateVariable (StudentID), GO TO QEXIT.
     Q4.
     D-end.
         GO TO C-rep.
     C-end.
     G.  MOVE clock TO FinishTime (StudentID).
         SUBTRACT StartTime (StudentID) FROM FinishTime (StudentID)
             GIVING StudentTime.
     QEXIT.
         EXIT PROGRAM.
     A-end.
```

13.8 Recognition Problems.

At the time of executing a condition associated with either a selection or repetition there may not be enough information available to be assured that the outcome of the condition is correct. This is a recognition problem. There are at least three techniques available for solving recognition problems, and these will be discussed in this section.

Backtracking

With a recognition problem it is not always possible to make the correct decision as to which path, in the case of a selection, or number of iterations, in the case of repetition, to execute in the absence of further information. The program designer must reason the course of action to be taken and incorporate this hypothesis into the design of the program. During program execution the hypothesis will either be proved right or wrong. If the hypothesis is right processing continues, however, if the hypothesis is proved to be wrong the computer must be directed to go back or backtrack, to the point in the program where the decision was made and continue processing on the basis of the alternative decision.

If the hypothesis is proved to be wrong, then data might have been processed that should not have been processed. The effects of processing this data on the predicted results would be regarded as being *harmful*, and it would be necessary to restore the data to its state prior to the wrong decision being made. However, if the hypothesis proved to be wrong and data has been processed prior to backtracking then the effect might be *beneficial* if the data is required, regardless of the outcome, or the effect might be *neutral* if it does not matter whether the data is processed or not.

When backtracking is used to solve recognition problems the technique is developed in two stages. The first stage is to consider the implications of backtracking on the expected results, this implies investigating the possible side effects that can occur and making a hypothesis on the basis of the least harmful side effects that can be generated. The second stage is to amend the schematic logic based upon the decisions made in the first stage.

As an example, the hotel register file used in earlier examples, is to be validated for correct batches of records. A good batch of records is defined as every record in the batch having the same end of week date as the header record in the batch. For every good batch of records the end of week date and number of registrations in that week will be output to a good file, otherwise every error record in each error batch will be output to an error file.

The detailed program structure and schematic logic, as the solution to this problem, follows on the next page.

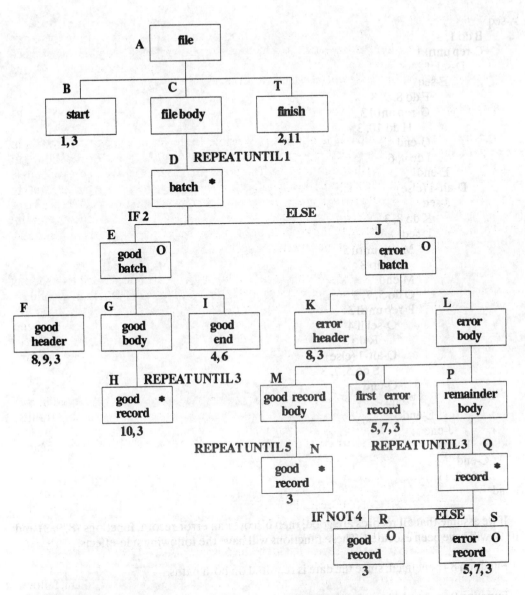

Functions
1. Open files
2. Close files
3. Read register file
4. Format good record for output
5. Format error record for output
6. Write record to good report
7. Write record to error report
8. Store date in temporary store
9. Initialise number of registrations to zero
10. Increase registrations by 1
11. Stop

Conditions
1. End of file
2. All records in batch have same header date
3. Guest details = spaces OR (1)
4. Header date NOT = record date
5. Guest details NOT = spaces AND (4) OR (1)

```
A-seq
     B do 1, 3
     C-rep until 1
        D-sel if 2
           E-seq
              F do 8, 9, 3
              G-rep until 3
                 H do 10, 3
              G-end
              I do 4, 6
           E-end
        D-alt-1 (else)
           J-seq
              K do 8, 3
              L-seq
                 M-rep until 5
                    N do 3
                 M-end
                 O do 5, 7, 3
                 P-rep until 3
                    Q-sel if 4
                       R do 3
                    Q-alt-1 (else)
                       S do 5, 7, 3
                    Q-end
                 P-end
              L-end
           J-end
        D-end
     C-end
     T do 2, 11
A-end
```

If we assume that all records are good, then discover an error record, functions (8, 9, 3) and (10, 3) will have been executed. These functions will have the following side-effects.

Function 8 - beneficial, since the date is required on both paths.

Function 9 - neutral, since the registration is not required on the other path.

Function 3 - beneficial, since a record is required regardless of the path taken.

Function 10 - neutral, for the same reason as function 9.

If we assume that every batch is in error and then discover that some batches are good, functions (8, 3) and (3) will have been executed. These functions will cause the following side effects.

Functions 8, 3 - beneficial, for the same reason given earlier.

Function 3 - harmful, since all the records in a good batch would be read without recording the number of registrations.

The side-effects when opting for the good batch are beneficial and neutral, whereas those for the error batch are beneficial and harmful. The path chosen with the least harmful side effects will determine the hypothesis, therefore, we shall assume that all the records in the hotel register file belong to good batches.

The amendments to the schematic logic are such that the component at which the recognition problem occurs has sel and alt replaced by *posit* and *admit* respectively. To posit is to lay down a hypothesis: we are laying down the hypothesis that all records form good batches; if it turns out that the hypothesis is wrong, we will admit that the record is in error.

In processing records from a good batch, if an error record is discovered, then it will be necessary to quit the good path and backtrack and admit that the hypothesis was wrong.

In backtracking to the error path it may be discovered that functions have already been executed that occur on the error path. These duplicate functions must be deleted. The schematic logic is modified as follows.

```
A-seq
     B do 1, 3
     C-rep until 1
        D-posit
           E-seq
              F do 8, 9, 3 quit D-posit if error record
              G-iter until 3
                 H do 10, 3 quit D-posit if error record
              G-end
              I do 4, 6
           E-end
        D-admit
           J-seq
              K do 8, 3 (duplicate functions are deleted)
              L-seq
                 .
                 .
                 .
```

The following segment of COBOL code illustrates how backtracking is implemented in the Procedure Division. Notice that condition 2 (all records in the batch have the same header date) cannot be coded since not all the records in the batch have been read at that point in the program. The amendment to quit D-posit has been implemented by using IF and GO TO statements.

PROCEDURE DIVISION.

.

.

D-posit.
E-seq.
F.
    MOVE RecordDate TO HeaderDate.
    MOVE ZERO TO registrations.
    READ register AT END MOVE 'T' TO EOF.
* quit D-posit if error record
    IF HeaderDate NOT = RecordDate
    AND GuestDetails NOT = SPACES GO TO D-admit.
G-rep.
    IF GuestDetails = SPACES OR EndOfFile GO TO G-end.
H.   ADD 1 TO registrations.
    READ register AT END MOVE 'T' TO EOF.
* quit D-posit if error record
    IF HeaderDate NOT = RecordDate
    AND GuestDetails NOT = SPACES GO TO D-admit.
    GO TO G-rep.
G-end.

.

.

D-admit.
J-seq.
L-seq.

.

.

Multiple Read-Ahead

Multiple read-ahead implies reading several records from a file prior to the evaluation of a condition that would, in a single read-ahead situation, cause a recognition problem. Multiple read- ahead can provide a better solution to a recognition problem than backtracking, when several physical records make up a single logical record and all parts are needed together for processing, or where each record is processed in its own right, but information from the records that follow is required in order to evaluate some condition.

The following worked example serves to illustrate the technique of multiple read-ahead.

An insurance company, specialising in motor insurance, keeps a file on all its policy holders. There may be one or more logical records relating to each policy holder. The first record for each policy holder contains personal details about the insured person. Subsequent records, if applicable, contain details of all driving convictions against the policy holder. There is a separate record for each conviction. The file is to be split into two new files, one file containing the details of policy holders with no previous convictions and the other file containing the details of convicted motorists. Design a program structure to solve this problem. Assume that two record areas R1 and R2 are used for reading two records ahead in the file.

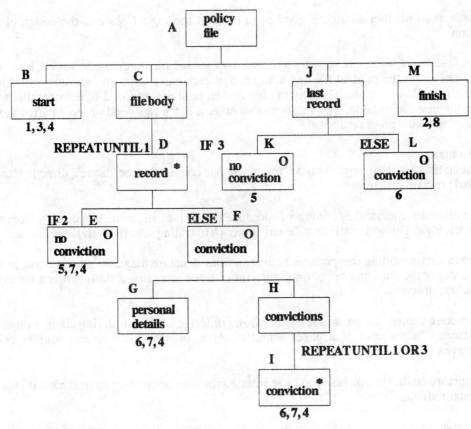

Functions
1. Open files
2. Close files
3. Read policy file into area R1
4. Read policy file into area R2
5. Write record R1 to non-convicted motorists file
6. Write record R1 to convicted motorists file
7. Move record area R2 to record area R1
8. Stop

Conditions
1. End of file
2. Policy holder in R1 NOT = policy holder in R2
3. Record area R1 does not contain a conviction record

Processing a file twice

The name of the technique is self-explanatory. In the example used to illustrate backtracking in this section, the hotel register file is read and each record is written to a new file, with a new record added to the end of each batch indicating whether the batch was good or in error. The new file is then sorted so that each new record precedes each batch. The sorted file is then processed for a second time and the indicator record allows the decision to be made as to whether a batch is good or in error at the logical place in the design of the program.

An alternative technique to writing records to a second file that must be sorted, is to read the batches from the original file and at the end of each batch write an indicator record into either a new file or a table. The original file is then read for a second time in parallel with either the new file or table, which indicates whether a batch was good or was in error at the logical place in the program design.

13.9 Summary

A schematic logic, that represents an in-line or flat coding, can be derived directly from a detailed program structure.

An alternative method of coding a Procedure Division exists, by coding directly from the schematic logic. This will involve a different approach to coding selections and repetitions.

When corresponding components between initial structure diagrams do not occur in the same order or the same number of times then the components cause a clash between the input and output structures.

Structure clashes can be caused by the wrong ordering of data, ordering clash; a physical boundary as in the case of a page, boundary clash; or data from several sources being interleaved, interleaving clash.

Structure clashes can be resolved by reordering the data or creating an intermediate file of re-structured data.

If program inversion is used the intermediate file need not be created, and one program becomes a subprogram of the other with the relevant data being passed from the subprogram to the calling program.

COBOL supports the idea of subprograms. Subprograms communicate data via a LINKAGE SECTION.

An inverted subprogram can be re-entered at different points in the subprogram by using a state-variable to store the position of the re-entry. The control of the re-entry position is achieved through a GO TO DEPENDING ON statement.

When an interleaving clash is resolved using an inverted subprogram, it is necessary to introduce a state-vector table to store the state-variable and local data for each item using the re-entrant subprogram.

When not enough information is available at run-time to implement a decision in either a selective or repetitive component then a recognition problem exits.

There are at least three methods of overcoming recognition problems - backtracking, multiple read-ahead or reading a file twice.

Keywords

Schematic logic, flat or in-line code;
GO TO, GO TO DEPENDING ON;
Ordering, boundary and interleaving clashes;
Program Inversion, subprogram;
State Variable, State-vector;
LINKAGE SECTION, CALL, EXIT PROGRAM
USING;
Backtracking, side effects, beneficial, neutral, harmful;
posit, admit, quit;
multiple read-ahead, processing file twice.

13.10 Questions.

1. Translate the detailed program structures in (a) and (b) into two respective schematic logic algorithms.

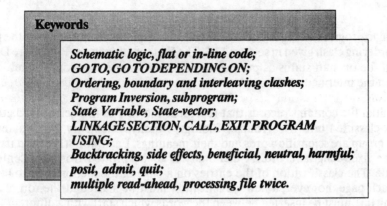

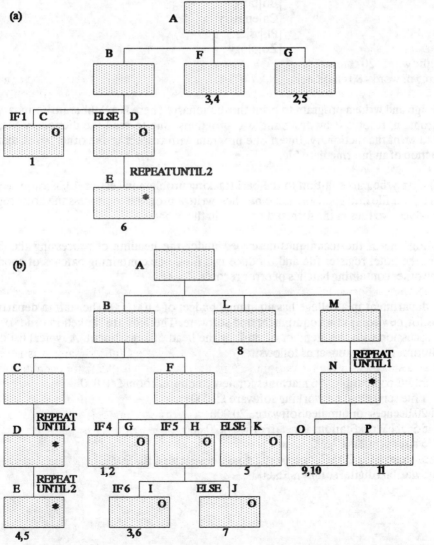

2. Write a single program, using flat or in-line code, to implement the design of the program to resolve the ordering clash given in section 13.3. The first function in the Procedure Division is to sort the staff file on staff status as primary key and staff name as secondary key. This sorted file is in effect the intermediate file.

[3]. A sequential file contains records that represent the entries in a scientific dictionary. The dictionary is classified into five groups - Biology, Botany, Chemistry, Physics and Zoology. Within each group are scientific words and their meanings. Each word (key) and its meaning is stored in one fixed-length record. A dictionary is to be printed from the contents of the sequential file. The classification of the entries on a page of the dictionary is to be printed at the top of each page, however, a new classification must be started at the top of a new page and one blank line must be inserted between the words which start with a different letter of the alphabet. The format of a record is:

Classification code - 2 characters   [Bi]ology
                                    [Bo]tany
                                    [Ch]emistry
                                    [Ph]ysics
                                    [Zo]ology
Scientific word - 20 characters
Meaning of word - 80 characters

Design and write a program to print the dictionary. There is a deliberate boundary clash in this problem, resolve it by designing two programs, one to read the dictionary file, and the other to print the dictionary. Invert one program with respect to the other, so as to avoid the production of an intermediate file.

[4].(a) Using the part solution to the backtracking problem in section 13.8, for processing the hotel register file into good and error batches, write a program to process the hotel register file and produce two files in the format described in the problem.

(b) Using one of the techniques described under the heading of processing the file twice, process the hotel register file and produce two files, one containing batches of good records and the other containing batches of error records.

[5]. A department in a college has an annual budget of £100,000. The staff in department put in bids for new computing equipment and software. The bids are ranked in order of priority, after discussion with the member of staff, by the head of department. A typical list of bids, in priority order, might appear as follows:

    20 PC compatible 486 machines for new computer room £40,000
    1 file server and networking software £5,000
    20 licences for bundled software £20,000
    5 SUN WorkStations for staff offices £20,000
    5 laser printers £7,500
    5 licences for CASE tools to run on SUN systems £10,000
    5 flat-bed digital scanners £5,000

    .

    .

    .

If each of these bids is stored in one fixed-length record, in priority order, on a sequential file, write a program to produce the following reports. Notice from the first report, if a bid cannot be paid in full, then the bid is rejected, and a residue of unspent money is allocated to the report. All bids that are rejected are written to the second report.

Successful Bids for Equipment and Software	
20 PC compatible 486 machines for new computer room	£40,000
1 file server and networking software	£5,000
20 licences for bundled software	£20,000
5 SUN Workstations for staff offices	£20,000
5 laser printers	£7,500
Residue not spent	£7,500
Total	£100,000

Unsuccessful bids for Equipment and Software	
5 licences for CASE tools to run on SUN systems	£10,000
5 flat-bed digital scanners	£5,000
.	
.	
.	

Hint. There is a recognition problem, in the repetitive part of the design of the program. This can be resolved through backtracking.

6. Invent a suitable test data file for the example given in section 13.8 under the heading of multiple read-ahead. Write a program from the given design to split the test data into two files, one file for motorists with no convictions and the other file for motorists with convictions.

Code each record to distinguish between convicted and non-convicted motorists. Hint - use 0 for no conviction and 1 for a conviction in a separate field called RecordCode.

14

Structured Programming with COBOL-85

This chapter brings together many of the enhancements of the language that provide a basis for writing structured computer programs in a similar way to using, say, a block-structured language.

14.1 Scope Terminators.

Scope terminators serve to delimit the scope of certain Procedure Division statements. Scope terminators are of two types: explicit and implicit. The explicit scope terminators are the following.

END-ADD	END-MULTIPLY	END-SEARCH
END-CALL	END-PERFORM	END-START
END-COMPUTE	END-READ	END-STRING
END-DELETE	END-RECEIVE	END-SUBTRACT
END-DIVIDE	END-RETURN	END-UNSTRING
END-EVALUATE	END-REWRITE	END-WRITE
END-IF		

The implicit scope terminators are the following.

At the end of any sentence, the separator period which terminates the scope of all previous statements not yet terminated.

Within any statement containing another statement, the next phrase of the containing statement following the contained statement terminates the scope of any unterminated contained statement. Examples of such phrases are ELSE and WHEN.

When statements are nested within other statements, a separator period which terminates the sentence also implicitly terminates all nested statements.

Scope terminators are optional in most cases, and termination by a period is still valid. However, there are exceptions to this rule, and these will be brought to the reader's attention at the appropriate time.

Never use an explicit scope terminator followed by an implicit period terminator.

14.2 Selection.

The only COBOL statement that has been used throughout the book to provide for selection has been the IF .. ELSE .. statement. This has enabled the programmer to perform multi-way branching and, when used with a GO TO statement, to control an exit from a loop! How has the COBOL-85 Standard for the language enhanced an already extremely powerful statement? The answer is, in two ways.

Firstly the IF .. ELSE .. statement has been tidied-up so that it appears to be similar in structure to the same statement used in block-structured languages such as Pascal, Modula-2, Ada, etc. The new format for the statement is:

```
IF condition THEN     { {statement-1} ...  }
                      { NEXT SENTENCE      }
    ELSE {statement-2} ... [END-IF]
    ELSE NEXT SENTENCE
    END-IF
```

This can be used in the form

```
IF MusicCode = 'A' THEN
    MOVE "popular" TO Title-2
ELSE
    IF MusicCode = 'B' THEN
        MOVE "jazz" TO Title-2
    ELSE
        MOVE "classical" TO Title-2
    END-IF
END-IF
```

Notice that the word THEN has appeared to improve the readability of the statement, and that each IF statement is terminated using END-IF.

Secondly, there is no need to nest several IF .. ELSE .. statements when a multi-way selection is to be made since COBOL-85 contains an EVALUATE statement. A simplified format of the EVALUATE statement follows.

```
EVALUATE identifier
{WHEN ⌠identifier-2⌡imperative-statement-1} ...
      ⌊literal-1  ⌋
[WHEN OTHER imperative-statement-2]
[END-EVALUATE]
```

This can be applied to the previous example of nested IF's to produce the following code.

```
EVALUATE MusicCode
    WHEN 'A' MOVE "popular" TO Title-2
    WHEN 'B' MOVE "jazz" TO Title-2
    WHEN OTHER MOVE "classical" TO Title-2
END-EVALUATE
```

In the music cassettes example given in chapter 9, the value of MusicCode was specified as being either A, B or C. When the EVALUATE statement is used here, MusicCode is assumed to contain one of the three alphabetic characters, such that when MusicCode is 'A' the string literal "popular" will be moved to Title-2; when MusicCode is 'B' the string literal "jazz" will be moved to Title-2; and if MusicCode is any other letter, 'C' by default, then the string literal "classical" is moved to Title-2.

The EVALUATE statement, as used above, closely resembles a CASE statement found in several block-structured languages. The statement, however, does have a more complex format as depicted in Appendix II.

14.3 Repetition.
The in-line, so called because it produces flat-code, PERFORM statement can be adapted to behave as either a while .. do, repeat .. until, or for .. do loop found in block-structured languages. A format of the in-line PERFORM statement is:

```
PERFORM [WITH TEST  ⎰BEFORE⎱] UNTIL condition
                    ⎱AFTER ⎰
  {imperative-statement} ...
END-PERFORM
```

By default, the condition is tested first, before each execution of the imperative statements. This implies that the PERFORM statement functions in the same way as a *while .. do* loop.

If the WITH TEST AFTER optional clause is used then the imperative statements will be executed once before the condition is tested. In this mode the PERFORM statement functions in the same way as a *repeat .. until* loop.

Example of a PERFORM loop equivalent to a *while .. do* loop

```
MOVE ZERO TO RecordCount.
READ DataFile INTO Record-1 AT END MOVE 'T' TO EOF.
PERFORM UNTIL EndOfFile
    DISPLAY Record-1
    ADD 1 TO RecordCount
    READ DataFile INTO Record-1 AT END MOVE 'T' TO EOF END-READ
END-PERFORM
DISPLAY 'number of records in file ', RecordCount.
```

In this example, if DataFile is empty then EndOfFile will be set to [T]rue and the statements within the loop will never be executed. As a result the number of records in the file will be displayed as 0.

The reader's attention is drawn to the use of implicit and explicit scope terminators. The syntax of the PERFORM UNTIL .. END-PERFORM statement would not be valid if each, or any, of the statements DISPLAY, ADD and READ were terminated by a period. The statements DISPLAY and ADD could have the appropriate explicit scope delimiters appended, END-DISPLAY and END-ADD respectively. However, the verb ADD implicitly terminates the DISPLAY statement and the verb READ implicitly terminates the ADD statement, therefore, there is no need to append END-DISPLAY and END-ADD.

But what about the second READ statement in the PERFORM loop, why is an END-READ appended to it? Ask yourself the question, "what delimits the AT END .. option of the READ statement?" Without the END-READ the END-PERFORM would be the terminator. But END-PERFORM is not an implicit terminator in the same way as the ADD or READ verbs, and furthermore, END-PERFORM is not the correct scope terminator for READ. A period after the AT END .. option would be wrong since it would cause the syntax of the PERFORM statement to be invalid. The answer is simple use the correct scope terminator for READ, END-READ.

Notice that statements outside the PERFORM .. UNTIL loop are terminated by periods. This is fine since they are not nested within another statement.

Example of a PERFORM statement equivalent to a *repeat .. until* statement.

```
DATA DIVISION.
77 MenuCode PIC A.
        88 LegalCode VALUES 'A', 'D', 'I', 'Q'.
        .
        .
PROCEDURE DIVISION.
        .
        PERFORM WITH TEST AFTER UNTIL LegalCode
                DISPLAY ClearScreen
                DISPLAY "do you want to"
                DISPLAY "[A]mend a record"
                DISPLAY "[D]elete a record"
                DISPLAY "[I]nsert a record"
                DISPLAY "[Q]uit the system"
                DISPLAY "input code A, D, I or Q"
                ACCEPT MenuCode END-ACCEPT
        END-PERFORM
        .
        .
```

In this example the user is invited to type, in response to a menu, a single character code, the computer tests the validity of the code after the statements of the PERFORM loop have been executed. If the code is not 'A', 'D', 'I' or 'Q' then the menu is output again and the user requested to type the code.

An alternative format of the in-line PERFORM statement that is equivalent to a for .. do loop is:

PERFORM [WITH TEST $\begin{Bmatrix} \text{BEFORE} \\ \text{AFTER} \end{Bmatrix}$]
VARYING item-1 FROM item-2 BY item-3 UNTIL condition-1
[AFTER item-4 FROM item-5 BY item-6 UNTIL condition-2] ...
[imperative statement] ...
END-PERFORM

A segment of code to provide a simple counting facility could be coded as:

```
PERFORM WITH TEST AFTER VARYING counter FROM 1 BY 1 UNTIL counter = 5
        DISPLAY counter WITH NO ADVANCING
END-PERFORM
```

and would display the following output: 1 2 3 4 5

14.4 Flat Code Revisited.

The purpose behind this section is to take the worked example on music cassette sales, from chapter 9, and present the program in a re-coded form using the selection and repetition statements (control statements) discussed in this chapter.

The functions, conditions and schematic logic are presented again for the reader's convenience.

Functions.

1. Open files
2. Close files
3. Read file
4. Write line of report
5. Stop
6. Move record-1 for output
7. Move 'popular' to record-2
8. Move 'jazz' to record-2
9. Move 'classical' to record-2
10. Move record-2 for output
11. Move record-3 for output
12. Move stock number and total quantity from store to record-4
13. Move record-4 for output
14. Add quantity to total quantity
15. Initialise total quantity to zero
16. Store music code
17. Store stock number
18. Move hyphens to record-1 for underlining

Conditions.

1. End of file
2. not same music code or (1)
3. not same stock number or (2)
4. music code = 'A'
5. music code = 'B'

Schematic Logic

```
A-seq
      B do 1,3,15,16,17
      C do 6,4,18,4
      D-rep until 1
        E-seq
          F-sel if 4
            G do 7
          F-alt-1 if 5
            H do 8
          F-alt-2 (else)
            I do 9
          F-end
          J do 10,4,11,4
          K-rep until 2
            L-seq
              M-rep until 3
                N do 14,3
              M-end
```

```
                O do 12,13,4,17,15
             L-end
          K-end
          P do 16
       E-end
    D-end
    Q do 2,5
A-end
```

The schematic logic has been modified to offer a more natural form for coding a Procedure Division. All the labels in the schematic logic have been removed since these cannot be used as paragraph names when using flat code and COBOL-85 control statements. The selections and their endings are represented using IF .. THEN .. ELSE .. END-IF statements and the repetitions are represented using the in-line PERFORM .. UNTIL .. END-PERFORM statements. The function numbers are replaced by the functions.

```
Open files
Read file
Initialise total quantity to zero
Store music code
Store stock number
Move record-1 for output
Write line of report
Move hyphens to record-1 for underlining
Write line of report
PERFORM UNTIL End of file
      IF music code = 'A' THEN
          Move 'popular' to record-2
      ELSE
          IF music code = 'B' THEN
              Move 'jazz' to record-2
          ELSE
              Move 'classical' to record-2
          END-IF
      END-IF
      Move record-2 for output
      Write line of report
      Move record-3 for output
      Write line of report
      PERFORM UNTIL End of file   OR not same music code
          PERFORM UNTIL End of file   OR not same music code
                                      OR not same stock number
              Add quantity to total quantity
              Read file
          END-PERFORM
          Move stock number and total quantity from store to record-4
          Move record-4 for output
          Write line of report
          Store stock number
```

```
                Initialise total quantity to zero
        END-PERFORM
            Store music code
    END-PERFORM
    Close files
    Stop
```

The program for the music cassette sales problem follows, with the Procedure Division coded directly from the modified schematic logic, using flat code and the control statements described in the chapter.

```
            IDENTIFICATION DIVISION.
            PROGRAM-ID. Music.

            ENVIRONMENT DIVISION.
            INPUT-OUTPUT SECTION.
            FILE-CONTROL.
                SELECT MusicData ASSIGN TO PFMS.
                SELECT MusicReport ASSIGN TO PFMS.

            DATA DIVISION.
            FILE SECTION.
            FD MusicData, COMPRESSED.
            01 Record-FS.
                02 MusicCode PIC A.
                02 StockNumber PIC 9(4).
                02 quantity PIC 9999.
            FD MusicReport, COMPRESSED.
            01 ReportOut.
                02 FILLER PIC X.
                02 LineImage PIC X(79).

            WORKING-STORAGE SECTION.
            01 Record-1-WS.
                02 FILLER PIC X(20) VALUE IS SPACES.
                02 title-1 PIC X(21) VALUE IS 'CASSETTE DISTRIBUTION'.
            01 Record-2-WS.
                02 FILLER PIC X(20) VALUE IS SPACES.
                02 FILLER PIC X(6) VALUE IS 'TYPE: '.
                02 title-2 PIC A(9).
            01 Record-3-WS.
                02 FILLER PIC X(20) VALUE IS SPACES.
                02 FILLER PIC X(21) VALUE IS 'STOCK-NUMBER QUANTITY'.
            01 Record-4-WS.
                02 FILLER PIC X(20) VALUE IS SPACES.
                02 StockNumber-WS PIC 9(4).
```

```
          02 FILLER PIC X(10) VALUE IS SPACES.
          02 Quantity-WS PIC ZZZ9.


      77 StockNumber-Store PIC 9(4).
      77 MusicCode-Store PIC A.
      77 EOF PIC A VALUE IS 'F'.
          88 EndOfFile VALUE 'T'.
      77 TotalQuantity PIC 9999 VALUE IS ZERO.



      PROCEDURE DIVISION.

          OPEN INPUT MusicData
               OUTPUT MusicReport.
          READ MusicData AT END MOVE 'T' TO EOF.

          MOVE MusicCode TO MusicCode-Store.
          MOVE StockNumber TO StockNumber-Store.
          MOVE Record-1-WS TO LineImage.
          WRITE ReportOut AFTER ADVANCING PAGE.
          MOVE ALL '-' TO Title-1.
          MOVE Record-1-WS TO LineImage.
          WRITE ReportOut AFTER ADVANCING 1 LINE.

          PERFORM UNTIL EndOfFile

              EVALUATE MusicCode
                  WHEN 'A' MOVE "POPULAR" TO Title-2
                  WHEN 'B' MOVE "JAZZ" TO Title-2
                  WHEN OTHER MOVE "CLASSICAL" TO Title-2
              END-EVALUATE

              MOVE Record-2-WS TO LineImage
              WRITE ReportOut AFTER ADVANCING 2 LINES
              MOVE Record-3-WS TO LineImage
              WRITE ReportOut AFTER ADVANCING 2 LINES

              PERFORM UNTIL MusicCode NOT = MusicCode-store
                      OR EndOfFile

                  PERFORM UNTIL StockNumber NOT = StockNumber-Store
                          OR MusicCode NOT = MusicCode-Store
                          OR EndOfFile

                      ADD quantity TO TotalQuantity
                      READ MusicData AT END MOVE 'T' TO EOF END-READ
```

```
                    END-PERFORM

              MOVE StockNumber-Store TO StockNumber-WS
              MOVE TotalQuantity TO quantity-WS
              MOVE record-4-WS TO LineImage
              WRITE ReportOut AFTER ADVANCING 1 LINE
              MOVE StockNumber TO StockNumber-Store
              MOVE ZERO TO TotalQuantity

           END-PERFORM

           MOVE MusicCode TO MusicCode-Store

        END-PERFORM

        CLOSE MusicData, MusicReport.
        STOP RUN.
```

14.5 Subprogram Library.

This section is an extension of the topic of separately compiled subprograms introduced in the last chapter.

In studying the use of a subprogram in program inversion it is possible to make an observation that is unique to COBOL subprograms, compared with, say, procedures or functions found in block-structured languages. A COBOL subprogram maintains its own state. Remember that a state variable QS was introduced into the inverted subprogram to control the re-entry point of the computer. Every call to the subprogram would rely upon the value of QS to direct the computer to a new re-entry point. This was only possible because the value QS was set, prior to exiting the subprogram, and was the same value upon re-entry into the subprogram after the next call had been executed. In other words the value of QS had not changed and neither had the values of the other variables in the subprogram. The state of the subprogram was maintained from one call to the next.

With either a procedure or a function in a block-structured language, the state of either is not maintained, and upon every call to the procedure or function the initial values of the variables are available. This effect can also be achieved in COBOL subprograms by using either CANCEL or INITIAL.

The CANCEL statement ensures that the named program will be restored to its initial state the next time it is called, by releasing the storage space of a called program and all its subprograms. The format of the CANCEL statement is:

CANCEL {item-1} ...

A CANCEL statement must be positioned in the calling program, and should be executed after a called program has exited.

COBOL-85 provides an alternative way of restoring a subprogram to its initial state by declaring INITIAL in the PROGRAM-ID heading. The format of this is:

PROGRAM-ID. program-name [IS INITIAL PROGRAM]

This will ensure that the program is restored to its initial state prior to re-entry, and will, therefore, behave in the same way as a procedure or function from a block-structured language.

Data is communicated to a COBOL subprogram through the data names declared in the CALL .. USING .. statement of the calling program, the PROCEDURE DIVISION USING .. statement of the subprogram and the corresponding data names in the LINKAGE SECTION of the subprogram. All data names in the calling program are treated as variable parameters. This implies that the data names can be used to send data to a subprogram as well as receive data from a subprogram. By contrast a data name in the calling program that only sends data is known as a value parameter. COBOL classifies, by default, all data names to be variable parameters in a CALL statement.

However, it is possible to specify from the calling program how a parameter is to be treated. The parameters within a CALL statement can be qualified using BY REFERENCE for a variable parameter, and BY CONTENT for a value parameter. This implies that the parameters for the same subprogram can be allowed to change between value and variable parameters during different calls to the same subprogram.

For example:

```
CALL "subprogram" USING  BY CONTENT alpha, beta
                         BY REFERENCE gamma.

        .
        .
CALL "subprogram" USING  BY REFERENCE alpha
                         BY CONTENT beta, gamma.
```

Subprograms that have been compiled, tested, and documented can be catalogued and stored in a software library available for all to use. In the following example three subprograms have been incorporated into a software library for general use. The catalogue entry for these three programs follows.

Name of library file: **Cat001.BIN**

Name of program: **"AgeCalc".**

Purpose: **To calculate the current age of a person from their date of birth.**

Restrictions: **The age is calculated in years (as a whole number). This program only applies to the twentieth century.**

Input parameter: **date-LS in the format YYMMDD.**

Output parameters: **age as an unsigned two-digit number. NoError as a flag set at [T]rue if the calculation is valid, otherwise, set at [F]alse.**

Order of parameters as presented in Linkage Section:

```
LINKAGE SECTION.
input parameter
01 date-LS.
    02 YY-LS PIC 99.
    02 MM-LS PIC 99.
    02 DD-LS PIC 99.
output parameters
01 age PIC 99.
01 NoError PIC A.
```

Name of library file: **Cat002.BIN**

Name of program: "TestDate".

Purpose: **To validate the numeric range of the fields of a date.**

Restrictions: **Only applicable to dates in the twentieth century. Date must be in the format YYMMDD with no embedded spaces.**

Input parameter: **date-LS in the format YYMMDD.**

Output parameter: **NoError as a flag set at [T]rue if the calculation is valid, otherwise, set at [F]alse.**

Order of parameters as presented in Linkage Section:

```
LINKAGE SECTION
input parameter
01 date-LS.
    02 YY-LS PIC 99.
    02 MM-LS PIC 99.
        88 MonthIndex VALUE 1 THRU 12.
        88 FebIndex VALUE 2.
    02 DD-LS PIC 99.
output parameter
01 NoError PIC A.
```

Name of library file: **Cat003.BIN**

Name of program: "SortData".

Purpose: **To sort the contents of a one-dimensional table into ascending order. Sorting**

algorithm used is a selection sort.

Restrictions: **Each cell contains a record of 80 characters. Minimum number of cells 2, maximum number of cells 999. Record is sorted on maximum 80 characters as primary key.**

Input parameters: **Name of the table, RecordTable, and the number of cells it contains, SizeOfTable.**

Output parameter: **RecordTable containing the sorted records.**

Order of parameters as presented in Linkage Section:

LINKAGE SECTION.
input parameter
01 SizeOfTable PIC 999.
input/output parameter
01 RecordTable.
  02 item PIC X(80) OCCURS 2 TO 999 TIMES DEPENDING ON SizeOfTable.

To use each of the library subprograms they must be loaded from the library during link/ loading. Prime use the command BIND to link/ load program files. If a COBOL program named Control uses the three library subprograms then they will be link/ loaded as follows.

```
OK, BIND Control
    :LOAD Control
    :LOAD Cat001
    :LOAD Cat002
    :LOAD Cat003
    :LI COBOL85LIB
    :LI
BIND COMPLETE
    :FILE
OK,
```

The control program that uses the files is then executed using the command:

OK, R Control

The control program accesses the library subprograms using a CALL to each program followed by the appropriate parameters. For example:

```
CALL "TestDate" USING BY CONTENT Birthdate,
                      BY REFERENCE ErrorFlag.
CALL "AgeCalc" USING  BY CONTENT Birthdate,
                      BY REFERENCE age, ErrorFlag.
CALL "SortData" USING BY CONTENT SizeOfTable,
                      BY REFERENCE RecordTable.
```

Notice that the names of the parameters do not need to be the same as the names given in the catalogue. However, the order in which the names are used must be the same as defined in the catalogue. The respective picture clauses for the parameters must be the same as those defined in the catalogue.

The library catalogue-entry for each subprogram has become an interface for each subprogram. There is no need for the library user to be aware of how each of the subprograms is implemented, a detailed knowledge of the coding is of no importance here. By introducing the catalogue-entry, level of interface, we have created a level of abstraction from the subprograms that is suitable for either the software system builder or programmer to understand what each subprogram does and how to use the subprogram.

Since the subprograms are stored in the library in their compiled format, the library user cannot gain access to the COBOL source code and change the routines in the library. The information contained in the library subprograms is hidden from the user.

A programmer is free to create and document new library subprograms that are either independent of all the subprograms in the library or re-use some of the existing library subprograms.

To continue this example, a sequential file contains fixed-length records with the format:

```
01 Record-1.
   02 Birthdate.
      03 YY PIC 99.
      03 MM PIC 99.
      03 DD PIC 99.
   02 Name PIC X(20).
```

A program is to be constructed that will perform the following operations.

Read each record in the file and validate each date of birth. Records that contain a valid date of birth, have the age of the person calculated, and if no errors are present the age of the person and name of the person is written to a second file.

Read the newly created file and store each record in respective cells of a one-dimensional table.

Sort the contents of the table into ascending order of age.

Write the sorted contents of the table to the last file created and display a report on those people who are in the age range 18 to 30 years.

The program to perform these operations follows.

```
IDENTIFICATION DIVISION.
PROGRAM-ID. MainOne.

ENVIRONMENT DIVISION.
INPUT-OUTPUT SECTION.
FILE-CONTROL.
    SELECT personnel ASSIGN TO PFMS.
    SELECT NewFile ASSIGN TO PFMS.

DATA DIVISION.
FILE SECTION.
FD personnel, COMPRESSED.
01 Record-1.
    02 Birthdate.
        03 YY PIC 99.
        03 MM PIC 99.
        03 DD PIC 99.
    02 name PIC X(20).
FD NewFile, COMPRESSED.
01 Record-2.
    02 NewAge PIC 99.
    02 NewName PIC X(20).

WORKING-STORAGE SECTION.
01 SizeOfTable PIC 999.
01 RecordTable.
    02 item PIC X(80) OCCURS 2 TO 999 TIMES
                    DEPENDING ON SizeOfTable,
                    INDEXED BY RecordIndex.

01 EOF PIC A VALUE 'F'.
    88 EndOfFile VALUE 'T'.
01 ErrorFlag PIC A.
    88 NoError VALUE 'T'.
01  age PIC 99.

PROCEDURE DIVISION.

* read the personnel file and create the new file

    SET RecordIndex TO ZERO.
    OPEN INPUT personnel, OUTPUT NewFile.
    READ personnel AT END MOVE 'T' TO EOF.
    PERFORM UNTIL EndOfFile
        CALL "TestDate" USING BY CONTENT BirthDate,
                        BY REFERENCE ErrorFlag
```

```
            IF NoError THEN
                CALL "AgeCalc" USING BY CONTENT Birthdate,
                                    BY REFERENCE age, ErrorFlag
                IF NoError THEN
                    MOVE age TO NewAge
                    MOVE name TO NewName
                    WRITE Record-2
                    SET RecordIndex UP BY 1
                END-IF
            END-IF
            READ personnel AT END MOVE 'T' TO EOF END-READ
        END-PERFORM
        CLOSE personnel, NewFile.
        MOVE RecordIndex TO SizeOfTable.


* transfer the contents of NewFile to a table and
* sort the contents of the table
        OPEN INPUT NewFile.
        MOVE 'F' TO EOF.
        PERFORM VARYING RecordIndex FROM 1 BY 1
                    UNTIL RecordIndex > SizeOfTable
                    OR EndOfFile
            READ NewFile AT END MOVE 'T' TO EOF END-READ
            MOVE Record-2 TO item (RecordIndex)
        END-PERFORM
        CLOSE NewFile.
        CALL "SortData" USING BY CONTENT SizeOfTable,
                            BY REFERENCE RecordTable.


* write the contents of the sorted file back to NewFile
* and display a report on those personnel in the specified
* age range

        OPEN OUTPUT NewFile.
        DISPLAY "Report on personnel in age range 18 - 30 years".
        DISPLAY SPACE
        DISPLAY "   age", SPACE, "name of personnel".
        PERFORM VARYING RecordIndex FROM 1 BY 1
                UNTIL RecordIndex > SizeOfTable
            MOVE item (RecordIndex) TO Record-2
            WRITE Record-2
            IF NewAge > = 18 AND <= 30 THEN
                DISPLAY NewAge, SPACE, SPACE NewName
            END-IF
        END-PERFORM
        CLOSE NewFile.
        STOP RUN.
```

The contents of the files used in this program and the displayed report follows.

Contents of personnel file

650617Appleton J.M
660718Axford B
531011Devereux J
480625Bailey T
650229Evans M
801030Mackenzie P.H
740329Bainbridge R
651310Elliot P
651210Fullerton F
700612Dunford C
480318Buzby B
200614Henderson G
220112Harmon T
451131Phillips L
631010Butler N
680408Barrett D.A
710820Irons J
731224Christmas F
800101Happy N.Y
720919Junner P

Results from program being run

Contents of NewFile file   Report on personnel in age range 18 - 30 years

10Mackenzie P.H   age name of personnel
11Happy N.Y   18   Junner P
17Bainbridge R   19   Irons J
17Christmas F   20   Dunford C
18Junner P   23   Barrett D.A
19Irons J   24   Axford B
20Dunford C   25   Appleton J.M
23Barrett D.A   25   Fullerton F
24Axford B   27   Butler N
25Appleton J.M
25Fullerton F
27Butler N
37Devereux J
42Bailey T
43Buzby B
69Harmon T
70Henderson G

14.6 Nested Subprograms.

A new feature to COBOL, through the 1985 revision of the Standard, will permit a subprogram to be embedded or nested within a COBOL program. This feature is a further step towards structured programming in so much as it is possible to mimic the features of procedure and functions found in block-structured languages such as Pascal, Modula-2 and Ada.

A nested subprogram must be coded after the last statement of the Procedure Division of the main control program. A new statement having the format:

END PROGRAM name-of-program

must be the final statement after each nested program and after all the nested programs to mark the end of the main or control program. Notice that END PROGRAM is not hyphenated, and is not classified as a scope terminator.

To pass control to a nested subprogram the CALL statement is used in the same way as for a separately compiled subprogram. Parameter passing between a controlling program and subprograms is via the same mechanism as with separately compiled subprograms. The CALL statement in the calling program and the Procedure Division heading in the called program will both have the USING phrase appended, containing the parameter list. This parameter list must also be present in the LINKAGE SECTION of the called program.

Figures 14.1, 14.2 and 14.3 illustrate how different subprograms can be nested within a main or controlling program. From these examples it is important to appreciate the following facts.

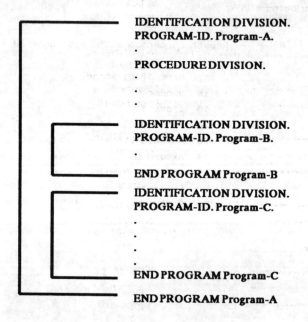

IDENTIFICATION DIVISION.
PROGRAM-ID. Program-A.
.
PROCEDURE DIVISION.
.
.
.

IDENTIFICATION DIVISION.
PROGRAM-ID. Program-B.
.
END PROGRAM Program-B

IDENTIFICATION DIVISION.
PROGRAM-ID. Program-C.
.
.
.
END PROGRAM Program-C

END PROGRAM Program-A

Figure 14.1 Programs B and C are directly contained within program-A.

Program-A can call either Program-B or Program-C

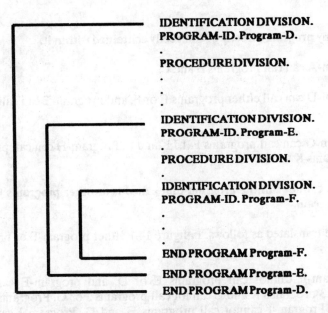

Figure 14.2. Program-E is directly contained within Program-D. Program-F is directly contained within Program-E and indirectly contained within Program-D. Program-D can call Program-E or Program-F. Program-E can call Program-F.

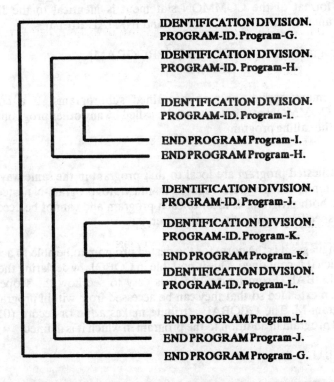

Figure 14.3 Programs H and J are directly contained within Program-G. Program-I is directly contained within Program-H and indirectly contained within Program-G. Programs K and L are directly contained within Program-J, and indirectly contained within Program-G.

A program can call any program directly or indirectly contained within it.

In figure 14.1 program-A can call programs B and C.

In figure 14.2 program-D can call either programs E or F, and program-E can call program F.

In figure 14.3 program-G can call programs H,I,J,K and L. Program-H can call program-I. Program-J can call programs K and L.

A contained program cannot call the program that called it or other programs indirectly contained within that program.

This statement can be translated as follows. In figure 14.1 either program-B or program-C cannot call program-A.

In figure 14.2 program-F cannot call programs E or D, and program-E cannot call program-D. In figure 14.3 programs K and L cannot call programs J or G. Programs J and H cannot call program G. Program-I cannot call programs H and G. Program-J cannot call program-I, since I is indirectly contained within G.

These rules applying to calling subprograms can be relaxed if the subprogram is defined as being COMMON. The format of the COMMON statement is identical to the INITIAL statement and a subprogram may have both COMMON and INITIAL attributes.

$$\text{PROGRAM-ID. program-name [IS} \begin{Bmatrix} \text{COMMON} \\ \text{INITIAL} \end{Bmatrix} \text{PROGRAM] ...}$$

The COMMON statement applies only to contained subprograms. If a contained subprogram includes the COMMON attribute, it may be called by any other program directly or indirectly contained in the calling program.

14.7 Visibility of Data.

Data names declared in a nested program are local to that program in the same way as data declared in a separately compiled subprogram. Figure 14.4 illustrates program-N nested within Program-M. The data for both programs is local to each program and cannot be accessed by the other program unless specifically passed as a parameter.

In block-structured languages it is the norm for the nested program to be able to access the data of the program in which it is contained. This is possible in COBOL by declaring the data of the outer program as GLOBAL. From figure 14.5 it is easy to see how the scope of the variables X and Y has been extended so that they can be accessed from within program-N as well as from within program-M. The GLOBAL attribute makes a file or record (01 entry) available to any contained program in addition to the program in which it is defined.

The format is: IS **GLOBAL**

and can be used at either an FD entry, or an 01 entry. For example:

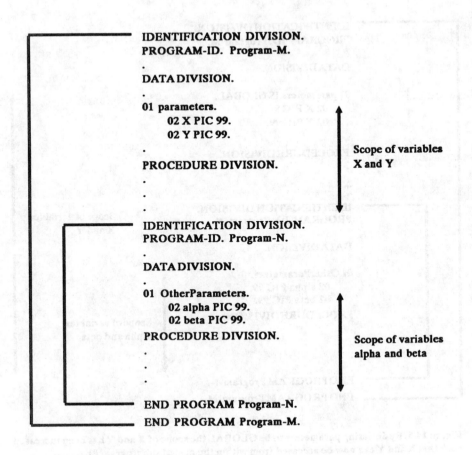

Figure 14.4. All variables are local to their respective programs by default.
Despite Program-N being directly contained within Program-M, the variables
of Program-M, X and Y, CANNOT be accessed within Program-N.

FD DataFile IS GLOBAL, COMPRESSED.
01 Record-1 IS GLOBAL.

Note if GLOBAL is specified at the FD level then it also applies to the record description
for the file as well as the file itself. GLOBAL can be used in both the File Section and/ or
Working-Storage Section.

A clause that is similar to GLOBAL, and can also be used at the FD and 01 levels, is
EXTERNAL. GLOBAL and EXTERNAL are not the same. The EXTERNAL attribute
causes storage of the file or record to be allocated external to the program. Such an item is
then available to any program, nested or separately compiled subprogram, that defines an item
as EXTERNAL.

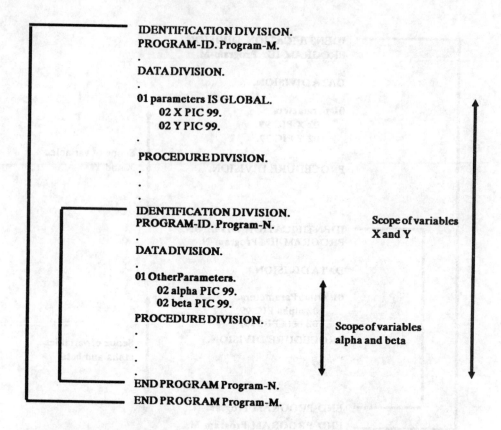

IDENTIFICATION DIVISION.
PROGRAM-ID. Program-M.
.
DATA DIVISION.
.
01 parameters IS GLOBAL.
    02 X PIC 99.
    02 Y PIC 99.
.
PROCEDURE DIVISION.
.
.
IDENTIFICATION DIVISION.
PROGRAM-ID. Program-N.
.
DATA DIVISION.
.
01 OtherParameters.
    02 alpha PIC 99.
    02 beta PIC 99.
PROCEDURE DIVISION.
.
.
.
END PROGRAM Program-N.
END PROGRAM Program-M.

Scope of variables
X and Y

Scope of variables
alpha and beta

Figure 14.5. By declaring parameters to be GLOBAL the scope of X and Y has been increased such that X and Y can now be accessed from within the nested subprogram Program-N. The variables alpha and beta still remain local to Program-N.

14.8 Worked Example.

This example is an extension of the previous example to display the names and ages of people in the age range 18 to 30 years. The program illustrates how the previous program can be re-coded to contain nested subprograms and calls to previously compiled subprograms.

By way of illustration only, the source listings of the three subprograms previously described in the library catalogue are listed here.

```
IDENTIFICATION DIVISION.
PROGRAM-ID. AgeCalc IS INITIAL PROGRAM.

* Purpose: To calculate the current age of a person from their
*          date of birth.
* Restrictions: The age is calculated in years (as a whole
*               number).
*               This program only applies to the twentieth century.
* Input parameter: date-LS in the format YYMMDD.
* Output parameters: age as an unsigned two-digit number.
```

```
*                       NoError as a flag set at [T]rue if the calculation
*                       is valid, otherwise, set at [F]alse.

DATA DIVISION.
WORKING-STORAGE SECTION.
01 TodaysDate.
    02 yy-today PIC 99.
    02 mm-today PIC 99.
    02 dd-today PIC 99.


LINKAGE SECTION.
01 date-LS.
    02 YY-LS PIC 99.
    02 MM-LS PIC 99.
    02 DD-LS PIC 99.
01 age PIC 99.
01 NoError PIC A.


PROCEDURE DIVISION USING date-LS, age, NoError.
* initialise error flag to [T]rue
    MOVE 'T' TO NoError.
* get today's date
    ACCEPT TodaysDate FROM DATE.
* test for date in future
    IF date-LS > TodaysDate THEN
        MOVE 'F' TO NoError
    ELSE
* calculate age in years only
        IF YY-LS < yy-today THEN
            IF MM-LS < mm-today
            OR ( MM-LS = mm-today AND DD-LS < = dd-today ) THEN
                SUBTRACT YY-LS FROM yy-today GIVING age
            ELSE
                IF ( MM-LS = mm-today AND DD-LS > dd-today )
                OR MM-LS > mm-today THEN
                    SUBTRACT 1, YY-LS FROM yy-today GIVING age
                END-IF
            END-IF
        ELSE
            MOVE ZERO TO age
        END-IF
    END-IF

    EXIT PROGRAM.
```

```
        IDENTIFICATION DIVISION.
        PROGRAM-ID. TestDate IS INITIAL PROGRAM.

      * Purpose: To validate the numeric range of the fields of a date.
      * Restrictions: Only applicable to dates in the twentieth century.
      *             Date must be in the format YYMMDD with no embedded spaces.
      * Input parameter: date-LS in the format YYMMDD.
      * Output parameter: NoError as a flag set at [T]rue if the date is valid,
      * otherwise set at [F]alse.

        DATA DIVISION.
        WORKING-STORAGE SECTION.
        01 DayList PIC X(24) VALUE "312831303130313130313031".
        01 DayTable REDEFINES DayList.
            02 MaxDays PIC 99 OCCURS 12 TIMES.

        77 LY PIC A.
            88 LeapYear VALUE 'T'.
        77 NewYear PIC 9(4).
        77 YearRemainder PIC 9.
        77 answer PIC 9(4).

        LINKAGE SECTION.
        01 date-LS.
            02 YY-LS PIC 99.
            02 MM-LS PIC 99.
                88 MonthIndex VALUE 1 THRU 12.
                88 FebIndex VALUE 2.
            02 DD-LS PIC 99.
        01 NoError PIC A.
            88 NoErrors VALUE 'T'.

        PROCEDURE DIVISION USING date-LS, NoError.
      * initialise error flag to [T]rue
            MOVE 'T' TO NoError.
      * test for non-numeric date
          IF date-LS NOT NUMERIC THEN
              MOVE 'F' TO NoError
          ELSE
      * test for leap year
              ADD 1900 TO YY-LS GIVING NewYear
              DIVIDE 4 INTO NewYear GIVING answer
              REMAINDER YearRemainder
              IF YearRemainder = 0 AND YY-LS NOT = ZERO THEN
                  MOVE 'T' TO LY
              ELSE
                  MOVE 'F' TO LY
              END-IF
```

```
* test for valid month
        IF NOT MonthIndex THEN
            MOVE 'F' TO NoError
        END-IF
* test for valid maximum number of days in a month
        IF LeapYear AND FebIndex THEN
            IF DD-LS < 1 OR > 29 THEN
                MOVE 'F' TO NoError
            END-IF
        END-IF
        IF NoErrors AND NOT LeapYear THEN
                IF DD-LS < 1 OR > MaxDays (MM-LS)
                    MOVE 'F' TO NoError
                END-IF
        END-IF
    END-IF

    EXIT PROGRAM.



IDENTIFICATION DIVISION.
PROGRAM-ID. SortData IS INITIAL PROGRAM.

* Purpose: To sort the contents of a one-dimensional table into
*          ascending order. Sorting algorithm used is a selection
*          sort.
* Restrictions: Each cell contains a record of 80 characters.
*               Minimum number of cells 2, maximum number of cells 999.
*               Record is sorted on maximum 80 characters as primary key.
* Input parameters: Name of table, RecordTable, and the number of
*                   cells it contains, SizeOfTable.
* Ouput parameter: Recordtable containing the sorted records.

DATA DIVISION.
WORKING-STORAGE SECTION.
77 subscript-1 PIC 999.
77 subscript-2 PIC 999.
77 TemporaryStore PIC X(80).
77 SwapPosition PIC 999.
77 largest PIC X(80).

LINKAGE SECTION.
01 SizeOfTable PIC 999.
01 RecordTable.
   02 item PIC X(80) OCCURS 2 TO 999 TIMES
                 DEPENDING ON SizeOfTable.
```

```
PROCEDURE DIVISION USING SizeOfTable, RecordTable.

    PERFORM VARYING subscript-1 FROM SizeOfTable BY -1
    UNTIL subscript-1 < 1
        MOVE SPACES TO largest
        PERFORM VARYING subscript-2 FROM 1 BY 1
                UNTIL subscript-2 > subscript-1
            IF item (subscript-2) > largest THEN
                MOVE item (subscript-2) TO largest
                MOVE subscript-2 TO SwapPosition
            END-IF
        END-PERFORM
        MOVE item (subscript-1) TO TemporaryStore
        MOVE largest TO item (subscript-1)
        MOVE TemporaryStore TO item (SwapPosition)
    END-PERFORM

    EXIT PROGRAM.
```

The main control program used in the last example has been re- coded to include nested subprograms. Notice that the control program is considerably shorter, and the nested subprograms have clearly defined functions.

```
IDENTIFICATION DIVISION.
PROGRAM-ID. NewOne.

ENVIRONMENT DIVISION.
INPUT-OUTPUT SECTION.
FILE-CONTROL.
    SELECT personnel ASSIGN TO PFMS.
    SELECT NewFile ASSIGN TO PFMS.

DATA DIVISION.
FILE SECTION.
FD personnel, IS GLOBAL, COMPRESSED.
01 Record-1.
```

```
        02 Birthdate.
            03 YY PIC 99.
            03 MM PIC 99.
            03 DD PIC 99.
        02 name PIC X(20).
FD NewFile, IS GLOBAL, COMPRESSED.
01 Record-2.
    02 NewAge PIC 99.
    02 NameOfPerson PIC X(20).


WORKING-STORAGE SECTION.
01 SizeOfTable PIC 999 IS GLOBAL.
01 RecordTable IS GLOBAL.
    02 item PIC X(80) OCCURS 2 TO 999 TIMES
                        DEPENDING ON SizeOfTable,
                        INDEXED BY RecordIndex.
01 EOF PIC A VALUE 'F' IS GLOBAL.
    88 EndOfFile VALUE 'T'.


PROCEDURE DIVISION.
    CALL "unit1"
    CALL "unit2"
    CALL "unit3"
    STOP RUN.


* --------------- nested subprogram unit1 --------------------


IDENTIFICATION DIVISION.
PROGRAM-ID. unit1 IS INITIAL PROGRAM.


WORKING-STORAGE SECTION.
01 ErrorFlag PIC A.
    88 NoError VALUE 'T'.
01 age PIC 99.


PROCEDURE DIVISION.

* read the personnel file and create the new file

    SET RecordIndex TO ZERO.
    OPEN INPUT personnel, OUTPUT NewFile.
    READ personnel AT END MOVE 'T' TO EOF.
    PERFORM UNTIL EndOfFile
        CALL "TestDate" USING BY CONTENT BirthDate,
                            BY REFERENCE ErrorFlag
```

```
                    IF NoError THEN
                        CALL "AgeCalc" USING BY CONTENT Birthdate,
                                              BY REFERENCE age, ErrorFlag
                        IF NoError THEN
                            MOVE age TO NewAge
                            MOVE name TO NewName
                            WRITE Record-2
                            SET RecordIndex UP BY 1
                        END-IF
                    END-IF
                    READ personnel AT END MOVE 'T' TO EOF END-READ
                END-PERFORM
                CLOSE personnel, NewFile.
                MOVE RecordIndex TO SizeOfTable.

                EXIT PROGRAM.
                END PROGRAM unit1.
*   --------------------- end of unit 1 -------------------


*   --------------- nested subprogram unit2 ---------------


    IDENTIFICATION DIVISION.
    PROGRAM-ID.  unit2  IS INITIAL PROGRAM.

    PROCEDURE DIVISION.

*   transfer the contents of NewFile to a table and
*   sort the contents of the table

        OPEN INPUT NewFile.
        PERFORM VARYING RecordIndex FROM 1 BY 1
        UNTIL RecordIndex > SizeOfTable OR EndOfFile
            READ NewFile AT END MOVE 'T' TO EOF END-READ
            MOVE Record-2 TO item (RecordIndex)
        END-PERFORM
        CLOSE NewFile.
        CALL "SortData" USING BY CONTENT SizeOfTable,
                             BY REFERENCE RecordTable.
        EXIT PROGRAM.
        END PROGRAM unit2.
*   ------------------------- end of unit 2 ----------------------


*   -------------------- nested subprogram unit3 ---------------


    IDENTIFICATION DIVISION.
    PROGRAM-ID.  unit3  IS INITIAL.
```

```
        PROCEDURE DIVISION.

    *   write the contents of the sorted file back to NewFile
    *   and display a report on those personnel in the specified
    *   age range

            OPEN OUTPUT NewFile.
            DISPLAY "Report on personnel in age range 18 - 30 years".
            DISPLAY SPACE.
            DISPLAY "   age", SPACE, "name of personnel".
            PERFORM VARYING RecordIndex FROM 1 BY 1
                    UNTIL RecordIndex > SizeOfTable
            MOVE item (RecordIndex) TO Record-2
            WRITE Record-2
            IF NewAge > = 18 AND <= 30 THEN
                    DISPLAY NewAge, SPACE, SPACE, NewName
            END-IF
            END-PERFORM
            CLOSE NewFile.
            EXIT PROGRAM.
            END PROGRAM unit3.
    *   ------------------------- end of unit3 -------------------------


            END PROGRAM NewOne.
    *   ------------------------- end of newone -------------------------
```

The results from running this program are identical to the previous program.

14.9 Summary.
Scope terminators are either explicit or implicit. Their purpose is to mark the end of a statement.

Selection statements have been enhanced with IF .. THEN .. ELSE .. END-IF and EVALUATE .. WHEN .. END-EVALUATE. The latter statement is similar to a case statement found in block- structured languages.

Repetition statements have been enhanced with an in-line PERFORM .. END-PERFORM. This retains all the features of the previously defined hierarchical PERFORM statements.

It is possible through both the control statements and nested subprograms, introduced into COBOL-85, to code programs in a similar style to that found in block-structured languages. The code used becomes flat or in-line code.

Libraries of re-usable software can be created using separately compiled subprograms.

A new feature of COBOL-85 is the ability to nest subprograms. It is possible to force nested subprogram to behave in the same way as procedures/ functions found in block-structured languages.

The state of a subprogram upon re-entry can be set to the initial state of the subprogram.

Parameters from a calling program can be either value parameters or variable parameters.

The scope of data in nested programs can be controlled by the use of the GLOBAL attribute. All data in subprograms is local to the subprogram by default.

The rules governing which nested subprogram may call another nested subprogram can be relaxed by using the COMMON attribute.

Nested subprograms cannot be recursive or allow for mutual recursion.

A modern view of producing software systems suggests that when building software components a designer/ programmer should incorporate the following ideas:

(i) data abstraction - combining a data type with a set of operations on that data type;

(ii) allow each data structure and its associated operations to be encapsulated into an independent program unit;

(iii) provide for abstraction and information hiding from the implementation of the program unit.

These ideas are all possible, to a limited extent, in COBOL-85.

Keywords

Explicit and implicit scope terminators;
IF .. THEN .., EVALUATE ..;
In-line PERFORM;
Separately compiled subprogram;
Subprogram Library; Nested Subprograms;
CANCEL, INITIAL, BY CONTENT,
BY REFERENCE, END PROGRAM;
COMMON, GLOBAL, EXTERNAL.

14.10 Questions.

[1]. Using the control statements for selection and repetition discussed in this chapter re-code, as flat code, the car sales program given in chapter 9, section 9.3.

[2]. Using the control statements and nested subprograms discussed in this chapter, re-code the

solution to the interleaving problem presented in chapter 13, section 13.7.

[3]. A sequential file contains information about members of a swimming club. Each fixed-length record contains information on the name, sex, date of birth and last three competition results for each member of the club. A typical record description would appear as:

```
01 ClubMember.
      02 name PIC X(15).
      02 sex PIC A.
      02 DateOfBirth.
            03 YY PIC 99.
            03 MM PIC 99.
            03 DD PIC 99.
      02 results.
            03 place PIC 9 OCCURS 3 TIMES.
```

The last entry, results, would be coded with (1) first place, (2) second place, (3) third place or (0) not placed or absent from the competition in the previous three competitions. For example, the value of results as 102 would imply that the member's last three results were first, not placed, and third respectively.

The file of members is to be used to create two new files of swimmers. A file of male swimmers in the age range 16 to 18 years inclusive, and a file of female swimmers in the age range 14 to 16 years inclusive. The files will contain the names of the eligible members and the total number of points scored over the last three competitions.

A points system is used to signify how well each swimmer did in the last three competitions. Three points are awarded for first place, two points for second place, and one point for third place. No points are awarded for not being placed or being absent from a competition. For example a member with two first places and one second place would be awarded eight points.

From the two newly created files of eligible members, a selection for one male and one female swimming team is made. Both teams must have three members with the highest number of points scored over the last three competitions.

Write a program to solve the problem, using both nested subprograms and the library subprograms given in this chapter.

[4]. Devise a bank cheque writing program using nested subprograms, in which an amount of money in Sterling, up to £999,999, is input and converted into words. Only convert the £'s into words and not the pence. For example £123.45 would be converted to one hundred twenty three pounds 45p. You may omit the £ sign in the input data.

You are advised to use the following nested subprograms.

Program-ID. "units".
Input parameter. Single digit.
Purpose - to convert the digits 1 .. 9 inclusive to words one .. nine respectively. Do not include zero.

Program-ID. "teens".
Input parameter. Single digit.
Purpose - to convert the digits 0 .. 9 inclusive to words ten .. nineteen respectively.

Program-ID. "tens".
Input parameter. Single digit.
Purpose - to convert the digits 2 .. 9 inclusive to words twenty .. ninety respectively.

Program-ID. "convert".
Input parameter. Three digits representing hundreds of pounds or thousands of pounds.
Purpose - to split up a three-digit number into hundreds, tens and units.

15

Software Development Tools

The purpose of this chapter is to make the reader aware of the existence of software development tools that support Jackson Structured Programming and the production of COBOL source code.

An introduction is given to the use of two software packages, JSP-COBOL and PDF. JSP-COBOL was developed by Michael Jackson Systems Ltd, and PDF was developed by the Computer Science & Systems Division of the Harwell Laboratory. Both products are commercially available from:

Learmonth & Burchett Management Systems Plc
Evelyn House, 62 Oxford Street, London W1N 9LF

15.1 An Introduction to JSP-COBOL.

As an introduction to the product JSP-COBOL the author has taken extracts from the document *JSP-COBOL A Technical Overview*, since this succinctly sums up the nature of the product.

"JSP-COBOL is a precompiler. It accepts a program design expressed in JSP structure text, and produces a COBOL program ready for compilation, together with documentation of the design." ...

The precompiler combines JSP with COBOL to obtain the following benefits.

"JSP-COBOL supports the JSP method directly, accepting as input the product of the JSP design steps.

JSP-COBOL checks its input to ensure correct use of the JSP method and correct use of its design language.

JSP-COBOL produces documentation of JSP programs, including fully formatted listing, structure diagrams, and other outputs.

JSP-COBOL mechanises the work of producing COBOL program coding, including the coding necessary to combine simple programs into complex run units.

JSP-COBOL accepts and uses COBOL operations, data types, and conditions, familiar to programmers from conventional COBOL programming.

JSP-COBOL allows the programmer to take advantage of all the database-management, transaction-handling, and file-organisation interfaces that are available in the COBOL language.

JSP-COBOL allows programs to be moved easily from one environment to another, from an old machine to a new machine or from a testing environment to a production environment.

JSP-COBOL provides a built-in macro feature that allows the readability of COBOL to be retained, while greatly reducing the amount that must be written. Macros can also be used to achieve compatibility between different implementation requirements and different COBOL compilers." ...

Figure 15.1 illustrates the JSP-COBOL Inputs and Outputs, this diagram is also taken from the JSP-COBOL A Technical Overview document.

15.2 Input File.

Figure 15.1 indicates that the JSP Program Design is prepared at a keyboard and communicated to the JSP-COBOL Processor. The listing of the file that follows was prepared under these conditions and stored on disc under the filename jspcob2.jsp. This is an input file to the JSP-COBOL Processor. In scanning through the file the reader should recognise the program design from the problem specified in chapter 10, section 10.2 on file updating.

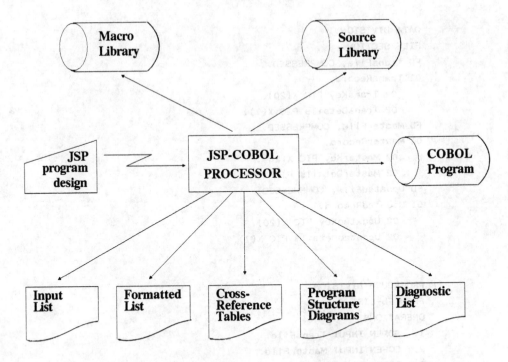

Figure 15.1 JSP-COBOL Inputs and Outputs, as represented in the Technical Overview

```
JSP PSA
JSP DFORM=2029
JSP TBPIC=30
JSP TBRDF=30
JSP TBVAL=45
JSP LNWDT=100
JSP LNCNT=60
JSP LNWDT2=100
JSP LNCNT2=60


IDENTIFICATION DIVISION.
PROGRAM-ID. FileUpdate.

ENVIRONMENT DIVISION.
INPUT-OUTPUT SECTION.
FILE-CONTROL.
    SELECT TransFile ASSIGN TO PFMS.
    SELECT MasterFile ASSIGN TO PFMS.
    SELECT UpdatedFile ASSIGN TO PFMS.

IMPLEMENTATION SECTION.
MI FileUpdate.
    MAKE FU-LIST CONTROLLER.
```

```
DATA DIVISION.
FILE SECTION.
FD TransFile, COMPRESSED.
01 TransRecord.
    02 TransKey PIC X(20).
    02 TransDetails PIC X(7).
FD MasterFile, COMPRESSED.
01 MasterRecord.
    02 MasterKey PIC X(20).
    02 MasterDetails PIC X(7).
FD UpdatedFile, COMPRESSED.
01 UpdatedRecord.
    02 UpdatedKey PIC X(20).
    02 UpdatedDetails PIC X(7).


PROCEDURE DIVISION.
PRGM FU-LIST.
OPERATIONS.
1.    SOPEN INPUT TransFile.
2.    SOPEN INPUT MasterFile.
3.    SOPEN OUTPUT UpdatedFile.
4.    SCLOSE INPUT TransFile.
5.    SCLOSE INPUT MasterFile.
6.    SCLOSE OUTPUT UpdatedFile.
7.    SREAD TransFile AT END MOVE HIGH-VALUES TO TransKey.
8.    SREAD MasterFile AT END MOVE HIGH-VALUES TO MasterKey.
9.    SWRITE UpdatedRecord FROM TransRecord.
10. SWRITE UpdatedRecord FROM MasterRecord.
STRUCTURE.
P-FU-LIST      SEQ DO 1, 2, 3, 7, 8
P-FILE-BODY    ITR U ((TransFile-EOF) AND (MasterFile-EOF))
P-RECORD       SEL (TransKey < MasterKey)
               DO 9, 7
P-RECORD       ALT (TransKey = MasterKey)
P-TRANS-MAST SEL (TransDetails NOT = SPACES)
               DO 9, 7, 8
P-TRANS-MAST ALT (ELSE) DO 7, 8
P-TRANS-MAST END
P-RECORD       ALT (ELSE) DO 10, 8
P-RECORD       END
P-FILE-BODY    END
               DO 4, 5, 6
P-FU-LIST      END
```

Upon inspecting the input file there are obviously new areas of code that have not been covered in the book.

JSP-COBOL Options

The operation of the JSP-COBOL processor can be controlled by including user options. These options can affect the efficiency with which the processor runs, the printed output which it will produce, the sequence numbering of the generated program and the nature of the generated code, and the expansion of the input text.

Options are included at the head of the input file after the JSP options statement. Either a single option or multiple options may appear after the JSP statement on one or many lines.

A standard default is preset for each option. No JSP statement is therefore required, unless these standard defaults are unsuitable.

As an example of the use of options, the options listed in the JSP input file have the following meanings.

JSP PSA - structure diagrams are always to be produced irrespective of the severity of any errors.

JSP DFORM=2029 - specifies the form of the structure diagram, where 2029 is coded to mean (2) nodes are to have outlines; (0) diagrams are to be split into sub-trees that fit on one page; (2) maximum number of lines that can appear in a node; (9) maximum number of characters that can appear in a line of text in a node.

JSP TBPIC=30 - specifies that the PICTURE clauses are to be aligned from column 30 in both the generated COBOL code and the formatted input-list.

JSP TBRDF=30 - similar to TBPIC but refers to the REDEFINES clause.

JSP TBVAL=45 - similar to TBPIC but refers to the VALUE clause.

JSP LNWDT=100 - specifies the width of the print line.

JSP LNCNT=60 - specifies the number of lines, excluding page headings, that will be printed on a sheet.

JSP LNWDT2=100 - same as LNWDT

JSP LNCNT2=60 - same as LNCNT

Implementation Section

The Implementation Section of the Environment Division allows arbitrary implementations to be specified for the program and for external files.

An Implementation Section is required in this program, as for all JSP-COBOL programs, to specify the controlling program. Since there is only one program it may seem somewhat artificial to include such an entry. However, when two or more programs are included, as in program inversion, one program is treated as the control program and the other(s) as the subprogram(s).

IMPLEMENTATION SECTION.
MI FileUpdate.
          MAKE FU-LIST CONTROLLER.

This entry simply states that the computer must start execution of the program at paragraph FU-LIST, hence the entry after the Procedure Division PRGM FU-LIST.

PROCEDURE DIVISION.
PRGM FU-LIST.

The Implementation Section is NOT a valid COBOL section and does not appear in the COBOL code that is generated by the processor.

The detailed program structure, functions and conditions lists from chapter 10 have been included over the page, to make cross-referencing between the JSP-COBOL input file and the design easier for the reader.

If the reader compares the functions with those listed under the heading of OPERATIONS then clearly there are some differences in the way the functions have been translated into COBOL statements. For instance, what is SOPEN, SCLOSE, SREAD and SWRITE?

These are JSP-COBOL file processing operations, similar to OPEN, CLOSE, READ and WRITE, however, they permit a more consistent and general treatment of files, permitting files to be assigned to programs as well as to devices.

The SREAD operation sets a level-88 condition name indicating the result of the operation. When the end of a file is encountered a filename-EOF condition name, in the example TransFile-EOF and MasterFile-EOF, is automatically set at TRUE. The syntax of SREAD also permits an action to be taken when the end of file is reached. In this example it has been necessary to move HIGH- VALUES to the corresponding key when the end of a file has been detected.

Notice that the operation to finish processing (STOP RUN) is omitted from the list of operations. This is because the JSP- COBOL processor will provide the appropriate operation automatically at the end of the program. The choice of appropriate operation depends on whether a file is assigned to the program.

Unlike the functions list being translated into an operations list under the heading of OPERATIONS in the Procedure Division, the conditions found in the conditions list are coded directly into what appears to be a schematic logic, but is known as structure text.

The reader should notice a similarity between the derivation of a schematic logic from a detailed program structure and the derivation of the structure text from the detailed program structure. The method of derivation is identical, only the notation has changed.

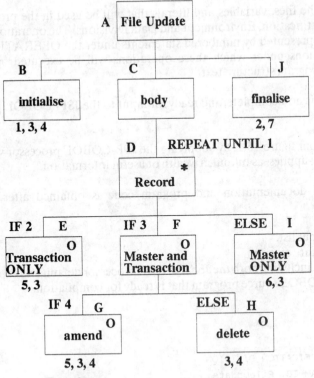

Functions.

1. Open files
2. Close files
3. Read transaction file
4. Read master file
5. Write transaction record to updated file
6. Write master record to updated file
7. Stop

Conditions.

1. End of file trans and End of file master
2. Key trans < Key master
3. Key trans = Key master
4. Transaction fields contain spaces

In place of rep (repetition) in a schematic logic ITR (iteration) has been substituted in the structure text. The letter U after ITR implies UNTIL. Hence C-rep until 1 is consistent with P-FILE-BODY ITR U ((TransFile-EOF) AND (MasterFile-EOF)).

Notice that for selection, SEL and ALT are both used in the same way as in the schematic logic. In the structure text only the conditions for the selection are coded, the IF and ELSE statements do not appear.

To summarise the information in this section. The input file contains all the data declarations for the files, variables and literals that will be used in the program, through the entries in the Identification, Environment and Data Divisions. The operations to be performed on the files are represented by numbered statements under the OPERATIONS heading. The order and conditions under which these operations will be executed by the computer is conveyed in the program structure text.

This input file is now complete, and ready for input to the JSP- COBOL processor.

15.3 Output Files.

As can be seen from figure 15.1, by supplying the JSP-COBOL processor with just one input file, the processor supplies, as output, a wealth of useful information.

The following documentation and program code is obtained after the input file is processed.

(i) A formatted-input list.
(ii) Program Structure diagram.
(iii) Diagnostic list including both the JSP-COBOL processor default and explicit options.
(iv) A complete COBOL source program that is ready for compilation.

```
000200 IDENTIFICATION DIVISION.
000300 PROGRAM-ID. FileUpdate.
000500 ENVIRONMENT DIVISION.
000600 INPUT-OUTPUT SECTION.
000700 FILE-CONTROL.
000800     SELECT TransFile ASSIGN TO PFMS.
000900     SELECT MasterFile ASSIGN TO PFMS.
001000     SELECT UpdatedFile ASSIGN TO PFMS.
001200 IMPLEMENTATION SECTION.
001300 MI  FileUpdate.
001400     MAKE FU-LIST CONTROLLER.
001800 DATA DIVISION.
001900 FILE SECTION.
002000 FD  TransFile, COMPRESSED.
002100 01  TransRecord.
002200 02  TransKey                        PIC X(20).
002300 02  TransDetails                    PIC X(7).
002400 FD  MasterFile, COMPRESSED.
002500 01  MasterRecord.
002600 02  MasterKey                       PIC X(20).
002700 02  MasterDetails                   PIC X(7).
002800 FD  UpdatedFile, COMPRESSED.
002900 01  UpdatedRecord.
003000 02  UpdatedKey                      PIC X(20).
003100 02  UpdatedDetails                  PIC X(7).
```

```
003400 PROCEDURE DIVISION.
003500 PRGM FU-LIST.
003600 OPERATIONS.
003700 1.    SOPEN INPUT TransFile.
003800 2.    SOPEN INPUT MasterFile.
003900 3.    SOPEN OUTPUT UpdatedFile.
004000 4.    SCLOSE INPUT TransFile.
004100 5.    SCLOSE INPUT MasterFile.
004200 6.    SCLOSE OUTPUT UpdatedFile.
004300 7.    SREAD TransFile AT END MOVE HIGH-VALUES TO TransKey.
004400 8.    SREAD MasterFile AT END MOVE HIGH-VALUES TO MasterKey.
004500 9.    SWRITE UpdatedRecord FROM TransRecord.
004600 10.   SWRITE UpdatedRecord FROM MasterRecord.
004700 STRUCTURE.
004800 P-FU-LIST SEQ
004800    DO 1    SOPEN INPUT TransFile.
004800       2    SOPEN INPUT MasterFile.
004800       3    SOPEN OUTPUT UpdatedFile.
004800       7    SREAD TransFile AT END MOVE HIGH-VALUES TO TransKey.
004800       8    SREAD MasterFile AT END MOVE HIGH-VALUES TO MasterKey.
004900 P-FILE-BODY ITR UNTIL ((TransFile-EOF) AND
004900                              (MasterFile-EOF))
005000    P-RECORD SEL (TransKey < MasterKey)
005100       DO 9    SWRITE UpdatedRecord FROM TransRecord.
005100          7    SREAD TransFile AT END MOVE HIGH-VALUES TO TransKey.
005200    P-RECORD ALT (TransKey = MasterKey)
005300       P-TRANS-MAST SEL (TransDetails NOT = SPACES)
005400          DO 9    SWRITE UpdatedRecord FROM TransRecord.
005400             7    SREAD TransFile AT END MOVE HIGH-VALUES TO TransKey.
005400             8    SREAD MasterFile AT END MOVE HIGH-VALUES TO MasterKey.
005500       P-TRANS-MAST ALT (ELSE)
005500          DO 7    SREAD TransFile AT END MOVE HIGH-VALUES TO TransKey.
005500             8    SREAD MasterFile AT END MOVE HIGH-VALUES TO MasterKey.
005600       P-TRANS-MAST END
005700    P-RECORD ALT (ELSE)
005700       DO 10   SWRITE UpdatedRecord FROM MasterRecord.
005700          8    SREAD MasterFile AT END MOVE HIGH-VALUES TO MasterKey.
005800    P-RECORD END
005900 P-FILE-BODY END
006000 DO 4    SCLOSE INPUT TransFile.
006000    5    SCLOSE INPUT MasterFile.
006000    6    SCLOSE OUTPUT UpdatedFile.
006100 P-FU-LIST END
```

SHEET 1

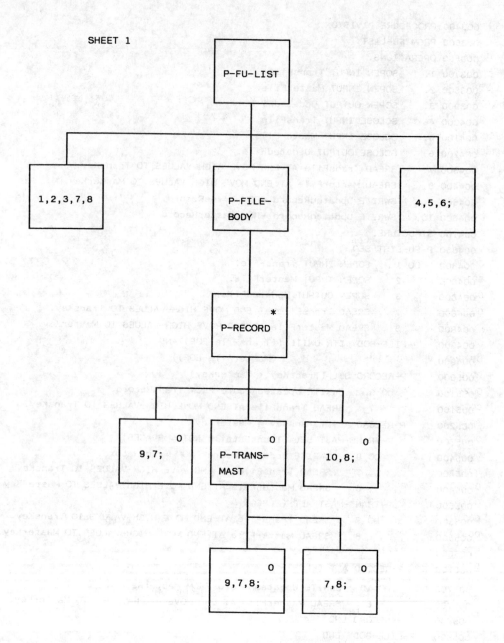

SUCCESSFUL - NO SYNTAX ERRORS.

```
  BAS   COP   MAC NOCID IPAPO OPQUO NUM=100 NOSEQ    NOJCL PUNCH=COB - MSDOS/LVL-II
NOPFC  CLW NOFLE   XLN   PSA NOCXL   TERM   FMTFL   FMTPF
  GTR NOOPT   TES VNSEL=2 VNFILE=2
NOTRA TRAABBR NOTRAIN NOTRAOUT NOPFL PFLMAX=0010 NOPFLSEQ NOPFLQUIT NOPFLRST
  PPD   OPL   INT   DGP DFORM=2029 CHSET=4 TBCOMP=49 TBOCC=49 TBPIC=30 TBRDF=30
LNWDT=100 LNCNT=060 SPACE1 LNWDT2=100 LNCNT2=060 CLP=5 FLP=1 XLP=5 PSP=1 CXLP=5
WKBLK=01022 WKBUF=30 TBVAL=45
```

```
    000200 IDENTIFICATION DIVISION.
    000300 PROGRAM-ID. FileUpdate.
    000500 ENVIRONMENT DIVISION.
    000600 INPUT-OUTPUT SECTION.
    000700 FILE-CONTROL. SELECT TransFile ASSIGN PFMS.
    000900     SELECT MasterFile ASSIGN PFMS.
    001000     SELECT UpdatedFile ASSIGN PFMS.
    001800 DATA DIVISION.
    001900 FILE SECTION.
    002000 FD  TransFile, COMPRESSED.
    002100 01  TransRecord.
    002200  02  TransKey          PIC X(20).
    002300  02  TransDetails      PIC X(7).
    002400 FD  MasterFile, COMPRESSED.
    002500 01  MasterRecord.
    002600  02  MasterKey         PIC X(20).
    002700  02  MasterDetails     PIC X(7).
    002800 FD  UpdatedFile, COMPRESSED.
    002900 01  UpdatedRecord.
    003000  02  UpdatedKey        PIC X(20).
    003100  02  UpdatedDetails    PIC X(7).
    003101 WORKING-STORAGE SECTION.
    003102 01  TransFile-COMM.
    003103     04  TransFile-OPCD  PIC XX.
    003104     04  TransFile-RES   PIC X.
    003105     88  TransFile-EOF                    VALUE "1".
    003106     88  TransFile-OK                     VALUE "4".
    003107 01  MasterFile-COMM.
    003108     04  MasterFile-OPCD PIC XX.
    003109     04  MasterFile-RES  PIC X.
    003110     88  MasterFile-EOF                   VALUE "1".
    003111     88  MasterFile-OK                    VALUE "4".
    003112 01  UpdatedFile-COMM.
    003113     04  UpdatedFile-OPCD PIC XX.
    003114     04  UpdatedFile-RES PIC X.
    003115     88  UpdatedFile-EOF                  VALUE "1".
    003116     88  UpdatedFile-OK                   VALUE "4".
```

```
003400 PROCEDURE DIVISION.
003401 JSP-MAIN SECTION.
003402 JSP-INVOKE. PERFORM FU-LIST.
003403 JSP-SUSPEND. STOP RUN.
003500 FU-LIST SECTION.
004800 P-FU-LIST-SEQ. OPEN INPUT TransFile.
004801     MOVE "4" TO TransFile-RES.
004802     OPEN INPUT MasterFile.
004803     MOVE "4" TO MasterFile-RES.
004804     OPEN OUTPUT UpdatedFile.
004805     READ TransFile AT END MOVE "1" TO TransFile-RES.
004806     IF TransFile-EOF MOVE HIGH-VALUES TO TransKey.
004807     READ MasterFile AT END MOVE "1" TO MasterFile-RES.
004808     IF MasterFile-EOF MOVE HIGH-VALUES TO MasterKey.
004900 P-FILE-BODY-ITR. IF (TransFile-EOF) AND (MasterFile-EOF) GO TO
004901     P-FILE-BODY-END.
005000     IF TransKey < MasterKey NEXT SENTENCE ELSE GO TO
005001     P-RECORD-ALT-001.
005100     WRITE UpdatedRecord FROM TransRecord.
005101     READ TransFile AT END MOVE "1" TO TransFile-RES.
005102     IF TransFile-EOF MOVE HIGH-VALUES TO TransKey.
005200     GO TO P-FILE-BODY-ITR.
005201 P-RECORD-ALT-001. IF TransKey = MasterKey NEXT SENTENCE ELSE
005202     GO TO P-RECORD-ALT-002.
005300     IF TransDetails NOT = SPACES NEXT SENTENCE ELSE GO TO
005301     P-TRANS-MAST-ALT-001.
005400     WRITE UpdatedRecord FROM TransRecord.
005401     READ TransFile AT END MOVE "1" TO TransFile-RES.
005402     IF TransFile-EOF MOVE HIGH-VALUES TO TransKey.
005403     READ MasterFile AT END MOVE "1" TO MasterFile-RES.
005404     IF MasterFile-EOF MOVE HIGH-VALUES TO MasterKey.
005500     GO TO P-FILE-BODY-ITR.
005501 P-TRANS-MAST-ALT-001. READ TransFile AT END MOVE "1" TO
005502     TransFile-RES.
005503     IF TransFile-EOF MOVE HIGH-VALUES TO TransKey.
005504     READ MasterFile AT END MOVE "1" TO MasterFile-RES.
005505     IF MasterFile-EOF MOVE HIGH-VALUES TO MasterKey.
005700     GO TO P-FILE-BODY-ITR.
005701 P-RECORD-ALT-002. WRITE UpdatedRecord FROM MasterRecord.
005702     READ MasterFile AT END MOVE "1" TO MasterFile-RES.
005703     IF MasterFile-EOF MOVE HIGH-VALUES TO MasterKey.
005900     GO TO P-FILE-BODY-ITR.
005901 P-FILE-BODY-END. CLOSE TransFile.
006000     CLOSE MasterFile.
006001     CLOSE UpdatedFile.
006002 FU-LIST-EXIT. EXIT.
```

The version of JSP-COBOL used in this chapter was designed to run on an IBM PC or compatible. The input file was created using an editor on the IBM PC, and the resultant COBOL source program file, output by the JSP-COBOL processor on the IBM PC, was transferred to the PRIME computer and compiled without errors using the PRIME COBOL-85 compiler.

The compiled program was run on the PRIME computer, using the same data file and giving the same results, as described in chapter 10.

Notice from the COBOL source program that the processor has used sections in the Procedure Division. A few words on sections will be given here in order to give the reader a clear insight into the working of the processor-produced source code.

A Procedure Division may be divided into sections. If sections are used each section must contain at least one paragraph and individual paragraphs within sections should not be performed or branched to from outside the section. If sections are used then no isolated paragraphs may be declared outside sections.

In the generated COBOL program the JSP-COBOL system has produced two sections. The first is a JSP-MAIN SECTION acting as a block of code that controls the other sections. However, since there is only one other section, FU-LIST SECTION, the computer is directed to PERFORM FU-LIST from the JSP-MAIN SECTION and upon returning to this section STOP RUN is executed.

The reader is recommended to trace through the derived source code to gain an understanding of the translation, into Standard COBOL, of such statements as SOPEN, SCLOSE, SREAD and SWRITE.

15.4 Macro Features.

The JSP-COBOL macro facility allows simple text replacement macros. The primary purpose of a macro is to reduce the amount of program text to be written. A macro definition may be local or global. A local definition may appear anywhere in the input text, but must precede any call to the defined macro. A global definition must be present in the macro library.

A small JSP-COBOL macro definition follows, used to generate the first few lines of the program given in the last section. This is stored in the macro library under the name HEAD.MAC.

```
$ML &HEAD &P1 &P2 &P3 &P4 &P5 &P6 =
IDENTIFICATION DIVISION.
PROGRAM-ID. &P1.
AUTHOR. B.J.Holmes.
INSTALLATION. Oxford Polytechnic.
DATE-WRITTEN. &P2.
DATE-COMPILED. &P3.
SECURITY. &P4.
```

```
ENVIRONMENT DIVISION.
CONFIGURATION SECTION.
SOURCE-COMPUTER. &P5.
OBJECT-COMPUTER. &P6.
INPUT-OUTPUT SECTION.
FILE-CONTROL.
$MEND
```

The parameters of this macro are &P1, &P2, &P3, &P4, &P5 and &P6 where:

&P1 is the name of the program;

&P2 and &P3 are the date the program was written and the date the program was compiled, respectively;

&P4 is a remarks string literal;

&P5 and &P6 are the names of the source and object computer, respectively.

The macro is called by using the statement: *&HEAD FileUpdate 28/2/91 28/2/91 none IBM-PC Prime-950* as depicted in the short extract of the beginning of a COBOL program.

```
&HEAD FileUpdate 28/2/91 28/2/91 none IBM-PC Prime-950
    SELECT TransFile ASSIGN TO PFMS.
    SELECT MasterFile ASSIGN TO PFMS.
    SELECT UpdatedFile ASSIGN TO PFMS.
```

and it generates the following opening statements of the program.

```
000100 IDENTIFICATION DIVISION.
000100 PROGRAM-ID. FileUpdate.
000100 AUTHOR. B.J.Holmes.
000100 INSTALLATION. Oxford Polytechnic.
000100 DATE-WRITTEN. 28/2/91.
000100 DATE-COMPILED. 28/2/91.
000100 SECURITY. none.
000100 ENVIRONMENT DIVISION.
000100 CONFIGURATION SECTION.
000100 SOURCE-COMPUTER. IBM-PC.
000100 OBJECT-COMPUTER. Prime-950.
000100 INPUT-OUTPUT SECTION.
000100 FILE-CONTROL.
000200     SELECT TransFile ASSIGN TO PFMS.
000300     SELECT MasterFile ASSIGN TO PFMS.
000400     SELECT UpdatedFile ASSIGN TO PFMS.
```

15.5 Internal Data Files.

Consider again the hotel register problem in chapter 13, this involved a boundary clash, and a method of solving the problem was to write two programs. The first read the register file and produced an intermediate file containing the extra lines needed by the report, and the second program read the intermediate file and produced a paginated report. A second solution required that the intermediate file was never created, and the first program became a subprogram of the second. The first program would read records from the register file and pass each record back, as a parameter, to the second program.

The reader will probably agree that the first solution, although longer to program, was easier to understand and implement. The second solution involved inverting the first program with respect to the second and making the first program a re-entrant subprogram.

It is possible using JSP-COBOL to have the best from both solutions. Two programs are designed on the basis of an intermediate file, yet the intermediate file is not physically created. One program is automatically inverted with respect to the other, and the inverted routine is automatically coded as a re-entrant subroutine. Both programs share the same Identification, Environment and Data Divisions so the amount of coding is reduced.

The intermediate file is declared using *SELECT intermediate ASSIGN TO SI-S-Rdat*, where **SI-S** is a JSP-COBOL code meaning Single Internal Sequential file and Rdat becomes a subprogram. The file SI-S-Rdat is purely internal to the program and cannot be accessed from outside of the program.

The full documentation, using JSP-COBOL, of the solution to the hotel register problem follows. Notice that it has been necessary to introduce a paper control character P-Control in the ReportRecord, and move either 1 or a space to it, in order to supply the correct lineprinter control character for the vertical positioning of the paper. Normally in COBOL it would be sufficient to state WRITE ReportRecord AFTER ADVANCING PAGE, or WRITE ReportRecord AFTER ADVANCING 1 LINE. There is no option in the SWRITE format for advancing the paper in the lineprinter.

```
JSP PSA
JSP DFORM=2029
JSP TBPIC=30
JSP TBRDF=30
JSP TBVAL=45
JSP LNWDT=132
JSP LNCNT=60
JSP LNWDT2=132
JSP LNCNT2=60


IDENTIFICATION DIVISION.
PROGRAM-ID. Hotel.


ENVIRONMENT DIVISION.
INPUT-OUTPUT SECTION.
```

```
FILE-CONTROL.
      SELECT register ASSIGN TO PFMS.
      SELECT intermediate ASSIGN TO SI-S-RDat.
      SELECT HotelReport ASSIGN TO PFMS.

IMPLEMENTATION SECTION.
MI Hotel.
      MAKE WRep CONTROLLER.

DATA DIVISION.
FILE SECTION.
FD register, COMPRESSED.
01 RegisterRecord.
      02 date-RR PIC 9(6).
      02 day-RR PIC 9.
      02 details-RR PIC X(73).


FD intermediate, COMPRESSED.
01 RDatRecord.
      02 date-RD PIC 9(6).
      02 day-RD PIC 9.
      02 details-RD PIC X(73).


FD HotelReport, COMPRESSED.
01 ReportRecord.
      02 P-Control PIC X.
      02 LineImage PIC X(79).

WORKING-STORAGE SECTION.
01 Record-1-WS.
      02 FILLER PIC X(13) VALUE IS "Week Ending".
      02 HeaderDate PIC 99BB99BB99.
01 Record-2-WS.
      02 DayName PIC X(4).
      02 Guest-Details-WS-1 PIC X(73).
01 Record-3-WS.
      02 FILLER PIC X(21) VALUE IS "SUNMONTUEWEDTHUFRISAT".
01 Record-4-WS REDEFINES Record-3-WS.
      02 NameOfDay PIC X(3) OCCURS 7 TIMES.
01 Record-5-WS.
      02 FILLER PIC X(6) VALUE IS "Total".
      02 RegCount PIC Z9.


77 LineCount PIC 99.
77 DateStore PIC 9(6).
77 DateStore-RR PIC 9(6).
77 DayStore PIC 9.
77 RegistrationCount PIC 99.
```

```
 PROCEDURE DIVISION.
 PRGM WRep.

 OPERATIONS.
 1.  SOPEN INPUT intermediate.
 2.  SOPEN OUTPUT HotelReport.
 3.  SCLOSE INPUT intermediate.
 4.  SCLOSE OUTPUT HotelReport.
 5.  SREAD intermediate.
 6.  SWRITE ReportRecord.
 7.  MOVE date-RD TO HeaderDate.
 8.  MOVE Record-1-WS TO LineImage.
 9.  MOVE 1 TO P-Control.
 10. MOVE NameOfDay (day-RD) TO DayName.
 11. MOVE details-RD TO Guest-Details-WS-1.
 12. MOVE Record-2-WS TO LineImage.
 13. MOVE SPACE TO P-Control.
 14. MOVE date-RD TO DateStore.
 15. MOVE ZERO TO LineCount.
 16. ADD 1 TO LineCount.
 STRUCTURE.
 P-report          SEQ    DO 1, 2, 5
 P-report-body     ITR  U (intermediate-EOF)
 P-week            SEQ    DO 14, 5
 P-week-body       ITR  U ((intermediate-EOF) OR
                            (date-RD NOT = DateStore))
 P-page            SEQ    DO 15, 7, 8, 9, 6
 P-page-body       ITR  U ((intermediate-EOF) OR
                            (date-RD NOT = DateStore) OR
                            (LineCount NOT < 60))
                          DO 16, 10, 11, 12, 13, 6, 5
 P-page-body       END
 P-page            END
 P-week-body       END
 P-week            END
 P-report-body     END    DO 3, 4
 P-report          END


 PRGM RDat.
 OPERATIONS.
 1.  SOPEN INPUT register.
 2.  SOPEN OUTPUT intermediate.
 3.  SCLOSE INPUT register.
 4.  SCLOSE OUTPUT intermediate.
 5.  SREAD register.
 6.  SWRITE RDatRecord.
 7.  MOVE RegistrationCount TO RegCount.
```

```
 8. MOVE Record-5-WS TO details-RD.
 9. MOVE RegisterRecord TO RDatRecord.
10. MOVE ZERO TO RegistrationCount.
11. ADD 1 TO RegistrationCount.
12. MOVE date-RR TO DateStore-RR.
13. MOVE day-RR TO DayStore.
STRUCTURE.
P-intermediate-file    SEQ        DO 1, 2, 5
P-file-body            ITR  U     (register-EOF)
P-week                 SEQ        DO 12, 9, 6, 5
P-week-body            ITR  U     ((register-EOF) OR
                                  (date-RR NOT = DateStore))
P-day                  SEQ        DO 13, 10
P-day-body             ITR  U     ((register-EOF) OR
                                  (date-RR NOT = DateStore) OR
                                  (day-RR NOT = DayStore))
                                  DO 9, 6, 11, 5
P-day-body             END        DO 7, 8, 6
P-day                  END
P-week-body            END
P-week                 END
P-file-body            END        DO 3, 4
P-intermediate-file    END
```

```
000200 IDENTIFICATION DIVISION.
000300 PROGRAM-ID. Hotel.
000500 ENVIRONMENT DIVISION.
000600 INPUT-OUTPUT SECTION.
000700 FILE-CONTROL.
000800     SELECT register ASSIGN TO PFMS.
000900     SELECT intermediate ASSIGN TO SI-S-RDat.
001000     SELECT HotelReport ASSIGN TO PFMS.
001200 IMPLEMENTATION SECTION.
001300 MI   Hotel.
001400     MAKE WRep CONTROLLER.
001600 DATA DIVISION.
001700 FILE SECTION.
001800 FD   register, COMPRESSED.
001900 01   RegisterRecord.
002000 02   date-RR                      PIC 9(6).
002100 02   day-RR                       PIC 9.
002200 02   details-RR                   PIC X(73).
```

```
002400 FD    intermediate, COMPRESSED.
002500 01    RDatRecord.
002600  02   date-RD                          PIC 9(6).
002700  02   day-RD                           PIC 9.
002800  02   details-RD                       PIC X(73).
003000 FD    HotelReport, COMPRESSED.
003100 01    ReportRecord.
003200  02   P-Control                        PIC X.
003300  02   LineImage                        PIC X(79).
003500 WORKING-STORAGE SECTION.
003600 01    Record-1-WS.
003700  02   FILLER                           PIC X(13)
             VALUE IS 'Week Ending'.
003800  02   HeaderDate                       PIC 99BB99BB99.
003900 01    Record-2-WS.
004000  02   DayName                          PIC X(4).
004100  02   Guest-Details-WS-1               PIC X(73).
004200 01    Record-3-WS.
004300  02   FILLER                           PIC X(21)
             VALUE IS 'SUNMONTUEWEDTHUFRISAT'.
004400 01    Record-4-WS                      REDEFINES Record-3-WS.
004500  02   NameOfDay                        PIC X(3)
             OCCURS 7 TIMES.
004600 01    Record-5-WS.
004700  02   FILLER                           PIC X(6)
             VALUE IS 'Total'.
004800  02   RegCount                         PIC Z9.
005000 77    LineCount                        PIC 99.
005100 77    DateStore                        PIC 9(6).
005200 77    DateStore-RR                     PIC 9(6).
005300 77    DayStore                         PIC 9.
005400 77    RegistrationCount                PIC 99.
005600 PROCEDURE DIVISION.
005700 PRGM WRep.
005800 OPERATIONS.
005900 1.    SOPEN INPUT intermediate.
006000 2.    SOPEN OUTPUT HotelReport.
006100 3.    SCLOSE INPUT intermediate.
006200 4.    SCLOSE OUTPUT HotelReport.
006300 5.    SREAD intermediate.
006400 6.    SWRITE ReportRecord.
006500 7.    MOVE date-RD TO HeaderDate.
006600 8.    MOVE Record-1-WS TO LineImage.
006700 9.    MOVE 1 TO P-Control.
006800 10.   MOVE NameOfDay (day-RD) TO DayName.
006900 11.   MOVE details-RD TO Guest-Details-WS-1.
```

```
007000 12.    MOVE Record-2-WS TO LineImage.
007100 13.    MOVE SPACE TO P-Control.
007200 14.    MOVE date-RD TO DateStore.
007300 15.    MOVE ZERO TO LineCount.
007400 16.    ADD 1 TO LineCount.
007500 STRUCTURE.
007600 P-report SEQ
007600    DO 1     SOPEN INPUT intermediate.
007600       2     SOPEN OUTPUT HotelReport.
007600       5     SREAD intermediate.
007700    P-report-body ITR UNTIL (intermediate-EOF)
007800      P-week SEQ
007800        DO 14    MOVE date-RD TO DateStore.
007800           5     SREAD intermediate.
007900        P-week-body ITR UNTIL ((intermediate-EOF) OR
008000                          (date-RD NOT = DateStore))
008100          P-page SEQ
008100            DO 15    MOVE ZERO TO LineCount.
008100               7     MOVE date-RD TO HeaderDate.
008100               8     MOVE Record-1-WS TO LineImage.
008100               9     MOVE 1 TO P-Control.
008100               6     SWRITE ReportRecord.
008200            P-page-body ITR UNTIL ((intermediate-EOF) OR
008300                          (date-RD NOT = DateStore) OR
008400                          (LineCount NOT < 60))
008500              DO 16    ADD 1 TO LineCount.
008500                 10    MOVE NameOfDay (day-RD) TO DayName.
008500                 11    MOVE details-RD TO Guest-Details-WS-1.
008500                 12    MOVE Record-2-WS TO LineImage.
008500                 13    MOVE SPACE TO P-Control.
008500                 6     SWRITE ReportRecord.
008500                 5     SREAD intermediate.
008600            P-page-body END
008700          P-page END
008800        P-week-body END
008900      P-week END
009000    P-report-body END
009000    DO 3     SCLOSE INPUT intermediate.
009000       4     SCLOSE OUTPUT HotelReport.
009100 P-report END
009300 PRGM RDat.
009400 OPERATIONS.
009500 1.    SOPEN INPUT register.
009600 2.    SOPEN OUTPUT intermediate.
009700 3.    SCLOSE INPUT register.
009800 4.    SCLOSE OUTPUT intermediate.
009900 5.    SREAD register.
```

```
010000 6.      SWRITE RDatRecord.
010100 7.      MOVE RegistrationCount TO RegCount.
010200 8.      MOVE Record-5-WS TO details-RD.
010300 9.      MOVE RegisterRecord TO RDatRecord.
010400 10.     MOVE ZERO TO RegistrationCount.
010500 11.     ADD 1 TO RegistrationCount.
010600 12.     MOVE date-RR TO DateStore-RR.
010700 13.     MOVE day-RR TO DayStore.
010800 STRUCTURE.
010900 P-intermediate-file SEQ
010900    DO 1    SOPEN INPUT register.
010900       2    SOPEN OUTPUT intermediate.
010900       5    SREAD register.
011000    P-file-body ITR UNTIL (register-EOF)

011100      P-week SEQ
011100       DO 12   MOVE date-RR TO DateStore-RR.
011100          9    MOVE RegisterRecord TO RDatRecord.
011100          6    SWRITE RDatRecord.
011100          5    SREAD register.
011200        P-week-body ITR UNTIL ((register-EOF) OR
011300                               (date-RR NOT = DateStore))
011400         P-day SEQ
011400          DO 13   MOVE day-RR TO DayStore.
011400             10   MOVE ZERO TO RegistrationCount.
011500          P-day-body ITR UNTIL ((register-EOF) OR
011600                                (date-RR NOT = DateStore) OR
011700                                (day-RR NOT = DayStore))
011800           DO 9    MOVE RegisterRecord TO RDatRecord.
011800              6    SWRITE RDatRecord.
011800             11    ADD 1 TO RegistrationCount.
011800              5    SREAD register.
011900          P-day-body END
011900           DO 7    MOVE RegistrationCount TO RegCount.
011900              8    MOVE Record-5-WS TO details-RD.
011900              6    SWRITE RDatRecord.
012000         P-day END
012100        P-week-body END
012200      P-week END
012300    P-file-body END
012300    DO 3    SCLOSE INPUT register.
012300       4    SCLOSE OUTPUT intermediate.
012400 P-intermediate-file END
```

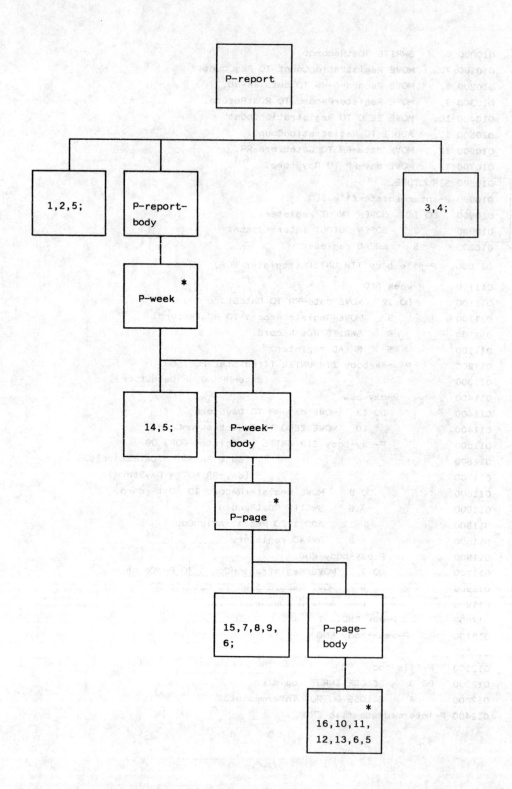

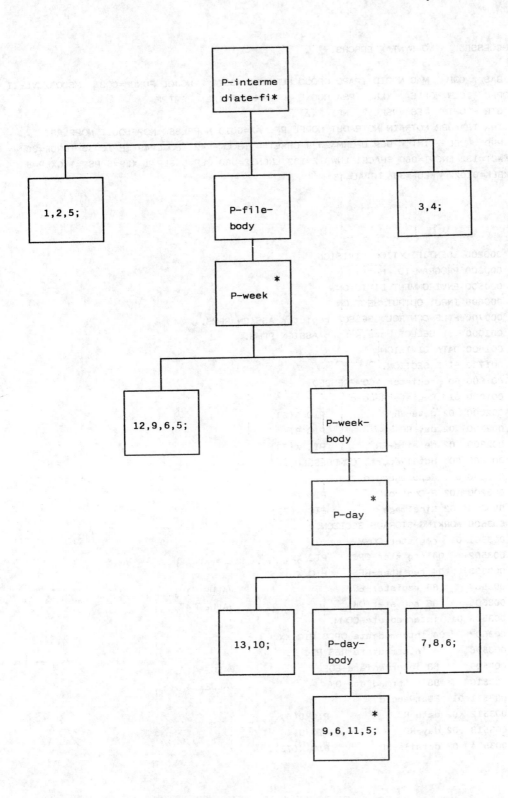

SUCCESSFUL - NO SYNTAX ERRORS.

```
 BAS   COP   MAC NOCID IPAPO OPQUO NUM=100 NOSEQ    NOJCL PUNCH=COB - MSDOS/LVL-II
NOPFC   CLW NOFLE   XLN   PSA NOCXL   TERM   FMTFL   FMTPF
  GTR NOOPT    TES VNSEL=2 VNFILE=2
NOTRA TRAABBR NOTRAIN NOTRAOUT NOPFL PFLMAX=0010 NOPFLSEQ NOPFLQUIT NOPFLRST
  PPD   OPL   INT   DGP DFORM=2029 CHSET=4 TBCOMP=49 TBOCC=49 TBPIC=30 TBRDF=30
LNWDT=132 LNCNT=060 SPACE1 LNWDT2=132 LNCNT2=060 CLP=5 FLP=1 XLP=5 PSP=1 CXLP=5
WKBLK=01022 WKBUF=30  TBVAL=45
```

```
000200 IDENTIFICATION DIVISION.
000300 PROGRAM-ID. Hotel.
000500 ENVIRONMENT DIVISION.
000600 INPUT-OUTPUT SECTION.
000700 FILE-CONTROL. SELECT register ASSIGN PFMS.
001000      SELECT HotelReport ASSIGN PFMS.
001600 DATA DIVISION.
001700 FILE SECTION.
001800 FD  register, COMPRESSED.
001900 01  RegisterRecord.
002000  02 date-RR          PIC 9(6).
002100  02 day-RR           PIC 9.
002200  02 details-RR        PIC X(73).
003000 FD  HotelReport, COMPRESSED.
003100 01  ReportRecord.
003200  02 P-Control        PIC X.
003300  02 LineImage        PIC X(79).
003500 WORKING-STORAGE SECTION.
003501 01  register-COMM.
003502    04 register-OPCD   PIC XX.
003503    04 register-RES    PIC X.
003504      88 register-EOF              VALUE "1".
003505      88 register-OK               VALUE "4".
003506 01  intermediate-COMM.
003507    04 intermediate-OPCD PIC XX.
003508    04 intermediate-RES PIC X.
003509      88 intermediate-EOF          VALUE "1".
003510      88 intermediate-OK           VALUE "4".
003511 01  RDatRecord.
003512  02 date-RD          PIC 9(6).
003513  02 day-RD           PIC 9.
003514  02 details-RD        PIC X(73).
```

```
003515 01   HotelReport-COMM.
003516      04 HotelReport-OPCD PIC XX.
003517      04 HotelReport-RES PIC X.
003518       88 HotelReport-EOF            VALUE "1".
003519       88 HotelReport-OK             VALUE "4".
003520 01   RDat-QS          PIC S9(4)       COMP VALUE 1.
003600 01   Record-1-WS.
003700 02   FILLER           PIC X(13)      VALUE IS 'Week Ending'.
003800 02   HeaderDate       PIC 99BB99BB99.
003900 01   Record-2-WS.
004000 02   DayName          PIC X(4).
004100 02   Guest-Details-WS-1 PIC X(73).
004200 01   Record-3-WS.
004300 02   FILLER           PIC X(21)      VALUE IS
004301       'SUNMONTUEWEDTHUFRISAT'.
004400 01   Record-4-WS      REDEFINES Record-3-WS.
004500 02   NameOfDay        PIC X(3)          OCCURS 7 TIMES.
004600 01   Record-5-WS.
004700 02   FILLER           PIC X(6)       VALUE IS 'Total'.
004800 02   RegCount         PIC Z9.
005000 77   LineCount        PIC 99.
005100 77   DateStore        PIC 9(6).
005200 77   DateStore-RR     PIC 9(6).
005300 77   DayStore         PIC 9.
005400 77   RegistrationCount PIC 99.
005600 PROCEDURE DIVISION.
005601 JSP-MAIN SECTION.
005602 JSP-INVOKE. PERFORM WRep.
005603 JSP-SUSPEND. STOP RUN.
005700 WRep SECTION.
007600 P-report-SEQ. PERFORM RDat.
007601      OPEN OUTPUT HotelReport.
007602      PERFORM RDat.
007700 P-report-body-ITR. IF intermediate-EOF GO TO P-report-body-END.
007800      MOVE date-RD TO DateStore.
007801      PERFORM RDat.
007900 P-week-body-ITR. IF (intermediate-EOF) OR (date-RD NOT =
008000      DateStore) GO TO P-report-body-ITR.
008100      MOVE ZERO TO LineCount.
008101      MOVE date-RD TO HeaderDate.
008102      MOVE Record-1-WS TO LineImage.
008103      MOVE 1 TO P-Control.
008104      WRITE ReportRecord.
008200 P-page-body-ITR. IF (intermediate-EOF) OR (date-RD NOT =
008300      DateStore) OR (LineCount NOT < 60) GO TO P-week-body-ITR.
008500      ADD 1 TO LineCount.
```

```
008501      MOVE NameOfDay (day-RD) TO DayName.
008502      MOVE details-RD TO Guest-Details-WS-1.
008503      MOVE Record-2-WS TO LineImage.
008504      MOVE SPACE TO P-Control.
008505      WRITE ReportRecord.
008506      PERFORM RDat.
008600      GO TO P-page-body-ITR.
009000 P-report-body-END. PERFORM RDat.
009001      CLOSE HotelReport.
009002 WRep-EXIT. EXIT.
009300 RDat SECTION.
009301 RDat-Q000. GO TO P-intermediate-file-SEQ RDat-Q002 RDat-Q003
009302      RDat-Q004 P-week-body-ITR P-intermediate-file-END
009303      DEPENDING ON RDat-QS.
010900 P-intermediate-file-SEQ. OPEN INPUT register.
010901      MOVE "4" TO register-RES.
010902      MOVE "4" TO intermediate-RES.
010903      MOVE 002 TO RDat-QS GO TO RDat-EXIT.
010904 RDat-Q002. READ register AT END MOVE "1" TO register-RES.
011000 P-file-body-ITR. IF register-EOF GO TO P-file-body-END.
011100      MOVE date-RR TO DateStore-RR.
011101      MOVE RegisterRecord TO RDatRecord.
011102      MOVE 003 TO RDat-QS GO TO RDat-EXIT.
011103 RDat-Q003. READ register AT END MOVE "1" TO register-RES.
011200 P-week-body-ITR. IF (register-EOF) OR (date-RR NOT = DateStore)
011300      GO TO P-file-body-ITR.
011400      MOVE day-RR TO DayStore.
011401      MOVE ZERO TO RegistrationCount.
011500 P-day-body-ITR. IF (register-EOF) OR (date-RR NOT = DateStore) OR
011700      (day-RR NOT = DayStore) GO TO P-day-body-END.
011800      MOVE RegisterRecord TO RDatRecord.
011801      MOVE 004 TO RDat-QS GO TO RDat-EXIT.
011802 RDat-Q004. ADD 1 TO RegistrationCount.
011803      READ register AT END MOVE "1" TO register-RES.
011900      GO TO P-day-body-ITR.
011901 P-day-body-END. MOVE RegistrationCount TO RegCount.
011902      MOVE Record-5-WS TO details-RD.
011903      MOVE 005 TO RDat-QS GO TO RDat-EXIT.
012300 P-file-body-END. CLOSE register.
012301      MOVE "1" TO intermediate-RES.
012302      MOVE 006 TO RDat-QS GO TO RDat-EXIT.
012400 P-intermediate-file-END. MOVE +1 TO RDat-QS.
012401 RDat-EXIT. EXIT.
```

15.6 An Introduction to PDF.

The remainder of this chapter should provide the reader with a fundamental understanding of a second Jackson Structured Programming tool known as Program Development Facility, or PDF for short. The version of PDF described in this chapter is version 2.1 suitable for an IBM PC.

PDF enables a user to perform the following functions.

To draw and edit data structure diagrams on the screen of a visual display unit.

The data structure diagrams can be expanded into detailed program structures containing operations (functions) and conditions.

Several interconnecting structure diagrams can be joined together to form a larger more complex structure.

When a detailed program structure diagram is complete it is possible to automatically generate the Procedure Division of a COBOL program using the code generator. The user has the choice of whether to generate flat code as illustrated in chapter 13, or flat code using COBOL-85 control structures, as illustrated in chapter 14.

The system will also output, on command, a paginated detailed program structure diagram, and a paginated structure text containing operations, conditions and the first three divisions of a COBOL program.

15.7 Constructing a Structure Diagram.

Before any attempt is made to use PDF it is recommended that the programmer has already derived, using pencil-and-paper, a detailed program structure with the functions coded into COBOL statements and the conditions coded into COBOL conditions. The detailed program structure used in this worked example is the sales of music cassettes example taken from chapter 9, and is reprinted on the next page.

The PDF package once installed, in this example on an IBM PC, is invoked using the command *PDF filename*. If the filename is a new file the user will be presented with the picture of a root node on the screen, and this will have been designated as the current node.

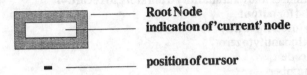

Root Node
indication of 'current' node

position of cursor

Notice the shaded rectangle is the node and the blank rectangle contained within, is an indication that this node has been designated as the current node.

Where do we go from here? Many of the interactions with the PDF system are through keys that have been designated for special functions. Figure 15.2 indicates the typical layout of part of a PC keyboard, and shows how the function and numeric keypad keys are labelled to interact with the PDF system.

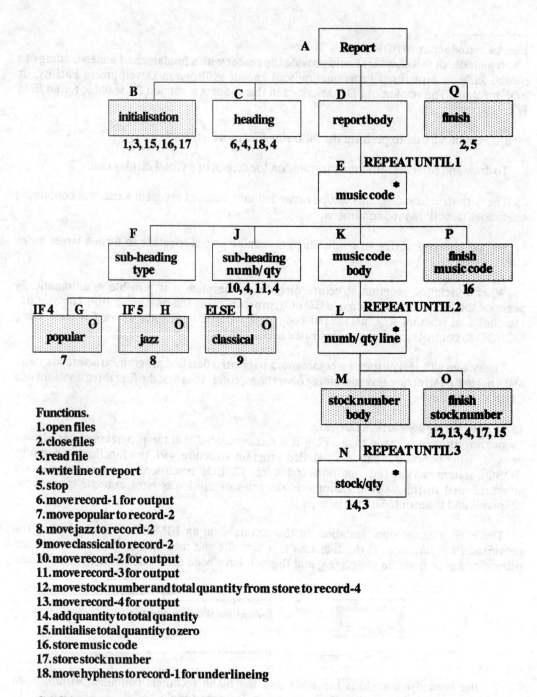

Functions.
1. open files
2. close files
3. read file
4. write line of report
5. stop
6. move record-1 for output
7. move popular to record-2
8. move jazz to record-2
9. move classical to record-2
10. move record-2 for output
11. move record-3 for output
12. move stock number and total quantity from store to record-4
13. move record-4 for output
14. add quantity to total quantity
15. initialise total quantity to zero
16. store music code
17. store stock number
18. move hyphens to record-1 for underlineing

Conditions.
1. end of file
2. not same music code or (1)
3. not same stock number or (2)
4. music code = A
5. music code = B

EDIT COND help	EDIT OPLIST list	COND tab up	JOIN tab down	PAGE tab left	VIEW tab right	ATTBIB current up	SEQ current down	SEL current left	ITER current right
F1	F2	F3	F4	F5	F6	F7	F8	F9	F10

Use SHIFT key to get to the functions written in upper case letters

7 scroll home	8 scroll up	9 set current scroll current
4 scroll left	5 exit help	6 scroll right

— scroll slower name

1 exit help cut	2 scroll down	3 exit help paste

scroll faster

0 Insert Node	• Delete Node Enter

Numeric Keypad

tidy	command	size
F8	F9	F10

Use the ALT key together with functions keys F8, F9 and F10.

Figure 15.2 Typical layout of operations associated with function keys and numeric keypad on an IBM PC.

To build a diagram of nodes requires that the cursor is roughly positioned at the place on the screen where the next node is to be generated. Cursor movement is made easy through the use of the cursor tab function keys F3, F4, F5 and F6. A node is generated at the position of the cursor by pressing the 0 key on the numeric keypad, labelled in figure 15.2 as Insert Node. Further nodes may be created in the same way, tabbing the cursor to a new position on the screen and pressing key 0 on the numeric keypad.

All the nodes that are generated are siblings of the parent node, marked as the current node. In order to progress the development of the structure diagram, to further levels it is necessary to change the position of the current node. Moving the indicator (blank rectangle) through the structure diagram is possible by using the function keys F7, F8, F9 and F10. Hence, once a new current node has been designated it is possible to construct further levels in the structure diagram.

Figure 15.3 illustrates how the function keys can be used to build the nodes of a structure diagram.

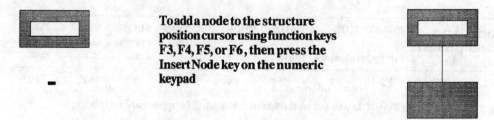

To add a node to the structure position cursor using function keys F3, F4, F5, or F6, then press the Insert Node key on the numeric keypad

Further nodes may be added to the structure by moving the cursor to the position of the new node to be inserted, then pressing the Insert Node key on the numeric keypad.

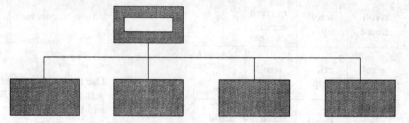

It is vital to remember that the production of the nodes is with respect to the 'current' node. To insert nodes beneath this structure, with respect to a new node, will involve moving the position of the 'current' node. Movement of the 'current node is through the function keys F7, F8, F9 or F10. For example, by pressing F8 (current down), F10 (current right) and F10 (current right) again causes the 'current' position to change by moving through three nodes. The final position is shown below.

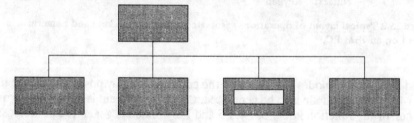

More nodes can be inserted with respect to the 'current' node by carrying out the instructions given above.

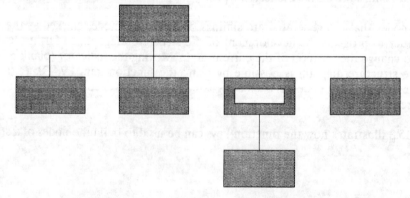

Figure 15.3 Inserting nodes into a structure diagram.

Having built the outline of a structure diagram in nodes only, it is necessary to embellish the diagram with comments, symbols, operation numbers (function numbers) and conditions. This is simple as long as you remember that every node to be embellished MUST first be designated as the current node. Comments and operation numbers are added to the diagram by pressing the minus (-) key on the numeric keypad, marked Name in figure 15.2. On the lower portion of the screen the user is invited to type the information that is to be printed inside the node on the screen. A user may type function numbers, for example, 1,3,15,16,17 or comments such as report body. This text will be printed inside the current node.

Symbols such as o (selection), * (repetition) and other attributes such as ! (quit), - (optimise out), + (recover) and ? (posit) are printed in the appropriate current node by pressing the SHIFT key and F9, F10 and F7 keys as indicated in figure 15.2. The respective symbol is then drawn in on the node.

Unlike the detailed program structure diagrams that appear throughout the book, the conditions associated with the selections and repetitions do not appear on a PDF generated detailed program structure. However, the conditions do exist behind the scenes!

Having selected the current node, which must be either a condition or selection, the SHIFT and F3 keys are pressed and the user is invited to type the corresponding condition in a lower-window on the screen. The first line of the condition is taken as a comment line, second and subsequent lines are used for the conditions that will eventually be converted into program code.

The operations of adding comments, symbols and conditions to the structure diagram are summarised in figure 15.4 over the page.

15.8 Editing Functions and Conditions.
The detailed program structure may at this stage appear to be complete, however, the functions need to be created and filed before the structure is ready for translating into a textural form and eventually into a COBOL program.

Unlike the creation of the conditions, the functions are entered into the system using an editor. However, there is no need to break out of the PDF system to create the functions. By pressing the keys SHIFT and F2 it is possible to edit the operation (functions) list.

On the first attempt at creating a list of functions the user is confronted with a screen that contains the following outline information.

```
- - - - - - - - - - - - top - - - - - - - - - - - - -
~ ~ ~ T ~ ~ ~ ~ ~ ~ ~ ~ ~ ~ ~ ~ ~
- - - - - - - - - - - bottom - - - - - - - - - - - -
```

The functions are typed between the ~ ~ ~ line and line marked bottom. The letter T is a tab position.

The functions are input as follows.

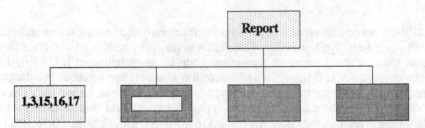

Function numbers and comments are entered into respective nodes by making the node the 'current' node and pressing the minus key on the numeric keypad, the system will respond with the prompt New name: and the appropriate text is then typed at the keyboard.

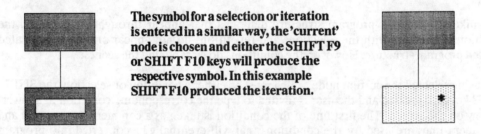

The symbol for a selection or iteration is entered in a similar way, the 'current' node is chosen and either the SHIFT F9 or SHIFT F10 keys will produce the respective symbol. In this example SHIFT F10 produced the iteration.

Conditions associated with selections or iterations are entered into the system in a similar manner. A node that contains either the selection or iteration symbol, is chosen and made the 'current' node. By pressing the SHIFT F3 key the user is invited to type the condition. This condition is stored in a PDF system file, and can be viewed by selecting the appropriate component, making it 'current' and pressing the F2 key. The conditions associated with the component are then displayed. These conditions can be edited by pressing SHIFT F1 and changed.

Functions are entered into the system by pressing SHIFT F2. To examine the functions associated with a curent node press the F2 key.

Figure 15.4 Inserting text and symbols into the nodes.

```
- - - - - - - - - - - - top - - - - - - - - - - - -
~ ~ ~ T ~ ~ ~ ~ ~ ~ ~ ~ ~ ~ ~ ~ ~
1           OPEN INPUT MusicData, OUTPUT MusicReport.
2           CLOSE MusicData, MusicReport.
3           READ MusicData AT END MOVE 'T' TO EOF.
4           WRITE ReportOut.
5           STOP RUN.
.
.
.
- - - - - - - - - - bottom - - - - - - - - - - -
```

Each function number corresponds with the function number depicted in the structure diagram.

If a COBOL program is to be generated from the structure diagram then it is necessary to create the remaining Divisions as a header to the operations file. These Divisions are entered between the line marked top and the ~ ~ ~ line. In this illustration only a skeletal outline of the Divisions has been given.

```
- - - - - - - - - - -top - - - - - - - - -
        IDENTIFICATION DIVISION.
        PROGRAM-ID. Music1.
        ENVIRONMENT DIVISION.
        INPUT-OUTPUT SECTION.
        FILE-CONTROL.
                SELECT MusicData ASSIGN TO PFMS.
        .

        DATA DIVISION.
        .

        .

        PROCEDURE DIVISION.
~ ~ ~T~ ~ ~ ~ ~ ~ ~ ~ ~ ~ ~ ~ ~ ~
1               OPEN INPUT MusicData, OUTPUT MusicReport.
2               CLOSE MusicData, MusicReport.
3               READ MusicData AT END MOVE 'T' TO EOF.
4               Write ReportOut.
5               STOP RUN.

        .

        .

        .

- - - - - - - - - - - bottom - - - - - - - - -
```

The text file that has been created is then filed using the keys SHIFT F2.

This file can be edited as required by using the keys SHIFT F2, and the screen cursor moved about the text file as though the text was in a window editor.

If a condition is to be edited, the appropriate node containing the condition must be designated the current node. Using the keys SHIFT F1 the appropriate condition can be edited.

All conditions and functions can be inspected without the need for invoking the editor (SHIFT F1 or F2 respectively), by designating the appropriate elementary node or condition node as the current node and pressing F2. The appropriate functions or conditions will be displayed in a lower window on the screen.

When the structure diagram is complete it can be saved by pressing the ALT and F9 keys and using the command SAVE filename. In this example SAVE Music1 or SAVE Music2. To leave the system use the command EXIT.

To re-load the program structure and associated functions and conditions files use PDF filename, in this example PDF Music1 or PDF Music2. The program structure diagram will then appear on the screen.

15.9 Output from the PDF Structure Diagram.

When the detailed program structure diagram has been completed it is possible to generate three forms of documentation. A structure text, structure diagram and complete COBOL program.

Commands are issued to the PDF system by pressing the ALT and F9 keys. From within a lower window a user is invited to enter a suitable command.

The command TEXT Music1 will generate the following file.

```
 1 Report               seq
 2                       ¦ OPEN INPUT MusicData, OUTPUT MusicReport.
 3                       ¦ READ MusicData AT END MOVE 'T' TO EOF.
 4                       ¦ MOVE ZERO TO TotalQuantity.
 5                       ¦ MOVE MusicCode TO MusicCode-Store.
 6                       ¦ MOVE StockNumber TO StockNumber-Store.
 7                       ¦ MOVE Record-1-WS TO LineImage.
 8                       ¦ WRITE ReportOut.
 9                       ¦ MOVE ALL '-' TO title-1.
10                       ¦
11                       ¦ MOVE Record-1-WS TO LineImage.
12                       ¦ WRITE ReportOut.
13 report body          itr while Not end of music file
14   music code           seq
15     sub heading          sel popular
16       popular              seq
17                              ¦ MOVE "POPULAR" TO title-2.
18       popular              end
19     sub heading          alt jazz
20       jazz                 seq
21                              ¦ MOVE "JAZZ" TO title-2.
22       jazz                 end
23     sub heading          alt classical
24       classical            seq
25                              ¦ MOVE "CLASSICAL" TO title-2.
26       classical            end
27     sub heading          end
28                       ¦ MOVE Record-2-WS TO LineImage.
29                       ¦ WRITE ReportOut.
30                       ¦ MOVE Record-3-WS TO LineImage.
31                       ¦ WRITE ReportOut.
```

```
32        music code body          itr while test for change of music code
33          numb qty line            seq
34            stock body               itr while test for change of stock number
35              line                     seq
36                                         ¦ ADD quantity TO TotalQuantity.
37                                         ¦ READ MusicData AT END MOVE 'T' TO EOF.
38              line                     end
39            stock body             end
40                                     ¦ MOVE StockNumber-Store TO StockNumber-WS,
41                                     ¦ MOVE TotalQuantity TO quantity-WS.
42                                     ¦ MOVE Record-4-WS TO LineImage.
43                                     ¦ WRITE ReportOut.
44                                     ¦ MOVE StockNumber TO StockNumber-Store.
45                                     ¦ MOVE ZERO TO TotalQuantity.
46          numb qty line            end
47        music code body          end
48                                   ¦ MOVE MusicCode TO MusicCode-Store.
49      music code               end
50    report body              end
51                              ¦ CLOSE MusicData, MusicReport.
52                              ¦ STOP RUN.
53 Report                      end
54        IDENTIFICATION DIVISION.
55        Program-ID. Music1.
56
57        ENVIRONMENT DIVISION.
58        INPUT-OUTPUT SECTION.
59        FILE-CONTROL.
60            SELECT MusicData ASSIGN TO PFMS.
61            SELECT MusicReport ASSIGN TO PFMS.
62
63        DATA DIVISION.
64        FILE SECTION.
65        FD MusicData, COMPRESSED.
66        01 Record-FS.
67            02 MusicCode PIC A.
68            02 StockNumber PIC 9(4).
69            02 quantity PIC 9999.
70        FD MusicReport, COMPRESSED.
71        01 ReportOut.
72            02 FILLER PIC X.
73            02 LineImage PIC X(79).
74
75        WORKING-STORAGE SECTION.
76        01 Record-1-WS.
77            02 FILLER PIC X(20) VALUE IS SPACES.
78            02 title-1 PIC X(21) VALUE IS "CASSETTE DISTRIBUTION".
```

```
79          01 Record-2-WS.
80              02 FILLER PIC X(20) VALUE IS SPACES.
81              02 FILLER PIC X(6) VALUE IS "TYPE: ".
82              02 title-2 PIC A(9).
83          01 Record-3-WS.
84              02 FILLER PIC X(20) VALUE IS SPACES.
85              02 FILLER PIC X(21) VALUE IS "STOCK-NUMBER QUANTITY".
86          01 Record-4-WS.
87              02 FILLER PIC X(20) VALUE IS SPACES.
88              02 StockNumber-WS PIC 9(4).
89              02 FILLER PIC X(10) VALUE IS SPACES.
90              02 Quantity-WS PIC ZZZ9.
91

92          77 StockNumber-Store PIC 9(4).
93          77 MusicCode-Store PIC A.
94          77 EOF PIC A VALUE IS 'F'.
95              88 EndOfFile VALUE 'T'.
96          77 TotalQuantity PIC 9999 VALUE IS ZERO.
97          PROCEDURE DIVISION.


98       1. OPEN INPUT MusicData, OUTPUT MusicReport.
99       2. CLOSE MusicData, MusicReport.
100      3. READ MusicData AT END MOVE 'T' TO EOF.
101      4. WRITE ReportOut.
102      5. STOP RUN.
103      6. MOVE Record-1-WS TO LineImage.
104      7. MOVE "POPULAR" TO title-2.
105      8. MOVE "JAZZ" TO title-2.
106      9. MOVE "CLASSICAL" TO title-2.
107     10. MOVE Record-2-WS TO LineImage.
108     11. MOVE Record-3-WS TO LineImage.
109     12. MOVE StockNumber-Store TO StockNumber-WS,
110         MOVE TotalQuantity TO quantity-WS.
111     13. MOVE Record-4-WS TO LineImage.
112     14. ADD quantity TO TotalQuantity.
113     15. MOVE ZERO TO TotalQuantity.
114     16. MOVE MusicCode TO MusicCode-Store.
115     17. MOVE StockNumber TO StockNumber-Store.
116     18. MOVE ALL '-' TO title-1.
117
```

```
118 report body\music code
119                                 Not end of music file
120                                 NOT EndOfFile
121 sub heading\popular
122                                 popular
123                                 MusicCode = 'A'
```

```
124 sub heading\jazz
125                               jazz
126                               MusicCode = 'B'
127 sub heading\classical
128                               classical
129                               MusicCode = 'C'
130 music code body\numb qty line
131                               test for change of music code
132                               MusicCode = MusicCode-store
133                               AND NOT EndOfFile
134 stock body\line
135                               test for change of stock number
136                               StockNumber = StockNumber-Store
137                               AND MusicCode = MusicCode-Store
138                               AND NOT EndOfFile
```

The command PRINT Music1 will generate the following diagram.

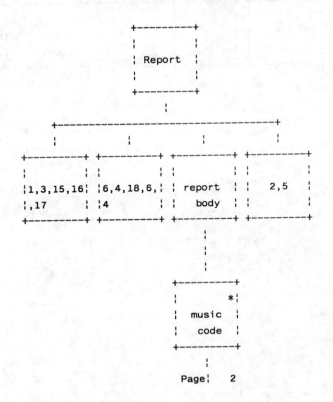

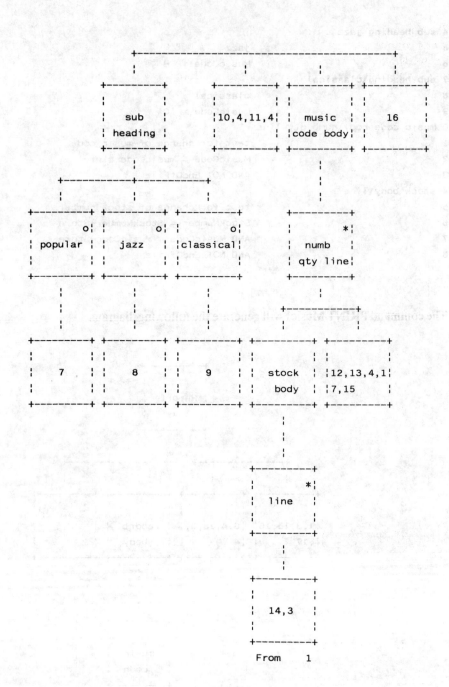

The command CODE Music1 PRODUCE FLAT COMMENT OFF will generate the following complete COBOL program. Notice the parameter FLAT causes flat or in-line code similar to that described in chapter 13. The parameter COMMENT OFF prevents the source program from being filled with comments taken from every comment in the detailed program structure.

```
      IDENTIFICATION DIVISION.
*     MUSIC1  IBM-PC PDF V2.1H   9-APR-91 14:04:38
      Program-ID. Music1.

      ENVIRONMENT DIVISION.
      INPUT-OUTPUT SECTION.
      FILE-CONTROL.
          SELECT MusicData ASSIGN TO PFMS.
          SELECT MusicReport ASSIGN TO PFMS.


      DATA DIVISION.
      FILE SECTION.
      FD MusicData, COMPRESSED.
      01 Record-FS.
          02 MusicCode PIC A.
          02 StockNumber PIC 9(4).
          02 quantity PIC 9999.
      FD MusicReport, COMPRESSED.
      01 ReportOut.
          02 FILLER PIC X.
          02 LineImage PIC X(79).


      WORKING-STORAGE SECTION.
      01 Record-1-WS.
          02 FILLER PIC X(20) VALUE IS SPACES.
          02 title-1 PIC X(21) VALUE IS "CASSETTE DISTRIBUTION".
      01 Record-2-WS.
          02 FILLER PIC X(20) VALUE IS SPACES.
          02 FILLER PIC X(6) VALUE IS "TYPE: ".
          02 title-2 PIC A(9).
      01 Record-3-WS.
          02 FILLER PIC X(20) VALUE IS SPACES.
          02 FILLER PIC X(21) VALUE IS "STOCK-NUMBER QUANTITY".
      01 Record-4-WS.
          02 FILLER PIC X(20) VALUE IS SPACES.
          02 StockNumber-WS PIC 9(4).
          02 FILLER PIC X(10) VALUE IS SPACES.
          02 Quantity-WS PIC ZZZ9.

      77 StockNumber-Store PIC 9(4).
      77 MusicCode-Store PIC A.
```

```
77 EOF PIC A VALUE IS 'F'.
    88 EndOfFile VALUE 'T'.
77 TotalQuantity PIC 9999 VALUE IS ZERO.
PROCEDURE DIVISION.
        OPEN INPUT MusicData, OUTPUT MusicReport.
        READ MusicData AT END MOVE 'T' TO EOF.
        MOVE ZERO TO TotalQuantity.
        MOVE MusicCode TO MusicCode-Store.
        MOVE StockNumber TO StockNumber-Store.
        MOVE Record-1-WS TO LineImage.
        WRITE ReportOut.
        MOVE ALL '-' TO title-1.

        MOVE Record-1-WS TO LineImage.
        WRITE ReportOut.
P1005.
        IF NOT (NOT EndOfFile) GO TO P2005.
            IF NOT (MusicCode = 'A') GO TO P0007.
                MOVE "POPULAR" TO title-2.
            GO TO P0011.
P0007.
            IF NOT (MusicCode = 'B') GO TO P0009.
                MOVE "JAZZ" TO title-2.
            GO TO P0011.
P0009.
                MOVE "CLASSICAL" TO title-2.
P0011.
        MOVE Record-2-WS TO LineImage.
        WRITE ReportOut.
        MOVE Record-3-WS TO LineImage.
        WRITE ReportOut.
P1015.
        IF NOT (MusicCode = MusicCode-store
        AND NOT EndOfFile) GO TO P2015.
P1017.
            IF NOT (StockNumber = StockNumber-Store
            AND MusicCode = MusicCode-Store
            AND NOT EndOfFile) GO TO P2017.
                ADD quantity TO TotalQuantity.
                READ MusicData AT END MOVE 'T' TO EOF.
            GO TO P1017.
P2017.
            MOVE StockNumber-Store TO StockNumber-WS,
            MOVE TotalQuantity TO quantity-WS.
            MOVE Record-4-WS TO LineImage.
            WRITE ReportOut.
            MOVE StockNumber TO StockNumber-Store.
            MOVE ZERO TO TotalQuantity.
```

```
                GO TO P1015.
   P2015.
                MOVE MusicCode TO MusicCode-Store.
         GO TO P1005.
   P2005.
         CLOSE MusicData, MusicReport.
         STOP RUN.
```

The command CODE Music2 PRODUCE STRUCT COMMENT ON will generate another complete COBOL source program. The Procedure Division code generated this time is still flat or in-line code, but it uses the COBOL-85 control structures. It has been necessary to modify the READ function in this example to include an END-READ, otherwise the code would contain a syntax error. The COMMENT parameter has been switched to ON in this example so that the reader can see how many comments are generated. Only the Procedure Division has been printed since the other three Divisions are identical to the program listing for Music1.

```
   PROCEDURE DIVISION.
   *
   *    ( Report -
         OPEN INPUT MusicData, OUTPUT MusicReport
         READ MusicData AT END MOVE 'T' TO EOF END-READ
         MOVE ZERO TO TotalQuantity
         MOVE MusicCode TO MusicCode-Store
         MOVE StockNumber TO StockNumber-Store
         MOVE Record-1-WS TO LineImage
         WRITE ReportOut
         MOVE ALL '-' TO title-1

         MOVE Record-1-WS TO LineImage
         WRITE ReportOut
   *
   *       ( report body -
         PERFORM UNTIL NOT (NOT EndOfFile)
   *
   *          ( music code -
   *
   *             ( sub heading -
             IF (MusicCode = 'A')
   *
   *                ( popular -
                    MOVE "POPULAR" TO title-2
   *                - popular )
   *
   *                - sub heading -
             ELSE
```

```
                    IF (MusicCode = 'B')
*
*                       ( jazz -
                            MOVE "JAZZ" TO title-2
*                        - jazz )
*
*                    - sub heading -
                    ELSE
*
*                       ( classical -
                            MOVE "CLASSICAL" TO title-2
*                        - classical )
*
                        END-IF
                    END-IF
*                    - sub heading )
*
                    MOVE Record-2-WS TO LineImage
                    WRITE ReportOut
                    MOVE Record-3-WS TO LineImage
                    WRITE ReportOut
*
*                    ( music code body -
                    PERFORM UNTIL NOT (MusicCode = MusicCode-store
                    AND NOT EndOfFile)
*
*                        ( numb qty line -
*
*                            ( stock body -
                            PERFORM UNTIL NOT (
                            StockNumber = StockNumber-Store
                            AND MusicCode = MusicCode-Store
                            AND NOT EndOfFile)
*
*                                ( line -
                                    ADD quantity TO TotalQuantity
                            READ MusicData AT END MOVE 'T' TO EOF END-READ
*                                - line )
*
                            END-PERFORM
*                            - stock body )
*
                            MOVE StockNumber-Store TO StockNumber-WS,
                            MOVE TotalQuantity TO quantity-WS
                            MOVE Record-4-WS TO LineImage
                            WRITE ReportOut
                            MOVE StockNumber TO StockNumber-Store
```

```
                        MOVE ZERO TO TotalQuantity
   *              - numb qty line )
   *

                  END-PERFORM
   *              - music code body )
   *

                        MOVE MusicCode TO MusicCode-Store
   *           - music code )
   *

              END-PERFORM
   *          - report body )
   *

              CLOSE MusicData, MusicReport
              STOP RUN
   *     - Report )
   *
```

15.10 Further Features of PDF.

When a structure diagram has been drawn it may be possible that some of the connections between nodes appear to be 'dog-legged', owing to the fact that the screen cursor was not correctly lined- up. When such a scruffy diagram is produced it can be tidied-up by pressing the ALT and F8 keys. The result is to remove all the 'dog-legs' and produce a well proportioned structure diagram.

Several structure diagrams can be pasted together using the PASTE subtree command to form one large structure diagram. Alternatively, parts of a structure diagram may be removed by using the CUT subtree command.

If a structure diagram is too large to fit on the screen it can be viewed in its entirety by pressing the ALT and F10 keys, this will give the user an image of the structure of the diagram, with the size of the nodes greatly reduced. Pressing ALT and F10 again will toggle the diagram back to the normal size, and only a portion will be visible on the screen.

There are HELP screens for both PDF commands and PDF function keys. For example HELP CODE will give information about using the code generator. Alternatively by pressing F1, having already invoked a function, it is possible to obtain information about a chosen function.

It is possible, but not necessary, to use a Microsoft mouse with the PDF system. The mouse menu provided has two movement modes, the cursor mode to simulate cursor up, cursor down, cursor left and cursor right. Scrolling the screen is possible if the SHIFT key is pressed in conjunction with moving the mouse. The tree mode simulates current up, current down, current left and current right.

Clicking on the left button causes the scroll current key to be simulated or if clicked with SHIFT pressed causes the set current function to be invoked. Clicking on the right button causes the scroll home key to be simulated.

16

Miscellaneous Features

This final chapter introduces the reader to an assortment of features found in COBOL that can either improve program execution time, or improve program coding facilities.

16.1 Data Validation Statements.

Class Conditions

A picture clause is used to define an item of data as being numeric, alphabetic or alphanumeric, however, to ensure that the data stored using such a description, is of the correct type, a class test can be made.

The general format of the class condition is:

$$\text{identifier-1 IS [NOT]} \begin{Bmatrix} \text{NUMERIC} \\ \text{ALPHABETIC} \\ \text{ALPHABETIC-LOWER} \\ \text{ALPHABETIC-UPPER} \\ \text{class-name} \end{Bmatrix}$$

For example, to ensure that a value with a description of *02 datum PIC 999* is numeric, the following test can be made in the Procedure Division.

A-rep.
        IF datum NUMERIC GO TO A-end.
        DISPLAY "ERROR - data not numeric", datum.
        .
        .
A-end.

If a value with a description of *02 datum PIC A(10)* was to be tested for the alphabetic type a Procedure Division entry would be modified to:

A-rep.
        IF datum ALPHABETIC GO TO A-end.
        DISPLAY "ERROR - data not alphabetic", datum.
        .
        .
A-end.

If a specific test for upper-case alphabetic or lower-case alphabetic is required then ALPHABETIC-UPPER or ALPHABETIC-LOWER would be used respectively.

Class names are defined in the SPECIAL-NAMES paragraph of the Environment Division.

For example,

SPECIAL-NAMES.
        CLASS vowel IS 'A', 'E', 'I', 'O', 'U'.

A Procedure Division statement to test a letter for being a vowel could be coded as IF vowel ...

The class condition NUMERIC must only be used on a data descriptor that is designated as being numeric, and the class conditions ALPHABETIC, ALPHABETIC-UPPER and ALPHABETIC-LOWER must only be used on a data descriptor that is designated as being alphabetic.

Sign Conditions

Sign conditions are used to determine if a numeric item is positive, negative or zero.

The format of the sign condition is:

$$\text{identifier-1 IS [NOT]} \begin{Bmatrix} \text{POSITIVE} \\ \text{NEGATIVE} \\ \text{ZERO} \end{Bmatrix}$$

Where identifier-1 can be a numeric datum or an expression that equates to a numeric value.

The Inspect Statement

The INSPECT statement can be used to check every character in an item of data, and replace specified characters with other characters, and/or count the number of characters in part of, or throughout, the item of data.

A common error that can occur when entering numbers into a computer is to introduce spaces in place of zeros. For example, a date might be input as b1b184 instead of 010184. The INSPECT statement can be used to detect the spaces present in the date and replace the spaces by zeros.

The general format of the INSPECT statement is given in Appendix II, however, only a simplified version of format-2, is required for processing the date. If the date is defined in Working- Storage as *02 date-WS PIC 9(6)* then the Procedure Division statement

INSPECT date-WS REPLACING SPACES BY ZEROS

would be sufficient to edit **b1b184** to 010184 during run-time.

In another example, if the format of an unsigned number is five digits to the left of the decimal point, and two digits to the right of the decimal point, then the format of a number can be checked by using a simplified version of the INSPECT statement given as format-1 in Appendix II.

If necessary Working-Storage Section entries are:

77 DecimalNumber PIC X(8).
77 DigitCount PIC 9.
        88 MaxDigits VALUE 5.

The test in the Procedure Division to ensure that the decimal point is in the correct place is:

```
        ACCEPT DecimalNumber.
        INSPECT DecimalNumber TALLYING DigitCount FOR CHARACTERS BEFORE
        INITIAL '.'.
A-rep.
        IF MaxDigits GO TO A-end.
            DISPLAY "ERROR - re-type number"
            ACCEPT DecimalNumber.
            INSPECT DecimalNumber TALLYING DigitCount FOR
            CHARACTERS BEFORE INITIAL '.'.
        GO TO A-rep.
A-end.
```

Notice that it is the responsibility of the programmer to define an identifier that can be used by the INSPECT statement for keeping a tally of the number of characters before the delimiting character.

16.2 Internal Storage of Numbers.

Display Mode

In every program example throughout the book the way in which numbers have been stored in the main memory of the computer has been using the DISPLAY mode. This has been done to simplify the amount of coding, since this mode of storage is used by default.

In the DISPLAY mode each character (digit) is stored in one byte of memory using either the ASCII (7 bit) or EBCDIC (8 bit) code for each character. For example if an item of data is described in Working-Storage as 02 datum PIC 999, and the value of datum was 138, the number would occupy three bytes of memory.

The computer, however, cannot perform arithmetic on an item of data stored in the DISPLAY mode. The computer must first convert the number to a mode of storage suitable for arithmetic use. In practice this means that the number will be converted to either a pure binary or packed decimal representation. Once the arithmetic on the number is complete the computer converts the number back to a DISPLAY mode.

This conversion from DISPLAY to computational mode and back to DISPLAY mode can waste time especially if the conversion has to be performed for many thousands of numbers. Furthermore, the amount of memory required to store a number in DISPLAY mode is generally greater than in computational mode.

A USAGE clause can be appended to an elementary or group item to specify the mode in which numbers are stored. The format of the USAGE clause is:

```
[USAGE IS] ⎧ BINARY          ⎫
           ⎪ COMPUTATIONAL   ⎪
           ⎨ COMP            ⎬
           ⎪ DISPLAY         ⎪
           ⎪ INDEX           ⎪
           ⎩ PACKED-DECIMAL  ⎭
```

Computer manufacturers have the option to specify different computational modes. For example, the common modes are:

COMPUTATIONAL as a pure binary representation, and COMPUTATIONAL-3 as a packed-decimal representation.

Manufacturers such as IBM and PRIME also include

COMPUTATIONAL-1 as a single precision floating-point representation, and COMPUTATIONAL-2 as a double precision floating-point representation, in addition to COMPUTATIONAL and COMPUTATIONAL-3.

Computational Mode

The COMPUTATIONAL mode uses a fixed number of bytes to store integers in a pure binary format. For example, PRIME use two bytes (16 bits) to store numbers described as COMPUTATIONAL. The range of signed integers that can be represented in this format is -32,768 to +32,767.

Since a fixed number of bytes is always used when an item of data is described as COMPUTATIONAL, there is no need to specify a picture clause for such items of data.

For example, 01 Parameters USAGE COMPUTATIONAL.
               02 datum-1.
               02 datum-2.

or 77 datum-3 USAGE IS COMPUTATIONAL.

The INDEX mode of storage is the same as for storing positive integers using the COMPUTATIONAL mode. An index does not have to be defined using a level number, however, if it is defined by a level number then no picture clause is required.

For example, 02 PositionIndex USAGE IS INDEX.

Computational-3 Mode

The COMPUTATIONAL-3 mode is used to store real numbers (numbers containing a decimal fraction). Each digit is represented using a Binary Coded Decimal (BCD) code. The table in figure 16.1 illustrates how each digit is represented using a four-bit binary code.

If a picture clause contains n 9's in describing a datum, then (n/2) + 1 bytes of storage are required for that datum. Four bits are always set aside for the sign of the number irrespective of whether S has been used in the picture string.

For example, if -142.76 is to be stored using a picture string of S9(4)V99, then four bytes of store will be used as shown in figure 16.2.

Decimal Number	BCD code
0	0000
1	0001
2	0010
3	0011
4	0100
5	0101
6	0110
7	0111
8	1000
9	1001

Figure 16.1 Decimal digits and BCD equivalent numbers

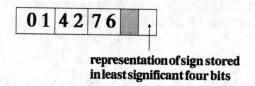

representation of sign stored
in least significant four bits

Figure 16.2 Storage of numbers using BCD representation

Note - unless the number of 9's in the picture string is odd there will be four bits wasted. The position of the decimal point is given in the picture string and is, therefore, not stored as part of the number.

COMPUTATIONAL-1 and COMPUTATIONAL-2 modes will not be considered here since they are seldom used in commercial applications.

Never use COMPUTATIONAL or COMPUTATIONAL-3 on data that is being input or output. Only use these modes for data that requires to be processed using arithmetic statements. Generally the result of displaying a datum, defined as COMPUTATIONAL or COMPUTATIONAL-3, on the screen of a vdu, will result in meaningless characters being displayed. The datum for display must first be moved to a field described as being USAGE DISPLAY (by default) before any attempt is made to output the information.

Synchronized Clause.

The efficiency of program execution can also be improved if a datum is stored in its own multiple word area of memory and is not allowed to share words with another datum. The SYNCHRONIZED clause specifies the alignment of an elementary item on a natural memory boundary. The general format is:

$$\begin{Bmatrix} \text{SYNCHRONIZED} \\ \text{SYNC} \end{Bmatrix} \begin{Bmatrix} \text{LEFT} \\ \text{RIGHT} \end{Bmatrix}$$

For example, 01 Record-1.
                02 A PIC 9 VALUE 1.
                02 B PIC 99 VALUE 12.
                02 C PIC 999 VALUE 123.

Assuming a natural boundary of two bytes the value of A, B and C would be stored over memory boundaries as:

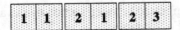

However, if each picture clause has SYNCHRONIZED RIGHT appended to it, the effect is as follows.

Alternatively SYNCHRONIZED LEFT would have the effect shown below.

SYNCHRONIZED without the RIGHT/LEFT option specifies that the elementary item is to be positioned between memory boundaries in such a way as to affect efficient utilization of the elementary data item.

16.3 Duplicate Identifiers.

In every example in this book duplicate identifiers have not been used in order to avoid confusion. However, duplicate variable names and paragraph names are permitted in COBOL programs provided the names are qualified.

Qualification

An identifier that is not unique, when used in the Procedure Division, must be followed by either IN or OF and the higher order name to which it belongs. For example two records may be described as:

01 Record-1.
        02 name.
                03 surname PIC X(20).
                03 initials PIC AA.
        02 address PIC X(50).
01 Record-2.
        02 name.
                03 surname PIC X(20).
                03 initials PIC AA.
        02 address PIC X(50).

If address is to be moved from Record-1 to Record-2 the statement **MOVE address IN Record-1 TO address IN Record-2**, must be used.

If surname was to be moved from Record-1 to Record-2 the statement **MOVE surname IN name IN Record-1 TO surname IN name IN Record-2** would be used. Alternatively if surname and initials are to be moved from Record-1 to Record-2 the statement **MOVE name IN Record-1 TO name IN Record-2** would be used.

Paragraph names can be duplicated between section names as long as the paragraph name is qualified by the section name. For example,

```
PROCEDURE DIVISION.
FIRST SECTION.
A-rep.
        .
        .
        .
        GO TO A-rep OF FIRST.
A-end.
SECOND SECTION.
A-rep.
        .
        .
        .
        GO TO A-rep OF SECOND.
A-end.
```

Corresponding Option

Fields that have the same names between two records can have the contents of these fields either moved, added or subtracted by including a CORRESPONDING option. If one record is defined as:

```
01 Record-1.
        02 tax PIC 9(4)V99.
        02 allowance PIC 9(4)V99.
        02 GrossSalary PIC 9(5)V99.
```

and a second record as:

```
01 Record-2.
        02 GrossSalary PIC 9(5).
        02 FILLER PIC X(10) VALUE SPACES.
        02 allowance PIC 9(4)V99.
        02 FILLER PIC X(10) VALUE SPACES.
        02 tax PIC 9(4)V99.
```

then **MOVE CORRESPONDING Record-1 TO Record-2** has the same effect as:

MOVE tax IN Record-1 TO tax IN Record-2
MOVE allowance IN Record-1 TO allowance IN Record-2
MOVE GrossSalary IN Record-1 TO GrossSalary IN Record-2.

If GrossSalary, allowance and tax have edited picture fields in Record-2, then the data would be edited as the result of the move. If the values in Record-1 are to be either added or subtracted from the values in Record-2 then **ADD CORRESPONDING Record-1 TO Record-2**, or **SUBTRACT CORRESPONDING Record-1 FROM Record-2** would be used respectively. Both the ROUNDED and ON SIZE ERROR options can be appended to these statements.

For example, if Record-1 and Record-2 contain the following values:

	tax	allowance	GrossSalary
Record-1	085050	120000	0945095
Record-2	915050	130000	08500

then the execution of the statement

ADD CORRESPONDING Record-1 TO Record-2 ROUNDED
ON SIZE ERROR DISPLAY "DATA SIZE ERROR - RUN ABORTED", STOP RUN.

will result in the following changes to the data.

	tax	allowance	GrossSalary
Record-1	085050	120000	0945095
Record-2	915050	250000	17951

and the message DATA SIZE ERROR - RUN ABORTED being displayed since the value for tax was computed as 1000100 and is too large for the PICTURE 9(4)V99. The original value for tax in Record-2 has not been changed. The picture for GrossSalary in Record-2 is 9(5), therefore, ROUNDED option has been used to give an answer of 17951 and not 17950.95.

16.4 String Processing.
The STRING statement concatenates (joins together), two or more strings to form one string. The following example uses a simplified format of the STRING statement compared with the format given in Appendix II.

For example, the format of a record on a file described as:

```
01 Record-1.
       02 surname PIC X(20).
       02 initials.
           03 FirstLetter PIC A.
           03 SecondLetter PIC A.
       02 TelephoneNumber.
           03 exchange PIC X(20).
           03 PhoneNo PIC 9(7).
```

If these picture strings were used to output the information, a large number of spaces between the surname and initials and exchange and number would occur. There would also be a lack of separation between initials and exchange. For example,

Bloggs**bbbbbbbbbbbbbbb**HCOxford**bbbbbbbbbbbbbb**2198764

This format for, say, a telephone directory would not be acceptable. A much improved output might be:

Bloggs**b**H.C**bbbbbbbbbbbbbbbb**Oxford**b**2198764**bbbbbbbbbbbbb**

This format is achieved if the output record is changed to:

```
01 Record-1.
      02 subscribers PIC X(25).
      02 TeleNumber PIC X(28).
```

and the following Procedure Division code is used.

STRING surname, SPACE, FirstLetter, '.', SecondLetter DELIMITED BY SPACES INTO subscribers, and

STRING exchange, SPACE, PhoneNo DELIMITED BY SPACES INTO TeleNumber.

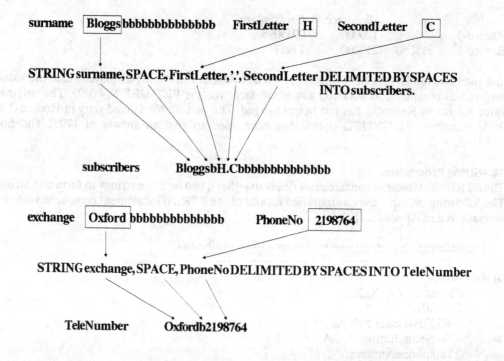

The UNSTRING statement serves the opposite purpose to STRING. The statement separates a long string into two or more shorter strings. For example, when the ACCEPT statement is used for entering a number, the number must be input at a keyboard in an identical format to the picture clause. This implies that leading and trailing zeros must be present and a decimal point must not be used. A number can, however, be input as an alphanumeric string on a free format, allowing a decimal point to be inserted and leading and trailing zeros to be omitted. If a datum is given a picture of X(10) and the string "13.76" is stored under the identifier datum, then to convert this value to a numeric type would require the following code.

```
WORKING-STORAGE SECTION.
01 DecimalNumber.
      02 integer PIC 9(7).
      02 fraction PIC XX.
77 datum PIC X(10).
77 ConvertedNumber PIC 9(7)V99.


PROCEDURE DIVISION.
A-seq.
      ACCEPT datum.
      UNSTRING datum DELIMITED BY '.' OR SPACE INTO integer, fraction.
      INSPECT fraction REPLACING SPACES BY ZEROS.
      MOVE DecimalNumber TO ConvertedNumber.
      .
      .
```

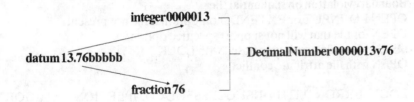

16.5 File Status Values.

After every file input/output statement is executed, a two-character status code is generated by the system, to inform whether the statement was successful or not. If the execution of the statement was not successful then the value of the code can be translated into the reason for failure.

The status code can be saved in a field named in the Environment Division in the FILE-CONTROL paragraph using the sentence:

```
FILE-CONTROL.
SELECT ...
      [FILE STATUS IS data-name-1].
```

ANS specified specific status codes for COBOL 85, however, many compilers use their own definitions. These status codes follow.

Code   Meaning

SUCCESSFUL COMPLETION CATEGORY
00   Successful completion
02   Duplicate alternate key detected or created
04   Successful READ, but length indicators do not match
05   OPEN executed; optional file not present; created if I-O or EXTEND
07   Successful, but not on tape, so tape options ignored

AT END WITH UNSUCCESSFUL COMPLETION CATEGORY
10   End of file on sequential read; optional file not present
14   Boundary violation on relative file

INVALID KEY WITH UNSUCCESSFUL COMPLETION CATEGORY
21   Sequence error; record in indexed file out of sequence
22   Duplicate key condition
23   Record not found
24   Boundary violation on indexed file

PERMANENT ERROR WITH UNSUCCESSFUL COMPLETION CATEGORY
30   Permanent error, no more information
34   Boundary violation on sequential file
35   OPEN I-O, INPUT or EXTEND; non-optional file not present
37   OPEN for file that will not support specified option
38   OPEN when file previously closed with LOCK
39   OPEN with file attribute conflict

LOGIC ERROR WITH UNSUCCESSFUL COMPLETION CATEGORY
41   OPEN for file already open
42   CLOSE for file not open
43   REWRITE or DELETE; last input/output not successful READ
44   Boundary violation
46   Sequential read not valid because no next record
47   READ or START on file not open in valid mode
48   WRITE on file not open in valid mode
49   REWRITE or DELETE on file not open in valid mode

IMPLEMENTOR DEFINED CONDITION CATEGORY
9x   As defined by implementor; cannot duplicate any other status

16.6 Declaratives Section.

The DECLARATIVES SECTION specifies procedures to be executed when an input/output statement is not successfully completed. The Declaratives Section when included in the Procedure Division must be written directly after the Division heading and before any procedural sections or paragraphs. The format of the Declaratives Section is:

PROCEDURE DIVISION.
[DECLARATIVES.
{section-name **SECTION.**
    USE statement.
[paragraph-name.
    [sentence] ...] ... } ...
END DECLARATIVES.]
{section-name **SECTION**
[paragraph-name.
    [sentence] ...] ... } ...

The USE statement is a compiler-directing sentence that causes the compiler to take a specific action during compilation. USE covers three areas.

(i) Specific procedures for input and output error handling.

(ii) USE FOR DEBUGGING (only applicable when the debug module is present).

(iii) USE BEFORE REPORTING (only applicable when the report writer module is present).

Note both the DEBUG and REPORT modules are not included in this book.

Input and Output Error handling

The sections under the DECLARATIVES header provide a method for including procedures which are invoked when a condition occurs which cannot be tested by the programmer. Although the system automatically handles the checking and creation of standard labels, and execution error recovery in the case of input and output errors, additional procedures may be specified by the programmer. Since such procedures are only executed at the time an error in reading or writing occurs, they cannot appear in the regular sequence of procedural statements. Instead, they must appear in the Declaratives Section. Related procedures are preceded by a USE sentence.

Use Statement

The USE statement specifies procedures for input and output error handling, which are in addition to the standard procedures provided by the input and output control systems. The format of the USE statement is:

$$\text{USE AFTER STANDARD} \begin{Bmatrix} \text{EXCEPTION} \\ \text{ERROR} \end{Bmatrix} \text{PROCEDURE ON} \begin{Bmatrix} \text{filename} \\ \text{INPUT} \\ \text{OUTPUT} \\ \text{I-O} \end{Bmatrix}$$

The Declaratives Section is executed by the same mechanism that executes a PERFORM statement, after the standard I-O recovery procedures for the files designated in a program, or after the invalid key condition arises on a statement lacking an INVALID KEY clause. After the execution of the USE procedure control is returned to the invoking routine.

The following example illustrates the use of a Declaratives Section in conjunction with the file status codes for reporting and taking action on various situations. When a file input/output error has been detected, the computer will branch to the Declaratives Section and execute the appropriate paragraph according to the value of the status code.

```
ENVIRONMENT DIVISION.
.
FILE-CONTROL.
.
    FILE STATUS IS StatusCode.

DATA DIVISION.
.
WORKING-STORAGE SECTION.
77 StatusCode PIC XX.
    88 BadSequence VALUE '21'.
    88 DuplicateKey VALUE '22'.
    88 NoRecord VALUE '23'.
    88 DiscFull VALUE '24'.
.


PROCEDURE DIVISION.
DECLARATIVES.
StaffFileError SECTION.
    USE AFTER STANDARD ERROR PROCEDURE ON StaffFile.
StatusCheck.
    IF BadSequence PERFORM Status-21, GO TO DeclarativeExit.
    IF DuplicateKey PERFORM Status-22, GO TO DeclarativeExit.
    IF NoRecord PERFORM Status-23, GO TO DeclarativeExit.
    IF DiscFull PERFORM Status-24, GO TO DeclarativeExit.
    .

Status-21.
    .
Status-22.
    .
Status-23.
    .
Status-24.
    .
DeclarativeExit.
    EXIT.
END DECLARATIVES.

A-seq.
B.    OPEN I-O StaffFile, OUTPUT LogFile.
C.
    .
```

16.7 Merge Statement.

The MERGE statement combines two or more identically sequenced files on a set of specified keys, and during the process makes the records available, in merged order, to an output procedure or to an output file.

A simplified format for the MERGE statement is:

```
MERGE file-name-1 ON   ASCENDING KEY {data-name-1} ... } ...
                       DESCENDING
USING {file-name-2} ...
GIVING file-name-3
```

where file-name-1 must be described in an SD entry. Each file- name-2 is an input file, and these must all be in the same key sequence and defined with FD entries. File-name-3, if used, is the output file, it must be defined with an FD entry and will contain the merged records. None of the files named in the MERGE statement must be open immediately prior to the MERGE statement being executed.

Each data-name-1 is a key field. All key field entries must be included in a record description entry associated with file-name- 1. The key fields are listed in order of decreasing significance.

No file name can be repeated in a single MERGE statement.

The first program given in chapter 10, to merge two files is repeated here, in a simplified format, using the MERGE statement.

```
IDENTIFICATION DIVISION.
PROGRAM-ID. TwoWayMerge.

ENVIRONMENT DIVISION.
INPUT-OUTPUT SECTION.
FILE-CONTROL.
      SELECT File-A ASSIGN TO PFMS.
      SELECT File-B ASSIGN TO PFMS.
      SELECT File-C ASSIGN TO PFMS.
      SELECT Merge-File ASSIGN TO PFMS.

DATA DIVISION.
FILE SECTION.
FD File-A, COMPRESSED.
01 Record-A PIC X(27).
FD File-B, COMPRESSED.
01 Record-B PIC X(27).
FD File-C, COMPRESSED.
01 Record-C.
      02 FILLER PIC X(27).
SD Merge-File.
01 Record-Merge.
```

```
02 key-Merge PIC X(20).
02 details-Merge PIC X(7).
```

PROCEDURE DIVISION.
    MERGE Merge-File ON ASCENDING KEY key-Merge
    USING File-A, File-B GIVING File-C.
    STOP RUN.

16.8 Copy Statement.

The COPY statement is a compiler directing statement and provides a means of including pre-written COBOL source code anywhere in a source program at the time of compilation.

A simplified format of COPY is   **COPY** text-name-1 $\left[\begin{Bmatrix} \textbf{OF} \\ \textbf{IN} \end{Bmatrix} \right.$ library-name-1]

where text-name-1 must be a unique name on the same user's file area that contains the COBOL program if the library-name-1 is to be omitted. Otherwise library-name-1 must be specified and must be the file area that contains text-name-1.

For example, a sequential file named *StdEnvDiv* contains the following information.

```
CONFIGURATION SECTION.
SOURCE-COMPUTER. PRIME 750.
OBJECT-COMPUTER. PRIME 750.
SPECIAL-NAMES. CONSOLE IS TTY, CURRENCY SIGN IS '£'.
INPUT-OUTPUT SECTION.
FILE-CONTROL.
    SELECT InputFile ASSIGN TO PFMS.
    SELECT OutputFile ASSIGN TO PFMS.
```

The contents of this file can be copied into a source program as follows.

```
IDENTIFICATION DIVISION.
PROGRAM-ID. TestCopy.

ENVIRONMENT DIVISION. COPY StdEnvDiv.
DATA DIVISION.
FILE SECTION.
```

The compiled source listing reveals the copied code as follows.
```
(0001) IDENTIFICATION DIVISION.
(0002) PROGRAM-ID. TestCopy.
(0003)
(0004) ENVIRONMENT DIVISION. COPY StdEnvDiv.
[0001] CONFIGURATION SECTION.
[0002] SOURCE-COMPUTER. PRIME 750.
[0003] OBJECT-COMPUTER. PRIME 750.
[0004] SPECIAL-NAMES. CONSOLE IS TTY, CURRENCY SIGN IS '£'.
[0005] INPUT-OUTPUT SECTION.
```

[0006] FILE-CONTROL.
[0007]   SELECT InputFile ASSIGN TO PFMS.
[0008]   SELECT OutputFile ASSIGN TO PFMS.
(0004) ENVIRONMENT DIVISION. COPY StdEnvDiv.
(0005) DATA DIVISION.
(0006) FILE SECTION.

16.9 Obsolete Elements.

Through the evolution of the language it has become necessary to identify parts of the language that are no longer required. In the 1985 revision of COBOL several elements were declared as being obsolete. However, these elements have been left unchanged in the 1985 Standard, and are expected to be deleted from the Standard in the next revision of the language. In order to enhance the maintainability of the COBOL code that is produced, programmers are advised to avoid all obsolete elements unless they are required by the compiler or installation.

In the Identification Division the following paragraphs are obsolete.

AUTHOR, INSTALLATION, DATE-WRITTEN, DATE-COMPILED, SECURITY.

In the Environment Division the following clauses are obsolete.

MEMORY-SIZE clause of the OBJECT-COMPUTER paragraph.

RERUN and MULTIPLE FILE TAPE clauses of the I-O-CONTROL paragraph.

In the Data Division, file description entry, the following clauses are obsolete.

LABEL RECORDS, VALUE OF and DATA RECORDS.

In the Procedure Division the following statements and clauses are obsolete.

ALTER, KEY clause in the DISABLE and ENABLE statements in the Communication Module (not covered in this book), ENTER, GO TO statement optional procedure-name-1, REVERSED clause in the OPEN statement, STOP literal.

Complete Modules (not covered in this book) that are obsolete.

Segmentation and Debug modules.

In general the ALL literal, where the literal is numeric or edited numeric, is obsolete.

16.10 Summary of COBOL 85 Differences.

Many of the items that follow should be studied in conjuction with the syntax of the language elements given in Appendix II. The differences have been grouped by Division in order to facilitate cross-referencing.

In general lower-case letters can be used in COBOL programs and are treated as their corresponding upper-case equivalents.

Environment Division

The entry ALPHABET alphabet-name-1 IS STANDARD-2 is new. The ALPHABET clause names a character set or collating sequence to be used by the program. Alphabet-name-1 can be specified in the PROGRAM COLLATING SEQUENCE clause of the OBJECT-COMPUTER paragraph as well as in the COLLATING SEQUENCE clause of the SORT or MERGE statements (see Appendix II). STANDARD-2 refers to the International Reference version of the ISO 7-bit code.

Data Division

A FILLER may be omitted for group or elementary items that will not be referenced.

The leading 0 in a level number can be omitted.

Picture characters . (period) and , (comma) may appear as the rightmost character in a picture if immediately followed by the period terminating the elementary item description.

The contents of data-name-2 may be shorter than the contents of data-name-1 in the syntax data-name-1 REDEFINES data-name-2.

A VALUE clause can be used in the same data-description entry as the OCCURS clause.

The number of subscripts that a table may have has been increased from three to seven. In other words a table may now have up to seven dimensions.

Procedure Division

DAY-OF-WEEK in the ACCEPT clause is new, with DAY-OF-WEEK taking the value of 1 - Monday, 2 - Tuesday ... 7 - Sunday. For example, ACCEPT DayNumber FROM DAY-OF-WEEK, would move 3 into DayNumber if the name of the day in the week was Wednesday. DayNumber would be described using a picture of PIC 9.

The DISPLAY statement can have a WITH NO ADVANCING option to prevent the cursor from moving to the left-hand edge of the next line down the screen.

Scope delimiters can be used at the end of Procedural statements. This is delimit a statement where normally a period would have been used.

Any arithmetic statement may have more than one result field. Each named field will receive the same value, although each receiving field can be defined differently. Each receiving field can be followed by the ROUNDED option.

When using the ADD statement both TO and GIVING may be used in the same statement. For example, ADD tax TO SubTotal GIVING total.

De-editing is now possible, where an edited numeric item (alphanumeric) can be moved to a numeric field.

The INITIALIZE statement is new, and provides the facility to set selected types of data fields to predetermined values. For example, numeric data fields can be set to zero and alphanumeric data fields to spaces, unless otherwise specified.

77 GrandTotal PIC 9(4)V99.
77 NameOfArticle PIX X(20).

INITIALIZE GrandTotal, NameOfArticle would initialize GrandTotal to zero and NameOfArticle to twenty spaces. Alternatively,

01 Parameters.
      02 total-1 PIC 99.
      02 total-2 PIC 99.
      02 EOF-A PIC A.
      02 EOF-B PIC A.

INITIALIZE Parameters REPLACING NUMERIC BY ZERO, ALPHABETIC BY 'F' would initialise total-1 and total-2 to zero and EOF-A and EOF-B to 'F'.

The CONVERTING clause in an INSPECT statement is new. This has the effect of replacing one character with another character. For example,

INSPECT   LineOfText   CONVERTING   "abcdefghijklmnopqrstuvwxyz"   TO "ABCDEFGHIJKLMNOPQRSTUVWXYZ" would convert the characters in the item of data LineOfText from lower-case to upper-case.

Setting switches, defined in the Environment Division, to ON or OFF, and condition names in the Data Division to TRUE, by using the SET statement is new. For example,

ENVIRONMENT DIVISION.
.
SPECIAL-NAMES.
      SWITCH-1 IS BinaryToggle
      ON STATUS IS BitSet-1
      OFF STATUS IS BitSet-0.

DATA DIVISION.
.
77 EOF PIC A.
      88 EndOfFile VALUE 'F'.

PROCEDURE DIVISION.
.

      SET BinaryToggle TO ON.
      SET EndOfFile TO TRUE.
.

With the STRING statement OVERFLOW is executed if the receiving field is not long enough to hold all the sending fields. NOT ON OVERFLOW is new and is applicable if the receiving field is not filled at the end of execution of the STRING statement.

With selection statements the inclusion of THEN in an IF statement and the EVALUATE statement are both new.

The CONTINUE statement has no effect. It may be used to form dummy paragraphs, or can occur in place of any imperative or conditional statement. For example, CONTINUE may be used in an IF statement to replace NEXT SENTENCE.

The GO TO DEPENDING ON statement has been modified to include at least one paragraph or section name. Prior to the 1985 Standard at least two names were required.

In-line or flat coding has been made possible, without contrivance, by the introduction of the in-line PERFORM statement.

A STOP RUN now has the effect of automatically closing all files that had remained open in a program.

The SEARCH statement need not be coded in a separate paragraph.

In a MERGE statement the OUTPUT PROCEDURE need not be in a section or series of sections as previously defined.

A RETURN statement obtains a sorted or merged record from the sequencing (sorting) or combining (merging) operations. Although the RETURN statement is not new the option NOT AT END is new in COBOL 85. This gives the programmer the opportunity of stating what cause of action to take when not at the end of the file. The same NOT AT END option has also been included in READ statements.

The INPUT and OUTPUT PROCEDURES in a SORT statement need not be in a section as previously defined.

In inter-program communication the following statements are new: END PROGRAM, COMMON, INITIAL, EXTERNAL, GLOBAL, and EXCEPTION (in a CALL statement).

EXIT PROGRAM does not need to be the last or only statement in a paragraph.

COBOL Files

PADDING CHARACTER applies to sequential files and is an optional entry in the SELECT statement [PADDING CHARACTER IS item-1]. Where item-1 specifies a literal or data-name containing a single character to be used by the system for padding out records. The default is implementor defined.

RECORD DELIMITER applies to sequential files that contain variable-length records and is an is an optional entry in the SELECT statement:

$$\left[\text{RECORD DELIMITER IS} \begin{Bmatrix} \text{STANDARD-1} \\ \text{implementor-name-1} \end{Bmatrix} \right]$$

It specifies the code that marks the end of a record. The delimiter is not counted in the length of the record.

LABEL RECORDS clause in an FD entry is no longer required.

NOT INVALID KEY is new in file access statements for indexed- sequential and relative files. Applicable to DELETE, READ, REWRITE, START and WRITE statements.

In a START statement GREATER THAN OR EQUAL TO or > = is new.

Appendices

Computer Environment - section 1.11

1. Central Processing Unit, main memory, secondary storage units, input unit, output unit.

3. COBOL is a high-level language, therefore, the instructions are not in a machine recognisable form (machine code). A COBOL program must be translated into machine code using a compiler.

4. Phase 1 - creation of a COBOL program in text mode using an editor.

Phase 2 - translation of the program using a COBOL compiler.

Phase 3 - link/loading the machine code program with the necessary library routines to provide a run-time unit.

Phase 4 - execution of the run-time unit.

Structured Design - section 2.11

1.

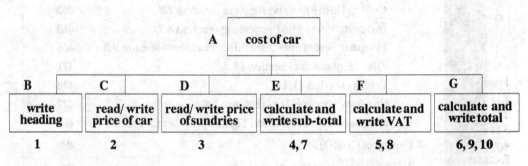

Functions

1. write heading
2. read/write basic price of car
3. read/write price of sundries
4. add price and sundries to give sub-total
5. calculate VAT @ 15% on sub-total
6. add sub-total and VAT to give total
7. write sub-total
8. write VAT
9. write total
10. finish

2.

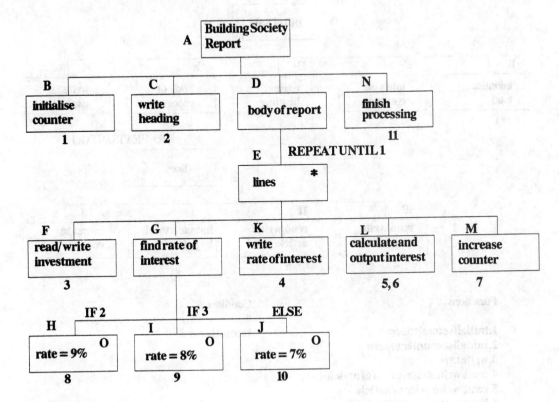

Functions

1. initialise counter to zero
2. write heading
3. read/write amount of investment
4. write rate of interest
5. calculate interest on investment
6. write interest
7. increase counter by 1
8. rate becomes 9%
9. rate becomes 8%
10. rate becomes 7%
11. finish

Conditions

1. counter = 5
2. investment > 20000
3. investment > 10000

3.

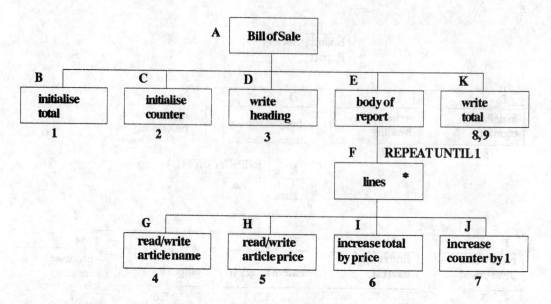

Functions

1. initialise total to zero
2. initialise counter to zero
3. write title
4. read/write description of article
5. read/write price of article
6. increase total by price
7. increase counter by 1
8. write total cost of srticle
9. finish

Conditions

1. counter = 5

4.

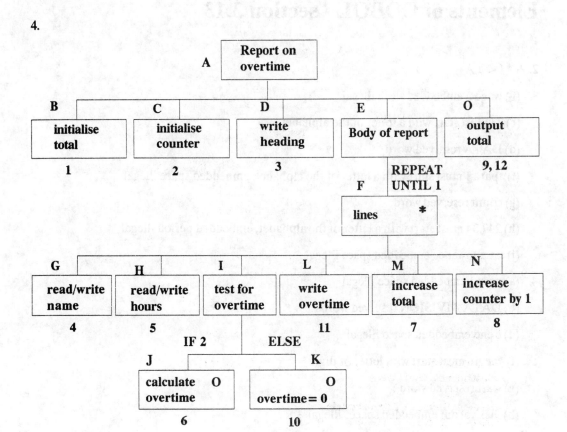

Functions

1. initialise total to zero
2. initialise counter to zero
3. write heading
4. read/ write name of employee
5. read/ write weekly hours worked
6. calculate overtime pay
7. add overtime pay to total
8. increase counter by 1
9. write total
10. overtime becomes zero
11. write overtime
12. finish

Conditions

1. counter = 7
2. hours > 40

Elements of COBOL - section 3.13

2. + * / < a A

3. (b) wage/3 embedded slash illegal

   (c) 23 must start with a letter of the alphabet

   (d) DATA reserved word

   (f) *para 1 must start with a letter of the alphabet, embedded space illegal

   (g) count reserved word

   (h) 247.34 must start with a letter of the alphabet, embedded period illegal

   (j) tax allowance embedded space illegal

4. (a) para 1 embedded space illegal

   (b) DATA DIVISION reserved words

   (d) c end embedded space illegal

   (f) *begin must start with letter or digit

   (g) start reserved word

   (h) max val out embedded spaces illegal

   (i) "a-seq" inverted commas illegal

5. (a) numeric (b) non-numeric (c) non-numeric

   (d) numeric (e) figurative (f) numeric

   (g) numeric (h) figurative (i) figurative

6. (a) comma illegal

   (b) embedded space illegal

   (c) end delimiter " not at end of literal

   (d) the combination of -. could cause an error, better to use -0.215

   (e) embedded space after point illegal

   (f) not a figurative literal

   (g) misssing delimiter

   (h) embedded space illegal

   (i) reserved word

7. (a) thirty-two (c) 1234 (f) ZERO

9. (a) Destination not a data name

(b) Two destination data names

(c) In pre-1985 compilers the inclusion of TO would give an error

(d) TIMES not a reserved word, should use BY

(e) Destination numeric literal

(f) Destination identifier missing

(g) COMPUTER not a reserved word, should use COMPUTE

10. (a)   a   b   c   d

36 36 36 36

(b)   a   b   c   d

10 14 29 89

(c)   a   b   c

24 98 122

(d)   x   y

17 15

(e)   u   v   w   x

29 32 84 -67

(f)   a   b

16 13

(g)   x   y   z

18 3 54

(h)   a   b

6   7

(i)   a   b

12 9

(j)   u   v   w   x

37 13 6 4

14. (a) Only one identifier must be present in an ACCEPT statement.

(b) PRINT not a reserved word, should be DISPLAY

(c) In pre-1985 compilers THEN would give an error

(d) If the PERFORM is intended to be an out-of-line statement it must refer to a paragraph and not an ADD statement. However, if this is an in-line PERFORM then the ADD statement is in the wrong place.

(e) GIVING should be used to specify destination for result of division.

15.   a b c

(a) 2 3 4

(b) 0 3 4

(c) 2 -1 4

(d) 0 3 4

16.   x y z

(a) 7 3 10

(b) 8 5 2

(c) 7 96 0

(d) 11 23 -7

17.

```
input a 4
input b 5
Hello World!
Hello World!
```

A Complete Program - section 4.7

1.

```
IDENTIFICATION DIVISION.
PROGRAM-ID. Cars.

DATA DIVISION.
WORKING-STORAGE SECTION.
77 Price-of-car PIC 9(5).
77 Price-of-sundries PIC 999.
```

```
77 sub-total PIC 9(5).
77 vat-amount PIC 9999.
77 Grand-total PIC 9(5).


PROCEDURE DIVISION.
A-seq.
    PERFORM B THROUGH G.

B.   DISPLAY "COST OF CAR".
     DISPLAY SPACE.
C.   DISPLAY "Price of vehicle ? " WITH NO ADVANCING.
     ACCEPT Price-of-car.
D.   DISPLAY "Price of sundries ? " WITH NO ADVANCING.
     ACCEPT Price-of-sundries.
E.   ADD Price-of-car TO Price-of-sundries GIVING sub-total.
     DISPLAY "Sub-total " sub-total.
F.   MULTIPLY 0.15 BY sub-total GIVING vat-amount.
     DISPLAY "VAT @ 15% " vat-amount.
G.   ADD sub-total TO vat-amount GIVING Grand-total.
     DISPLAY "Total " Grand-total.
     STOP RUN.
```

2.

```
IDENTIFICATION DIVISION.
PROGRAM-ID. BuildingSoc.

DATA DIVISION.
WORKING-STORAGE SECTION.
77 investment PIC 9(5).
77 interest PIC 9(4).
77 rate PIC 9.
77 counter PIC 9.

PROCEDURE DIVISION.
A-seq.
    PERFORM B THROUGH N.

B.   MOVE ZERO TO counter.
C.   DISPLAY "XYZ Building Society"
     DISPLAY SPACE.
D-rep.
    PERFORM E-seq UNTIL counter = 5.
N.   STOP RUN.
```

```
E-seq.
    PERFORM F THROUGH M.

F.   DISPLAY "amount of investment = " WITH NO ADVANCING
     ACCEPT investment
G-sel.
     IF investment > 20000
         PERFORM H
     ELSE
         IF investment > 10000
             PERFORM I
         ELSE
             PERFORM J.
K.   DISPLAY "rate of interest = " rate "%"
L.   COMPUTE   interest = rate * investment / 100
     DISPLAY "annual interest = " interest
M.   ADD 1 TO counter

H.   MOVE 9 TO rate.
I.   MOVE 8 TO rate.
J.   MOVE 7 TO rate.
```

3.

```
IDENTIFICATION DIVISION.
PROGRAM-ID. BillOfSale.

DATA DIVISION.
WORKING-STORAGE SECTION.
77 total PIC 999.
77 price PIC 99.
77 article PIC A(8).
77 counter PIC 9.

PROCEDURE DIVISION.
A-seq.
    PERFORM B THROUGH K.

B.   MOVE ZERO TO total.
C.   MOVE ZERO TO counter.
D.   DISPLAY "BILL OF SALE".
     DISPLAY SPACE.
E-rep.
    PERFORM F-seq until counter = 5.
```

```
K.   DISPLAY "TOTAL = ", total.
     STOP RUN.

F-seq.
     PERFORM G THROUGH J.

G.   DISPLAY "article ? " WITH NO ADVANCING.
     ACCEPT article.
H.   DISPLAY "price = " WITH NO ADVANCING.
     ACCEPT price.
I.   ADD price TO total.
J.   ADD 1 TO counter.
```

4.

```
IDENTIFICATION DIVISION.
PROGRAM-ID. TimeCards.

DATA DIVISION.
WORKING-STORAGE SECTION.
77 total PIC 9(4).
77 hours PIC 99.
77 overtime PIC 999.
77 counter PIC 9.
77 employee PIC A(7).

PROCEDURE DIVISION.
A-seq.
     PERFORM B THROUGH O.

B.   MOVE ZERO TO total.
C.   MOVE ZERO TO counter.
D.   DISPLAY "OVERTIME PAY".
     DISPLAY SPACE.
E-rep.
     PERFORM F-seq UNTIL counter = 7.
O.   DISPLAY "TOTAL OVERTIME = " total.
     STOP RUN.


F-seq.
     PERFORM G THROUGH N.

G.   DISPLAY "name ? " WITH NO ADVANCING.
     ACCEPT employee.
H.   DISPLAY "hours ? " WITH NO ADVANCING.
     ACCEPT hours.
```

```
I-sel.
    IF hours > 40
        COMPUTE overtime = (hours - 40) * 10
    ELSE
        MOVE ZERO TO overtime.
L.  DISPLAY "overtime = " overtime
M.  ADD overtime TO total
N.  ADD 1 TO counter
```

Program Development - section 5.9

1. The results obtained from executing the programs should be identical to the output reports shown for each question at the end of chapter 2.

Picture Editing - section 6.6

Note in the following answers the character **b** represents a space.

1.

bbbb67

bbb45,277.45

254.89

bb$457.34

$***,*95.89

bb$294.56CR

835bb

4573-

bb528

bb67+

bbb-23

bbbb-45.78

267,845.90

bbbb1456bb23

bbbb345.00

2.

$46,389.00

bbb$467.00

bbbbb$0.00

b$1,235.40

bbbbb$0.93

bbbb423.00

bbbbb-4.00

bbb+543.00

bbbbb-3.00

bbbb832.00

bbbb382.00

***4127.00bb

bbb08-

bbb67-

**65489.00CR

0012.34

bbbbbbb

****.00

bbbbbbb

**45.73

Coding Data Files and Reports - section 7.8

1.

```
FILE SECTION.
FD custom, COMPRESSED.
01 CustomerRec.
   02 AccountNo PIC 9(8).
   02 name.
       03 surname PIC X(20).
       03 forename PIC A(15).
   02 address.
       03 street PIC X(20).
       03 town PIC X(20).
       03 postcode PIC X(8).
   02 CreditLimit PIC 9(5).
   02 balance PIC 9(4)V99.
```

4.

```
WORKING-STORAGE   SECTION.
01 Record-1.
   02 FILLER PIC X(31) VALUE IS "SALES OF CARS (SOUTHERN REGION)".
01 Record-2.
   02 FILLER PIC X(8) VALUE IS "COUNTY: ".
   02 county-WS PIC A(15).
01 Record-3.
   02 FILLER PIC X(6) VALUE IS "TOWN: ".
   02 town-WS PIC A(15).
01 Record-4.
   02 model-WS PIC A(8).
   02 FILLER PIC X(9) VALUE IS SPACES.
   02 sale-WS PIC $$,$$$,$$9.
```

6.

```
WORKING-STORAGE   SECTION.
01 Record-1-WS.
   02 FILLER PIC X(18) VALUE IS "THE UNIVERSAL BANK".
01 Record-2-WS.
   02 FILLER PIC X(22) VALUE IS "STATEMENT OF ACCOUNT ".
   02 AccountNo-WS PIC 9(8)B9(7).
01 Record-3-WS.
   02 FILLER PIC X(51) VALUE IS "DATEbbDESCRIPTIONbbbbbDEBITbbbb
-  "bCREDITbbbbbbBALANCE".
01 Record-4-WS.
   02 date-WS PIC X(6).
   02 description-WS PIC X(12).
   02 debit-WS PIC ZZ,ZZ9.99.
   02 FILLER PIC XX VALUE IS SPACES.
   02 credit-WS PIC ZZ,ZZ9.99.
   02 FILLER PIC X(4) VALUE IS SPACES.
   02 balance-WS PIC ZZ,ZZ9.99.
```

```
01  Record-5-WS.
      02 FILLER PIC X(25) VALUE IS SPACES.
      02 FILLER PIC X(16) VALUE IS "FINAL BALANCE".
      02 FinalBalance-WS PIC £££,££9.99DB.
```

8.

```
ENVIRONMENT  DIVISION.
CONFIGURATION  SECTION.
SOURCE-COMPUTER. Prime 750.
OBJECT-COMPUTER. Prime 550.
SPECIAL-NAMES.
      CONSOLE IS TTY.
      PRINTER IS PRT.
      CURRENCY SIGN IS 'F'.
      DECIMAL-POINT IS COMMA.
INPUT-OUTPUT  SECTION.
FILE-CONTROL.
      SELECT alpha ASSIGN TO CR0.
      SELECT beta ASSIGN TO LP0.
      SELECT delta ASSIGN TO MT9,
      ORGANIZATION IS SEQUENTIAL.
      SELECT epsilon ASSIGN TO PFMS,
      ORGANIZATION IS SEQUENTIAL.
```

Introduction to file Processing - section 8.7

1. Unless the FullName contained the surname of an employee as the first part of the field, sorting on the primary key FullName would not be of any benefit to the classification and access to the data. Sorting the file on the secondary key sex is pointless since it would only categorise groups of females and groups of males with the same names!

Sorting the file on DateOfBirth as the primary key is not practical since the date is in the format DDMMYY, which might result in the following ordering of records.

```
010148
010236
010352
010434
     .
     .
```

The dates have been sorted into numerical ascending order, however, this has no relationship with the chronological ordering of the keys. Only if the format of the date was changed to YYMMDD would it be practical to sort the records on DateOfBirth as primary key. The result would then appear as:

```
340401
360201
480101
```

520301
.
.

The record of the eldest employee is then to be found at the beginning of the file.

3.

```
        IDENTIFICATION DIVISION.
        PROGRAM-ID. c8q3.

        ENVIRONMENT DIVISION.
        INPUT-OUTPUT SECTION.
        FILE-CONTROL.
            SELECT subscriber ASSIGN TO PFMS.
            SELECT SubReport ASSIGN TO PFMS.
            SELECT SubWork ASSIGN TO PFMS.
            SELECT SubSort ASSIGN TO PFMS.

        DATA DIVISION.
        FILE SECTION.
        SD SubWork.
        01 Record-1.
            02 SecondaryKey PIC X(21).
            02 FILLER PIC X(4).
            02 PrimaryKey PIC X(23).
            02 FILLER PIC X(12).
        FD subscriber, COMPRESSED.
        01 Record-2.
            02 FILLER PIC X(60).
        FD SubSort, COMPRESSED.
        01 Record-3.
            02 FullName.
                03 surname-3 PIC X(19).
                03 initial-1 PIC A.
                03 initial-2 PIC A.
                03 TITLE PIC A(4).
            02 TeleNumber.
                03 exchange PIC X(15).
                03 PhoneNumber PIC 9(8).
            02 PreviousRead PIC 9(6).
            02 PresentRead PIC 9(6).
        FD SubReport, COMPRESSED.
        01 ReportOut.
            02 FILLER PIC X.
            02 LineImage PIC X(119).
```

```cobol
WORKING-STORAGE SECTION.
01 Record-1-WS.
    02 FILLER PIC X(24) VALUE IS SPACES.
    02 FILLER PIC X(11) VALUE IS "SUBSCRIBERS".
01 Record-2-WS.
    02 FILLER PIC X(4) VALUE IS "NAME".
    02 FILLER PIC X(25) VALUE IS SPACES.
    02 FILLER PIC X(33) VALUE IS "TELEPHONE NUMBER        UNITS US
-   "ED".
01 Record-3-WS.
    02 TITLE-WS PIC X(5).
    02 initial-1-WS PIC A.
    02 FILLER PIC X VALUE IS ".".
    02 initial-2-WS PIC AA.
    02 surname-WS PIC X(20).
    02 TeleNumber-WS PIC X(25).
    02 UNITS-USED-WS PIC ZZZ,ZZ9.


77 UNITS-USED PIC S9(6).
77 EOF PIC A VALUE IS 'F'.
    88 EndOfFile VALUE 'T'.


PROCEDURE DIVISION.
A-seq.
    PERFORM B THROUGH G.

B.
    SORT SubWork ON ASCENDING KEY PrimaryKey, SecondaryKey
    USING subscriber
    GIVING SubSort.
C.  OPEN INPUT SubSort OUTPUT SubReport.
    READ SubSort AT END MOVE 'T' TO EOF.
D.  MOVE Record-1-WS TO LineImage.
    WRITE ReportOut AFTER ADVANCING PAGE.
    MOVE Record-2-WS TO LineImage.
    WRITE ReportOut AFTER ADVANCING 2 LINES.
    MOVE SPACES TO LineImage.
    WRITE ReportOut AFTER ADVANCING 1 LINE.
E-rep.
    PERFORM F UNTIL EndOfFile.
G.  CLOSE SubSort, SubReport.
    STOP RUN.
```

```
F.   MOVE TITLE TO TITLE-WS.
     MOVE initial-1 TO initial-1-WS.
     MOVE initial-2 TO initial-2-WS.
     MOVE surname-3 TO surname-WS.
     MOVE TeleNumber TO TeleNumber-WS.
     SUBTRACT PreviousRead FROM PresentRead GIVING UNITS-USED-WS.
     MOVE Record-3-WS TO LineImage.
     WRITE ReportOut AFTER ADVANCING 1 LINE.
     READ SubSort AT END MOVE 'T' TO EOF.
```

Program Structures from File Structures - section 9.8

1.

```
IDENTIFICATION DIVISION.
PROGRAM-ID. FileSort.

ENVIRONMENT DIVISION.
INPUT-OUTPUT SECTION.
FILE-CONTROL.
     SELECT MembersFile-SD ASSIGN TO PFMS.
     SELECT MembersFile ASSIGN TO PFMS.
     SELECT NewFile-sorted ASSIGN TO PFMS.
     SELECT ClubNotice ASSIGN TO PFMS.

DATA DIVISION.
FILE SECTION.
SD MembersFile-SD.
01 Record-SD.
     02 name-SD PIC X(30).
     02 sex-SD PIC A.
     02 league-SD.
         03 div-SD PIC 9.
         03 box-SD PIC A.
     02 FILLER PIC X(15).
```

```
FD MembersFile, COMPRESSED.
01 Record-1.
    02 FILLER PIC X(48).


FD NewFile-sorted, COMPRESSED.
01 Record-3.
    02 name PIC X(30).
    02 sex PIC A.
    02 league.
        03 div PIC 9.
        03 box PIC A.
    02 TeleNo PIC X(15).


FD ClubNotice, COMPRESSED.
01 ReportOut.
    02 FILLER PIC X.
    02 LineImage PIC X(79).

WORKING-STORAGE SECTION.
01 Record-1-WS.
    02 FILLER PIC X(15) VALUE IS SPACES.
    02 FILLER PIC X(22) VALUE IS "SQUASH CLUB MEMBERSHIP".
01 Record-2-WS.
    02 FILLER PIC X(9) VALUE IS "DIVISION ".
    02 div-WS PIC 9.
01 Record-3-WS.
    02 FILLER PIC X(4) VALUE IS "BOX ".
    02 box-WS PIC A.
01 Record-4-WS.
    02 title PIC AAA.
    02 name-WS PIC X(30).
    02 FILLER PIC X VALUE IS SPACE.
    02 TeleNo-WS PIC X(15).


 77 EOF PIC A VALUE IS 'F'.
    88 EndOfFile VALUE 'T'.
 77 div-STORE PIC 9.
 77 box-STORE PIC A.


PROCEDURE DIVISION.
A-seq.
    PERFORM B THROUGH Q.


B.  SORT MembersFile-SD
```

```
            ON ASCENDING KEY div-SD, box-SD, name-SD
      USING MembersFile
      GIVING NewFile-sorted.

 C.   OPEN INPUT NewFile-sorted,
           OUTPUT ClubNotice.
      READ NewFile-sorted AT END MOVE 'T' TO EOF.

 D.   MOVE Record-1-WS TO LineImage.
      WRITE ReportOut AFTER ADVANCING PAGE.
 E-rep.
      PERFORM F-seq UNTIL EndOfFile.
 Q.   CLOSE NewFile-sorted, ClubNotice.
      STOP RUN.


 F-seq.
      PERFORM G THROUGH H-rep.

 G.   MOVE div TO div-WS, div-STORE.
      MOVE Record-2-WS TO LineImage.
      WRITE ReportOut AFTER ADVANCING 2 LINES.
 H-rep.
      PERFORM I-seq UNTIL (div NOT = div-WS) OR EndOfFile.


 I-seq.
      PERFORM J THROUGH K-rep.


 J.   MOVE box TO box-WS, box-STORE.
      MOVE Record-3-WS TO LineImage.
      WRITE ReportOut AFTER ADVANCING 2 LINES.
 K-rep.
      PERFORM L-seq UNTIL (box NOT = box-WS) OR
                          (div NOT = div-WS) OR EndOfFile.


 L-seq.
      PERFORM M-sel THROUGH P.

 M-sel.
      IF sex = 'M'
         MOVE "Mr" TO title
      ELSE
         MOVE "Ms" TO title.
 P.   MOVE name TO name-WS.
      MOVE TeleNo TO TeleNo-WS.
      MOVE Record-4-WS TO LineImage.
      WRITE ReportOut AFTER ADVANCING 1 LINE.
      READ NewFile-sorted AT END MOVE 'T' TO EOF.
```

3.

```
            IDENTIFICATION DIVISION.
            PROGRAM-ID. C9Q3.

            ENVIRONMENT DIVISION.
            INPUT-OUTPUT SECTION.
            FILE-CONTROL.
                SELECT BookFile ASSIGN TO PFMS.
                SELECT LibraryReport ASSIGN TO PFMS.

            DATA DIVISION.
            FILE SECTION.
            FD BookFile, COMPRESSED.
            01 Record-1.
                02 BookTitle PIC X(30).
                02 authors PIC X(20).
                02 publisher PIC X(15).
                02 StatusCode PIC A.
                02 price PIC 99V99.
            FD LibraryReport, COMPRESSED.
            01 ReportOut.
                02 FILLER PIC X.
                02 LineImage PIC X(119).

            WORKING-STORAGE SECTION.
            01 Record-1-WS.
                02 FILLER PIC X(20) VALUE IS "LIBRARY BOOK DETAILS".
            01 Record-2-WS.
                02 FILLER PIC X(8) VALUE IS "STATUS: ".
                02 BookStatus PIC X(8).
            01 Record-3-WS.
                02 FILLER PIC X(73) VALUE IS "AUTHOR                TITLE
        -       "                 PUBLISHER      PRICE".
            01 Record-4-WS.
                02 Author-WS PIC X(21).
                02 title-WS PIC X(31).
                02 publisher-WS PIC X(16).
                02 price-WS PIC $$9.99.
            01 Record-5-WS.
                02 FILLER PIC X(52) VALUE IS SPACES.
                02 FILLER PIC X(8) VALUE IS "total   ".
                02 total-WS PIC $$$,$$$,$$9.99.

            77 EOF PIC A VALUE IS 'F'.
                88 EndOfFile VALUE 'T'.
            77 total PIC 9(8)V99.
            77 StatusStore PIC A.
```

```
PROCEDURE DIVISION.
A-seq.
    PERFORM B THROUGH R.


B.  OPEN INPUT BookFile
         OUTPUT LibraryReport.
    READ BookFile AT END MOVE 'T' TO EOF.
C.  MOVE Record-1-WS TO LineImage.
    WRITE ReportOut AFTER ADVANCING PAGE.
D-rep.
    PERFORM E-seq UNTIL EndOfFile.
R.  CLOSE BookFile, LibraryReport.
    STOP RUN.


E-seq.
    PERFORM F-seq THROUGH Q.


F-seq.
    PERFORM G-sel THROUGH L.
M.  MOVE StatusCode TO StatusStore.
    MOVE ZERO TO total.
N.  MOVE Record-3-WS TO LineImage.
    WRITE ReportOut AFTER ADVANCING 1 LINE.
O-rep.
    PERFORM P UNTIL EndOfFile OR
               (StatusCode NOT = StatusStore).
Q.  MOVE total TO total-WS.
    MOVE Record-5-WS TO LineImage.
    WRITE ReportOut AFTER ADVANCING 1 LINE.


G-sel.
    IF StatusCode = "A"
        PERFORM H
    ELSE
        IF StatusCode = "D"
            PERFORM I
        ELSE
            IF StatusCode = "E"
                PERFORM J
            ELSE
                PERFORM K.
L.  MOVE Record-2-WS TO LineImage.
    WRITE ReportOut AFTER ADVANCING 1 LINE.


P.  MOVE authors TO Author-WS.
    MOVE BookTitle TO title-WS.
```

```
        MOVE publisher TO publisher-WS.
        MOVE price TO price-WS.
        MOVE Record-4-WS TO LineImage.
        WRITE ReportOut AFTER ADVANCING 1 LINE.
        ADD price TO total.
        READ BookFile AT END MOVE 'T' TO EOF.

    H.  MOVE "ACTIVE" TO BookStatus.
    I.  MOVE "DAMAGED" TO BookStatus.
    J.  MOVE "EXTERNAL" TO BookStatus.
    K.  MOVE "LOST" TO BookStatus.
```

File Maintenance - section 10.5

2.

```
    IDENTIFICATION DIVISION.
    PROGRAM-ID. c10q2.

    ENVIRONMENT DIVISION.
    INPUT-OUTPUT SECTION.
    FILE-CONTROL.
        SELECT transaction ASSIGN TO PFMS.
        SELECT master ASSIGN TO PFMS.
        SELECT update ASSIGN TO PFMS.
        SELECT PaySlip ASSIGN TO PFMS.

    DATA DIVISION.
    FILE SECTION.
    FD transaction, COMPRESSED.
    01 Record-1.
        02 EmployeeNo PIC X(10).
        02 hours PIC 999.
    FD master, COMPRESSED.
    01 Record-2.
        02 employee PIC X(10).
        02 RateOfpay PIC 99V99.
        02 FixedAllowance PIC 999V99.
        02 TotalIncome PIC 9(5)V99.
        02 TotalTax PIC 9(5)V99.
        02 TotalPension PIC 9(4)V99.
        02 TotalNatIns PIC 9(4)V99.
```

```
FD update, COMPRESSED.
01 Record-3.
   02 FILLER PIC X(45).
FD PaySlip, COMPRESSED.
01 Record-4.
   02 FILLER PIC X.
   02 LINE-IMAGE PIC X(119).


WORKING-STORAGE SECTION.
01 Record-1-WS.
   02 FILLER PIC X(17) VALUE IS "EMPLOYEE NUMBER: ".
   02 EmployeeNo-WS PIC X(10).
01 Record-2-WS.
   02 FILLER PIC X(12) VALUE IS "GROSS WAGE: ".
   02 Gross-WS-OUT PIC $$$$9.99.
01 Record-3-WS.
   02 FILLER PIC X(39) VALUE IS SPACES.
   02 FILLER PIC X(9) VALUE IS "PENSION: ".
   02 Pension-WS-OUT PIC $$$9.99.
01 Record-4-WS.
   02 FILLER PIC X(39) VALUE IS SPACES.
   02 FILLER PIC X(9) VALUE IS "NAT.INS: ".
   02 NatIns-WS-OUT PIC $$$9.99.
01 Record-5-WS.
   02 FILLER PIC X(39) VALUE IS SPACES.
   02 FILLER PIC X(9) VALUE IS "TAX:".
   02 Tax-WS-OUT PIC $$$9.99.
01 Record-6-WS.
   02 FILLER PIC X(11) VALUE IS "NETT WAGE: ".
   02 NettWage-WS PIC $(5)9.99.


77 EOFA PIC A VALUE IS 'F'.
   88 EndOfFileA VALUE 'T'.
77 EOFB PIC A VALUE IS 'F'.
   88 EndOfFileB VALUE 'T'.
77 Gross-WS PIC 9(4)V99.
77 Pension-WS PIC 9(3)V99.
77 Tax-WS PIC 9(3)V99.
77 TaxABLE-Income-WS PIC 9(4)V99.
77 Nett-WS PIC 9(4)V99.
```

```
PROCEDURE DIVISION.
A-seq.
    PERFORM B THROUGH L.


B.  OPEN INPUT transaction, master
            OUTPUT update, PaySlip.
    READ transaction AT END MOVE 'T' TO EOFA,
    MOVE HIGH-VALUES TO EmployeeNo.
    READ master AT END MOVE 'T' TO EOFB,
    MOVE HIGH-VALUE TO employee.
C-rep.
    PERFORM D-sel UNTIL EndOfFileA AND EndOfFileB.
L.  CLOSE transaction, master, update, Payslip.
    STOP RUN.


D-sel.
    IF EmployeeNo = employee
        PERFORM F-seq
    ELSE
        IF EmployeeNo > employee
            PERFORM K
        ELSE
            PERFORM E.


F-seq.
    PERFORM G THROUGH J.


K.  Write Record-3 FROM record-2.
    READ master AT END MOVE 'T' TO EOFB,
                    MOVE HIGH-VALUES TO employee.


E.  DISPLAY "ERROR - TRANSACTION FILE KEY ", EmployeeNo.
    READ transaction AT END MOVE 'T' TO EOFA,
                    MOVE HIGH-VALUES TO employee.


G.  MULTIPLY RateOfpay BY hours GIVING Gross-WS.
    MULTIPLY 0.06 BY Gross-WS GIVING Pension-WS.
    SUBTRACT Pension-WS, FixedAllowance FROM Gross-WS
                    GIVING TaxABLE-Income-WS.
    MULTIPLY 0.3 BY TaxABLE-Income-WS GIVING Tax-WS.
    SUBTRACT Pension-WS, 10.5, Tax-WS FROM Gross-WS
                    GIVING Nett-WS.
H.  ADD Gross-WS TO TotalIncome.
    ADD Tax-WS TO TotalTax.
    ADD Pension-WS TO TotalPension.
    ADD 10.5 TO TotalNatIns.
    WRITE Record-3 FROM Record-2.
```

```
I.  MOVE EmployeeNo TO EmployeeNo-WS.
    MOVE Gross-WS TO Gross-WS-OUT.
    MOVE Pension-WS TO Pension-WS-OUT.
    MOVE 10.5 TO NatIns-WS-OUT.
    MOVE Tax-WS TO Tax-WS-OUT.
    MOVE Nett-WS TO NettWage-WS.
    MOVE Record-1-WS TO LINE-IMAGE.
    WRITE Record-4 AFTER ADVANCING PAGE.
    MOVE Record-2-WS TO LINE-IMAGE.
    WRITE Record-4 AFTER ADVANCING 2 LINES.
    MOVE Record-3-WS TO LINE-IMAGE.
    WRITE Record-4 AFTER ADVANCING 1 LINE.
    MOVE Record-4-WS TO LINE-IMAGE.
    WRITE Record-4 AFTER ADVANCING 1 LINE.
    MOVE Record-5-WS TO LINE-IMAGE.
    WRITE Record-4 AFTER ADVANCING 1 LINE.
    MOVE Record-6-WS TO LINE-IMAGE.
    WRITE Record-4 AFTER ADVANCING 1 LINE.
J.  READ transaction AT END MOVE 'T' TO EOFA,
                          MOVE HIGH-VALUES TO EmployeeNo.
    READ master AT END MOVE 'T' TO EOFB,
                          MOVE HIGH-VALUE TO employee.
```

Tables - section 11.11

1.

(a) OCCURS should not be used at level 01.

(b) Pre-1985 compilers would not allow OCCURS and VALUE in the same clause.

(c) DataX should not have a picture clause since the identifier represents the rows of the two-dimensional table and not the individual elements.

(d) OCCURS should not be used at level 77.

(e) REDEFINES should not be used in the FILE SECTION since it is enough to use different 01 level entries to describe the records of a file having an alternative format.

(f) REDEFINES should only be used to redefine an identifier at the same level.

(g) Use REDEFINES immediately after the description of the identifier to be redefined.

2.

(a)

```
01 Table-1.
    02 alpha PIC 999 OCCURS 50 TIMES.
```

(b)

```
01 Table-2.
    02 alpha OCCURS 10 TIMES.
        03 beta PIC 9(5)V99 OCCURS 3 TIMES.
```

(c)

```
01 Table-2.
    02 alpha OCCURS 10 TIMES.
        03 beta OCCURS 50 TIMES.
            04 gamma PIC X(20).
            04 delte PIC 999.
```

(d)

```
01 Table-3.
    02 Table-2 OCCURS 5 TIMES.
        03 Table-1 OCCURS 10 TIMES.
            04 epsilon PIC 999 OCCURS 8 TIMES.
```

3.

(a)

```
01 CountyString.
    02 FILLER PIC X(27) VALUE "CORNWALLbDORSETbbbHAMPSHIRE".
01 CountyTable REDEFINES CountyString.
    02 county PIC X(9) OCCURS 3 TIMES.
```

(b)

```
01 TownString.
    02 FILLER PIC X(33) VALUE "PENZANCEbbbTRURObbbbbbNEWQUAYbbbb".
    02 FILLER PIC X(33) VALUE "POOLEbbbbbbDORCHESTERbSHAFTESBURY".
    02 FILLER PIC X(33) VALUE "SOUTHAMPTONBASINGSTOKEWINCHESTERb".
01 TownTable REDEFINES TownString.
    02 counties OCCURS 3 TIMES.
        03 towns PIC X(11) OCCURS 3 TIMES.
```

(c)

```
01 PopulationString.
    02 FILLER PIC X(54) VALUE IS "019210018557015209012497401422505
"0495121480207349203566450".
01 TownPopulation REDEFINES PopulationString.
    02 CountyPopulation OCCURS 3 TIMES.
        03 population PIC 9(6) OCCURS 3 TIMES.
```

4.

```
PROCEDURE DIVISION.
A-seq.
    PERFORM B.
    PERFORM C VARYING subscript FROM 1 BY 1 UNTIL subscript > 3.
    PERFORM D VARYING subscript FROM 1 BY 1 UNTIL subscript > 3.
```

```
          PERFORM E THROUGH F.
          PERFORM C VARYING subscript FROM 1 BY 1 UNTIL subscript > 3.
          PERFORM G.
          PERFORM H VARYING subscript FROM 1 BY 1 UNTIL subscript > 3.
          PERFORM I VARYING RowSubscript FROM 1 BY 1 UNTIL RowSubscript > 3
              AFTER ColumnSubscript FROM 1 BY 1 UNTIL ColumnSubscript > 3.
          PERFORM J.
          STOP RUN.
      B.  ACCEPT CountyName. ACCEPT TownName.
      C.  IF CountyName = county (subscript)
              MOVE subscript TO RowSubscript.
      D.  IF TownName = towns (RowSubscript, subscript)
              MOVE subscript TO ColumnSubscript.
      E.  DISPLAY "population of " TownName " is "
          population (RowSubscript, ColumnSubscript).
      F.  ACCEPT CountyName.
      G.  MOVE ZERO TO CountyPop, TotalPop.
      H.  ADD population (RowSubscript, subscript) TO CountyPop.
      I.  ADD population (RowSubscript, ColumnSubscript) TO TotalPop.
      J.  COMPUTE PercentagePop = CountyPop / TotalPop * 100
          DISPLAY "percentage population for " CountyName " is " PercentagePop.
```

5. A catalogue of the errors in the segment of code follows.

In the clause 02 RECORD OCCURS 50 TIMES INDEXED BY I, the reserved word RECORD must not be used, and the statement does not need a period.

In the clause ASCENDING-KEY IS name(I), the hyphen is not required in ASCENDING KEY and name should not contain a parenthesised index.

The clause 04 TeleNumber PIC 9(12) has an incorrect level number, should be 03 since it is part of the record. The picture clause is also incorrect.

77 I PIC 99 is incorrect since the index I does not require a separate declaration.

MOVE 1 TO I is an illegal statement for an index.

InputName (I) is an illegal identifier since no table using InputName has been declared.

Since the contents of the table is not ordered SEARCH ALL should not be used, but substituted by SEARCH. TeleTable should be replaced by the equivalent legal replacement for RECORD and CHANGING should be replaced by VARYING.

The segment of code should be re-coded as:

```
      WORKING-STORAGE SECTION.
      01 TeleTable.
          02 Record-1 OCCURS 50 TIMES INDEXED BY I.
              03 name PIC X(12).
              03 TeleNumber PIC X(12).
      PROCEDURE DIVISION.
          SET I TO 1.
          ACCEPT InputName.
          SEARCH Record-1 VARYING I AT END DISPLAY "name not found"
          WHEN InputName = name (I) DISPLAY TeleNumber (I).
```

Random Access Files - section 12.8

1.

```
IDENTIFICATION DIVISION.
PROGRAM-ID. FileCreation.

ENVIRONMENT DIVISION.
INPUT-OUTPUT SECTION.
FILE-CONTROL.
    SELECT PoliceFile ASSIGN TO PFMS,
    ORGANIZATION IS INDEXED,
    ACCESS MODE IS DYNAMIC,
    RECORD KEY IS RegistrationNo,
    ALTERNATE RECORD KEY IS MMC WITH DUPLICATES.

DATA DIVISION.
FILE SECTION.
FD PoliceFile.
01 Record-1.
    02 RegistrationNo PIC X(7).
    02 DateOfRegistration PIC 9(4).
    02 MMC.
        03 manufacturer PIC X(10).
        03 model PIC X(10).
        03 colour PIC X(8).
    02 VehicleOwner PIC X(25).
    02 address PIC X(30).
    02 DateOfExpiry.
        03 MM PIC 99.
        03 YY PIC 99.

WORKING-STORAGE SECTION.
77 MenuCode PIC A.
    88 QuitSystem VALUE 'E', 'e'.
77 ErrorFlag PIC A.
    88 errors VALUE 'T'.
77 ClearScreen PIC X VALUE ''.

PROCEDURE DIVISION.
A-seq.
    PERFORM B.
    PERFORM C.
    PERFORM D-rep.
    PERFORM M.
```

```
B.   OPEN I-O PoliceFile.
C.   PERFORM FUNCTIONS-8-9.
D-rep.
     PERFORM E-seq UNTIL QuitSystem.
M.   CLOSE PoliceFile.
     STOP RUN.


E-seq.
     PERFORM F THROUGH L.


F.   PERFORM FUNCTIONS-11-12.
G-sel.
     IF MenuCode = 'A' OR 'a'
        PERFORM H-seq
     ELSE IF MenuCode = 'D' OR 'd'
             PERFORM I-seq
           ELSE
             PERFORM J-seq.


* paragraph K missing since no log file


L.   PERFORM FUNCTIONS-8-9.
H-seq.
     PERFORM HA THROUGH HF.


HA.  READ PoliceFile KEY IS RegistrationNo
     INVALID KEY MOVE 'T' TO ErrorFlag.
HB-rep.
     PERFORM HC-seq UNTIL NOT errors.
HF.  PERFORM FUNCTIONS-10-5.
     REWRITE Record-1 INVALID KEY MOVE 'T' TO ErrorFlag.


HC-seq.
     PERFORM HD THROUGH HE.


HD.  DISPLAY "ERROR - INVALID KEY"
     PERFORM FUNCTIONS-11-12.
HE.  READ PoliceFile KEY IS RegistrationNo
     INVALID KEY MOVE 'T' TO ErrorFlag.


I-seq.
     PERFORM IA THROUGH IB-rep.


IA.  DELETE PoliceFile
     INVALID KEY MOVE 'T' TO ErrorFlag.
```

```
IB-rep.
     PERFORM IC-seq UNTIL NOT errors.


IC-seq.
     PERFORM IE THROUGH IG.


IE. DISPLAY "ERROR - INVALID KEY"
     PERFORM FUNCTIONS-11-12.
IG. DELETE PoliceFile
     INVALID KEY MOVE 'T' TO ErrorFlag.
J-seq.
     PERFORM JA THROUGH JC-rep.


JA. PERFORM FUNCTIONS-10-5.
JB. WRITE Record-1
     INVALID KEY MOVE 'T' TO ErrorFlag.
JC-rep.
     PERFORM JD-seq UNTIL NOT errors.


JD-seq.
     PERFORM JE THROUGH JF.


JE. DISPLAY "ERROR - INVALID KEY"
     PERFORM FUNCTIONS-11-12.
JF. WRITE Record-1
     INVALID KEY MOVE 'T' TO ErrorFlag.


* ----------------------- subroutines --------------------


FUNCTIONS-8-9.
     DISPLAY ClearScreen.
     DISPLAY "Do you require to:"
     DISPLAY " "
     DISPLAY "[A]mend record"
     DISPLAY "[D]elete record"
     DISPLAY "[I]nsert record"
     DISPLAY "[E]xit from system".
     DISPLAY SPACE.
     DISPLAY "input code A,D,I or E " WITH NO ADVANCING.
     ACCEPT MenuCode.


FUNCTIONS-11-12.
     DISPLAY "input vehicle registration number".
     ACCEPT RegistrationNo.

     MOVE 'F' TO ErrorFlag.
```

```
FUNCTIONS-10-5.
    DISPLAY "input the following details"
    DISPLAY SPACE.
    DISPLAY "date of registration of vehicle as MMYY".
    ACCEPT DateOfRegistration.
    DISPLAY "manufacturer of vehicle".
    ACCEPT manufacturer.
    DISPLAY "model"
    ACCEPT model.
    DISPLAY "colour".
    ACCEPT colour.
    DISPLAY "owner of vehicle".
    ACCEPT VehicleOwner.
    DISPLAY "address".
    ACCEPT address.
    DISPLAY "date of expiry of licence as MMYY".
    ACCEPT DateOfExpiry.
```

2.
```
    IDENTIFICATION DIVISION.
    PROGRAM-ID. Interrogation.

    ENVIRONMENT DIVISION.
    INPUT-OUTPUT SECTION.
    FILE-CONTROL.
        SELECT PoliceFile ASSIGN TO PFMS,
        ORGANIZATION IS INDEXED,
        ACCESS MODE IS DYNAMIC,
        RECORD KEY IS RegistrationNo,
        ALTERNATE RECORD KEY IS MMC WITH DUPLICATES.

    DATA DIVISION.
    FILE SECTION.
    FD PoliceFile.
    01 Record-1.
        02 RegistrationNo PIC X(7).
        02 DateOfRegistration PIC 9(4).
        02 MMC.
            03 manufacturer PIC X(10).
            03 model PIC X(10).
            03 colour PIC X(8).
        02 VehicleOwner PIC X(25).
        02 address PIC X(30).
        02 DateOfExpiry.
            03 MM PIC 99.
            03 YY PIC 99.
```

```
WORKING-STORAGE SECTION.
77 MenuCode PIC 9.
   88 QuitSystem VALUE 4.
77 ErrorFlag PIC A.
   88 errors VALUE 'T'.
77 MMCStore PIC X(28).
77 EOF PIC A.
   88 EndOfFile VALUE 'T'.
77 ExpiryTime PIC S999.
77 ClearScreen PIC X VALUE ''.


01 date-WS.
   02 YY-WS PIC 99.
   02 MM-WS PIC 99.
   02 FILLER PIC XX.



PROCEDURE DIVISION.
A-seq.
     PERFORM B THROUGH K.


B.   OPEN INPUT PoliceFile.
C.   PERFORM FUNCTIONS-3-4.
D-rep.
     PERFORM E-seq UNTIL QuitSystem.
K.   CLOSE PoliceFile.
     STOP RUN.


E-seq.
     PERFORM F-sel THROUGH J.


F-sel.
     IF MenuCode = 1
        PERFORM G-seq
     ELSE IF MenuCode = 2
        PERFORM H-seq
     ELSE
        PERFORM I-seq.


J.   PERFORM FUNCTIONS-3-4.


G-seq.
     PERFORM GA THROUGH GD.


GA.  PERFORM FUNCTIONS-5-6.
     MOVE 'F' TO ErrorFlag.
```

```
            READ PoliceFile KEY IS RegistrationNo,
            INVALID KEY MOVE 'T' TO ErrorFlag.
    GB-rep.
            PERFORM GC UNTIL NOT errors.
    GD. PERFORM FUNCTION-10.


    GC. DISPLAY "ERROR - INVALID KEY".
            PERFORM FUNCTIONS-5-6.
            MOVE 'F' TO ErrorFlag.
            READ PoliceFile KEY IS RegistrationNo,
            INVALID KEY MOVE 'T' TO ErrorFlag.


    H-seq.
            PERFORM HA THROUGH HE-rep.


    HA. PERFORM FUNCTIONS-7-8-9.
            MOVE 'F' TO ErrorFlag.
            START PoliceFile KEY IS NOT LESS THAN MMC,
            INVALID KEY MOVE 'T' TO ErrorFlag.
    HB-rep.
            PERFORM HC UNTIL NOT errors.
    HD. MOVE MMC TO MMCStore.
            MOVE 'F' TO EOF.
            READ PoliceFile NEXT RECORD AT END MOVE 'T' TO EOF.
    HE-rep.
            PERFORM HF UNTIL EndOfFile OR MMC NOT = MMCStore.


    HC. DISPLAY "ERROR - INVALID KEY"
            PERFORM FUNCTIONS-5-6.
            MOVE 'F' TO ErrorFlag.
            START PoliceFile KEY IS NOT LESS THAN MMC,
            INVALID KEY MOVE 'T' TO ErrorFlag.
    HF. PERFORM FUNCTION-10.
            READ PoliceFile NEXT RECORD AT END MOVE 'T' TO EOF.


    I-seq.
            PERFORM IA THROUGH IB-rep.


    IA. MOVE 'F' TO EOF.
            ACCEPT date-WS FROM DATE.
            MOVE SPACES TO RegistrationNo.
            START PoliceFile KEY IS NOT LESS THAN RegistrationNo,
            INVALID KEY MOVE 'T' TO ErrorFlag.
            READ PoliceFile NEXT RECORD AT END MOVE 'T' TO EOF.
    IB-rep.
            PERFORM IC-seq UNTIL EndOfFile.
```

```
IC-seq.
    PERFORM IDD THROUGH IFF.


IDD.
    COMPUTE ExpiryTime = 12 * (YY - YY-WS) + (MM - MM-WS).
IE-sel.
    IF ExpiryTime < 0  PERFORM FUNCTION-10.
IFF.
    READ PoliceFile NEXT RECORD AT END MOVE 'T' TO EOF.



* -------------------- subroutines --------------------

FUNCTIONS-3-4.
    DISPLAY "Do you require record access on:"
    DISPLAY " "
    DISPLAY "1. Registration Number".
    DISPLAY "2. Manufacturer, model and colour".
    DISPLAY "3. Vehicles without excise licence".
    DISPLAY "4. EXIT from system".
    DISPLAY " "
    DISPLAY "input numeric code 1-4 " WITH NO ADVANCING.
    ACCEPT MenuCode.
    DISPLAY ClearScreen.


FUNCTIONS-5-6.
    DISPLAY "input registration number".
    ACCEPT RegistrationNo.


FUNCTIONS-7-8-9.
    DISPLAY "input manufacturer".
    ACCEPT manufacturer.
    DISPLAY "input model".
    ACCEPT model.
    DISPLAY "input colour".
    ACCEPT colour.


FUNCTION-10.
    DISPLAY "registration number:  " RegistrationNo.
    DISPLAY "date of registration: " DateOfRegistration.
    DISPLAY "manufacturer:         " manufacturer.
    DISPLAY "model:                " model.
    DISPLAY "colour:               " colour.
    DISPLAY "name of owner:        " VehicleOwner.
    DISPLAY "address:              " address.
    DISPLAY "excise expiry         " DateOfExpiry.
```

Program Implementation Techniques - section 13.10

1. (a)

```
A-seq
    B-sel if 1
        C do 1
    B-alt (else)
        D-rep until 2
            E do 6
        D-end
    B-end
    F do 3,4
    G do 2,5
A-end
```

(b)

```
A-seq
    B-seq
        C-rep until 1
            D-rep until 2
                E do 4,5
            D-end
        C-end
        F-sel if 4
            G do 1,2
        F-alt-1 if 5
            H-sel if 6
                I do 3,6
            H-alt (else)
                J do 7
            H-end
        F-alt-2 (else)
            K do 5
        F-end
    B-end
    L do 8
    M-rep until 1
        N-seq
            O do 9,10
            P do 11
        N-end
    M-end
A-end
```

2.

```
        IDENTIFICATION DIVISION.
        PROGRAM-ID. OrderClash.

        ENVIRONMENT DIVISION.
        INPUT-OUTPUT SECTION.
        FILE-CONTROL.
            SELECT SortNames ASSIGN TO PFMS.
            SELECT WorkFile ASSIGN TO PFMS.
            SELECT StaffNames ASSIGN TO PFMS.

        DATA DIVISION.
        FILE SECTION.
        SD WorkFile.
        01 Record-SD.
            02 name-SD PIC X(12).
            02 department-SD PIC A.
            02 StaffStatus-SD PIC A.
        FD SortNames, COMPRESSED.
        01 Record-1.
            02 FILLER PIC X(14).
        FD StaffNames, COMPRESSED.
        01 Record-2.
            02 name PIC X(12).
            02 department PIC A.
            02 StaffStatus PIC A.

        WORKING-STORAGE SECTION.
        77 EOF PIC A VALUE 'F'.
            88 EndOfFile VALUE 'T'.
        77 StatusStore PIC A.



        PROCEDURE DIVISION.
        A-seq.
        B.   SORT WorkFile ON ASCENDING KEY StaffStatus-SD
                        USING SortNames GIVING StaffNames.

        C.   OPEN INPUT StaffNames.
             READ StaffNames AT END MOVE 'T' TO EOF.
        D-rep.
             IF EndOfFile GO TO D-end.
        E-seq.
        F.      MOVE StaffStatus TO StatusStore.
                DISPLAY SPACE.
```

```
G-sel.
        IF StaffStatus NOT = 'H' GO TO G-alt-1.
H.          DISPLAY "Heads of Departments".
        GO TO G-end.
G-alt-1.
        IF StaffStatus NOT = 'L' GO TO G-alt-2.
I.          DISPLAY "Lecturers".
         GO TO G-end.
G-alt-2.
        IF StaffStatus NOT = 'S' GO TO G-alt-3.
J.          DISPLAY "Secretaries".
        GO TO G-end.
G-alt-3.
K.          DISPLAY "Technicians".
G-end.
L.      DISPLAY SPACE.
M-rep.
        IF EndOfFile OR
        StaffStatus NOT = StatusStore GO TO M-end.
N.          DISPLAY name.
            READ StaffNames AT END MOVE 'T' TO EOF.
        GO TO M-rep.

M-end.
E-end.
        GO TO D-rep.
D-end.
N.  CLOSE StaffNames, STOP RUN.
A-end.
```

6.

```
IDENTIFICATION DIVISION.
PROGRAM-ID. SplitFiles.

ENVIRONMENT DIVISION.
INPUT-OUTPUT SECTION.
FILE-CONTROL.
    SELECT motorists ASSIGN TO PFMS.
    SELECT convicted ASSIGN TO PFMS.
    SELECT NotConvicted ASSIGN TO PFMS.
```

```
DATA DIVISION.
FILE SECTION.
FD motorists, COMPRESSED.
01 Record-1.
    02 PolicyNumber PIC 9(8).
    02 RecordCode PIC 9.
    02 details PIC X(71).
FD convicted, COMPRESSED.
01 Record-2.
    02 FILLER PIC X(80).
FD NotConvicted, COMPRESSED.
01 Record-3.
    02 FILLER PIC X(80).


WORKING-STORAGE SECTION.
01 AreaR1.
    02 PolicyNumber-R1 PIC 9(8).
    02 RecordCode-R1 PIC 9.
    02 FILLER PIC X(71).
01 AreaR2.
    02 PolicyNumber-R2 PIC 9(8).
    02 RecordCode-R2 PIC 9.
    02 FILLER PIC X(71).
77 EOF  PIC A VALUE IS 'F'.
    88 EndOfFile VALUE 'T'.


PROCEDURE DIVISION.
A-seq.
B.
    OPEN INPUT motorists,
         OUTPUT convicted, NotConvicted.
    READ motorists INTO AreaR1 AT END MOVE 'T' TO EOF.
    READ motorists INTO AreaR2 AT END MOVE 'T' TO EOF.
C-rep.
    IF EndOfFile GO TO C-end.
D-sel.
        IF PolicyNumber-R1 = PolicyNumber-R2 GO TO D-alt.
        WRITE Record-3 FROM AreaR1.
        MOVE AreaR2 TO AreaR1.
        READ motorists INTO AreaR2 AT END MOVE 'T' TO EOF.
        GO TO D-end.
D-alt.
F-seq.
```

```
G.
        WRITE Record-2 FROM AreaR1.
        MOVE AreaR2 TO AreaR1.
        READ motorists INTO AreaR2 AT END MOVE 'T' TO EOF.
H-rep.
        IF RecordCode-R1 NOT = 1 OR EndOfFile GO TO H-end.
I.
        WRITE Record-2 FROM AreaR1.
        MOVE AreaR2 TO AreaR1.
        READ motorists INTO AreaR2 AT END MOVE 'T' TO EOF.
        GO TO H-rep.
H-end.
F-end.
D-end.
    GO TO C-rep.
C-end.
J-sel.
    IF RecordCode-R1 = 1 GO TO J-alt.
K.    WRITE Record-3 FROM AreaR1.
    GO TO J-end.
J-alt.
L.    WRITE Record-2 FROM AreaR1.
J-end.
M.   CLOSE motorists, convicted, NotConvicted. STOP RUN.
A-end.
```

Appendix II contains the general format of statements found in COBOL-85.

The reserved words are <u>underlined.</u>

```
IDENTIFICATION DIVISION.

PROGRAM-ID. program-name  [ IS  { | COMMON | }  PROGRAM ]
                                 { | INITIAL| }

[AUTHOR.  [comment-entry] ... ]

[INSTALLATION.  [comment-entry] ... ]

[DATE-WRITTEN.  [comment-entry] ... ]

[DATE-COMPILED.  [comment-entry] ... ]

[SECURITY.  [comment-entry] ... ]



[ENVIRONMENT DIVISION.

[CONFIGURATION SECTION.

[SOURCE-COMPUTER.  [computer-name  [WITH DEBUGGING MODE].]]

[OBJECT-COMPUTER.  [computer-name

    [PROGRAM COLLATING SEQUENCE IS alphabet-name-1]

    [SEGMENT-LIMIT IS segment-number].]]

[SPECIAL-NAMES.  [[implementor-name-1

   ( IS mnemonic-name-1  [ON STATUS IS condition-name-1  [OFF STATUS IS condition-name-2]] )
   ( IS mnemonic-name-2  [OFF STATUS IS condition-name-2  [ON STATUS IS condition-name-1]] )  ...
   ( ON STATUS IS condition-name-1  [OFF STATUS IS condition-name-2] )
   ( OFF STATUS IS condition-name-2  [ON STATUS IS condition-name-1] )

   [ALPHABET alphabet-name-1 IS

       (  STANDARD-1          )
       (  STANDARD-2          )
       (  NATIVE              )  ...
       (  implementor-name-2  )
       (           [ {THROUGH}  literal-2 ] )
       ( literal-1 [ {THRU   }           ] ) ...
       (           [ {ALSO literal-3} ... ] )
```

$$\left[\underline{\text{SYMBOLIC}} \text{ CHARACTERS} \left\{\left\{\{\text{symbolic-character-1}\} \ldots \begin{Bmatrix} \text{IS} \\ \text{ARE} \end{Bmatrix} \{\text{integer-1}\} \ldots \right\} \ldots\right.\right.$$

$$\left.\left. [\text{IN alphabet-name-2}] \right\} \right] \ldots$$

[CURRENCY SIGN IS literal-4]

[DECIMAL-POINT IS COMMA].]]]

[INPUT-OUTPUT SECTION.

  FILE-CONTROL.

    {file-control-entry} ...

  [I-O-CONTROL.

$$\left[\left[\underline{\text{SAME}} \begin{bmatrix} \underline{\text{RECORD}} \\ \underline{\text{SORT}} \\ \underline{\text{SORT-MERGE}} \end{bmatrix} \text{AREA FOR file-name-1 \{file-name-2\} } \ldots \right] \right] \ldots$$

    [MULTIPLE FILE TAPE CONTAINS

        {file-name-3 [POSITION IS integer-1] } ...] ... .]]]]

SEQUENTIAL FILE:

SELECT [OPTIONAL] file-name-1

  ASSIGN TO {implementor-name-1} ...

$$\left[\underline{\text{RESERVE}} \text{ integer-1} \begin{bmatrix} \text{AREA} \\ \text{AREAS} \end{bmatrix}\right]$$

  [[ORGANIZATION IS] SEQUENTIAL]

$$\left[\underline{\text{BLOCK}} \text{ CONTAINS [integer-2 } \underline{\text{TO}}] \text{ integer-3} \begin{Bmatrix} \underline{\text{RECORDS}} \\ \underline{\text{CHARACTERS}} \end{Bmatrix}\right]$$

  [CODE-SET IS alphabet-name-1]

$$\left[\underline{\text{PADDING}} \text{ CHARACTER IS } \begin{Bmatrix} \text{data-name-1} \\ \text{literal-1} \end{Bmatrix}\right]$$

$$\left[\underline{\text{RECORD}} \underline{\text{DELIMITER}} \text{ IS } \begin{Bmatrix} \underline{\text{STANDARD-1}} \\ \text{implementor-name-2} \end{Bmatrix}\right]$$

  [ACCESS MODE IS SEQUENTIAL]

  [FILE STATUS IS data-name-2].

RELATIVE FILE:

SELECT [OPTIONAL] file-name-1

   ASSIGN TO {implementor-name-1} ...

$$\left[\text{RESERVE integer-1} \begin{bmatrix} \text{AREA} \\ \text{AREAS} \end{bmatrix}\right]$$

[ORGANIZATION IS] RELATIVE

$$\left[\text{BLOCK CONTAINS [integer-2 TO] integer-3} \begin{Bmatrix} \text{RECORDS} \\ \text{CHARACTERS} \end{Bmatrix}\right]$$

$$\left[\text{RECORD DELIMITER IS} \begin{Bmatrix} \text{STANDARD-1} \\ \text{implementor-name-2} \end{Bmatrix}\right]$$

$$\left[\text{ACCESS MODE IS} \begin{Bmatrix} \text{SEQUENTIAL} & \text{[RELATIVE KEY IS data-name-1]} \\ \begin{Bmatrix} \text{RANDOM} \\ \text{DYNAMIC} \end{Bmatrix} & \text{RELATIVE KEY IS data-name-1} \end{Bmatrix}\right]$$

[FILE STATUS IS data-name-2].

INDEXED FILE:

SELECT [OPTIONAL] file-name-1

   ASSIGN TO {implementor-name-1} ...

$$\left[\text{RESERVE integer-1} \begin{bmatrix} \text{AREA} \\ \text{AREAS} \end{bmatrix}\right]$$

[ORGANIZATION IS] INDEXED

$$\left[\text{BLOCK CONTAINS [integer-2 TO] integer-3} \begin{Bmatrix} \text{RECORDS} \\ \text{CHARACTERS} \end{Bmatrix}\right]$$

$$\left[\text{RECORD DELIMITER IS} \begin{Bmatrix} \text{STANDARD-1} \\ \text{implementor-name-2} \end{Bmatrix}\right]$$

$$\left[\text{ACCESS MODE IS} \begin{Bmatrix} \text{SEQUENTIAL} \\ \text{RANDOM} \\ \text{DYNAMIC} \end{Bmatrix}\right]$$

RECORD KEY IS data-name-1

[ALTERNATE RECORD KEY IS data-name-2 [WITH DUPLICATES]] ...

[FILE STATUS IS data-name-3].

SORT OR MERGE FILE:

SELECT file-name-1 ASSIGN TO {implementor-name-1} ... .

```
[DATA DIVISION.

[FILE SECTION.

[file-description-entry

{record-description-entry} ... ] ...

[sort-merge-file-description-entry

{record-description-entry} ... ] ...

[report-file-description-entry] ... ]

[WORKING-STORAGE SECTION.

⎡77-level-description-entry⎤
⎣record-description-entry ⎦ ...

[LINKAGE SECTION.

⎡77-level-description-entry⎤
⎣record-description-entry ⎦ ...
```

SEQUENTIAL FILE:

```
FD  file-name-1

    [IS EXTERNAL]

    [IS GLOBAL]

    ⎡                                        ⎧RECORDS   ⎫⎤
    ⎢BLOCK CONTAINS [integer-1 TO] integer-2 ⎨CHARACTERS⎬⎥
    ⎣                                        ⎩          ⎭⎦

    ⎡       ⎧CONTAINS integer-3 CHARACTERS                                              ⎫⎤
    ⎢RECORD ⎨IS VARYING IN SIZE [[FROM integer-4] [TO integer-5] CHARACTERS]            ⎬⎥
    ⎢       ⎨     [DEPENDING ON data-name-1]                                            ⎬⎥
    ⎣       ⎩CONTAINS integer-6 TO integer-7 CHARACTERS                                 ⎭⎦

    ⎡      ⎧RECORD IS ⎫ ⎧STANDARD⎫⎤
    ⎢LABEL ⎨RECORDS ARE⎬ ⎨OMITTED ⎬⎥
    ⎣      ⎩          ⎭ ⎩        ⎭⎦

    ⎡                                  ⎧data-name-2⎫⎫    ⎤
    ⎢VALUE OF ⎨implementor-name-1 IS   ⎨literal-1  ⎬⎬ ...⎥
    ⎣                                  ⎩           ⎭⎭    ⎦

    ⎡     ⎧RECORD IS ⎫                ⎤
    ⎢DATA ⎨RECORDS ARE⎬ {data-name-3} ...⎥
    ⎣     ⎩          ⎭                ⎦

    ⎡         ⎧data-name-4⎫                          ⎧data-name-5⎫⎤
    ⎢LINAGE IS⎨integer-8  ⎬ LINES [WITH FOOTING AT   ⎨integer-9  ⎬⎥
    ⎣         ⎩           ⎭                          ⎩           ⎭⎦
```

$$\left[\text{LINES AT } \underline{\text{TOP}} \quad \left\{ \begin{array}{l} \text{data-name-6} \\ \text{integer-10} \end{array} \right\} \right] \left[\text{LINES AT } \underline{\text{BOTTOM}} \quad \left\{ \begin{array}{l} \text{data-name-7} \\ \text{integer-11} \end{array} \right\} \right] \right]$$

[<u>CODE-SET</u> IS alphabet-name-1]

[[<u>ACCESS</u> MODE IS] <u>SEQUENTIAL</u>]

[FILE <u>STATUS</u> IS data-name-8].

<u>INDEXED FILE</u>:

<u>FD</u> file-name-1

[IS <u>EXTERNAL</u>]

[IS <u>GLOBAL</u>]

$$\left[\underline{\text{BLOCK}} \text{ CONTAINS } [\text{integer-1 } \underline{\text{TO}}] \text{ integer-2} \left\{ \begin{array}{l} \underline{\text{RECORDS}} \\ \text{CHARACTERS} \end{array} \right\} \right]$$

$$\left[\underline{\text{RECORD}} \left\{ \begin{array}{l} \text{CONTAINS integer-3 CHARACTERS} \\ \text{IS } \underline{\text{VARYING}} \text{ IN SIZE } [[\text{FROM integer-4}] \ [\underline{\text{TO}} \text{ integer-5}] \text{ CHARACTERS}] \\ \qquad [\underline{\text{DEPENDING}} \text{ ON data-name-1}] \\ \text{CONTAINS integer-6 } \underline{\text{TO}} \text{ integer-7 CHARACTERS} \end{array} \right\} \right]$$

$$\left[\underline{\text{LABEL}} \left\{ \begin{array}{l} \underline{\text{RECORD}} \text{ IS} \\ \underline{\text{RECORDS}} \text{ ARE} \end{array} \right\} \left\{ \begin{array}{l} \underline{\text{STANDARD}} \\ \underline{\text{OMITTED}} \end{array} \right\} \right]$$

$$\left[\underline{\text{VALUE}} \ \underline{\text{OF}} \left\{ \text{implementor-name-1 IS} \left\{ \begin{array}{l} \text{data-name-2} \\ \text{literal-1} \end{array} \right\} \right\} \dots \right]$$

$$\left[\underline{\text{DATA}} \left\{ \begin{array}{l} \underline{\text{RECORD}} \text{ IS} \\ \underline{\text{RECORDS}} \text{ ARE} \end{array} \right\} \ \{\text{data-name-3}\} \ \dots \right]$$

$$\left[[\underline{\text{ACCESS}} \text{ MODE IS}] \left\{ \begin{array}{l} \underline{\text{SEQUENTIAL}} \\ \underline{\text{RANDOM}} \\ \underline{\text{DYNAMIC}} \end{array} \right\} \right]$$

<u>RECORD</u> <u>KEY</u> IS data-name-4

[<u>ALTERNATE</u> <u>RECORD</u> KEY IS data-name-5 [WITH <u>DUPLICATES</u>]] ...

[FILE <u>STATUS</u> IS data-name-6].

RELATIVE FILE:

FD file-name-1

[IS EXTERNAL]

[IS GLOBAL]

$$\left[\underline{BLOCK} \text{ CONTAINS } [\text{integer-1 } \underline{TO}] \text{ integer-2} \begin{Bmatrix} \underline{RECORDS} \\ CHARACTERS \end{Bmatrix} \right]$$

$$\left[\underline{RECORD} \begin{Bmatrix} \text{CONTAINS integer-3 CHARACTERS} \\ \text{IS } \underline{VARYING} \text{ IN SIZE } [[\text{FROM integer-4}] \ [\underline{TO} \text{ integer-5}] \text{ CHARACTERS}] \\ \qquad [\underline{DEPENDING} \text{ ON data-name-1}] \\ \text{CONTAINS integer-6 } \underline{TO} \text{ integer-7 CHARACTERS} \end{Bmatrix} \right]$$

$$\left[\underline{LABEL} \begin{Bmatrix} \underline{RECORD} \text{ IS} \\ \underline{RECORDS} \text{ ARE} \end{Bmatrix} \begin{Bmatrix} \underline{STANDARD} \\ \underline{OMITTED} \end{Bmatrix} \right]$$

$$\left[\underline{VALUE} \ \underline{OF} \begin{Bmatrix} \text{implementor-name-1 IS} \begin{Bmatrix} \text{data-name-2} \\ \text{literal-1} \end{Bmatrix} \end{Bmatrix} \dots \right]$$

$$\left[\underline{DATA} \begin{Bmatrix} \underline{RECORD} \text{ IS} \\ \underline{RECORDS} \text{ ARE} \end{Bmatrix} \{\text{data-name-3}\} \dots \right]$$

$$\left[[\underline{ACCESS} \text{ MODE IS}] \begin{Bmatrix} \underline{SEQUENTIAL} \quad [\underline{RELATIVE} \text{ KEY IS data-name-4}] \\ \begin{Bmatrix} \underline{RANDOM} \\ \underline{DYNAMIC} \end{Bmatrix} \underline{RELATIVE} \text{ KEY IS data-name-4} \end{Bmatrix} \right]$$

[FILE $\underline{STATUS}$ IS data-name-5].

SORT-MERGE FILE:

SD file-name-1

$$\left[\underline{RECORD} \begin{Bmatrix} \text{CONTAINS integer-1 CHARACTERS} \\ \text{IS } \underline{VARYING} \text{ IN SIZE } [[\text{FROM integer-2}] \ [\underline{TO} \text{ integer-3}] \text{ CHARACTERS}] \\ \qquad [\underline{DEPENDING} \text{ ON data-name-1}] \\ \text{CONTAINS integer-4 } \underline{TO} \text{ integer-5 CHARACTERS} \end{Bmatrix} \right]$$

$$\left[\underline{DATA} \begin{Bmatrix} \underline{RECORD} \text{ IS} \\ \underline{RECORDS} \text{ ARE} \end{Bmatrix} \{\text{data-name-2}\} \dots \right] .$$

FORMAT 1:

level-number $\begin{bmatrix} \text{data-name-1} \\ \underline{\text{FILLER}} \end{bmatrix}$

   [<u>REDEFINES</u> data-name-2]

   [IS <u>EXTERNAL</u>]

   [IS <u>GLOBAL</u>]

   $\left[\begin{Bmatrix} \underline{\text{PICTURE}} \\ \underline{\text{PIC}} \end{Bmatrix} \text{IS character-string} \right]$

   $\left[[\underline{\text{USAGE}}\ \text{IS}] \begin{Bmatrix} \underline{\text{COMPUTATIONAL}} \\ \underline{\text{COMP}} \\ \underline{\text{DISPLAY}} \\ \underline{\text{INDEX}} \end{Bmatrix} \right]$

   $\left[[\underline{\text{SIGN}}\ \text{IS}] \begin{Bmatrix} \underline{\text{LEADING}} \\ \underline{\text{TRAILING}} \end{Bmatrix} [\underline{\text{SEPARATE}}\ \text{CHARACTER}] \right]$

   $\left[\begin{array}{l} \underline{\text{OCCURS}}\ \text{integer-2 TIMES} \\[4pt] \qquad \left[\begin{Bmatrix} \underline{\text{ASCENDING}} \\ \underline{\text{DESCENDING}} \end{Bmatrix} \text{KEY IS \{data-name-3\}} \dots \right] \dots \\[10pt] \qquad [\underline{\text{INDEXED}}\ \text{BY \{index-name-1\}} \dots] \\[6pt] \underline{\text{OCCURS}}\ \text{integer-1}\ \underline{\text{TO}}\ \text{integer-2 TIMES}\ \underline{\text{DEPENDING}}\ \text{ON data-name-4} \\[4pt] \qquad \left[\begin{Bmatrix} \underline{\text{ASCENDING}} \\ \underline{\text{DESCENDING}} \end{Bmatrix} \text{KEY IS \{data-name-3\}} \dots \right] \dots \\[10pt] \qquad [\underline{\text{INDEXED}}\ \text{BY \{index-name-1\}} \dots]\ . \end{array} \right]$

   $\left[\begin{Bmatrix} \underline{\text{SYNCHRONIZED}} \\ \underline{\text{SYNC}} \end{Bmatrix} \begin{bmatrix} \underline{\text{LEFT}} \\ \underline{\text{RIGHT}} \end{bmatrix} \right]$

   $\left[\begin{Bmatrix} \underline{\text{JUSTIFIED}} \\ \underline{\text{JUST}} \end{Bmatrix} \text{RIGHT} \right]$

   [<u>BLANK</u> WHEN <u>ZERO</u>]

   [<u>VALUE</u> IS literal-1].

FORMAT 2:

66 data-name-1 <u>RENAMES</u> data-name-2 $\left[\begin{Bmatrix} \underline{\text{THROUGH}} \\ \underline{\text{THRU}} \end{Bmatrix} \text{data-name-3} \right]$.

FORMAT 3:

88 condition-name-1 $\begin{Bmatrix} \underline{\text{VALUE}}\ \text{IS} \\ \underline{\text{VALUES}}\ \text{ARE} \end{Bmatrix} \begin{Bmatrix} \text{literal-1} \left[\begin{Bmatrix} \underline{\text{THROUGH}} \\ \underline{\text{THRU}} \end{Bmatrix} \text{literal-2} \right] \end{Bmatrix} \dots$.

FORMAT 1:

[PROCEDURE DIVISION [USING {data-name-1} ...].

[DECLARATIVES.

{section-name SECTION [segment-number].

    USE statement.

[paragraph-name.

    [sentence] ...] ... } ...

END DECLARATIVES.]

{section-name SECTION [segment-number].

[paragraph-name.

    [sentence] ...] ... } ...]

FORMAT 2:

[PROCEDURE DIVISION [USING {data-name-1} ...].

{paragraph-name.

    [sentence] ... } ...]

GENERAL FORMAT FOR NESTED SOURCE PROGRAMS

IDENTIFICATION DIVISION.

PROGRAM-ID. program-name-1.

[ENVIRONMENT DIVISION. environment-division-content]

[DATA DIVISION. data-division-content]

[PROCEDURE DIVISION. procedure-division-content]

[[nested-source-program] ...

END PROGRAM program-name-1.]

GENERAL FORMAT FOR NESTED-SOURCE-PROGRAM

IDENTIFICATION DIVISION.

PROGRAM-ID. program-name-2 $\left[\text{IS} \left\{ \left| \begin{array}{c} \text{COMMON} \\ \text{INITIAL} \end{array} \right| \right\} \text{PROGRAM} \right]$.

[ENVIRONMENT DIVISION. environment-division-content]

[DATA DIVISION. data-division-content]

[PROCEDURE DIVISION. procedure-division-content]

[nested-source-program] ...

END PROGRAM program-name-2.

GENERAL FORMAT FOR A SEQUENCE OF SOURCE PROGRAMS

{IDENTIFICATION DIVISION.

PROGRAM-ID. program-name-3.

[ENVIRONMENT DIVISION. environment-division-content]

[DATA DIVISION. data-division-content]

[PROCEDURE DIVISION. procedure-division-content]

[nested-source-program] ...

END PROGRAM program-name-3.} ...

IDENTIFICATION DIVISION.

PROGRAM-ID. program-name-4.

[ENVIRONMENT DIVISION. environment-division-content]

[DATA DIVISION. data-division-content]

[PROCEDURE DIVISION. procedure-division-content]

[[nested-source-program] ...

END PROGRAM program-name-4.]

GENERAL FORMAT FOR COBOL VERBS

<u>ACCEPT</u> identifier-1 [<u>FROM</u> mnemonic-name-1]

<u>ACCEPT</u> identifier-2 <u>FROM</u> $\begin{Bmatrix} \underline{DATE} \\ \underline{DAY} \\ \underline{DAY-OF-WEEK} \\ \underline{TIME} \end{Bmatrix}$

<u>ACCEPT</u> cd-name-1 MESSAGE <u>COUNT</u>

<u>ADD</u> $\begin{Bmatrix} identifier-1 \\ literal-1 \end{Bmatrix}$ ... <u>TO</u> {identifier-2 [<u>ROUNDED</u>]} ...

   [ON <u>SIZE</u> <u>ERROR</u> imperative-statement-1 [<u>END-ADD</u>]]

<u>ADD</u> $\begin{Bmatrix} identifier-1 \\ literal-1 \end{Bmatrix}$ ... <u>TO</u> $\begin{Bmatrix} identifier-2 \\ literal-2 \end{Bmatrix}$

   <u>GIVING</u> {identifier-3 [<u>ROUNDED</u>]} ...

   [ON <u>SIZE</u> <u>ERROR</u> imperative-statement-1 [<u>END-ADD</u>]]

<u>ADD</u> $\begin{Bmatrix} \underline{CORRESPONDING} \\ \underline{CORR} \end{Bmatrix}$ identifier-1 <u>TO</u> identifier-2 [<u>ROUNDED</u>]

   [ON <u>SIZE</u> <u>ERROR</u> imperative-statement-1 [<u>END-ADD</u>]]

<u>CALL</u> $\begin{Bmatrix} identifier-1 \\ literal-1 \end{Bmatrix}$ $\left[\underline{USING} \begin{Bmatrix} [BY \underline{REFERENCE}] \quad \{data-name-1\} ... \\ BY \underline{CONTENT} \quad \{data-name-1\} ... \end{Bmatrix} ... \right]$

   [ON <u>OVERFLOW</u> imperative-statement-1 [<u>END-CALL</u>]]

<u>CANCEL</u> $\begin{Bmatrix} identifier-1 \\ literal-1 \end{Bmatrix}$

<u>CLOSE</u> $\begin{Bmatrix} file-name-1 & \left[\begin{Bmatrix} \underline{REEL} \\ \underline{UNIT} \end{Bmatrix} [FOR \underline{REMOVAL}] \\ WITH \begin{Bmatrix} \underline{NO} REWIND \\ \underline{LOCK} \end{Bmatrix} \end{Bmatrix} \right]$ ...

<u>CLOSE</u> {file-name-1 [WITH <u>LOCK</u>]} ...

```
COMPUTE  {identifier-1 [ROUNDED]} ... = arithmetic-expression-1

   [ON SIZE ERROR imperative-statement-1 [END-COMPUTE]]


CONTINUE

DELETE file-name-1 RECORD  [INVALID KEY imperative-statement-1 [END-DELETE]]

DISPLAY  {identifier-1}  ...  [UPON mnemonic-name-1]  [WITH NO ADVANCING]
         {literal-1   }


DIVIDE  {identifier-1}  INTO  {identifier-2 [ROUNDED]} ...
        {literal-1   }

   [ON SIZE ERROR imperative-statement-1 [END-DIVIDE]]


DIVIDE  {identifier-1}  INTO  {identifier-2}
        {literal-1   }        {literal-2   }

   GIVING  {identifier-3 [ROUNDED]} ...

   [ON SIZE ERROR imperative-statement-1 [END-DIVIDE]]


DIVIDE  {identifier-1}  BY  {identifier-2}
        {literal-1   }      {literal-2   }

   GIVING  {identifier-3 [ROUNDED]} ...

   [ON SIZE ERROR imperative-statement-1 [END-DIVIDE]]


DIVIDE  {identifier-1}  INTO  {identifier-2}  GIVING identifier-3 [ROUNDED]
        {literal-1   }        {literal-2   }

   REMAINDER identifier-4

   [ON SIZE ERROR imperative-statement-1 [END-DIVIDE]]

DIVIDE  {identifier-1}  BY  {identifier-2}  GIVING identifier-3 [ROUNDED]
        {literal-1   }      {literal-2   }

   REMAINDER identifier-4

   [ON SIZE ERROR imperative-statement-1 [END-DIVIDE]]
```

```
EVALUATE  ⎧identifier-1  ⎫
          ⎪literal-1     ⎪
          ⎨expression-1  ⎬ ...
          ⎪TRUE          ⎪
          ⎩FALSE         ⎭

   {{WHEN
        ⎧ ANY                                                                           ⎫
        ⎪ condition-1                                                                    ⎪
        ⎪ TRUE                                                                           ⎪   }      }
        ⎨ FALSE                                                                          ⎬ ... } ...
        ⎪        ⎧identifier-2          ⎫ ⎡⎧THROUGH⎫ ⎧identifier-3          ⎫⎤ ⎪   }      }
        ⎪ [NOT]  ⎨literal-2             ⎬ ⎢⎨THRU   ⎬ ⎨literal-3             ⎬⎥ ⎪
        ⎩        ⎩arithmetic-expression-1⎭ ⎣⎩       ⎭ ⎩arithmetic-expression-2⎭⎦ ⎭

        imperative-statement-1} ...

   [WHEN OTHER imperative-statement-2]

   [END-EVALUATE]



EXIT.

EXIT PROGRAM

GO TO procedure-name-1

GO TO {procedure-name-1} ...   DEPENDING ON identifier-1

IF condition-1 THEN  ⎧{statement-1} ...  ⎫
                     ⎨NEXT SENTENCE      ⎬
                     ⎩                   ⎭

     ⎧ELSE {statement-2} ... [END-IF]⎫
     ⎨ELSE NEXT SENTENCE             ⎬
     ⎩END-IF                         ⎭


INITIALIZE {identifier-1} ...

     ⎡          ⎧ALPHABETIC         ⎫                           ⎤
     ⎢          ⎪ALPHANUMERIC       ⎪                ⎧identifier-2⎫⎥
     ⎢REPLACING ⎨NUMERIC            ⎬ DATA BY        ⎨literal-1   ⎬⎥
     ⎢          ⎪ALPHANUMERIC-EDITED⎪                ⎩           ⎭⎥
     ⎣          ⎩NUMERIC-EDITED     ⎭                            ⎦

INSPECT identifier-1 TALLYING
  ⎧                 ⎧CHARACTERS ⎡⎧BEFORE⎫ INITIAL ⎧identifier-4⎫⎤ ...                                            ⎫
  ⎨identifier-2 FOR ⎨           ⎣⎩AFTER ⎭         ⎩literal-2   ⎭⎦                                                ⎬ ... ⎫
  ⎩                 ⎪⎧ALL    ⎫ ⎧identifier-3⎫ ⎡⎧BEFORE⎫ INITIAL ⎧identifier-4⎫⎤ ...⎫ ...                         ⎭      ⎬ ...
                    ⎩⎩LEADING⎭ ⎩literal-1   ⎭ ⎣⎩AFTER ⎭         ⎩literal-2   ⎭⎦   ⎭                                    ⎭
```

INSPECT identifier-1 <u>REPLACING</u>

$$\left\{ \begin{array}{l} \text{CHARACTERS } \underline{\text{BY}} \left\{ \begin{array}{l} \text{identifier-5} \\ \text{literal-3} \end{array} \right\} \left[\left\{ \begin{array}{l} \underline{\text{BEFORE}} \\ \underline{\text{AFTER}} \end{array} \right\} \text{INITIAL} \left\{ \begin{array}{l} \text{identifier-4} \\ \text{literal-2} \end{array} \right\} \right] \dots \\ \left\{ \begin{array}{l} \underline{\text{ALL}} \\ \underline{\text{LEADING}} \\ \underline{\text{FIRST}} \end{array} \right\} \left\{ \left\{ \begin{array}{l} \text{identifier-3} \\ \text{literal-1} \end{array} \right\} \underline{\text{BY}} \left\{ \begin{array}{l} \text{identifier-5} \\ \text{literal-3} \end{array} \right\} \left[\left\{ \begin{array}{l} \underline{\text{BEFORE}} \\ \underline{\text{AFTER}} \end{array} \right\} \text{INITIAL} \left\{ \begin{array}{l} \text{identifier-4} \\ \text{literal-2} \end{array} \right\} \right] \dots \right\} \dots \end{array} \right\} \dots$$

INSPECT identifier-1 <u>TALLYING</u>

$$\left\{ \text{identifier-2 } \underline{\text{FOR}} \left\{ \begin{array}{l} \underline{\text{CHARACTERS}} \left[\left\{ \begin{array}{l} \underline{\text{BEFORE}} \\ \underline{\text{AFTER}} \end{array} \right\} \text{INITIAL} \left\{ \begin{array}{l} \text{identifier-4} \\ \text{literal-2} \end{array} \right\} \right] \dots \\ \left\{ \begin{array}{l} \underline{\text{ALL}} \\ \underline{\text{LEADING}} \end{array} \right\} \left\{ \left\{ \begin{array}{l} \text{identifier-3} \\ \text{literal-1} \end{array} \right\} \left[\left\{ \begin{array}{l} \underline{\text{BEFORE}} \\ \underline{\text{AFTER}} \end{array} \right\} \text{INITIAL} \left\{ \begin{array}{l} \text{identifier-4} \\ \text{literal-2} \end{array} \right\} \right] \dots \right\} \dots \end{array} \right\} \dots \right\} \dots$$

<u>REPLACING</u>

$$\left\{ \begin{array}{l} \text{CHARACTERS } \underline{\text{BY}} \left\{ \begin{array}{l} \text{identifier-5} \\ \text{literal-3} \end{array} \right\} \left[\left\{ \begin{array}{l} \underline{\text{BEFORE}} \\ \underline{\text{AFTER}} \end{array} \right\} \text{INITIAL} \left\{ \begin{array}{l} \text{identifier-4} \\ \text{literal-2} \end{array} \right\} \right] \dots \\ \left\{ \begin{array}{l} \underline{\text{ALL}} \\ \underline{\text{LEADING}} \\ \underline{\text{FIRST}} \end{array} \right\} \left\{ \left\{ \begin{array}{l} \text{identifier-3} \\ \text{literal-1} \end{array} \right\} \underline{\text{BY}} \left\{ \begin{array}{l} \text{identifier-5} \\ \text{literal-3} \end{array} \right\} \left[\left\{ \begin{array}{l} \underline{\text{BEFORE}} \\ \underline{\text{AFTER}} \end{array} \right\} \text{INITIAL} \left\{ \begin{array}{l} \text{identifier-4} \\ \text{literal-2} \end{array} \right\} \right] \dots \right\} \dots \end{array} \right\} \dots$$

<u>INSPECT</u> identifier-1 <u>CONVERTING</u> $\left\{ \begin{array}{l} \text{identifier-6} \\ \text{literal-4} \end{array} \right\}$ <u>TO</u> $\left\{ \begin{array}{l} \text{identifier-7} \\ \text{literal-5} \end{array} \right\}$

$$\left[\left\{ \begin{array}{l} \underline{\text{BEFORE}} \\ \underline{\text{AFTER}} \end{array} \right\} \text{INITIAL} \left\{ \begin{array}{l} \text{identifier-4} \\ \text{literal-2} \end{array} \right\} \right] \dots$$

<u>MERGE</u> file-name-1 $\left\{ \text{ON} \left\{ \begin{array}{l} \underline{\text{ASCENDING}} \\ \underline{\text{DESCENDING}} \end{array} \right\} \text{KEY } \{\text{data-name-1}\} \dots \right\} \dots$

[COLLATING <u>SEQUENCE</u> IS alphabet-name-1]

<u>USING</u> file-name-2 {file-name-3} ...

$$\left\{ \begin{array}{l} \underline{\text{OUTPUT}} \ \underline{\text{PROCEDURE}} \text{ IS section-name-1} \left[\left\{ \begin{array}{l} \underline{\text{THROUGH}} \\ \underline{\text{THRU}} \end{array} \right\} \text{section-name-2} \right] \\ \underline{\text{GIVING}} \ \{\text{file-name-4}\} \dots \end{array} \right\}$$

<u>MOVE</u> $\left\{ \begin{array}{l} \text{identifier-1} \\ \text{literal-1} \end{array} \right\}$ <u>TO</u> {identifier-2} ...

<u>MOVE</u> $\left\{ \begin{array}{l} \underline{\text{CORRESPONDING}} \\ \underline{\text{CORR}} \end{array} \right\}$ identifier-1 <u>TO</u> identifier-2

<u>MULTIPLY</u> $\left\{ \begin{array}{l} \text{identifier-1} \\ \text{literal-1} \end{array} \right\}$ <u>BY</u> {identifier-2 [<u>ROUNDED</u>]} ...

[ON <u>SIZE</u> <u>ERROR</u> imperative-statement-1 [<u>END-MULTIPLY</u>]]

```
MULTIPLY {identifier-1} BY {identifier-2}
         {literal-1   }    {literal-2   }

   GIVING {identifier-3 [ROUNDED]} ...

   [ON SIZE ERROR imperative-statement-1 [END-MULTIPLY]]


OPEN {INPUT  {file-name-1 [WITH NO REWIND]} ... }
     {OUTPUT {file-name-2 [WITH NO REWIND]} ... } ...
     {I-O    {file-name-3} ...                   }
     {EXTEND {file-name-4} ...                   }


OPEN {INPUT  {file-name-1} ... }
     {OUTPUT {file-name-2} ... } ...
     {I-O    {file-name-3} ... }
     {EXTEND {file-name-4} ... }


OPEN {OUTPUT {file-name-1 [WITH NO REWIND]} ... } ...
     {EXTEND {file-name-2} ...                   }


PERFORM [procedure-name-1 [{THROUGH} procedure-name-2]]
                          [{THRU   }                   ]

   [imperative-statement-1 END-PERFORM]


PERFORM [procedure-name-1 [{THROUGH} procedure-name-2]]
                          [{THRU   }                   ]

   {identifier-1} TIMES [imperative-statement-1 END-PERFORM]
   {integer-1   }


PERFORM [procedure-name-1 [{THROUGH} procedure-name-2]]
                          [{THRU   }                   ]

   [WITH TEST {BEFORE}] UNTIL condition-1
   [          {AFTER }]

   [imperative-statement-1 END-PERFORM]


PERFORM [procedure-name-1 [{THROUGH} procedure-name-2]]
                          [{THRU   }                   ]

   [WITH TEST {BEFORE}]
   [          {AFTER }]
```

```
VARYING  {identifier-2}  FROM  {identifier-3}
         {index-name-1}        {index-name-2}
                               {literal-1}

     BY  {identifier-4}  UNTIL condition-1
         {literal-2}

   ┌                                                    ┐
   │ AFTER  {identifier-5}  FROM  {identifier-6}        │
   │        {index-name-3}        {index-name-4}        │
   │                              {literal-3}           │
   │                                                    │
   │    BY  {identifier-7}  UNTIL condition-2           │ ...
   │        {literal-4}                                 │
   └                                                    ┘

[imperative-statement-1 END-PERFORM]


READ file-name-1 [NEXT] RECORD [INTO identifier-1]

   [AT END imperative-statement-1 [END-READ]]


READ file-name-1 RECORD [INTO identifier-1]

   [INVALID KEY imperative-statement-1 [END-READ]]


READ file-name-1 RECORD [INTO identifier-1]

   [KEY IS data-name-1]

   [INVALID KEY imperative-statement-1 [END-READ]]


REWRITE record-name-1 [FROM identifier-1]


REWRITE record-name-1 [FROM identifier-1]

   [INVALID KEY imperative-statement-1 [END-REWRITE]]


SEARCH identifier-1 [VARYING  {identifier-2}]
                             {index-name-1}

   [AT END imperative-statement-1]

   {WHEN condition-1  {imperative-statement-2}} ...
                      {NEXT SENTENCE}

   [END-SEARCH]
```

```
SEARCH ALL identifier-1  [AT END imperative-statement-1]

          ⎧                  ⎧IS EQUAL TO⎫  ⎧identifier-3            ⎫⎫
          ⎪data-name-1       ⎨IS =       ⎬  ⎨literal-1              ⎬⎪
    WHEN  ⎨                  ⎩           ⎭  ⎩arithmetic-expression-1⎭⎪
          ⎪                                                          ⎪
          ⎩condition-name-1                                          ⎭

          ⎡     ⎧                  ⎧IS EQUAL TO⎫  ⎧identifier-4            ⎫⎫⎤
          ⎢     ⎪data-name-2       ⎨IS =       ⎬  ⎨literal-2              ⎬⎪⎥
          ⎢AND  ⎨                  ⎩           ⎭  ⎩arithmetic-expression-2⎭⎪⎥ ...
          ⎢     ⎪                                                          ⎪⎥
          ⎣     ⎩condition-name-2                                          ⎭⎦

    ⎧imperative-statement-2⎫
    ⎨NEXT SENTENCE         ⎬
    ⎩                      ⎭

    [END-SEARCH]

    SET  ⎧index-name-1⎫  ...  TO  ⎧index-name-2⎫
         ⎨identifier-1⎬          ⎨identifier-2⎬
         ⎩            ⎭          ⎩integer-1   ⎭


    SET  {index-name-3} ...  ⎧UP BY  ⎫  ⎧identifier-3⎫
                             ⎨DOWN BY⎬  ⎨integer-2   ⎬
                             ⎩       ⎭  ⎩            ⎭

    SET  ⎧{mnemonic-name-1} ...  TO  ⎧ON ⎫⎫ ...
         ⎨                            ⎨OFF⎬⎬
         ⎩                            ⎩   ⎭⎭

    SET  {condition-name-1} ...  TO TRUE


    SORT file-name-1  ⎧ON  ⎧ASCENDING ⎫⎫ KEY {data-name-1} ...⎫ ...
                      ⎨    ⎨DESCENDING⎬⎬                       ⎬
                      ⎩    ⎩          ⎭⎭                       ⎭

       [WITH DUPLICATES IN ORDER]

       [COLLATING SEQUENCE IS alphabet-name-1]

       ⎧INPUT PROCEDURE IS section-name-1  ⎡⎧THROUGH⎫  section-name-2⎤⎫
       ⎪                                   ⎣⎨THRU   ⎬                ⎦⎪
       ⎨                                    ⎩       ⎭                 ⎬
       ⎪USING {file-name-2} ...                                      ⎪
       ⎩                                                             ⎭

       ⎧OUTPUT PROCEDURE IS section-name-3  ⎡⎧THROUGH⎫  section-name-4⎤⎫
       ⎪                                    ⎣⎨THRU   ⎬                ⎦⎪
       ⎨                                     ⎩       ⎭                 ⎬
       ⎪GIVING {file-name-3} ...                                      ⎪
       ⎩                                                              ⎭
```

```
        ┌      ┌ IS EQUAL TO      ┐            ┐
        │      │ IS =             │            │
START file-name-1 │ KEY │ IS GREATER THAN  │ data-name-1 │
        │      │ IS >             │            │
        │      │ IS NOT LESS THAN │            │
        └      └ IS NOT <         ┘            ┘

   [INVALID KEY imperative-statement-1 [END-START]]


STOP  ⎰ RUN       ⎱
      ⎱ literal-1 ⎰


STRING ⎰ identifier-1 ⎱ ...  DELIMITED BY ⎧ identifier-2 ⎫ ...
       ⎱ literal-1    ⎰                   ⎨ literal-2    ⎬
                                          ⎩ SIZE         ⎭

   INTO identifier-3

   [WITH POINTER identifier-4]

   [ON OVERFLOW imperative-statement-1 [END-STRING]]


SUBTRACT ⎰ identifier-1 ⎱ ...  FROM {identifier-3 [ROUNDED]} ...
         ⎱ literal-1    ⎰

   [ON SIZE ERROR imperative-statement-1 [END-SUBTRACT]]


SUBTRACT ⎰ identifier-1 ⎱ ...  FROM ⎰ identifier-2 ⎱
         ⎱ literal-1    ⎰           ⎱ literal-2    ⎰

   GIVING {identifier-3 [ROUNDED]} ...

   [ON SIZE ERROR imperative-statement-1 [END-SUBTRACT]]


SUBTRACT ⎰ CORRESPONDING ⎱ identifier-1 FROM identifier-2 [ROUNDED]
         ⎱ CORR          ⎰

   [ON SIZE ERROR imperative-statement-1 [END-SUBTRACT]]

UNSTRING identifier-1

   ⎡ DELIMITED BY [ALL] ⎰ identifier-2 ⎱ ⎡ OR [ALL] ⎰ identifier-3 ⎱ ⎤ ... ⎤
   ⎣                    ⎱ literal-1    ⎰ ⎣          ⎱ literal-2    ⎰ ⎦     ⎦

   INTO {identifier-4 [DELIMITER IN identifier-5] [COUNT IN identifier-6]} ...

   [WITH POINTER identifier-7]

   [TALLYING IN identifier-8]

   [ON OVERFLOW imperative-statement-1 [END-UNSTRING]]
```

$$\underline{\text{USE}} \; [\underline{\text{GLOBAL}}] \; \underline{\text{AFTER}} \; \text{STANDARD} \; \begin{Bmatrix} \underline{\text{EXCEPTION}} \\ \underline{\text{ERROR}} \end{Bmatrix} \; \underline{\text{PROCEDURE}} \; \text{ON} \; \begin{Bmatrix} \{\text{file-name-1}\} \; \dots \\ \underline{\text{INPUT}} \\ \underline{\text{OUTPUT}} \\ \underline{\text{I-O}} \\ \underline{\text{EXTEND}} \end{Bmatrix} .$$

$$\underline{\text{WRITE}} \; \text{record-name-1} \; [\underline{\text{FROM}} \; \text{identifier-1}]$$

$$\left[\begin{Bmatrix} \underline{\text{BEFORE}} \\ \underline{\text{AFTER}} \end{Bmatrix} \; \text{ADVANCING} \; \begin{Bmatrix} \begin{Bmatrix} \text{identifier-2} \\ \text{integer-1} \end{Bmatrix} \begin{bmatrix} \text{LINE} \\ \text{LINES} \end{bmatrix} \\ \begin{Bmatrix} \text{mnemonic-name-1} \\ \underline{\text{PAGE}} \end{Bmatrix} \end{Bmatrix} \right]$$

$$\left[\text{AT} \; \begin{Bmatrix} \underline{\text{END-OF-PAGE}} \\ \underline{\text{EOP}} \end{Bmatrix} \; \text{imperative-statement-1} \; [\underline{\text{END-WRITE}}] \right]$$

$$\underline{\text{WRITE}} \; \text{record-name-1} \; [\underline{\text{FROM}} \; \text{identifier-1}]$$

$$[\underline{\text{INVALID}} \; \text{KEY} \; \text{imperative-statement-1} \; [\underline{\text{END-WRITE}}]]$$

GENERAL FORMAT FOR CONDITIONS

RELATION CONDITION:

$$\begin{Bmatrix} \text{identifier-1} \\ \text{literal-1} \\ \text{arithmetic-expression-1} \end{Bmatrix} \begin{Bmatrix} \text{IS} \; [\underline{\text{NOT}}] \; \underline{\text{GREATER}} \; \text{THAN} \\ \text{IS} \; [\underline{\text{NOT}}] \; > \\ \text{IS} \; [\underline{\text{NOT}}] \; \underline{\text{LESS}} \; \text{THAN} \\ \text{IS} \; [\underline{\text{NOT}}] \; < \\ \text{IS} \; [\underline{\text{NOT}}] \; \underline{\text{EQUAL}} \; \text{TO} \\ \text{IS} \; [\underline{\text{NOT}}] \; \underline{=} \end{Bmatrix} \begin{Bmatrix} \text{identifier-2} \\ \text{literal-2} \\ \text{arithmetic-expression-2} \end{Bmatrix}$$

CLASS CONDITION:

$$\text{identifier-1} \; \text{IS} \; [\underline{\text{NOT}}] \; \begin{Bmatrix} \underline{\text{NUMERIC}} \\ \underline{\text{ALPHABETIC}} \\ \underline{\text{ALPHABETIC-LOWER}} \\ \underline{\text{ALPHABETIC-UPPER}} \end{Bmatrix}$$

CONDITION-NAME CONDITION:

condition-name-1

SWITCH-STATUS CONDITION:

condition-name-1

SIGN CONDITION:

arithmetic-expression-1 IS [NOT] $\left\{ \begin{array}{l} \text{POSITIVE} \\ \text{NEGATIVE} \\ \text{ZERO} \end{array} \right\}$

NEGATED CONDITION:

NOT condition-1

COMBINED CONDITION:

condition-1 $\left\{ \left\{ \begin{array}{l} \text{AND} \\ \text{OR} \end{array} \right\} \text{ condition-2} \right\}$ ...

ABBREVIATED COMBINED RELATION CONDITION:

relation-condition $\left\{ \left\{ \begin{array}{l} \text{AND} \\ \text{OR} \end{array} \right\} \text{ [NOT] [relational-operator] object} \right\}$ ...

Appendix III contains a list of reserved words used in COBOL-85.

ACCEPT	COMPUTATIONAL	DIVIDE	FILLER
ACCESS	COMPUTE	DIVISION	FINAL
ADD	CONFIGURATION	DOWN	FIRST
ADVANCING	CONTAINS	DUPLICATES	FOOTING
AFTER	CONTENT	DYNAMIC	FOR
ALL	CONTINUE		FROM
ALPHABET	CONTROL	EGI	
ALPHABETIC	CONTROLS	ELSE	GENERATE
ALPHABETIC-LOWER	CONVERSION	EMI	GIVING
ALPHABETIC-UPPER	CONVERTING	ENABLE	GLOBAL
ALPHANUMERIC	COPY	END	GO
ALPHANUMERIC-EDITED	CORR	END-ADD	GREATER
ALSO	CORRESPONDING	END-CALL	GROUP
ALTERNATE	COUNT	END-COMPUTE	
AND	CURRENCY	END-DELETE	HEADING
ANY		END-DIVIDE	HIGH-VALUE
ARE	DATA	END-EVALUATE	HIGH-VALUES
AREA	DATE	END-IF	
AREAS	DATE-COMPILED	END-MULTIPLY	I-O
ASCENDING	DATE-WRITTEN	END-OF-PAGE	I-O-CONTROL
ASSIGN	DAY	END-PERFORM	IDENTIFICATION
AT	DAY-OF-WEEK	END-READ	IF
AUTHOR	DE	END-RECEIVE	IN
	DEBUG-CONTENTS	END-RETURN	INDEX
BEFORE	DEBUG-ITEM	END-REWRITE	INDEXED
BLANK	DEBUG-LENGTH	END-SEARCH	INDICATE
BLOCK	DEBUG-NAME	END-START	INITIAL
BOTTOM	DEBUG-NUMERIC-CONTENTS	END-STRING	INITIALIZE
BY	DEBUG-SIZE	END-SUBTRACT	INITIATE
	DEBUG-START	END-UNSTRING	INPUT
CALL	DEBUG-SUB	END-WRITE	INPUT-OUTPUT
CANCEL	DEBUG-SUB-ITEM	ENVIRONMENT	INSPECT
CD	DEBUG-SUB-N	EOP	INSTALLATION
CF	DEBUG-SUB-NUM	EQUAL	INTO
CH	DEBUGGING	ERROR	INVALID
CHARACTER	DECIMAL-POINT	ESI	IS
CHARACTERS	DECLARATIVES	EVALUATE	
CLOSE	DELETE	EXCEPTION	JUST
CODE	DELIMITED	EXIT	JUSTIFIED
CODE-SET	DELIMITER	EXTEND	
COLLATING	DEPENDING	EXTERNAL	KEY
COLUMN	DESCENDING		
COMMA	DESTINATION	FALSE	LABEL
COMMON	DETAIL	FD	LAST
COMMUNICATION	DISABLE	FILE	LEADING
COMP	DISPLAY	FILE-CONTROL	LEFT

LENGTH	PERFORM	RH	TAPE
LESS	PF	RIGHT	TERMINAL
LIMIT	PH	ROUNDED	TERMINATE
LIMITS	PIC	RUN	TEST
LINAGE	PICTURE		TEXT
LINAGE-COUNTER	PLUS	SAME	THAN
LINE	POINTER	SD	THEN
LINE-COUNTER	POSITION	SEARCH	THROUGH
LINES	POSITIVE	SECTION	THRU
LINKAGE	PRINTING	SECURITY	TIME
LOCK	PROCEDURE	SEGMENT	TIMES
LOW-VALUE	PROCEDURES	SEGMENT-LIMIT	TO
LOW-VALUES	PROGRAM	SELECT	TOP
	PROGRAM-ID	SEND	TRAILING
MERGE	PURGE	SENTENCE	TRUE
MESSAGE		SEPARATE	TYPE
MODE	QUEUE	SEQUENCE	
MOVE	QUOTE	SEQUENTIAL	UNIT
MULTIPLE	QUOTES	SET	UNSTRING
MULTIPLY		SIGN	UNTIL
	RANDOM	SIZE	UP
NATIVE	RD	SORT	UPON
NEGATIVE	READ	SORT-MERGE	USAGE
NEXT	RECEIVE	SOURCE	USE
NO	RECORD	SOURCE-COMPUTER	USING
NOT	RECORDS	SPACE	
NUMBER	REDEFINES	SPACES	VALUE
NUMERIC	REEL	SPECIAL-NAMES	VALUES
NUMERIC-EDITED	REFERENCE	STANDARD	VARYING
	REFERENCE-MODIFIER	STANDARD-1	
OBJECT-COMPUTER	REFERENCES	STANDARD-2	WHEN
OCCURS	RELATIVE	START	WITH
OF	RELEASE	STATUS	WORKING-STORAGE
OFF	REMAINDER	STOP	WRITE
OMITTED	REMOVAL	STRING	
ON	RENAMES	SUB-QUEUE-1	ZERO
OPEN	REPLACE	SUB-QUEUE-2	ZEROES
OPTIONAL	REPLACING	SUB-QUEUE-3	ZEROS
OR	REPORT	SUBTRACT	
ORDER	REPORTING	SUM	+
ORGANIZATION	REPORTS	SUPPRESS	-
OTHER	RESERVE	SYMBOLIC	*
OUTPUT	RESET	SYNC	/
OVERFLOW	RETURN	SYNCHRONIZED	**
	REWIND		>
PADDING	REWRITE	TABLE	<
PAGE	RF	TALLYING	=
PAGE-COUNTER			

Bibliography

Ashley & Fernandez, COBOL Wizard, Wiley, 1987

Central Computer and Telecommunications Agency, Structured Design Method, 1983

Harwell Laboratory, Program Development Facility User Guide (version 2.1), 1988

Holmes, B.J. Structured Programming in COBOL, First Edition, DP Publications, 1984

Jackson, M.A. Principles of Program Design, Academic Press, 1975

Michael Jackson Systems Ltd, JSP-COBOL

    - A Technical Overview

    - Language Description & Operating Characteristics, 1976-1984

    - User Guide Version 2.2, 1984

Prime Computer Inc, COBOL-85 Reference Guide, release 1.0-22.0 Doc 10166-1LA

Technical Committee X3J4, Draft proposed revised X3.23 American National Standard Programming Language COBOL, 1981

Tyrrell, COBOL from Pascal, Macmillan, 1989

Index